**Library of
Davidson College**

STYLE

Photograph of Harriett Hawkins by Bill Waldron.

STYLE

Essays on Renaissance and Restoration
Literature and Culture
in Memory of Harriett Hawkins

Edited by
Allen Michie and Eric Buckley

Newark: University of Delaware Press

© 2005 by Rosemont Publishing & Printing Corp.

All rights reserved. Authorization to photocopy items for internal or personal use, or the internal or personal use of specific clients, is granted by the copyright owner, provided that a base fee of $10.00, plus eight cents per page, per copy is paid directly to the Copyright Clearance Center, 222 Rosewood Drive, Danvers, Massachusetts 01923. [0-87413-909-0/05 $10.00 + 8¢, pp, pc.]

Other than as indicated in the foregoing, this book may not be reproduced, in whole or in part, in any form (except as permitted by Sections 107 and 108 of the U.S. Copyright Law, and except for brief quotes appearing in reviews in the public press).

Associated University Presses
2010 Eastpark Boulevard
Cranbury, NJ 08512

The paper used in this publication meets the requirements of the American National Standard for Permanence of Paper for Printed Library Materials Z39.48-1984.

Library of Congress Cataloging-in-Publication Data

Style : essays on renaissance and restoration restoration literature and culture in memory of Harriett Hawkins / edited by Allen Michie and Eric Buckley.
    p. cm.
"Harriett Hawkins : a bibliography": p.
Includes bibliographical references and index.
ISBN 0-87413-909-0 (alk. paper)
  1. English literature—Early modern, 1500–1700—History and criticism. 2. English literature—Early modern, 1500–1700—History and criticism—Theory, etc. 3. Hawkins, Harriett—Knowledge—Literature. I. Michie, Allen, 1963– II. Buckley, Eric. III. Hawkins, Harriett.
PR423.S79   2005
820.9′003—dc22   2004024701

PRINTED IN THE UNITED STATES OF AMERICA

"To a T"
by David Norbrook
In Memoriam
Harriett Hawkins Buckley, 1934–1995

"There was a star danced, and under that was I born"—Order of Service, Oxford Crematorium

>Those twinned Ts, Harriett,
>shaped by a genial star,
>turned such a pirouette
>the Cross's downward bar
>can't still the dancing toes
>as, echoing your chord,
>we watch the curtains close
>and, bemused, half-applaud.

Contents

Preface	9
Part I: The Style of Scholarship and a Scholarship of Style: A Tribute to Harriett Hawkins	
Harriett Hawkins: A Bibliography	25
Harriett Hawkins's Renaissance ARTHUR KINNEY	30
Harriett Hawkins and the Criticism of the 1970s: Interpretation, Theory, and Iconoclasm ROBERT MARKLEY	42
A Literary Deadlock: The Destruction of the "Bower of Bliss" in Spenser's *The Faerie Queene* HARRIETT HAWKINS	55
The Seductions of *Comus* HARRIETT HAWKINS	60
Part II: Single Authors and Singular Styles	
Henry Vaughan's Poetry: Pointful Vagueness and the Merging of Contraries JOHN CAREY	69
Shakespeare and Magical Grammar LINDA WOODBRIDGE	84
Shakespeare's Eloquence MAURICE CHARNEY	99
Hamlet's Dramatic Soliloquies RICHARD LEVIN	113
Denzil Holles and the Stylistic Development of the Early English Memoir MARTINE WATSON BROWNLEY	135
"New Philosophy Calls All in Doubt": Chaos Theory and the Fractal Poetics of John Donne ALLEN MICHIE	150

Part III: Fashion, Culture, and Politics

"An artificiall following of nature": Dryden, Etherege, and the Perfection of Art   181
MICHAEL NEILL

Discourses on Health and Leisure and Modern Constructions of Holidays at the Restoration Spas   202
MANUEL J. GÓMEZ-LARA

Jewish History and Christian Providence in Elizabethan England: The Contexts of Thomas Legge's *Solymitana Clades (The Destruction of Jerusalem)*, c. 1579–88   228
PAULINA KEWES

The Prince's Choice   267
TERENCE HAWKES

Notes on Contributors   279
Bibliography   282
Index   291

Preface

THE FIRST WORDS OF HARRIETT HAWKINS'S FIRST BOOK ARE A QUOTAtion from John Dryden:

> The purity of phrase, the clearness of conception and expression, the boldness maintained to majesty, the significancy and sound of words, not strained into bombast, but justly elevated; in short, those very words and thoughts, which cannot be changed, but for the worse, must of necessity escape our transient view upon the theatre; and yet without all these a play may take. For if either the story move us, or the actor help the lameness of it with his performance, or now and then a glittering beam of wit or passion strike through the obscurity of the poem, any of these are sufficient to effect a present liking, but not to fix a lasting admiration; for nothing but truth can long continue; and time is the surest judge of truth.[1]

For Dryden, as for Hawkins, "truth" is something that emerges from an ongoing dialectic. In two of her major works, *Likenesses of Truth in Elizabethan and Restoration Drama* and *The Devil's Party: Critical Counter-Interpretations of Shakespearian Drama*, Hawkins argues that "truth" is no less the sole property of bald, humorless, and limpid sermonizing as it is the property of ornate, witty, and obtuse poetry or prose. A "glittering beam of wit of passion" is often all it takes to transform obscurity into clarity, but "lasting admiration" is something that cannot be purchased cheaply by "purity of phrase" or "boldness maintained to majesty." Perhaps Hawkins used Dryden's words from "An Essay on Dramatic Poesy" to set the tone for her book, and by extension the remainder of her career, to illustrate how true style is in the service of, and is in turn served by, a verdict of lasting worth. This is the difference between "style" and its lesser cousin, "fashion." Both are cultural constructions, both can be vessels for "truth," but, as both Dryden and Hawkins make clear, they have significantly different relationships to *time*. The essays in this volume are all written in honor of Hawkins as evidence of her own lasting worth and continuing influence on Renaissance and Restoration studies. But they also address Dryden's challenge for modern readers to cast a cold eye back on the past, to evaluate how elements of literary style from the age of Dryden and his predecessors have held up to our standards for "lasting admiration" and even "truth."

Style is as difficult to define as it is ubiquitous in our presentations of Renaissance and Restoration art and culture. It is virtually impossible to conceive of the Renaissance without thinking almost immediately of style—it is perhaps the most self-consciously ornamental and rigorously individualistic period in British cultural history. The very word "Renaissance," meaning of course "rebirth," brings to mind baroque elaboration, rhetorical polish, symbolic power sewn into the flowering aristocratic clothing, Senecan bombast, Elizabethan lyricism, and Machiavellian *panache*. Likewise, the Restoration is defined as much by its sense of style as by its historical bookends. Representative government and Calvinist theology both survived the fall of Cromwell and the return of Charles II, but the manners, methods, materials, and motives of the court still seem to us nearly as radically and refreshingly different from the years immediately preceding the Restoration as they seemed to the citizens of London at the time.

Yet "style" remains elusive, something that tends to slip away from precise measurement and definition. It remains linked to personal *taste*, something that forms both the life of literary enjoyment and the death of more-or-less objective literary history. As a result, style has become something we often speak of in the classroom or with one another, often with great enthusiasm and affection, but also something we seldom write about anymore (apart from discussions of "stylistics," a narrow branch of rhetorical analysis). Recent advances in historicist criticism, however, have made it easier for us to see how all virtually all aspects of literature intersect at some level with virtually all aspects of the history of culture. Style, often relegated to the ironically "unfashionable" bin of the disgraced New Criticism, should be no different. We are therefore in a unique position now to redefine "style" as much more than simply an author's patented quirks or the casual taste of the town.

Style, as these essays collectively demonstrate, can be seen as a fertile juncture of culture, politics, technique, fashion, history, science, theology, and genre. After all, it takes more than one ingredient to cook a style. Fashion alone is meaningless without an economics of scale to accompany it; technique is meaningless without a context of canonical works against which it can be measured; and rhetoric is meaningless without an ethics or a theology for its persuasive power to endorse. Style is inherently interdisciplinary, heteroglossic and, of course, it is inherently *interesting*. Style is where history meets cultural context meets personality meets reader response. It is both the beginning and end of inspiration and appeal: it is what artists seek to imitate and build upon in other artists, and what readers remember long after they have grown fuzzy on the content and details of an argument.

Literary history has assigned each conventional literary period, and cultural movement within each period, its characteristic style: the elegiac tone of Anglo Saxon epic poetry, the elegant artificiality of pastorals, the erotic brooding of gothic novels, etc. Yet style seems to break down into smaller and smaller units the closer we look at the individual works. Ann Radcliffe's gothic brooding seems considerably more sublime and picturesque than the violent occultism of Matthew Lewis, which is different still from the passionate longing of Emily Brontë and the archetypal heroic questing in Herman Melville's *Moby Dick* (of course, individual chapters, even sentences, of *Moby Dick* show dramatically different styles and techniques). Different styles on the small scale often work together to create the kinds of cultural generalizations we often make on the larger scale: Christopher Marlowe's sweeping passages of wild ambition and Robert Herrick's precise attention to small objects of delicate beauty, for example, both share stylistic traits of seventeenth-century Humanism.

The essays in this volume are marked by their awareness that style is a consideration of scale, not of kind. Close examination of individual texts and individual authors alternates with broader considerations of culture, politics, and history. Taken together, the essays point to the Renaissance and Restoration as two periods that find unity in underlying assumptions about the value of highly individual expression and the high stakes of aesthetic debate for transcending matters of transient fashion and tradition-bound genres.

The essays fall into three parts. The first section, "The Style of Scholarship and the Scholarship of Style: A Tribute to Harriett Hawkins," begins with two essays that demonstrate how Renaissance style as a subject of literary criticism can parallel, and perhaps even influence, the stylishness and appeal of the criticism itself. Harriett Hawkins's life and career are a case in point. The first essay is by Arthur Kinney, professor at the University of Massachusetts and director of its Renaissance Center there, which holds the repository of Hawkins's publications and papers. Professor Kinney summarizes Hawkins's major works and assesses their influence on the field of Renaissance studies, pointing out how Hawkins herself plays into the dichotomy she sometimes used in her work on Shakespeare criticism, how "the fox knows many things, but the hedgehog knows one big thing." According to Kinney, Harriett was the kind to follow the style of the fox while clinging to the style of the hedgehog for a central thesis that is found throughout her major work: hedgehogs have it all wrong. Robert Markley shows exactly how this works in one particular respect: in "Harriett Hawkins and the Criticism of the 1970s: Interpretation, Theory, and Iconoclasm," Markley details how Hawkins's unusual and prescient stance on the healthy ethical pluralism of Restoration comedy was a radical departure in a critical atmosphere that emphasized narrowly moralistic readings.

The section concludes with two short pieces by Hawkins herself. Since Kinney and Markley account for the contribution of her major scholarship, it seems appropriate to provide representative samples of Hawkins's legendary prowess at undergraduate teaching. These essays were written for an Oxford journal she cared a great deal about in the final years of her life, *The English Review*, a publication aimed at English sixth-formers considering university study in English at Oxford and elsewhere. Both selections deal in various ways with the dialectical style of specific passages from Spenser and Milton. They illustrate in microcosm what both Kinney and Markley claim for her more extended works: Hawkins constantly has an eye for dialectics and debate, for the ways in which the author's meaning and the reader's pleasure is found in the play of opposing forces, sometimes found in words of the same sentence. These exercises in practical criticism more than hold their own in a volume such as this, surrounded by highly advanced scholarship, but they work equally well on the level of an informed general readership. Hawkins always knew, as Dryden did, that "the clearness of conception and expression, the boldness maintained to majesty, the significancy and sound of words, not strained into bombast, but justly elevated" is all that effective literary criticism has ever really needed, then as now.

The second part of the volume is entitled "Single Authors and Singular Styles," a section devoted to studies of the development and lasting influence of the individuality and subjectivity so characteristic of Renaissance and Restoration poetics. Whereas value was often placed on traditional, familiar genres and subjects in Renaissance writing, the bar was correspondingly raised on the heightened expectations for unique treatments and fresh perspectives (much like yet another jazz musician taking a solo on yet another chorus of "Stardust"). The authors in this section therefore look for ways in which the fingerprint of an author's imagery, language, rhetoric, and frames of reference matters greatly to that author's canonization, continued relevance, and what he or she can tell us about Renaissance and Restoration aesthetics.

Sometimes even the best critics make value judgments on style that go further than questions of individual taste and personal preference, blinding them to all that an unusual literary technique can make possible. T. S. Eliot once dismissed the poetry of Henry Vaughan on the basis of his "vague, adolescent, fitful and retrogressive" portrayals of emotion. John Carey, in his essay "Henry Vaughan's Poetry: Pointful Vagueness and the Merging of Contraries," begins with this passage from Eliot to claim that Vaughan has never received the proper recognition he deserves. Viewed from the right perspective and with an open imagination, Vaughan's peculiarities of linguistics and imagery clarify rather than obfuscate his verse. His unusual word choices override usual oppositions, so that contraries like night & light, heat & cold, stasis & agitation, etc., are reconciled.

Artful rhetoric, Carey argues, can help create an aura of mysticism. Something similar happens in Shakespeare's works, but as the result of a slightly different spin on Vaughan's same style of select omissions and indirect language. In her essay "Shakespeare and Magical Grammar," Linda Woodbridge claims that many of Shakespeare's plays preserve elements of magical beliefs carried over from an earlier age. Since cultural beliefs sometimes encode themselves in the very grammar of language, a choice of literary style in later generations becomes in part a choice of cultural reference. Shakespeare preserves the traditional superstition that danger arises from drawing attention to someone or something by naming him/her/it. This is seen especially in the use of pronouns rather than nouns that name directly; the use of passive verbs to evade naming who performed the action; the use of euphemisms to avoid naming the action itself; the use of epithets or praise-names rather than proper names; and the use of synonyms and other substitutive devices.

Maurice Charney also claims that Shakespeare sometimes communicates most effectively through what he does *not* say. In "Shakespeare's Eloquence," a version of the Shakespeare Birthday speech given at the Merchantile Library, Charney illustrates the idea that Shakespeare's eloquence may not be just in the words he wrote, but also in the intensely dramatic scenes or parts of scenes that rely on nonverbal eloquence. At times Shakespeare's style is most effective when the language he uses is not particularly impressive in itself. One of Shakespeare's most magical lines, for example, is Lear's simple "Pray you undo this button. Thank you, sir." Actions, too, often speak louder than words. Charney argues for a definition of "eloquence" that is inclusive of the entire range of rhetorical and literary techniques that make Shakespeare's most effective scenes truly "dramatic."

Richard Levin locates Shakespeare's eloquence very differently in "Hamlet's Dramatic Soliloquies," using the examples of Hamlet's seven great speeches to define the "dramatic" in two senses: each soliloquy is an integral part of the surrounding dramatic action and is therefore inseparable from it, and each one contains within itself a small dramatic action. The style of the soliloquies also serves the structure and characterization of the play by marking the ends of episodes and suggesting character motivation (among other things).

The investigation into how an author's individual style serves, and is served by, the structure and development of genre is continued by Martine Watson Brownley in "Denzil Holles and the Stylistic Development of the Early English Memoir." Brownley demonstrates how Holles's "Discourse" exhibits all of the primary literary qualities of the seventeenth-century English memoir, but at the same time by virtue of its distinctive language it reflects the conflicted relationship to historical discourse that rapidly destabilized the memoir over the relatively brief course of its development. In Holles's hands, therefore, the early English memoir negotiates its uneasy relationship to historical discourse into stylistic possibilities that help make possible the emerging English novel.

Allen Michie draws upon Harriett Hawkins's innovative interdisciplinary theory in her final book, *Strange Attractors: Literature, Culture, and Chaos Theory*, to outline a new aesthetic for the poetry of John Donne that emphasizes very different kinds of instability, emerging properties, and perhaps even "magic." In "'New philosophy calls all in doubt': Chaos Theory and the Fractal Poetics of John Donne," Michie claims that many characteristics of Donne's style and imagery give his poetry much in common with the natural and mathematical systems described so well by recent chaos theory: it is dynamic, nonlinear, complex, adaptive, and turbulent. The basic elements of chaos theory and fractal geometry are summarized and explained for the benefit of nonspecialists, sensitive dependence on initial conditions, strange attractors, self-similarity across scale, and phase transitions. Each element applies to Donne's poetry and prose to the extent that chaos theory can pull together many otherwise disconnected strands of Donne's art and thought.

The third part of the book, "Style and Culture," includes essays that address the cross-pollinating influence of Renaissance style on fashion, politics, and aesthetics. Michael Neill writes in "'As loose and free as nature': Etherege, Dryden and the 'perfection of art'" that two otherwise very different works, Dryden's "Essay of Dramatic Poesy" and Etherege's comedy "The Man of Mode," are both structured as elaborate but mockingly inconclusive debates on the relationship between art and nature. Each debate is illustrated with numerous exemplars of art and artifice, and the pettiness of differences is highlighted by a style of parallelism that juxtaposes the debates to actual civil warfare. While not making claims that Etherege was directly influenced by Dryden's "Essay," this essay argues that the symmetry between the two works, despite the generic difference that separates them, reveals structures of thought and feeling in Restoration culture.

M. J. Gómez Lara, in "Discourses on Health and Leisure and Modern Constructions of Holidays at the Restoration Spas," also pinpoints how Restoration culture intersects with aesthetic fashion in the form of social metaphors and ironic dialectics. He uses theories of cultural geography and anthropology to examine the life of spas in the late seventeenth century, demonstrating how their depictions in pamphlets and poems satirize, challenge, or maintain discriminatory social categories. The literary renderings of this cultural landscape feed back into Restoration society by privileging a stylish, fashionable environment suitable for the enactment of larger social conflicts.

Paulina Kewes discusses the serious social conflicts of English colonialism in Ireland and the treatment of British Jews in her essay "Jewish History and Christian Providence in Elizabethan England: The Contexts of Thomas Legge's *Solymitana Clades (The Destruction of Jerusalem)*, c. 1579–88." The subtle political parallels in Legge's overlooked play pull out double identifications from the audience, creating sympathies with both Roman and Jewish characters that call us to question our own ethical standards. Legge's style of characterization and plotting holds up to scrutiny the entire process of making, transmitting, and representing history.

Such processes are ongoing, nor is colonialism only a thing of the past. Just as Legge's narrative style posed challenges to the authority of colonial rule during the Renaissance, so does Renaissance literature still maintain a political dimension today. Terence Hawkes uses a collection of Shakespeare's verse selected by Prince Charles titled *The Prince's Choice* to examine how Shakespeare is conscripted into service by a modern monarchical establishment keenly conscious of its own need for cultural support. Characters claiming the title of "Prince of Wales" in the early modern "Great Britain" project form the central concern of Shakespeare's history plays, just as in our time the present day responds in kind and uses Shakespeare's cultural cachet as fuel for an authoritative royal style.

Biographical Note

Harriett Bloker Hawkins was born in Memphis, Tennessee on April 29, 1934, and grew up on the banks of the Mississippi River in Caruthersville, Missouri. She relished escape at the local cinema, where the now-classic films she saw there made a permanent impact on her imagination, her scholarly open-mindedness to popular culture, and her personal sense of style. Most who knew her believed they had met a movie star who had been too busy with grander things to get around to being in any movies.

Hawkins attended Tulane University, and even as a secretary and part-time undergraduate there, she attended the lectures of Richard Fogle and was invited to join his select after-hours circle of faculty and graduate students. She thought her physical education classes a waste of her time and tuition, skipped them all, and dared the university not to give her a degree. She graduated with the prizes for Shakespeare studies, dramatic literature, and overall excellence in the Department of English.

She then attended Washington University on a National Defense fellowship and graduated with a Ph.D. in 1964, winning the prize for best graduate student just as she had for best undergraduate. She then spent two years teaching at Swarthmore College before joining the full-time faculty at Vassar College in 1966. She won grants from the National Endowment for the Humanities and the Huntington Library, and her first book, *Likenesses of Truth in Elizabethan and Restoration Drama*, appeared under the Clarendon imprint from Oxford University Press in 1972.

A Guggenheim Fellowship in 1975 came close upon her full professorship at Vassar. *Poetic Freedom and Poetic Truth* followed that same year, winning the Rose Mary Crawshay Prize from the British Academy and being listed as one of the "Books of the Year" in the London *Observer*. Research and consultations for her doctoral thesis had taken her several times to Oxford, and by now she had become a familiar and welcomed fixture at Linacre College, where friends who remember her there say she played a key role in setting the intellectual and social tone for Oxford's newest college. Her marriage to Eric Buckley, Printer to the University at Oxford University Press, took her away from Vassar in 1979, and by 1982 she was appointed Senior Research Fellow at Linacre.

Hawkins was happy and productive in Oxford. She supervised graduate students, lectured to undergraduates, served as faculty and speaker for various summer programs, was Visiting Professor at Emory for a semester in 1987, and enjoyed being on vacation in exotic places from Egypt to Antarctica as much as she enjoyed being at home in Headington with Eric and (as she put it in the flyleaf to *Classics and Trash*) her "tyrannical tortoise-shell cat."

Three turns at reviewing the year's Shakespeare scholarship for the *Shakespeare Survey* resulted in *The Devil's Party: Critical Counter-Interpretations of Shakespearian Drama*. The first two essays in this volume review the impact of Hawkins' first three books on the field of Renaissance and Restoration studies, so there is no need to go into detail here. A word should be said for Hawkins's later works, however. The following years saw Hawkins expanding her range of interest, making greater use of her considerable teaching experience to write for general audiences. She allowed herself to speak more freely about the undeniable links she had always seen between literature, popular culture, and science (all written prior to, or at the early stages of, the rise of interdisciplinary studies).

Measure for Measure: A Critical Introduction was written in 1987 for the Harvester New Critical Introductions to Shakespeare series. In 1992 she joined the editorial board of *The English Review*, a journal aimed at English secondary school students to inform and inspire them about literary study. Hawkins helped to revive the lagging publication, bringing to it a new energy and an all-star list of contributors who had difficulty saying "no" to her requests, especially when they were reinforced with her own example (see the reprinted essays in this volume). Several years' worth of popular guest lectures blended into *Classics and Trash: Traditions and Taboos in High Literature and Popular Modern Genres*, which appeared in 1990 and is in many ways Hawkins's most creative and nearly autobiographical work. She poured into it her wealth of literary reference, along with her committed feminism and all her affection for the popular culture that shaped her own aesthetics, from the most recent West End musicals to those childhood experiences at the Caruthersville cinema that never left her.

Her final book, *Strange Attractors: Literature, Culture and Chaos Theory*, was her greatest stretch. She immersed herself in an entirely new field of study, the nonlinear dynamics of chaotic and complex systems. Anchored by a characteristically witty parallel between *Paradise Lost* and *Jurassic Park*, Hawkins wrote of both chaos theory and a range of "high" and popular literature with clarity and catching enthusiasm. Of all her honors and accolades, she was perhaps most proud of her invitation to speak to the Oxford University physics department on the relationship between chaos theory and the arts.

Hawkins was a legendary teacher. Ready with a quote from her formidable memory to match any occasion, she was able to reach many generations of students of all age groups and social backgrounds. Her scholarship on Shakespeare was impeccable, but in the classroom the dramatic arts were just that to her—always dramatic and always an art.

Hawkins died from complications of cancer surgery on September 18, 1995. Her close friend John Bamborough, the first Principal of Linacre College who did so much for her career from its earliest stages, paid her his last service with a eulogy at her funeral in Oxford. His conclusion is a fitting introduction for the essays on the chosen theme for this volume:

> One always felt better for meeting Harriett; she was a source of colour in one's existence. . . . While the rest of us muster round for the daily battle of life in our drab khaki battledress, Harriett came on parade in full-dress uniform, with a scarlet tunic, and a plume in her helmet. . . . She was fond of an Arabic saying, which she quotes more than once in her writing: "What need you of the black tents of the tribe, you who have the crimson pavilion of my heart?" That is where her memorial will be: in the pavilions of our hearts.

Acknowledgments

The editors wish to thank the entire staff of the Center for Renaissance Studies at the University of Massachusetts for their assistance with the compilation of the bibliography, which is drawn from the repository of Hawkins's works and papers maintained by the Center, which readers of this book are invited to visit. Hawkins would be pleased to know that her life's work is preserved in such beautiful and professional surroundings, kept side by side with the collected works and papers of her own mentor and friend, Dame Helen Gardner. The director of the center, Arthur Kinney, offered early advice, encouragement, and even guest lodgings that directly led to the organization and publication of this volume.

John Carey offered his time and expertise beyond the substantial contribution of his own scholarship. Sophie Goldsworthy, Chief Editor of Humanities at Oxford University Press, offered valuable suggestions, and Sarah Poynting of the *English Review* offered essential assistance with permissions for reprinting Hawkins's two essays. The editors also wish to thank Colette Ryder-Hall for her able and prompt assistance with the manuscript, and Alistair Buckley for his enthusiasm and help with long-distance communications. Financial support for editorial work and research was liberally provided by the provost's office and English department of Iowa State University.

It is a great tribute to Hawkins that she maintained an astonishing assembly of loyal friends and colleagues. Many of them who work in Renaissance and/or Restoration studies were contacted about this volume, and *all* of them gave offers of support and encouragement even if they were reluctantly unable to contribute essays at the time on our particular theme. The editors wish to thank Jonathan Bate, Catherine Belsey, Julia Briggs, Sue Coker Brothers, Christopher Butler, Cecile Williamson Carey, Beth Darlington, Robert DeMaria, Katherine Duncan-Jones, Christopher Grose, Werner Habicht, Cicely Havely, the late Christopher Hill, Emrys Jones, James F. Jones, Roger Lonsdale, Anthony Nuttal, Helen Powers, Harry Rusche, Ron Schuchard, Kathleen Scott, Evert Sprinchorn, Joseph Summers, Michael Wutz, and especially Bonnie Wheeler. For those whom we have failed to contact who would have liked to make a contribution in Hawkins's memory, we apologize for the inadvertent omission, and we thank each of you for generous thoughts.

Our earliest, most enthusiastic, and generous supporter has been Juliana Michie, who joins the editors in feeling that this book is a fitting eulogy to her sister in the native language of scholarship that she spoke in so eloquently herself.

Note

1. Hawkins, *Likenesses of Truth in Elizabethan and Restoration Drama* (Oxford: Clarendon Press, 1972), vii.

STYLE

I
The Style of Scholarship and a Scholarship of Style: A Tribute to Harriett Hawkins

Harriett Hawkins: A Bibliography

Hawkins, Harriett. "'All the World's a Stage': Some Illustrations of the *Theatrum Mundi*." *Shakespeare Quarterly* 17 (1966): 174–78.
———. "Apparition Poems by Robert Frost." *The English Review* 4, no. 2 (November 1993): 12–15.
———. "As We Read the Living?" *Essays in Criticism* 24, no. 1 (January 1974): 94–104.
———. *Classics and Trash: Traditions and Taboos in "High" Literature and Popular Modern Genres*. Toronto: University of Toronto Press, 1990.
———. "'Conjectures and Refutations': The Positive Use of Negative Feedback in Criticism and Performance." In *Shakespeare: Man of the Theater: Proceedings of the Second Congress of the International Shakespeare Association, 1981*, edited by Jay L. Halio, Kenneth Muir, and D. J. Palmer, 105–13. Newark: University of Delaware Press, 1983.
———. "Critical Counter-Interpretations of Shakespearean Drama: Some Variants of the Dialectical Process." In *Reconciliations: Studies in Honor of Richard Haster Fogel*, edited by Mary Lynn Johnson and Seraphia D. Leyda. *Romantic Reassessment* 96, 3–16. Salzburg: Institut für Anglistik und Amerikanistik, Universität Salzburg, 1983.
———. *The Devil's Party: Critical Counter-Interpretations of Shakespearian Drama*. Oxford: Clarendon Press, 1985.
———. "'The Devil's Party': Virtues and Vices in *Measure for Measure*." In *Shakespeare Survey* 31, edited by Kenneth Muir, 105–13. Cambridge: Cambridge University Press, 1978.
———. "Disrupting Tribal Difference: Critical and Artistic Responses to Shakespeare's Radical Romanticism." *Studies in the Literary Imagination* 26, no. 1 (Spring 1993): 115–26.
———. "Dramatic Judgment in *King Lear*." In *Shakespeare: The Tragedies: New Perspectives*. Twentieth Century Views, 163–74. Englewood Cliffs, N.J.: Prentice-Hall, 1984.
———. "The Dyer's Hand" (Review of *Shakespeare and the English Romantic Imagination* by Jonathan Bate). *Essays in Criticism* 37, no. 2 (April 1987): 170–78.
———. "The 'Example Theory' and the Providentialist Approach to Restoration Drama: Some Questions of Validity and Applicability." *The Eighteenth Century: Theory and Interpretation* 24, no. 2 (1983): 103–14.

———. "Fabulous Counterfeits: Dramatic Construction and Dramatic Perspectives in *The Spanish Tragedy, A Midsummer Night's Dream, and The Tempest.*" *Shakespeare Studies* 6 (1970): 51–65, edited by J. Leeds Barroll and William C. Brown.

———. "Five Poetic Worlds: A Study of the Relationship Between Thematic Content and Dramatic Construction in Representative Works of Ben Jonson." Ph.D. Diss. St. Louis: Washington University, 1964.

———. "Folly, Incurable Disease, and *Volpone.*" *Studies in English Literature 1500–1900* 8, no. 2 (Spring 1968): 335–48.

———. "From *King Lear* to *King Kong* and Back: Shakespeare and Popular Modern Genres." In *"Bad" Shakespeare: Revaluations of the Shakespeare Canon*, edited by Maurice Charney, 37–55. Rutherford, N.J.: Fairleigh Dickinson, 1988.

———. "The House of Fame (Review of *Feasting with Panthers, or The Importance of Being Famous* by Peter Conrad)." *Oxford Magazine*, no. 118 (Second Week, Trinity Term 1995): 10–11.

———. "The Idea of a Theatre in Jonson's *The New Inn.*" *Renaissance Drama* 9 (1966), 205–26.

———. "Jonson's Use of Traditional Dream Theory in *The Vision of Delight.*" *Modern Philology* 64, no. 4 (May 1967): 285–92.

———. *Likenesses of Truth in Elizabethan and Restoration Drama*. Oxford: Clarendon Press, 1972.

———. "A Literary Deadlock: The Destruction of the 'Bower of Bliss' in Spenser's *The Faerie Queene.*" *The English Review* 3, no. 3 (February 1993): 22–24.

———. "Maidens and Monsters in Modern Popular Culture: *The Silence of the Lambs* and *Beauty and the Beast.*" *Textual Practice* 7, no. 2 (Summer 1993): 258–66.

———. *Measure for Measure*: A CRITICAL INTRODUCTION. Brighton: Harvester, 1987.

———. "'Merrie England?': Contradictory Interpretations of the Corpus Christie Plays." *English* 29 (1980): 189–200.

———. "The Morality of Elizabethan Drama: Some Footnotes to Plato." In *English Renaissance Studies: Presented to Dame Helen Gardner in Honour of Her Seventieth Birthday*, edited by John Carey, 12–32. Oxford: Clarendon Press, 1980.

———. "Mortality, Morality, and Modernity in *The Broken Heart*: Some Dramatic and Critical Counter-Arguments." In *John Ford: Critical Re-Visions*, edited by Michael Neill, 129–52. Cambridge: Cambridge University Press, 1988.

———. "Myth and Morals (Review of *The Rapes of Lucretia* by Ian Donaldson)." *Essays in Criticism* 34, no. 1 (January 1984): 79–87.

———. "Paradigms Lost: Chaos, Milton and *Jurassic Park.*" *Textual Practice* 8, no. 2 (Summer 1994): 255–67.

———. "Parts and Partners in *Macbeth* and *Antony and Cleopatra.*" *The English Review* 2, no. 1 (September 1991): 11–15.

———. *Poetic Freedom and Poetic Truth*. Oxford: Clarendon Press, 1975.

———. "Reply to 'Spenser's Wanton Maidens' by Arlene Okerlund." Papers of the Modern Language Association 88, no. 5 (October 1973): 1185–87.

———. "Review of *The Action of English Comedy: Studies in the Encounter of Abstraction and Experience from Shakespeare to Shaw* by A. N. Kaul, and *The World Upside Down: Comedy from Jonson to Fielding* by Ian Donaldson." *Review of English Studies* new series 22 (November 1971): 517–20.

———. "Review of *An Approach to Congreve* by Aubrey Williams." *Review of English Studies* 32 new series, no. 125 (February 1981): 80–83.

———. "Review of *Dialectical Criticism and Renaissance Literature* by Michael McCanles." *Notes and Queries* 23, no. 4 (April 1976): 185–86.

———. "Review of *The Ethos of Restoration Comedy* by Ben Ross Schneider, Jr." *Review of English Studies* new series 23 (May 1972): 209–11.

———. "Review of *The Golden Age of English Drama* by S. Gorley Putt." *Review of English Studies* 35, no. 138 (May 1984): 221–22.

———. "Review of *Literary Creations: Conventional Characters in the Drama of Shakespeare and His Contemporaries* by G. M. Pinciss, and *Shifting Perspectives and the Sytlish Style: Mannerism in Shakespeare and His Jacobean Contemporaries* by John Greenwood." *Review of English Studies* 42 (1991): 105–6.

———. "Review of *The Motives of Eloquence: Literary Rhetoric in the Renaissance* by Richard A. Lanham." *Modern Language Review* 74 (January 1979): 139–41.

———. "Review of *The Ornament of Action: Text and Performance in Restoration Comedy* by Peter Holland." *Review of English Studies* 31, no. 124 (November 1980): 467–68.

———. "Review of *Passion Lends Them Power: A Study of Shakespeare's Love Tragedies* by Derick R. C. Marsh and *Shakespeare: Seven Tragedies: The Dramatist's Manipulation of Response* by E. A. J. Honigmann." *Review of English Studies* 28, no. 3 (August 1977): 334–37.

———. "Review of *Restoration Literature: Critical Approaches*, edited by Harold Love." *Review of English Studies* 24, no. 94 (May 1973): 213–15.

———. "Review of *Shakespeare Survey* 34, edited by Stanley Wells." *Review of English Studies* 35, no. 140 (November 1984): 531–33.

———. "Review of *Shakespeare's Tragedies of Love: An Examination of the Possibility of Common Readings of "Romeo and Juliet," "Othello," "King Lear," and "Antony and Cleopatra,"* by H.A. Mason." *Review of English Studies* 24, no. 96 (November 1973): 473–76.

———. "Review of *Shylock: Four Hundred Years in the Life of a Legend* by John Gross." *The English Review* 4, no. 1 (September 1993): 31–33.

———. "Review of *The Tragic Plane* by H. A. Mason, *The Subject of Tragedy: Identity and Difference in Renaissance Drama* by Catherine Belsey, and *Renaissance Tragedy and the Senecan Tradition: Anger's*

Privilege by Gordon Braden." *Review of English Studies* 38, no. 150 (May 1987): 277–80.

———. "Review of *Unconformities in Shakespeare's History Plays* by Kristian Smidt." *Review of English Studies* 35, no. 140 (November 1984): 532–33.

———. "Review of *The Uses of Division: Unity and Disharmony in Literature* by John Bayley." *Review of English Studies* 28, no. 112 (November 1977): 503–5.

———. "The Seductions of 'Comus'." *The English Review* 6, no. 2 (November 1995): 17–19.

———. "Shakespeare's Radical Romanticism: The Popular Tradition and the Challenge to Tribalism." In *Shakespeare in the New Europe*, edited by Boika Sokolova, Michael Hallaway, and Derek Roper. Sheffield: Sheffield Academic Press, 1994.

———. "Shared Dreams: Reproducing *Gone with the Wind*." In *Novel Images: Literature in Performance*, edited by Peter Reynolds, 122–38. London: Routledge, 1993.

———. *Strange Attractors: Literature, Culture and Chaos Theory*. New York: Prentice Hall/Harvester Wheatsheaf, 1995.

———. "Tara! Tara! Tara! (Review of *Scarlett: The Sequel to Margaret Mitchell's "Gone with the Wind"* by Alexandra Ripley)." *The Modern Review* 1, no. 2 (Winter 1991–92): 32.

———. "Thank You, Dr Lecter (Review of *The Silence of the Lambs*, directed by Jonathan Demme)." *The Modern Review* 1, no. 1 (Autumn 1991): 30–31.

———. "Twentieth-Century Appropriations of *The Tempest*." *The English Review* 3, no. 2 (November 1992): 18–22.

———. "The Two Most Beautiful Milkmaids in the World." In *KM 80: A Birthday Album for Kenneth Muir*, 68–71. Liverpool: Liverpool University Press, 1987.

———. "Venus Genus (Review of *Sexual Personae* by Camille Paglia)." *The Listener* 123, no. 3159 (5 April 1990): 30.

———. "The Victim's Side: Chaucer's *Clerk's Tale* and Webster's *Duchess of Malfi*." *Signs: Journal of Women in Culture and Society* 1, no. 2 (Winter 1975): 339–61.

———. "What Kind of Pre-Contract Had Angelo?: A Note on Some Non-Problems in Elizabethan Drama." *College English* 36, no. 2 (October 1974): 173–79.

———. "What Neoclassical Criticism Tells Us About What Shakespeare Does not Do." In *Shakespearean Comedy*, edited by Maurice Charney, 37–46. New York: New York Literary Forum, 1980.

———. "The Wonderful World of Carl Jung (Review of *Snow White and the Seven Dwarfs*, directed by Walt Disney)." *The Modern Review* 1, no. 3 (Spring 1992): 33.

———. "The Year's Contributions to Shakespearean Study: Critical Studies." In *Shakespeare Survey* 33, edited by Kenneth Muir, 181–94. Cambridge: Cambridge University Press, 1980.

———. "The Year's Contributions to Shakespearean Study: Critical Studies." In *Shakespeare Survey* 34, edited by Stanley Wells, 161–77. Cambridge: Cambridge University Press, 1981.
———. "The Year's Contributions to Shakespearean Study: Critical Studies." In *Shakespeare Survey* 35, edited by Stanley Wells, 153–79. Cambridge: Cambridge University Press, 1982.
Hawkins, Harriett, and Eric Buckley ("Margot Marlowe"). "Setting *A Midsummer Night's Dream* in the Third Reich." *Spectator*, 1981, 27 June 1981, 30.

Harriett Hawkins's Renaissance

Arthur Kinney

> You are confusing two concepts: *the solution of a problem* and *the correct posing of a question*. Only the second is obligatory for an artist. Not a single problem is solved in *Anna Karenina* and *Eugène Onegin*, but you find these works quite satisfactory . . . because all the questions in them are correctly posed . . . The court is obliged to pose the questions correctly, but it's up to the jurors to answer them, each juror according to his own taste.
> —Anton Chekhov

CORRECTLY POSING QUESTIONS RATHER THAN SOLVING THEM IS Harriett Hawkins's chief legacy. The passage from Chekhov arguing that this was the task of the artist she transformed into the task of the literary critic, and she quoted this passage many times in her works; it appears, for instance, as the epigraph to Chapter 1 of her booklength study of Shakespeare's *Measure for Measure*. But the questions she posed were often fresh and penetrating. Answers were another matter; for her, they were always multiple and often individual: she could analyze a passage or a character or an idea in a literary text with dazzling observation, but she always stopped short of offering any final interpretation. This followed another critical maxim she always observed: "For us," she comments in *Poetic Freedom and Poetic Truth*, "the very act of perception entails interpretation, and so carries with it the danger of misinterpretation."[1] The notion is prompted by misunderstandings within Shakespeare: the death of Cinna the poet, not Cinna the conspirator; the fatal unexpected meeting of Romeo and Count Paris in the graveyard; the great good fortune of Fortinbras who is handed a kingdom he might well have fought to gain. These sudden reversals of fortune, both bad and good, startle us as spectators or readers as they startle the characters themselves, who have misperceived and so misjudged their situations and, in turn, pose questions but do not solve the problem for us. We might label them *aporias*, although Hawkins, who resolutely placed text before theory, simply found them moments needing interpretation, aware of many interpretations, and always cognizant of misperceptions.

This is illustrated more elaborately in a passage on how dukes use their deputies, taken from Machiavelli's *Il Principe* and used to introduce issues unresolved in *Measure for Measure*:

> When the duke [Cesare Borgia] took over the Romagna, he found it had been controlled by impotent masters . . . so that the whole province was full of robbers, feuds and lawlessness of every description. To establish peace and reduce the land to obedience, he decided good government was needed; and he named Messer Remirro de Orco, a cruel and vigorous man, to whom he gave absolute powers. In short order this man pacified and unified the whole district, winning thereby great renown. But then the duke decided such excessive authority was no longer necessary, and feared it might become odious; so he set up a civil court in the middle of the province, with an excellent judge and a representative from each city. And because he knew that the recent harshness had generated some hatred, in order to clear the minds of the people and gain them over to his cause completely, he determined to make plain that whatever cruelty had occurred had come, not from him, but from the brutal character of the minister. Taking a proper occasion, therefore, he had him placed on the public square of Cesena one morning, in two pieces, with a piece of wood beside him and a bloody knife. The ferocity of this scene left the people at once stunned and satisfied.[2]

The passage veers toward, then away, from the Duke and Angelo, his appointed surrogate, but it seems close enough to have possibly influenced Shakespeare or to at least have resonated in the minds of some of his readers. The initial situation is in many ways analogous, but the ending is not. What does it mean to suggest? poor leadership and judgment on the part of Borgia? betrayal? vengeance? justice? another tyranny? How might we unscramble "stunned" alongside "satisfied"? Hawkins uses this as an opening context for *Measure for Measure* in a way typical for her: she sees resonances and dissonances both, and the divergence—she might well have said dialectic—opens up multiple considerations, any one of which or any combination of which is potentially relevant and so, in its way, satisfying. Machiavelli is useful because he poses relevant questions—and he is free of rewarding any reading preference.

The title of Shakespeare's play clearly seems biblical, and Hawkins traces it to Mark 4:21–24:

> And he said unto them, Is a candle brought to be put under a bushel, or under a bed? and not to be set on a candlestick?

> For there is nothing hid, which shall not be manifested; neither was any thing kept secret, but that it should come abroad.
> If any man have ears to hear, let him hear.
> And he said unto them, Take heed what ye hear: with what measure ye mete, it shall be measured to you.

The usual passage cited is from Luke 6:37—"Judge not, and ye shall not be judged"—but for Hawkins that would be too admonitory and restrictive; the passage she prefers is far more ambiguous and even obscure (when applied to the play) since what is given is reciprocal to what was given and Mark does not name that. Mark's gospel, then, opens up meanings rather than closes them down. *Measure for Measure* was in many ways Hawkins's play, and her triumphant readings and rereadings became a centerpiece of her Shakespearean criticism. This may largely be because, for her, it was a play of so many questions:

> How important—or unimportant—is chastity? And what constitutes rape? How grievous a violation is it to be blackmailed or tricked into bed with someone you, personally, would not choose to have sexual intercourse with? Given a conflict between Christian virtues (like chastity and charity), which should take precedence? Should a brother allow his sister to prostitute herself in order to save him? Should a young novice sacrifice her chastity, and so jeopardise what she believes to be her immortal soul, in order to save her brother's life? And if she will not do so, should she encourage another woman to do it for her?
> And what about the rule of law? Does the scriptural commandment, "Judge not that ye be not judged" apply to princes and magistrates who are professionally bound to laws of the land? If so, *or* if not—"'twas my fault to give the people scope"—is it right for the Duke to deputise Angelo to "strike and gall" the people for what he, himself, had bid them do?—"For we bid this be done, / When evil deeds have their permissive pass / And not the punishment" (I.ii.37–39). And what if certain laws "set down in heaven", or on earth, conflict with the biological and psychological laws of human nature? How socially disruptive, or socially acceptable, is premarital sex? Or organised prostitution? And what about shot-gun weddings? Isn't the free consent of both parties just as important in marriage as in sex? How binding is a legal certificate if there is not a marriage of true minds?[3]

These are, essentially, *textual* questions. They are not performative. The point needs to be made, because Hawkins wrote these words in the rising tide of theatrical and performance criticism. She eschewed that for the text itself. She also wrote in the early days of the New Historicism—and after Josephine Waters Bennett had written a provocative and influential book arguing that the play was written for royal performance and the Duke was Shakespeare's staging of James I and VI. For Hawkins, such a reading would have been both too limiting and too directive; it would also have been too ideological. She refuted such criticism openly in *Classics and Trash*, and she used Karl Marx to do so!

> As Karl Marx observed, it is not at all difficult to see any work of art as the product of a given social, historical and technological stage of development or in terms of a reigning ideology. What Marx himself believed it was far more difficult—and far more important—to account for was why Greek art and Shakespearian drama have continued to give succeeding generations such great pleasure and why, to ages and nations in very different stages of social and technological development—as well as in states with dialectically opposite ideologies—they "still prevail as standards and models beyond attainment."[4]

Hawkins would pay no mind to those critics who prioritized or eliminated possible meanings that a text could reasonably yield to an informed and sensitive reader. She cites Karl Popper in *The Devil's Party* as closer to her lines of investigation: "Repeated observations and experiments function in science as *tests* of our conjectures or hypotheses, i.e. as attempted refutations . . . It is easy to obtain confirmations, or verifications, for nearly every theory—if we look for confirmations," Popper writes. "Confirming evidence should not count *when it is the result of a genuine test of the theory*; and this means that it can be presented as a serious but unsuccessful attempt to falsify the theory" so that even negative feedback of an idea or critical interpretation could be possible and refutation should be sought, not dismissed.[5] But her rather more obscure allusions to the work of Norman Rabkin on Shakespeare, which draws on Neils Bohr's sense of complementarity, is perhaps nearer as a resource for her thought. What such a principle of criticism gave to Rabkin and thus in turn to Hawkins was a kind of balancing act, in which ideas were held in suspension, in equipoise, in a kind of ongoing equivocation (*Macbeth*, in fact, seems to be another favorite Shakespearean play of hers). Yet I think that behind both Popper and Bohr was Heisenberg's principle of indeterminacy. That too was abroad as Hawkins plied her profession of literary critic, although I find no mention of him in her work. Indeed, Hawkins's work on Shakespeare anticipated Michael Frayn's recent play: *Copenhagen* where Bohr and Heisenberg mysteriously meet in 1941 and, later on, Bohr and his wife entertain, serially and repetitively, possible reasons for Heisenberg's unexpected visit while working on atomic physics for the Gestapo. Hawkins would, I think, have seen this play as a concentrated paradigm of her critical method as, late in life, she was drawn to chaos theory for much the same reasons. The dance of literary sensibility and interpretive reason over texts is unending.

II

"It seems to me," Hawkins contends in *Poetic Freedom and Poetic Truth*, "that the pursuit of objectivity has itself proved destructive to good criticism because it tends to require some form of authority apart from the individual texts themselves which can dictate how we all ought to think about those texts, or how we ought to respond to them."[6] Conversely, the texts themselves provide their own interpretations *and* their counter-interpretations. Her study of *Measure for Measure* is grounded in both. So "Isabella's searing refusal to lay down the treasure of her body to Angelo is charged with an erotic power that might well evoke a gleam in the eye of the most depraved marquis in the audience";[7] furthermore, the language betrays Isabella's own masturbatory inclinations:

> were I under the terms of death,
> Th' impression of keen whips I'd wear as rubies,
> And strip myself to death as to a bed,
> That longing have been sick for, ere I'd yield
> My body up to shame.
> (II. iv. 100–104)

Julietta's sexual complicity with Claudio, that is, her sexual consummation, is termed "wrong," "a sin," "a most offenceful act," an "evil," by the Duke and yet it is precisely the sin (or act) of Mariana with Angelo which is seen by the Duke as sinless:

> [Angelo] is your husband on a pre-contract,
> To bring you thus together 'tis no sin,
> Sith that the justice of your title to him
> Do flourish the deceit,
> (IV. i. 70–73)

yet Shakespeare is clear enough that this pre-contract is, if anything, more sincere than—and surely identical with—the contract between Julietta and Claudio. Again, "It is hard to imagine any bleaker reasons to 'Be absolute for death' than the ones that the Duke gives to Claudio," Hawkins tells us—"Yet in this life / Lie hid moe thousand deaths; yet death we fear, / That makes these odds all even." "But," Hawkins goes on, "*mutatis mutandis*, it is difficult to imagine any better reasons to be absolute for life than the ones that Claudio gives to Isabella:

> Ay, but to die, and go we know not where;
> To lie in cold obstruction, and to rot; . . .
> The weariest and most loathed worldly life
> That age, ache, penury, and imprisonment,
> Can lay on nature is a paradise
> To what we fear of death."
>
> (III.i.119–20; 130–33)[8]

Or, again, if Claudio is legally liable for the death penalty, then why not Angelo? And if Isabella allows Claudio to go to his own death for fornication, why does she later plead to the Duke to grant mercy to Angelo for the same immoral, criminal act—why does she condemn her own brother and defend the potential rapist? Those who deny such oppositions within the text—who try to place on it some "thematic unity, or hermeneutical allegory, or Brechtian alienation, or an Eliot-like detachment"[9]—supply *Measure for Measure* with a field theory of integrity that it simply does not provide. Rather, it is fundamentally dialectical, each quotation matched with its opposite:

> Thus, on the basis of counter-quotations from the same script, individual members of the audience—very like the individual characters portrayed on the stage—may arrive at diametrically opposite conclusions about the same issue: or remain torn between conflicting attitudes towards the same thing. . . . What it is almost impossible to do is to defend any one position or character or response—or interpretation of the play as a whole—*without* arguing against another one. The critical result is a tangle of intertwined, yet mutually contradictory, interpretations of the play based on different arguments for or against the various characters, all of which can be supported by quotations from the text itself, and so would appear to be equally valid.[10]

It would be a fundamental misreading, Hawkins argues, to erase such oppositions by selective evidence or prioritized concerns. It would, in fact, not only be critically counterproductive, but also fundamentally antidramatic and antitheatrical. Furthermore, she argues, Shakespeare did not mean us to read the play with a single and simple thesis, which is amply demonstrated by providing no external authority for reading the play and no internal one either.

This does not mean for Hawkins that *Measure for Measure*, or any other Shakespearean play, is *merely* a matter of sequential dialogue as dialectic with no shape—resembling the early Tudor plays of John Heywood or the early Elizabethan plays of John Lyly or the grammar-school exercises from which both sprang—but rather that such arguments and counterarguments, such conflicting evidence, is subsumed into a larger dramatic (although still dialectical) structure. "Thus, on the one hand, Shakespeare creates a desire to watch these characters face the tragic truths and consequences of their own decisions and desires and, on the other hand, creates a counterdesire to see how he—or the Duke—is going to save them from death, dishonour, each other, themselves, and so on."[11] In *Measure for Measure* this happens with a major, but subtle, shift in Act III when the play moves from "tragic psychological and social and biological realities to comic evasions and intrigues,"[12] when we move from the fears of Claudio and the firm unforgiveness of Isabella to the bed trick, from irrevocable justice to a kind of mercy that pardons the innocent Claudio, the duplicitous Angelo, and even the murderer Bernardine (who alone is intransigent and ungriefstricken, but who, also alone, did not know what he was doing, since he was drunk when he committed his crime). For Hawkins, though, such an arrangement, moving this "problem play" into the realm of comedy (marriage and forgiveness), is still crammed with multiple interpretations that make us aware of the two-part, dialectical structure of the whole. We can interpret characters, actions, and ideas, that is, but without any singular (or certain) answers: the interpretations continually pose the questions.

III

It is crucial to Hawkins's critical method that reading (or seeing) Shakespeare keeps us suspended in a kind of dialectic because it keeps open the possibility of new meanings and interpretations added to the multitude already advocated by various critics, some more sensibly and reliably than others. *The Devil's Party*, still her most powerful and influential book on Shakespeare, rests on just this premise. It is the keystone of Shakespearean art: "Shakespearian drama itself actually does allow the audience to experience any number of differing emotions simultaneously and may elicit a number of different responses (e.g., pity and terror and aesthetic admiration and moral disapproval)."[13] We can feel terror at the Ghost of Hamlet, sorrow for Ophelia, impatience with Hamlet, and joy with the First Gravedigger, but it is just such variety that gives power to Shakespeare and unfixes final meanings for any of his plays. Unfixing meaning liberates plays from powerful ideologies, which, for Hawkins in *The Devil's Party*, have oppressed the reading of plays by imposing Marxist, Christian, and Freudian readings among others. Assuming that one helpful approach for one play can work equally well for other plays likewise reduces them to disappointing (if desirably predictable) similarities. Such fixed perspectives, like ideologies, diminish and misconstrue the rich complexity of the plays. "Critics would swear that they had said something profoundly true about Shakespeare's *Hamlet*," for instance, but having "actually given us their own Romantic, or late-Victorian, or Modernist, or Post-Structuralist pseudo *Hamlets* . . . will be seen, and probably sneered at, as such, by successive generations."[14] In her own defense, and for illustration, she cites Friar Laurence from *Romeo and Juliet* on the creative powers of Nature:

> And from her womb children of diverse kind
> We sucking on her natural bosom find;
> Many for many virtues excellent,
> None but for some, and yet all different.
> O mickle is the powerful grace that lies
> In plants, herbs, stones, and their true qualities;
> For nought so vile that on earth doth live
> But to the earth some special good doth give.
>
> (II.ii.11–18)

It is typical of Hawkins's shrewd moves, for in aligning her sense of Shakespearean art with the processes of nature, she draws into her camp the various critics who have praised Shakespeare as the playwright of nature without reducing that proposition to sheer Romanticism or sentimentality.

But there is more at work here. By admitting many possibilities for understanding Shakespeare that are not necessarily similar or coherent, one with another, she opens up reading (and seeing) the plays to individual responses. She does this to advance another of her major critical claims: that we finally do not simply read or see a play but actually participate in it. By investing our own perspective and judgments, we anticipate developments and outcomes and what is (dramatically) at stake: posing interpretations as questions is our commitment to test meaning through our own intimate relationship with the text. In *The Devil's Party* (but not elsewhere) she develops this participation into a set of rules that guarantees its dynamic possibilities:

1. The drama may, simultaneously, elicit contradictory moral, aesthetic, and emotional responses towards a single character. . . .
2. Dramatic prose and poetry can be outrageously insolent and impudent to those in authority. . . .
3. Drama may encourage us to relish, on the stage, behaviour that, in real life, we would certainly deplore. . . .
4. The emphasis of the drama is, far more often than not, on the worst aspects of human nature, on sensational, spectacular vices. . . .
5. The greatest poets often hint, or imply, or come right out and say, that the gods themselves are sometimes cruelly or arbitrarily unjust to men and women—that good people are sometimes wretched, and wrong-doing sometimes pays . . . or, as Shakespeare puts it [in *King Lear*], "As flies to wanton boys are we to the gods"; and those who act "with best meaning" have sometimes "incurr ' d the worst."[15]

While this liberation of the reader, spectator, or critic provides the liberation of the meanings stored in a Shakespearean play, it does validate Plato's concern with poetry as having the power to free emotions, make men uncontrollable, and threaten the order of the state and of society. For Hawkins, this is the price of knowledge, of creative participation, and finally for comprehension of Shakespeare's art. A play "may not only look different to different people at the same time, and may seem entirely different to the same person at different times, but may also appear in different ways to the same individual at one and the same time."[16] Hamlet can be cruel to be kind. Iago can be honest to be dishonest. Hermione can return to life; Prospero can burn his books.

Hawkins locates a companionable voice in Hobbes's *Leviathan*:

> For though the nature of that we conceive, be the same; yet the diversity of our reception of it, in respect of different constitutions of body, and prejudices of opinion, gives everything a tincture of our different passions. . . . For one man calleth *Wisdome*, what another calleth *feare*; and one *cruelty*, what another *justice*; one *prodigality*, what another *magnanimity*. . . . From the same it proceedeth, that men give different names, to one and the same thing, from the difference of their own passions: As they that approve a private opinion, call it Opinion; but they that mislike it, Haerisie.[17]

Like Chekhov, she means to pose questions—and that only, her whole *ouevre* of a piece. Like Popper, she would have "conjectures boldly put forward for trial."

IV

There is one other principle operating in Hawkins's Shakespearean criticism. That is the playwright's peculiar sense of form, discussed in *The Devil's Party*.

> Like Hamlet's deliverance by pirates, many things in Shakespeare do seem "inconsequential" in the sense that they do not, necessarily, follow from what has gone before. There are accidental judgments, casual slaughters, and purposes mistook. For instance, the fact that Edmund falls, just as he rose, because of a letter, seems utterly, even poignantly, inconsequential. So does the death of the County Paris. And so does the death of Cordelia. It has been argued, by Maurice Morgann (among others) that in drama the "impression is the fact". And the main impression conveyed by Shakespeare's construction is that, at its best, it is not too good to be true to human experience. Very like some of their greatest characters, the zigzag motions of certain plays have resisted all critical efforts to clear them up, to smooth out their depressions and elevations, or to lend arguments not drawn from life to principles (or prejudices) that will shape, to tidy ends, what Brecht called the "lot of raw material" that Shakespeare "shovels onto the stage."[18]

Elsewhere, she writes that "With Shakespeare at his best, construction is not an art but a secret; and the secret of organic form remains inviolable."[19] She knows why he uses this secret, however, if not always how: it is to achieve that very zigzag that prevents clamping an ideology down on the text; rather, it reawakens life in a way that participatory readings can experience it, finally, without discomfort and usually without surprise.

In her last book before turning to chaos theory itself, *Classics and Trash: Traditions and Taboos in High Literature and Popular Modern Genres*, Hawkins finally exposes the reasons for her criticism. The multiplicity of responses, the freedom from ideologies, the dismissal of theory, the secret construction: all underwrite and promote participatory criticism. It is the very opposite of Brechtian alienation. But given their dialectical presentation and variable significances, Shakespeare's plays are open to all kinds of adaptation—Dryden's *All for Love*; Verdi's operas on *Otello* and *Falstaff*; *Nicholas Nickleby* and *Huckleberry Finn*; *The Boys from Syracuse*; *Kiss Me, Kate!* and *West Side Story*—showing their inner resources, their vitality and, not least, their versatility and resiliency. But Shakespeare's own works, inspiring others, are never swallowed up in these derivations. Rather, Shakespeare retains preeminence because his works, capable of changing meanings in changing times, have that multivocality that guarantees both timeliness and timelessness. Or, to revert to science, which Hawkins also admired, literary criticism follows the law of physics that for every stimulus (read play) there is a response; for every action, a reaction; but the responses and reactions are seldom, if ever, identical.

The Devil's Party begins with an epigraph from Archilochus that she used more than once: "The fox knows many things. The hedgehog knows one big thing."[20] She might then have been comparing Shakespeare to the fox—"he wrote without a direct moral purpose, and extolled the 'negative capacity' [in Keats's phrase] of the chameleon artist who can take as much delight 'in conceiving an Iago as an Imogen'[21]—and herself to the hedgehog, concentrating at the time as she was on the single body of Shakespeare's work. But the conclusion of that book belies this:

> The fact that the centuries-long search for some unified field theory—for some structural, or theological, or historical, or mimetic, or moralistic, or theoretical, or sexual, or psychoanalytical, perspective (or premise) that can comprehend the organization and characterization of Shakespearian drama—has proved as futile as the search for the Fountain of Youth, or the Philosopher's Stone, or the Maltese Falcon (some very interesting discoveries have been made along the way), should be cause for general celebration, not despair. It suggests that we are far better off with a multiplicity of approaches, and so opens everything up by liberating critics, teachers, students, and directors alike from the obligation to confirm the ubiquitous applicability of any given approach—whether with or without reference to those works that might better serve to refute it. The inexhaustible range of Shakespearian subjects and styles also explains why anyone, from the beginning student to the greatest living Shakespearian critic (and the best in our kind are but his students) who looks to the plays as a source of personal delight and instruction is bound to find innumerable topics for fruitful speculation.[22]

So this stylish critic is the foxy lady reading the foxy playwright. And she, given her sense of charity and style, would have us join her. The world can do without hedgehogs.

Notes

1. Harriett Hawkins, *Poetic Freedom and Poetic Truth* (Oxford: Clarendon Press, 1975), 18.
2. Harriett Hawkins, *Measure for Measure: A Critical Introduction* (Brighton: Harvester, 1987), 1–2.

3. Ibid., 12.
4. Harriett Hawkins, *Classics and Trash: Traditions and Taboos in "High" Literature and Popular Modern Genres* (Toronto: University of Toronto Press, 1990), 130.
5. Harriett Hawkins, *The Devil's Party: Critical Counter-Interpretations of Shakespearian Drama* (Oxford: Clarendon Press, 1985), 109.
6. Hawkins, *Poetic Freedom and Poetic Truth*, 23.
7. Hawkins, *Measure for Measure*, 27.
8. Ibid., 15.
9. Ibid., xiv.
10. Ibid., 16.
11. Ibid., 42.
12. Ibid., 87.
13. Hawkins, *The Devil's Party*, 3.
14. Ibid., 19.
15. Ibid., 47–48.
16. Ibid., 55.
17. Ibid., 82.
18. Ibid., 173.
19. Ibid., 175.
20. Ibid., 1.
21. Ibid., 2.
22. Ibid., 179.

Harriett Hawkins and the Criticism of the 1970s: Interpretation, Theory, and Iconoclasm

Robert Markley

It is difficult for me to believe that Harriett Hawkins published *Likenesses of Truth in Elizabethan and Restoration Drama* more than thirty years ago when I was student in her course on English drama to 1700 at Vassar College.[1] It is more difficult for me to reread her work now without hearing her classroom voice animating her prose—a voice at once witty, probing, assertive, and iconoclastic. To jump-start a class discussion on George Etherege's *The Man of Mode* she asked, "Isn't it interesting that Etherege decided to name his bitchy heroine after me?" Her penchant for asking seemingly off-the-wall and yet provocative questions was a hallmark of her teaching, and, as many readers of this essay know, of her critical writing as well. Such questions were intended to get her students and readers to react first and to formulate intellectual justifications for their responses only after they had registered the complexities that literature engenders.

For a critic who turned to popular culture and chaos theory in the 1990s, it is significant that her first two books, *Likenesses of Truth* (a phrase used by Ben Jonson to describe his plays) and *Poetic Freedom and Poetic Truth*, featured "truth" in their titles.[2] Hawkins's use of this now-suspect term, however, was not indicative of a moralism that she later rejected but a mark of her career-long commitment to complex aesthetic and moral heuristics. Challenging the New Critical orthodoxies of the 1970s that were obsessed with identifying "unifying themes" in the plays of Shakespeare and his contemporaries, both studies argued that literature mirrors and intervenes in complex sociopolitical realities. Hawkins granted to students, playgoers, and readers an interpretive iconoclasm and a stubborn resistance to the one-size-fits-all moralizing that characterized the criticism of many of her contemporaries. In arguing that these two books had a significant, though often underappreciated, influence on the development of the criticism of seventeenth-century drama, I make no pretenses to complete objectivity. Harriett Hawkins was as generous as she was brilliant. Long after we had both left Vassar, she helped me grope toward a dissertation topic; sent me copies of her work-in-progress and even her abandoned graduate school essays that she termed (with hilarious modesty) "bonecrushingly boring," and eventually ran interference for my first book with Oxford University Press as it labored through the editorial and production processes. My approach to Restoration comedy still owes a good deal to a mentor and friend who proved anything but bitchy.

In notes that I took in a class that Hawkins taught on *The Revengers Tragedy*, there is an underlined assertion: "Truth is corrosive." While I would love to take credit for this turn of phrase, it is likely either a direct quotation or my shorthand for her comments on the ways in which Cyril Tourneur's tragic farce makes hash of Jacobean pieties about truth and virtue. As her comment on Etherege's heroine implies, Hawkins suggests that truth is corrosive in at least two senses: it undermines moral, ideological, and political verities that serve the interests of those in power; and, in plays such as John Webster's *The Duchess of Malfi*, it measures the toll that the imposition of coercive moralities exacts on both its victims (the Duchess) and its perpetrators (her lycanthropic brother). If my rhetoric seems to nudge her work towards the critique of ideology that became prominent in the 1980s and 1990s, my characterization is deliberate: throughout her work, Hawkins insists on the ways in which aesthetic responses and moral judgments frequently tugged readers and audiences in different directions. Precisely because literature is characterized by the "persistent refusals" of poets and dramatists "to mirror the orthodoxies of the time," she maintains, it resists rules of extra-poetic justice and didactic demonstration. In this regard, it is telling that in her brilliant opening chapter of *Poetic Freedom and Poetic Truth*, she illustrates the arbitrary rewards and punishments of literary texts and history by quoting two long passages from Alexander Solzhenitsyn's *The First Circle*.[3] Her juxtaposition of Stalin's Gulag and the world of Thomas Middleton's and William Rowling's *The Changeling* exemplifies a critical method that recognizes the lengths to which humans will go both to defy religious and secular authorities—De Flores goes to his death still besotted with Beatrice-Joanna—and to bend their desires to conform to the injunctions of "truths" as arbitrary as they are corrosive.

Hawkins' insistence on "the divine right" of Chaucer, Shakespeare, Milton, and their contemporaries "to argue freely" against the orthodoxies of their era cleverly appropriates the rhetoric of seventeenth-century political and theological debates to provide a basis for her non-deterministic criticism. Like Milton, Hawkins is a voluntarist who emphasizes the irruption of the irrational, unpredictable, and arbitrary into the course of human affairs. The "poetic deadlocks" that characterize *Paradise Lost*, for example, offer no predictable resolution to the mutual recriminations of Adam and Eve after the fall, and no false hopes for those confronted by the spectacle of human suffering and evil that Michael describes in Book XI.[4] The skepticism that creeps into her later comments on the monological tendencies of some New Historicists and Anglo-American purveyors of French theory, in this regard, stems from her suspicion of critical orthodoxies of any sort. Her turn to chaos theory in *Strange Attractors*, then, represents an extension of the historical and theoretical commitments evident in her work of the 1970s: rather than rejecting New Historicism or Anglo-American feminism (as some commentators seem to think), Hawkins tried to ensure that the discourses of historical and theoretical analysis remain true to what she saw as the iconoclasm of great literature.

In part, her interpretation of early modern drama emerged dialogically in response to the thematic-oriented criticism of the 1960s and 1970s. *Likenesses of Truth* and *Poetic Freedom* challenge the formalism that dominated the study of Shakespeare and his contemporaries on both historical and theoretical grounds. To some extent, these books as well as articles such as "The 'Example Theory' and the Providentialist Approach to Restoration Drama" (1983) and "Players and Scorecards" (1984), both drew from and informed similar critiques offered by A. H. Scouten and Richard Levin.[5] But to a greater extent than either Scouten or Levin, Hawkins exposed the querulous drudgery of hunting for "central themes" and the strained logic of manufacturing "new" readings that somehow had escaped all previous critics and audiences. In some respects, her witty skepticism in debunking the paint-by-numbers techniques of New Critics had affinities with the approach of Stanley Fish in *Surprised by Sin* and *Self-Consuming Artifacts*.[6] Both Hawkins and Fish maintained that literature was experiential rather than didactic, and, in different ways, both suggested that English literature of the sixteenth and seventeenth centuries resisted the organic and holistic metaphors that dominated New Criticism. "Truth" and "freedom" in these four books are not timeless verities etched on well-wrought urns but products of self-doubt, bitter experience, and hard-won knowledge. However, while Fish was and is a product of the high-powered research university system (an icon of the hyper-professional who, like Morris Zapp, gains notoriety by playing himself), Hawkins spent her career outside the small world of academic stardom satirized by David Lodge—first at Vassar and later at Linacre College, Oxford. Her voice in the studies she published in the 1970s and 1980s is always that of a teacher who knows that she must entertain as well as instruct her audience, and who recognizes that entertainment is a serious business.

Ironically for a critic who taught and wrote mostly about Shakespeare and his contemporaries, Hawkins's influence on subsequent generations of scholars might best be judged by the changes she fostered in the criticism of Restoration comedy. In the 1960s and 1970s, Restoration drama was a small and marginalized subfield, dominated by theater historians and taught to undergraduates only as an afterthought in courses on the Renaissance. Its defenders were locked in what seemed a Sisyphean struggle to have the plays of Etherege, Wycherley, Congreve, and their contemporaries taken seriously as part of a formalist tradition of "great" literature. In itself, this state of affairs was hardly new. Since the eighteenth century, moralistic critics had lambasted the plays of Etherege, Wycherley, and Congreve for their blasphemy and immorality, and largely ignored the comedies of Aphra Behn, Thomas Otway, John Vanbrugh, and George Farquhar. In the first half of the twentieth century, a handful of scholars argued for the aesthetic value of one or more of these playwrights, but in the 1950s some critics began to assert the best Restoration comedies displayed the timeless aesthetic significance of great literature.[7] Dale Underwood, for example, maintained that Etherege's comedies reconciled the foundational oppositions of western culture—those of "Christianity and Christian humanism, the 'heroic' tradition, the honest-man tradition, and courtly love" on the one hand and "philosophical and moral libertinism, Machiavellian and Hobbesian concepts [of] the nature of man" on the other.[8] Norman Holland deftly traced the imagistic patterns at work in the plays of Etherege, Wycherley, and Congreve to argue that these first "modern" comedies registered a profound questioning of Renaissance humanism.[9] As valuable as these studies were, they tended to subordinate theatrical irony and complex satirical strategies to a kind of neoromanticism that valued literary texts for the insights they provided into a transhistorical and transcultural human condition.

By the time *Likenesses of Truth* appeared, such efforts to moralize Restoration comedy had reached a critical impasse between a limited contextualism and self-congratulatory theme-hunting: while the wit-battles endemic to the late seventeenth-century stage reflected right-way, wrong-way demonstrations of how to thrive socially, such conversations among heiresses, truewits, witwouds, and fops implied grander concerns about "the nature of man." These comedies therefore were curiously detached from the political uncertainties, diplomatic maneuverings, parliamentary and governmental crises, religious conflicts, wars, and the threat of wars that characterized the world outside the theater. For many formalist critics, history was a concern only to the extent that it buttressed their quest to uncover moral seriousness and aesthetic significance in comedies that many of their colleagues working in other periods dismissed as artificial and trivial. Contextualizing Restoration comedy consequently took the form of chasing down ideologically loaded and self-interested pronouncements in a handful of late seventeenth-century texts, including sermons, and treating them as unambiguous reflections of widely held beliefs and values. These monochromatic snapshots of seventeenth-century belief systems could then be used as guides to ferret out the serious purposes informing plays by Etherege, Wycherley, and Congreve.

In criticizing such ahistorical formalism, Hawkins zeroed in on the work of Aubrey Williams, a well-regarded editor and critic of Pope who had turned his attention to Restoration drama in the late 1960s. In a series of articles that culminated in his 1979 study, *An Approach to Congreve*, Williams argued that *The Old Batchelour*, *The Double-Dealer*, *Love for Love*, and *The Way of the World*—attacked for three hundred years for their immorality and blasphemy—actually exemplified the workings of providential order.[10] Not only were Congreve's comedies "patently religious" works, Williams argues, but their demonstrations that divine providence guided all human actions had been understood intuitively by a Restoration audience steeped in Christian doctrine. "Most Restoration plays," he writes, "whether adaptations, revivals, or original compositions were thought to reveal, or were made to reveal, the great patterns of Providence, and they reflect a specifically religious attitude towards life." To argue his case, Williams traces imagistic patterns of sin, contrition, redemption, and divinely ordained justice in Congreve's plays, and asserts more broadly that such Providential "patterns and images are to be found throughout the entire range of Restoration drama."[11] Methodologically, this was New Criticism taken to its logical extreme—not only could all Restoration plays be read to yield their central themes, these themes were foreordained by a unitary vision of "seventeenth-century theodicy." Each play, including Congreve's, provides "another example of the manifold literary guises by which God's ways could be justified to man."[12]

Rather than playing a tired game of critical one-upsmanship ("my reading trumps your reading"), Hawkins challenges Williams on both historical and theoretical grounds. Ignoring the work of Keith Thomas, Christopher Hill, and A. L. Morton, among other historians, Williams paints what she argues is a skewed portrait of Restoration society, downplaying both the skepticism rampant in the period and the very reasons—Civil War, plague, fire, and defeat—that Milton, among others, assumed that justifying the ways of God would be "awesomely difficult."[13] She questions Williams's choice of texts to support his view of Restoration "theodicy," and she attacks his interpretation of the Collier controversy. Faced with Jeremy Collier's charges that his plays ridiculed the clergy, made virtue boring, and presented vice as dazzlingly attractive, Congreve hemmed, hawed, and argued that Collier consistently took his examples out of context. Williams reads into Congreve's defense a providentialist counterargument that would have been obvious to readers; Hawkins insists that the dramatist's chief line of defense was invoking theatrical contexts: fools mouthing platitudes about Providence, like the cuckold Sir Paul Plyant in *The Double-Dealer*, are still fools. As obsessed in his own way as Collier with "stringing together scattered religious allusions" excised from Congreve's plays, Williams produces what Hawkins calls a "photo-negative reversal" of the clergyman's critique, taking as evidence of serious moral intent what Collier and other critics of the stage in 1698 found blasphemous, profane, and immoral.[14] More damningly, she argues that Williams's "interpretations of [Congreve's] plays (again like Collier's) tend to be predictable, humorless, moralistic, and . . . infuriatingly patronizing," unable to register the irony that marks, for example, Mirabel's scenes with Lady Wishfort.[15] Generic differences among heroic tragedy, comedy, and sermons get trampled under foot by Williams as much as by Collier, and his approach offers no way to distinguish Congreve's achievement from the efforts of dozens of other playwrights all churning out plays to the same religious end.

Williams's book, Hawkins contends, thus raises and begs crucial theoretical questions—that is, questions dealing with the values and assumptions that underlie his methods of reading Restoration drama. "Why," she asks, "is a literature which denies or rationalizes the injustice inherent in the ways of our world deemed to be more profoundly moral . . . than one which does not?" Quoting Milton's Archangel Michael—"So shall the world go on/ To good malignant, to bad men benign"—she then asks her readers to consider what lessons conceivably could be learned by audience members who, day in and day out, witness virtue rewarded and evil punished.[16] If all Restoration playgoers already believe in a divinity that shapes their ends, and patronize only theatrical representations that confirm their beliefs, then the drama becomes at best trivial or at worst delusional—teaching people that religious orthodoxy will ensure temporal rewards. In a sense, Hawkins's critique of Williams is a latter-day version of the eighteenth-century debate between Henry Fielding and Samuel Richardson: Virtue rewarded, she suggests, can be a self-serving means to defend the status quo. Invoking Bertolt Brecht's observation that the dominant viewpoint is the viewpoint of the dominators, she argues that providentialist design, as Williams conceives it, is a means to dodge individual, collective, and even religious responsibility "to do whatever one can to alleviate or to stop human suffering" and "obvious instances of temporal injustice."[17]

The article I have been discussing, "The 'Example Theory' and the Providentialist Approach to Restoration Drama," appeared in a special issue of *The Eighteenth Century: Theory and Interpretation* that included pieces by Michael Neill, Michael McKeon, and James Thompson.[18] This context, I think, is significant because it suggests the extent to which Hawkins by 1983 had helped to send her colleagues and students back to the literature of the seventeenth century more attuned to the ideological implications of truisms about Providence and upper-class virtue. One measure of her influence—if we take "influence" not as a causal mechanism but as an informing analytic—is to consider the sea changes that marked the careers of two of Aubrey Williams's prominent students, J. Douglas Canfield and James Thompson. Both began their scholarly careers as providentialists, following Williams in arguing that religious "patterns and images" played a crucial role in how seventeenth-century dramatists and audiences perceived the moral and social-cultural significance of the theater.[19] Within a few years, however, both were drawing far more on the works of Karl Marx and Louis Althusser in their readings of Restoration and eighteenth-century literature than they were on Williams or other New Critics.[20] In historicizing the Restoration, Canfield and Thompson joined a small army of other critics—Peter Holland, Laura Brown, Robert Hume, Harold Weber, myself, Brian Corman, Pat Gill, and Derek Hughes, among others—who, while offering often competing views of the late seventeenth-century stage, nonetheless rejected Williams's argument that playwrights, actors, cits, and dissolute aristocrats were (to borrow the title of the opening chapter of *An Approach to Congreve*) of one faith.[21] Of these critics, I am probably the one most versed in, and appreciative of, Harriett's work. But I would argue that an extremely interesting history of the recent criticism of seventeenth-century drama could be written by tracing a genealogy of the work of Williams's students and colleagues on the one hand and Hawkins's on the other. To some extent, works such as Raymond Tumbleson's *Catholicism in the English Protestant Imagination*, Desiree Hellegers's *Handmaid to Divinity* and Heidi Hutner's *Colonial Women* continue conversations that began thirty years ago in *Likenesses of Truth* and in the classes Hawkins taught at Vassar.[22]

Hawkins's methodological critique of Williams and other reductionists developed from her own analytical and teaching strategies. One of the touchstones of her criticism was the work of the Shakespearean scholar Derek Traversi. In a series of well-regarded studies in the 1950s and 1960s, Traversi argued that no dramatic image had any meaning beyond its immediate theatrical context. Shakespeare's language is specific to the moment of its utterance. Consequently, critics who string together images taken from different speakers at different points in a play or plays are imposing ahistorical notions of aesthetic and ideational coherence on Shakespeare's plays. Renaissance playgoers, Traversi maintains, were not neoformalists and did not play "connect the dots" with, say, images of blood in *Julius Caesar* to make sense of Shakespeare's tragedy.[23] In extending Traversi's approach, Hawkins insists that Renaissance and Restoration plays are not organized thematically, and that the scholarly search for thematic coherence inevitably proves heavy-handed and coercive. No hypothetical model of an undifferentiated seventeenth-century audience can describe individual responses to characters knowingly or even gleefully transgressing the moral and religious standards of the period, and no amount of after-the-fact ingenuity or moralizing about Renaissance conceptions of paternal authority can undermine the emotional effects of theatrical master strokes such as Romeo's and Juliet's death scene.

Long before Hawkins began invoking chaos theory, her analyses of seventeenth-century drama explored ways to justify individual interpretive freedom within the boundaries defined by always complex and changing generic expectations. The metaphors that appear frequently in her work are those of chance, uncertainty, and, in her analysis of *The Man of Mode*, game playing and gambling.[24]

Etherege's final comedy, she argues, is a game of chance: Harriett must be "bitchy" because she has to play her hand by stoking Dorimant's interest while retaining her only trump card—her virginity. The differences among Harriett, Belinda, and Mrs. Loveit have little to do with moral virtue, true love, or even physical attractiveness; they are playing the same game, and Harriett is astute enough to recognize that her wit is her most valuable asset. Wit, though, is not measured by her conformity to an abstract ideal, but by her success as an actress, her delight in her ability to dissemble. Of all of Etherege's critics, Hawkins was the first to emphasize that the parodic language of wit destabilizes the relationships between actor and role, original and mimic, and truewit and witwoud. In her analysis of Congreve's *Love for Love*, she places a good deal of weight on Angelica's lines to Valentine, "Wou'd any thing, but a Madman complain of Uncertainty? Uncertainty and Expectation are the Joys of Life."[25] In an important sense, her criticism was always about uncertainty and strange attractors, the unpredictable emergence of order from chaos, and the ability of literary works to embody the scientific realization that physical reality is always in a "state of persistent instability."[26] This instability is not a postmodern artifact, a sea-change that overtook western culture in the 1970s or 80s, but, she maintains, the dynamic conditions of social and personal identity. "Security," to quote Congreve's Angelica again, "is an insipid thing" (IV.i.788), and the reductiveness of theme-hunting never seemed more insipid than it did in Hawkins's critiques of its circular logic and forced ingenuity.

Hawkins's methodological comments were often illuminated and extended by examples drawn from the physical sciences. At the end of her article on the limitations of the "example theory," she cites Francis Bacon on the necessity of considering evidence that does not fit preconceived models: "'to conclude, upon an enumeration of particulars, without instance contradictory, is no conclusion, but a conjecture.'"[27] In putting pressure on her own conceptions of "truth" and "freedom" as she explores the social and ideological grounds of literary interpretation, she counters the simplistic models of the scientific method that too often had dominated New Criticism, and that were making their way into discussions of literary theory in the 1970s and 1980s.

Stumbling in the hazy theoretical twilight cast by redactions of French theory, many critics appropriated metaphors from the sciences with little forethought or understanding of the disciplinary context of complex concepts such as relativism, entropy, and chaos theory. American semioticians often talked as though interpretive rules could be designed to the specifications of a Gradgrind, and some avatars of deconstruction found all texts collapsing into black holes of their imagination. The "new pragmatists," on the other hand, took it for granted that "theory" in the sciences and social sciences was, in Stanley Fish's phrase, "formal, abstract, general, and invariant"—a rigid, all-explanatory system that programmed responses to individual phenomena, including literary texts.[28] Such narrow views of how scientific theory actually governed what could be said about phenomena led to a "pragmatic" rejection of all efforts to explore the ways in which the ground rules of interpretation could be negotiated. In contrast, Hawkins frequently invokes examples of the ways in which scientific "theory" is subject to indeterminate, and often ironic, qualification. At the beginning of her essay on dramatic exposition, she uses an example that she also employed in the classroom.

> Discussing the immemorial cry of the teacher to the student looking through the microscope for the first time—"Why can't you draw what you see!"—the biologist Peter Medawar notes that "The teacher has forgotten and the student will soon forget, that what he sees conveys no information until he knows beforehand the kind of thing he is expected to see." And as A. H. Scouten once reminded me, Medawar's observation was conclusively confirmed by James Thurber, who, innocently gazing into a microscope, really did draw what he saw. "Do you know what you've done?" cried Thurber's instructor, "You've drawn a picture of your own eye!"

If critics who ignore the principles of dramatic exposition "often tend, in effect, to draw pictures of their own eyes," Hawkins's cautionary tale also serves as a useful metaphor for the limits of theory: abstract, general, and invariant certainty lies only in the (reflected) eye of the beholder.[29] At the same time, she maintains, a framework for perception and knowledge-making—a dynamic and flexible structure of expectations—is essential in order for observers to learn anything at all. Rather than rejecting a caricature of scientific theory under the banner of interpretive pragmatism, Hawkins cleverly asks her readers to consider the seemingly bedrock conditions of contemporary critical activity.

Hawkins, however, was never primarily a theoretician. Her criticism was full of references to popular films, junk novels, and the seeming ephemera of material culture. In the classroom as well as her writing, the works of Shakespeare, Milton, Chaucer, Marlowe, Etherege, and Congreve were cultural texts that might provoke thought but first and foremost were meant to be enjoyed. The masterworks of literature could be praised for their aesthetic value, but their significance does not lie in their conforming to abstract schema or after-the-fact analyses but in the "truths" that audiences and readers continue to find them dialogic, disruptive, thought-provoking, and fun. This kind of iconoclasm never goes out of fashion; and it is my guess that Hawkins' works of the 1970s will survive as valuable historical markers of the turn in criticism of Restoration drama away from an arid formalism and toward the complex contextualization that defines the best critical work being done in the twenty-first century.

The last letter I received from Harriett Hawkins was absolutely characteristic. It praised (too lavishly) my work on nondeterministic science in the seventeenth century and then mocked her own book on literature and chaos theory. "As usual," she concluded, "I'm still learning from my students." For all her emphasis on the harshness of the ways of our world and all her skill in countering the arguments of posturing formalists, her enjoyment of intellectual debate never compromised her generosity and wit. The "strangely combined pleasure of aesthetic pleasure and experiential recognition" that she attributed to the fractal sets of chaos theory might serve as a good metaphor for her own work.[30] Her witty refusal to be seduced by her own readings remains an object lesson for all critics and teachers who are tempted to think that their interpretations will stand like the inscription of Ozymandias. Many years ago, one of my classmates skipped Hawkins's class on *The Duchess of Malfi* and wanted my synopsis of that day's discussion. My future as an English professor apparently foreordained by Providence, I launched into a long exposition. After a few minutes, my friend cut me off with these words: "Sorry, but you can't do Harriett without the soundtrack." For many of us, the soundtrack is still playing.

Notes

1. Harriett Hawkins, *Likenesses of Truth in Elizabethan and Restoration Drama* (Oxford: Clarendon Press, 1972).

2. Harriett Hawkins, *Poetic Freedom and Poetic Truth: Chaucer, Shakespeare, Marlowe, Milton* (Oxford: Clarendon Press, 1976). Her later works include *Classics and Trash: Traditions and Taboos in High Literature and Popular Modern Genres* (Toronto: University of Toronto Press, 1990), and *Strange Attractors: Literature, Culture, and Chaos Theory* (New York: Prentice-Hall, 1995).

3. Hawkins, *Poetic Freedom*, xi, 5–6.

4. Ibid., 69.

5. Harriett Hawkins, "The 'Example Theory' and the Providentialist Approach to Restoration Drama: Some Questions of Validity and Applicability," *The Eighteenth Century: Theory and Interpretation* 24 (1983):103–14, and "'Players and Scorecards': Some Principles of Exposition in English Drama," in *From Renaissance to Restoration: Metamorphoses of the Drama*, ed. Robert Markley and Laurie Finke (Cleveland: Bellflower Press, 1984), 16–32. See particularly Arthur H. Scouten, "Notes Toward a History of Restoration Comedy," *Philological Quarterly* 45 (1966), 62–70; and Richard Levin, *New Readings vs. Old Plays: Recent Trends in the Reinterpretation of Renaissance Drama* (Chicago: University of Chicago Press, 1979).

6. Stanley Fish, *Surprised by Sin: The Reader in "Paradise Lost"* (Baltimore: Johns Hopkins University Press, 1967), and *Self-Consuming Artifacts: The Experience of Seventeenth-Century Literature* (Berkeley and Los Angeles: University of California Press, 1972).

7. On the critical reception of Restoration comedy, see John T. Harwood, *Critics, Values, and Restoration Comedy* (Carbondale: Southern Illinois University Press, 1982); Frances M. Kavenik, *British Drama, 1660–1779: A Critical History* (New York: Twayne, 1995), and Robert Markley, "The Canon and Its Critics," in *The Cambridge Companion to English Restoration Theatre*, ed. Deborah Payne Fisk (Cambridge: Cambridge University Press, 2000), 226–42.

8. Dale Underwood, *Etherege and the Seventeenth Century Comedy of Manners* (New Haven: Yale University Press, 1957), 8.

9. Norman Holland, *The First Modern Comedies: The Significance of Etherege, Wycherley, and Congreve* (Cambridge: Harvard University Press, 1959).

10. Aubrey Williams, *An Approach to Congreve* (New Haven: Yale University Press, 1979).

11. Ibid., 4, 54, 12.

12. Ibid., 12.

13. Hawkins, "The 'Example Theory,'" 108.

14. Ibid., 110.

15. Ibid.

16. Ibid., 111.

17. Ibid., 112.

18. Neill, "Heroic Heads and Humble Tails: Sex, Politics, and the Restoration Comic Rake," *The Eighteenth Century: Theory and Interpretation* 24 (1983), 115–39; McKeon, "Marxist Criticism and *Marriage a la Mode*," 141–62; and Thompson, "Histories of Restoration Drama," 163–72.

19. See Canfield, *Nicholas Rowe and Christian Tragedy* (Gainesville: University of Florida Press, 1977), and Thompson, *Language in Wycherley's Plays: Seventeenth-Century Language Theory and Drama* (Tuscaloosa: University of Alabama Press, 1984).

20. Canfield, *Tricksters and Estates: On the Ideology of Restoration Comedy* (Lexington: University of Kentucky Press, 1997); Thompson, "Dryden's *Conquest of Granada* and the Dutch Wars," *The Eighteenth Century: Theory and Interpretation* 31 (1990), 211–26, and *Models of Value: Eighteenth-Century Political Economy and the Novel* (Durham: Duke University Press, 1996).

21. Peter Holland, *The Ornament of Action: Text and Performance in Restoration Comedy* (Cambridge: Cambridge University Press, 1979); Laura Brown, *English Dramatic Form, 1660–1760: An Essay in Generic History* (New Haven: Yale University Press, 1981); Robert Hume, *The Rakish Stage: Studies in English Drama, 1660–1800* (Carbondale: Southern Illinois University Press, 1983); Har-

old Weber, *The Restoration Rake-Hero: Transformations in Sexual Understanding in Seventeenth-Century England* (Madison: University of Wisconsin Press, 1986); Robert Markley, *Two-Edg'd Weapons: Style and Ideology in the Comedies of Etherege, Wycherley, and Congreve* (Oxford: Clarendon Press, 1988); Brian Corman, *Genre and Generic Change in English Comedy, 1660–1710* (Toronto: University of Toronto Press, 1993); Pat Gill, *Interpreting Ladies: Women, Wit, and Morality in the Restoration Comedy of Manners* (Athens: University of Georgia Press, 1994); and Derek Hughes, *English Drama 1660–1700* (Oxford: Clarendon Press, 1996).

22. Tumbleson, *Catholicism in the English Protestant Imagination: Nationalism, Religion, and Literature 1600–1745* (Cambridge: Cambridge University Press, 1998); Hellegers, *Handmaid to Divinity: Natural Philosophy, Poetry, and Gender in Seventeenth-Century England* (Norman: University of Oklahoma Press, 2000); and Hutner, *Colonial Women: Race and Culture in Stuart Drama* (New York: Oxford University Press, 2001).

23. Derek Traversi, *Shakespeare: From 'Richard II' to 'Henry V'* (Stanford: Stanford University Press, 1957), *Shakespeare: The Roman Plays* (Stanford: Stanford University Press, 1963), *Shakespeare: The Last Phase* (Stanford: Stanford University Press, 1965), and *An Approach to Shakespeare* (New York: Doubleday, 1969).

24. Hawkins, *Likenesses of Truth*, 72–97.

25. *The Complete Plays of William Congreve*, ed. Herbert Davis (Chicago: University of Chicago Press, 1967), IV.i.785–6. See Hawkins, *Likenesses of Truth*, 98–114.

26. Hawkins, *Strange Attractors*, 2.

27. Hawkins, "The 'Example Theory,'" 114.

28. See Stanley Fish, "Consequences," in *Against Theory: Literary Studies and the New Pragmatism*, ed. W. J. T. Mitchell (Chicago: University of Chicago Press, 1985), 8.

29. Hawkins, "'Players and Scorecards': Some Principles of Exposition in English Drama," 17–18. The quotation from Medawar is from his "Hypothesis and Imagination," *The Art of the Soluble* (London: Methuen, 1967), 133 (cited on p. 31, n. 1).

30. Hawkins, *Strange Attractors*, 166.

A Literary Deadlock: The Destruction of the "Bower of Bliss" in Spenser's *The Faerie Queene*

(Reprinted from *The English Review*, February 1993)

Harriett Hawkins

THE CONTEXT OF THE CONFLICT

A BEAUTIFUL ENCHANTRESS, HER MALE LOVER/VICTIM, AND HIS RESCUE from the spell of her sensuality by traditionally 'masculine' virtues such as military honor, tribal duty, temperance and reason, have continually haunted the literary imagination. Classical examples are the Goddess Venus urging Mars to make love, not war, and the seductive Circe, whose charms turned men into beasts as well as their counterparts in the Judeo-Christian tradition from the Old Testament Delilah to Milton's Dalila. Successive variations on the central conflict between 'feminine' beauty/sensuality/emotion and 'masculine' duty/practicality/reason include the Shakespearian confrontation between Egypt as embodied in the enchanting Cleopatra, and Rome as personified by the politic Octavius. See, for instance, the Roman Pompey's lines equating Cleopatra's beauty and sensuality with witchcraft, addictive drugs, a kind of enslavement, a bestial wallowing in gluttony and sloth, and ultimately with oblivion:

> Let witchcraft join with beauty, lust with both;
> Tie up the libertine [Antony] in a field of feasts . . .
> That sleep and feeding may prorogue his honour
> Even till a Lethe'd dullness—[1]

Two centuries later, in a contest comparable to the one between Antony's 'serpent of old Nile' and her archfoe Octavius, Keats portrayed an irreconcilable conflict between the lovely serpent-woman Lamia and her archenemy, the coldly rational philosopher Apollonius, who contend for the body and soul of the hero, Lycius. On the one hand, as the subject of these conflicts, the male enchanted by the beautiful temptress (Antony, Lycius) is portrayed as emotionally, erotically, enviably blessed. For instance, when Antony says he wishes he had never seen Cleopatra, Enobarbus protests: "O, Sir, you had then left unseen a wonderful piece of work, which not to have been blest withal would have discredited your travel."[2] On the other hand, the enraptured lover risks being emotionally softened, addicted to sensuality, deflected from his duty in the larger world. Thus his 'manhood' will be destroyed by the goddess of love, unless he heroically summons the 'masculine' qualities (reason, resolution, ruthlessness) required to dispel her enchantment, to destroy her power and if necessary destroy her along with it.

The Spenserian Deadlock

Edmund Spenser's description of the destruction of the Circe-like seductress Acrasia, by Guyon, the Knight of Temperance in Book II, Canto xii of *The Faerie Queene,* binds classical mythology with successive English portrayals of this major conflict. Shakespeare, Milton (in *Comus* and *Paradise Lost* as well as *Samson Agonistes*) and Keats alike look back to Spenser. But what is most crucial to Spenser's portrayal of the confrontation is the ambivalence with which he presents the destruction of "feminine" beauty, sensuality and artifice (all associated with poetry) by ruthless, repressive, censorious "masculine" (and profoundly anti-poetic) virtue. Thus Spenser's poem confronts the reader with a moral and aesthetic deadlock wherein poetic beauty and moral virtue are at odds. To appreciate the complexity of the conundrum, you need only contrast Spenser's glorious description of his enchantress, Acrasia, with the lines depicting the brutal and violent destruction of her Bower.

Long before Sir Guyon enters the Bower of Bliss on his search-and-destroy mission, Spenser's readers are informed that the arch-enemy of Temperance, the enchantress Acrasia, has the power to turn men into beasts. In the climax of Book II we enter her garden of sensual delights along with Guyon, whose duty is to capture the enchantress and liberate her victims. But we (and he) first see Acrasia reclining on a bed of roses with her sleeping lover, Verdant, in a scene of such poetic beauty that it turns Spenser's readers, if not Sir Guyon himself, into enchanted observers:

> Upon a bed of Roses she was layd,
> As faint through heat, or dight to pleasant sin,
> And was arayed, or rather disarayed,
> All in a vele of silk and silver thin,
> That hid no whit her alablaster skin,
> But rather shewd more white, if more might bee:
> More subtile web Arachne cannot spin,
> Nor the fine nets, which oft we woven see
> Of scorched deaw, do not in th'aire more lightly flee.[3]

Note the poetic paradoxes: pleasant/sin; arayed/disarayed, the alluring veil that does not veil but rather reveals Acrasia's alabaster skin. She's wearing silver silk that sparkles like a spider's web—thus implying a comparison of Acrasia to a spider and her victim to a fly caught in her web. But the net is fine, blows freely in the wind.

What is the effect of this beauty and sensuality on the Knight of Temperance? Like a resentful voyeur condemning a beautiful woman because of the desire she arouses in him, the perspective (of Guyon? of the male viewer-reader?) changes to that of a rapacious peeping Tom with "hungry eyes," who looks at Acrasia's breast as open to "spoil"—to be taken (despoiled?) like the spoils of war:

> Her snowy brest was bare to readie spoyle
> Of hungry eies, which n'ote therewith be fild,
> And yet through languour of her late sweet toil,
> Few drops, more cleare than Nectar, forth distild,
> That like pure Orient perles adowne it trild,
> And her faire eyes sweet smyling in delight,
> Moistened their fierie beames, with which she thrilled
> Frail harts, yet quenched not; like starry light,
> Which sparckling on the silent waves, does seem more bright.[4]

This stanza makes the viewer seem the character most guilty of lust, while the sweet delight with which Acrasia looks at her young lover seems comparatively innocent. She does not view him with "hungry eyes", as ready spoil. Nor do her eyes glitter with triumph at the reduction of her victim to sensual sloth. They smile down like starlight, beautifully, harmlessly sparkling on silent waves. Then, having just had Acrasia's beauty and sensuality so vividly and even poignantly described, we are officially instructed that the scene is one of "foul" "lewd" lust, and that we should see Acrasia's young lover as pitiable, his condition as "horrible":

> The young man sleeping by her, seemed to bee
> Some goodly swayne of honourable place,

> That certes it great pittie was to see
> Him his nobilitie so foule deface; . . . .
> But in lewd loves, and wasteful luxuree,
> His dayes, his goods, his bodie he did spend:
> O horrible enchantment, that him so did blend.[5]

As originally portrayed by Spenser's own poetry, the loveliness of Acrasia and her bower seem far more powerfully and memorably evoked than their wasteful luxury, their superficiality, and their power to destroy "masculine" honor. But so long as the personification of Temperance, Guyon himself, remains free from criticism, there would be no serious problem so far as Spenser's moral conclusion is concerned. The message of the episode might seem rather pat and obvious, but it would, at least, be absolutely straightforward. Glorious, yet destructively "feminine" (and effeminate-making?) sensuality should be brought to terms by "manly" temperance. But suddenly, Spenser himself inserts a stanza wherein temperance takes the form of a tempestuous and brutally destructive rage:

> But all those pleasant bowers and Palace brave,
> Guyon broke down, with rigour pitiless,
> Nor aught their goodly workmanship might save
> Them from the tempest of his wrathfulness,
> But that their bliss he turned to balefulness:
> Their groves he felled, their gardens did deface,
> Their arbors spoil, their Cabinets suppress,
> Their banquet houses burn, their buildings raze,
> And of the fairest late, now made the foulest place.[6]

Why does Spenser describe the destruction of the bower in terms of such oppositions as these?

pleasant bowers	rigour pitiless
goodly workmanship	tempest of wrathfulness
bliss	balefulness
groves	felled
garden	defaced
arbors	spoiled
cabinets	suppressed
banquet houses	burned
building	razed
what was the fairest place	now is the foulest place

Had he wished, Spenser surely could have shown the triumph of temperance over sensuality without making temperance itself turn into a pitiless fury that is out to burn, to spoil, to deface. In this stanza, lovely and harmless works of art and nature are ruined by what seems a kind of intemperate, self-righteous indulgence in sheer destruction for its own sake. Indeed, the column of words describing Guyon's actions suggest repression manifesting itself in violence.

In his description of Acrasia's bower and Guyon's destruction of it, Spenser thus creates a poetic deadlock. The slavishly sensual life may be a bestial one, yet puritanical attacks on beauty, poetry, art and sensuality may themselves take the forms of excess. Can (the poetry asks us) militant virtue/temperance/repression untempered by tender "feminine" emotion, itself turn a man into a brutal machine/instrument of destruction? Of course, independently of this stanza, Spenser should be allowed to score his series of unanswerably valid moral points about the virtues of moderation. Yet he himself chose to bless Acrasia's bower with the equally unanswerable arguments of poetry. You could thus argue that even as Spenser's morality is on the side of Guyon, his poetry is on the side of Acrasia. For that matter, ever since Plato banished poets from the Republic, poetry itself has been compared to a *femme fatale*, seducing and softening men with enchanting illusions, making them forget their primary duty as warriors. But is the "Terminator" behavior of Guyon a positive, or a negative alternative to Acrasia? The Spenserian deadlock offers no certain answer either way, and his poetry therefore resonates continually in ways that haunt the memory and cannot be dismissed from the mind.

Notes

1. *Antony and Cleopatra*, 2.1.22–26.
2. Ibid., 1.2.148–49.
3. *The Faerie Queene*, 2.12.77.
4. Ibid., 2.12.77–78.
5. Ibid., 2.12.79–80.
6. Ibid., 2.12.83.

The Seductions of *Comus*

Harriett Hawkins

(Reprinted from *The English Review*, November 1995)

(*Note:* The English Review, *aimed primarily at undergraduates, often presented two or more approaches to the same literary work. In this case, there were two articles on Milton's* Comus: *the first is a close reading of selected passages, and the second—reprinted here—is an argument for the modern relevance of the work for school-age readers.*)

VIRTUE THREATENED BY VICE, IN THE FORM OF A VERY ATTRACTIVE DRUG pusher, is the theme of the masque *Comus*. Separated from her two brothers in a forest, a beautiful young Lady meets what seems to be a friendly peasant (compare Eve's meeting with the seemingly friendly serpent in *Paradise Lost*) who turns out to be the arch-tempter Comus, son of Circe the enchantress and Bacchus the god of wine, who has inherited the power to turn human beings into beasts through slavish indulgence in sensual pleasures. The Lady is held captive by Comus, but steadfastly refuses to drink his addictive potion, and is finally rescued by her brothers with the aid of Sabrina, a goddess attendant on virtue in distress.

No plot could be simpler in moral outline, but in *Comus* Milton raises serious questions about the relationship between physical and spiritual virtue, and physical and spiritual rape. He also raises a crucial question which is as difficult to answer in 1995 as it was in 1634: "*Why* say no to pleasure?" So seductive are the speeches of Comus that this entertainment, originally commissioned to celebrate the virtues of the Earl of Bridgwater and his family and entitled simply, "A MASK/Presented at Ludlow Castle," has always been known by the name of its *villain*. There are interesting reasons why this is the case.

To test the allure of Comus, ask yourself whether you would accept—or why and how you would refuse—this invitation to his party:

> [Let us] welcome Joy and Feast,
> Midnight shout and revelry,
> Tipsy dance and Jollity . . .
> Strict Age and sour Severity
> With their grave Saws in slumber lie . . .
> Night hath better sweets to prove,
> *Venus* now wakes, and wak'ns Love,
> Come let us our rites begin,
> 'Tis only daylight that makes Sin.[1]

How could *anyone* turn down this offer of sensual delight without seeming a moralistic prig? And on what moral grounds should it be refused?

In *Comus,* as elsewhere in the works of Milton, if morality finally triumphs, it wins against the most powerful and seductive arguments that immorality can throw at it. Thus the counter-arguments presented both for and against unrestrained indulgence in the sensual pleasures offered by Comus inevitably evoke conflicting emotional and critical responses. These responses, which may vary from person to person and from historical time to time—and likewise may vary *within the same person* from time to time—make *Comus* anything but a simple text.

The Playboy Philosopher

In his seduction speeches, Comus insists to the Lady that her temperance is an insult to nature's bounty. As for her virginity, he asks, what is she saving it for? "Why should you be so cruel to yourself?" (679):

> . . . Lady, be not coy, and be not cozen'd
> With that same vaunted name Virginity.
> Beauty is nature's coin, must not be hoarded,
> But must be current, and the good thereof
> Consists in mutual and partak'n bliss . . .
> If you let slip time, like a neglected rose
> It withers on the stalk with languish'd head.
>
> (737–44)

He likewise advocates the profligate enjoyment of youth, beauty, wealth and power in conspicuous consumption and flamboyant display (compare some of today's playboy/playgirl aristocrats). Nature, he claims, is abundant "to please, and sate the curious taste" (713). Arguing against temperance, he insists that

> If all the world
> Should in a pet of temperance feed on Pulse,
> Drink the clear stream, and nothing wear but Frieze
> Th'all giver would be unthank't, would be unprais'd,
> Not half his riches known . . .
>
> (720–24)

As everyone has noted, it is by no means self-evident that these arguments are false, so it is important to have the Lady's counter-arguments (quoted below) that Nature's abundance is not designed to encourage intemperance, but to ensure that with the proper distribution of resources no one need go hungry. Yet the enchanter's persuasions to seize the day, to enjoy whatever we can, whenever we can, retain their seductive power. Is there anyone of us who has *not* felt the pressure of the identical arguments posited in modern language by the sons and daughters of Comus? Yet it is hard to cite anyone since who has expressed them so eloquently. Like Milton's Satan, Comus is such a supreme master of the art of seductive language that he is capable of tempting the reader, along with the Lady, to "be wise, and taste" from his cup:

> One sip of this
> Will bathe the drooping spirits in delight
> Beyond the bliss of dreams.
>
> (811–13)

Comus makes it easy to forget that his persuasion to unbridled self-indulgence, like the drink he offers, is a delicious distillation of all dangerous and addictive drugs combined in one.

Attendant Spirits

When she first encounters him in the forest, Comus appears to the Lady in the guise of a helpful and sympathetic shepherd-guide who offers no threat or harm, as if to suggest that vice initially presents itself as a harmless and humble servant, not a physically or spiritually enslaving master of our desires. Significantly, the good "Attendant Spirit" who aids the Lady's brothers also appears as a shepherd, as if to suggest how hard it is to distinguish between the guiding spirit who faithfully serves us, and the *seeming* servant or "attendant" (within or without) that will ultimately wield absolute power over us. Comus offers not liberty, but enslavement in his cup.

In *Comus,* the Lady is threatened with spiritual as well as physical rape. When the Lady extols "the sage/And serious doctrine of virginity" (783–86), she is not just describing physical chastity, she is also describing spiritual integrity. Physical integrity may be violated by force; spiritual integrity cannot be. Virtue "may be assail'd, but never hurt/Surprised by unjust force but not enthrall'd" (590–91). "Fool, do not boast," the Lady insists to Comus:

> Thou can'st not touch the freedom of my mind.
> With all thy charms, although this corporal rind
> Thou hast immancl'd.
>
> (662–64)

In this spectacle designed for family entertainment, a physical rape of the Lady does not, of course, take place. But the threat of rape is one of its central concerns. The nymph Sabrina, who comes to the Lady's rescue, was also the daughter of a powerful father, and she too was "a virgin pure" (825). To escape some form of violation with broadly sexual connotations, "the guiltless damsel" threw herself into the river Severn, "commending her fair innocence to the flood" (828–30). Having been transformed into the Goddess of the River, Sabrina displays a special solidarity with virgins threatened by rape:

> For maidenhood she loves, and will be swift
> To aid a virgin such as was herself
> In hard-besetting need.
>
> (855–57)

It is because of what they have in common, the text implies, that Sabrina is able to release the Lady. The Lady's young brothers also come to the rescue, and thus embody male chivalry in opposition to Comus as the male seducer/rapist. But the crucial protagonists in Milton's drama of projected rape, the embodiments of virtue (as well as the imperiled victims) in the text are women.

Sexual and Social Responsibility

The Lady's aristocratic virtues involve a strong sense of social responsibility. She is not a snob. When she meets Comus disguised as a shepherd, she observes that courtesy and honesty are "sooner found in lowly sheds with smoky rafters" than "in tap'stry Halls/ And Courts of Princes" (324–25). It is therefore significant that the scene in which Comus tempts the Lady is set in his "stately Palace set out with all manner of deliciousness; soft Music, Tables spread with all dainties. Comus appears with his rabble, and the Lady set in an enchanted Chair, to whom he offers his Glass" (p. 105). When she refuses him, the Lady *has* to sound like a prude:

> And wouldst thou seek to trap me here
> With likerish baits fit to ensnare a brute?
> Were it a drop for *Juno* when she banquets
> I would not taste thy treasonous offer; none
> But such as are good men can give good things,
> And that which is not good is not delicious
> To a well-govern'd and wise appetite.
>
> (699–705)

Compare how hard it is to resist peer pressure by just saying "No."

By contrast, Comus finds it *very* easy to put down all arguments against the pleasures he offers as "mere moral babble" (807). Note the way he makes virtue seem unattractive and boring. As described by Comus, "Lean and sallow Abstinence" (708) sounds unhealthy, anorexic. He argues that rich and gorgeous young people should show off their wealth and beauty at lavish feasts and parties: "It is for homely features to keep home/They had their name thence" (744–45).

But again, if you think virtue has a better answer than the outright rejection the Lady gives to vice, try to refute, point by point, Comus' most alluring arguments. Why not eat, drink and be merry? If you've got it, why not flaunt it? A better case for the self-indulgent pursuit of pleasure for its own sake has probably never been made. The persuasions of Comus are as seductive today as yesterday. And yet, as if inevitably, a still, small counter-voice insists, with the Lady, that there must be more to life than self-indulgence.

In opposition to Comus, the Lady delivers the lines that constitute Milton's major moral and political message:

> If every just man that now pines with want
> Had but a moderate and beseeming share
> Of that which lewdly-pampered Luxury
> Now heaps upon some few with vast excess
> Nature's full blessings would be well-dispensed
> In unsuperfluous even proportion.
>
> (767–72)

The Lady's arguments for a fairer distribution of nature's resources, and a fairer distribution of wealth, are never answered by Comus—he contemptuously puts them down as if they were the moral babbling of a politically correct prude. But which character, the text leaves us to decide, is really, truly, *right*? This spectacular, fantastical, aristocratic entertainment has to do with social justice as well as sexual politics, and it raises questions, even as it poses temptations, that are disturbingly familiar today.

Blake said that Milton, as a poet, was "of the Devil's party without knowing it," but although he poetically gives Comus his due, there is absolutely no question that morally Milton is on the side of the Angels. In *Areopagitica*, his classic defense of the freedom of the press against censorship, he tells us why it is so important for vice to be portrayed in all its power: "I cannot praise a fugitive and cloistered virtue, unexercised and unbreathed. . . . That virtue therefore which is but a youngling in the contemplation of evil, and *knows not the utmost that vice promises to her followers, and rejects it* [is] but a blank virtue." By contrast, tested virtue can "see and know" all the delights that vice may offer, and "yet abstain" (my italics).[2]

By giving the best, not the worst, arguments that can be leveled against virtue to his devils, Milton enables us to "see and know" and thus make an informed decision whether and why it is best to abstain. "Love virtue, she alone is free" proclaims the true Attendant Spirit at the end (1018). Reading Milton is an exercise in the freedom to choose between right and wrong, and he insists that in actively choosing virtue, not vice, lies true liberty. But he never pretends that making the right choice is easy.

Notes

1. John Milton, "A Masque (Comus)," in *Complete Poems and Major Prose*, ed. Merritt Y. Hughes (New York: Odyssey Press, 1957), lines 102–26. Subsequent line numbers are cited in the text.

2. John Milton, "Areopagitica," in *Complete Poems and Major Prose*, ed. Merritt Y. Hughes (New York: Odyssey Press, 1957), 728.

II
Single Authors and Singular Styles

Henry Vaughan's Poetry: Pointful Vagueness and the Merging of Contraries

John Carey

HENRY VAUGHAN'S POETRY HAS RECEIVED SPORADIC AND OFTEN ENlightening attention from critics. Its relation to his twin brother Thomas's Hermeticism has been teased out by, among others, his editors L. C. Martin and Alan Rudrum.[1] But its strangeness, its persistent capacity to elude ascertainable meaning, has received little comment even from a critic as perceptive as Stevie Davies, whose *Henry Vaughan* (1995) contains by far the most imaginative writing on Vaughan to date. Yet this strangeness, constantly observable in his syntax, and evident to any reader who takes time to notice, is Vaughan's hallmark. It is what makes his poetry distinguishable from that of other seventeenth-century devotional poets, including his mentor George Herbert, and this remains true even when he is using words and phrases quarried from Herbert.

In this article it is Vaughan's strangeness and how it operates upon the reader that I want to analyze. A useful starting point is an attack on Vaughan by T. S. Eliot published in the magazine *The Dial* in 1927. Disparaging and surprisingly ignorant (referring, for example, to Archbishop Laud's "cheerfulness and democracy"), this is a review of Edmund Blunden's *On the Poems of Henry Vaughan,* and it takes particular exception to Blunden's and (as Eliot sees it) Vaughan's reminiscence of childhood:

> It does not occur to Mr Blunden that this love of one's own childhood, a passion which he appears to share with Lamb and Vaughan, is anything but a token of greatness. We all know the mood; and we can all, if we choose to relax to that extent, indulge in the luxury of reminiscence of childhood; but if we are at all mature and conscious we refuse to indulge this weakness to the point of writing and poeticizing about it; we know that it is something to be buried and done with, though the corpse will from time to time find its way up to the surface. . . . This reminiscent humour of Vaughan, upon which Mr Blunden has pounced so delightedly, has always seemed to me one of the reasons for

his inferiority to the best of his contemporaries ... The emotion of Herbert is clear, definite, mature and sustained; whereas the emotion of Vaughan is vague, adolescent, fitful and retrogressive.[2]

There are several things here that might claim our attention. It is typical of Eliot's critical prejudice at the time to value definitiveness and precision, though they were not, in any evident sense, qualities of his own poetry. The unexpectedly violent image of the buried corpse recalls "The Waste Land" ("That corpse you planted last year in your garden,/Has it begun to sprout?"),[3] and Eliot's touchiness about childhood reminiscence may link in some defensive way with his own poignant memories of childhood vacations on the New England coast that infiltrate poems such as "Marina." It is noticeable that this focus has misled Eliot into supposing that Vaughan indulges in "the luxury of reminiscence of childhood" when in fact it is difficult to gather any facts about Vaughan's childhood from his poetry. What he refers to, rather, is the purity that (according to Pythagoreans, Platonists, and Hermeticists, and such church fathers as Origen and Cyril of Alexandria) the child's soul had known in heaven before birth.

However, it is Eliot's charge of vagueness that seems most worth pursuing. Despite the negative weighting that Eliot gives it, it reveals a sensitivity to something unfinished in Vaughan's formulations of meaning that is, I would argue, inseparable from his peculiar sources of power. When he writes about childhood, as in "The Retreat," the effort is not to refocus a past experience—not, as Eliot makes out, to reminisce—but, on the contrary, to access the poignancy of the vague, the lost. The symbol of a bird that has flown from its nest serves his purpose precisely because it embodies vagueness. No one knows where it is.

> He that hath found some fledg'd birds nest, may know
>   At first sight, if the bird be flown;
> But what fair Well, or Grove he sings in now,
>   That is to him unknown.[4]

The strange word here, of course, is "Well." Birds do not sing in wells. The word suggests coolness, depth, and diminishing echoes. The mysterious bird sinks mysteriously away from us into a darkness that our eyes cannot penetrate. But quite how "Well" is meant to justify its presence in the line remains as unknown as the bird's whereabouts. The word troubled Vaughan's editor L. C. Martin and he glossed it as "The neighbourhood of a well or fountain." Officious paraphrase of that kind removes the difficulty but only at the expense of destroying the poetry. Its achievement is to eliminate what makes the lines singular. To back up his supposition, Martin refers to other uses of the word "well" in Vaughan's poetry. But far from helping his case, they compound the damage. Vaughan seeking his savior in "The Search," for example, speculates upon

> What silent paths, what shades, and Cells,
> Faire, virgin-flowers and hallow'd *Wells*
> I should rove in . . .[5]

You cannot rove in wells, nor in flowers. Martin's solution, no doubt, would be to substitute "among" or "near" for "in." But "in" is what Vaughan writes, and its lack of intelligible cohesion with the words preceding it is essential to the Vaughan experience which proceeds from subtle disorientation and uncertainty.

These effects, it will be seen, are attained by quite small disruptions of expected word-usage. The Vaughanian vagueness is not, as Eliot implies, a feature of emotion. Indeed, it is not apparent from Eliot's critique how "clear" emotion would be distinguished from "vague." Rather it resides quite demonstrably in syntax, especially as it relates to the position and juxtaposition of referents. Prepositions, in particular, are exchanged and manipulated in ways that throw whole contexts into uncertainty. The start of the poem in which the fledged bird appears is one of Vaughan's high points, much anthologized, and its vagueness is painstakingly worked for:

> They are all gone into the world of light!
>   And I alone sit lingering here;
> Their very memory is fair and bright,
>   And my sad thoughts doth clear.
> It glows and glitters in my cloudy brest
>   Like stars upon some gloomy grove,
> Or those faint beams in which this hill is drest,
>   After the Sun's remove.
>
> I see them walking in an Air of glory,
>   Whose light doth trample on my days:
> My days, which are at best but dull and hoary,
> Meer glimmerings and decays.[6]

The movement of things in Vaughan's poems is frequently vague, as here. The motive verbs are simple and unspecific. People "walk" or "move" to and from nowhere very certain, and we are not always sure, as here, who it is that is moving. The whole passage with its "glimmerings" and "faint beams" is deliberately distanced from the precise, the fully seen. It shimmers like a mirage. Its moment of alerting specificity ("this hill") turns out to be unspecific, for we do not know what hill it is or why it is introduced. As in the fledged bird passage, however, the vagueness of meaning increases the emotional intensity. It suggests something yearned for but not fully knowable, or at any rate not fully communicable. The norms of expression break, as it were, under the power of desire—or this is how we are moved, as readers, to interpret it. Consequently vagueness and intensity become reconcilable; indeed, the intensity is dependent on the vagueness.

The verb "trample" is typical in this respect, being both violent and not quite clear in its signification. It is one of Vaughan's borrowings from Herbert, who writes in "Jordan II," "Nothing could seem too rich to clothe the sun / Much less those joys which trample on his head." In Herbert the trampling is largely metaphorical. "Trample on his head" is equivalent to "are superior to." In the relationship between the joys (of heaven) and the sun there is no question of anything being actually trodden underfoot. But in Vaughan we are not so sure. Light seems to become solid, like metal. We seem only a short step from Gerard Manley Hopkins's great gray drayhorse's "bright and battering sandal" in "Felix Randall." Perhaps there is a memory of St. Paul's citation of Isaiah: "How beautiful are the feet of them that preach the gospel of peace"[7]—a fleeting image of luminous beings treading mundane reality underfoot. Yet just how light can trample, and trample on "days," remains unspecific.

Vaughan's vagueness operates too in the reference to the "grove" (which is vaguely "some," not "a," grove). As often, a preposition is at the root of it. A memory glows and glitters like stars "upon" the grove. But what does "upon" mean? Are the stars shining above the grove? Or are they seen through the branches, and so seemingly imposed upon them like jewels set against a dark background? This might explain why, if the branches are moving, the stars seem to glow and glitter. But either way "upon" is a curious preposition. The combination of branches and stars brings to mind Keats's oak trees in "Hyperion": "Tall oaks, branch-charmed by the earnest stars."[8] But no one seems to know what that line means, either.

The aim of these observations is not to devalue Vaughan—quite the contrary. His displacements of orthodox syntax, often effected, as we have seen, by adjustment of minimal components such as prepositions, are vital to his distinctive poetic effect. They account, largely, for the impression his poetry gives of being at a remove from, or elevated above, ordinary reality. The argument about whether or not he had mystical experiences seems inevitably inconclusive. But the impulse to ascribe such experiences to him can be traced, I would argue, to syntactical features in the poetry of the sort I have been describing which, while retaining the appearance of meaning, carry it beyond logical elucidation. That these features so often depend on connectives such as prepositions points us to the conclusion that what is disrupted (or "strange") in the worldview the poetry reflects is not so much the objects of perception but how they relate to each other. The tendency of the poems to place agents and verbs in odd conjunction makes for the same effect. As we read, it is not so much the action, but the agent ascribed to it, that disconcerts; we therefore feel an inclination to ignore what Vaughan writes and substitute some inoffensive paraphrase. The opening of "Cock-Crowing" supplies an example:

> Father of lights! what Sunnie seed
> What glance of day hast thou confin'd
> Into this bird? To all the breed
> This busie Ray thou hast assign'd;
>   Their magnetisme works all night,
>   And dreams of Paradise and light.
>
> Their eyes watch for the morning hue,
> Their little grain expelling night
> So shines and sings, as if it knew
> The path unto the house of light.
>   It seems their candle, howe'r done,
>   Was tinn'd and lighted at the sunne.[9]

The Hermetic underpinnings of this poem—the belief in the seed or grain of divine light in creatures and the magnetism that draws them to astral bodies—have been amply glossed by Martin and others. But a strangeness that seems not to be traceable to these arcane beliefs, and which is, like those we have been considering, syntactical, is that at the end of the first stanza it is "magnetisme" that dreams, not the birds. Any hasty impulse we may have to silently reallocate the dreams to the cockerels robs the lines of the disorienting break from normal expectations of agency that characterizes Vaughan. The poem's syntax also prevents any simple or normal understanding of the "seed" or "grain" implanted in the birds. This seed or grain is also a "busy ray" that "shines." Whether it is composed of light or of solid matter is a question the poem makes us hesitant about answering. Further, the seed or grain "sings." Our normal conceptual divisions and categories are overridden. To express his vision, Vaughan must abrogate distinctions such as those between animate and inanimate and between material and immaterial (seeds do not sing, magnetism cannot dream, according to our accustomed categories).

I have suggested that Vaughan's syntactical disruptions convey to the reader a sense of divorce from normal reality. Vaughan's worldview seems, indeed, to have been highly idiosyncratic. He was not a Hermeticist in any simple sense. Some Hermetic ideas, such as man's godlike potential and the possibility of total mastery of nature, seem to have had no appeal for him. They were alien to his preoccupation with loss and yearning. More congenial was the animism integral to Hermeticism—the belief that plants, trees and even stones are conscious and sentient. In "The Bird," stones, like other creatures, worship God: "though poor stones have neither speech nor tongue, / While active winds and streams both run and speak, / Yet stones are deep in admiration."[10] Even the speechlessness of stones will, furthermore, cease at the Last Judgment, Vaughan foretells. Then the fact that they have been listening to us all the time, and observing our secret sins, will come out. God will call on them as witnesses against us.

> They hear, see, speak,
> And into loud discoveries break,
> As loud as blood . . .
> . . . Hence sand and dust
> Are shak'd for witnesses, and stones
> Which some think dead, shall all at once
> With one attesting voice detect
> Those secret sins we least suspect.[11]

These lines from "The Stone" are prefaced by a reference to Joshua 24:27, where the belief that stones hear and speak is given biblical corroboration: "And Joshua said unto all the people, Behold this stone shall be a witness unto us; for it hath heard all the words of the Lord which he spake unto us." Some modern critics seem unwilling to grant that Vaughan ascribes consciousness to minerals and vegetables.[12] But the evidence from the poetry is overwhelming. As he writes in "Rules and Lessons," "Each *Bush* / And *Oak* doth know *I AM*."[13] In "The Night" he contemplates Christ surrounded by nature, not a human temple, and watched by the plants:

> No mercy-seat of gold,
> No dead and dusty *Cherub,* nor carv'd stone,
> But his own living works did my Lord hold
>   And lodge alone;
> Where *trees* and *herbs* did watch and peep
> And wonder, while the *Jews* did sleep.[14]

In such a context it is unthinkable that Vaughan would indulge in whimsy or pretense. He writes as a Hermeticist, believing that the trees and herbs were filled with wonder as they watched Jesus. The biblical evidence for such an idea was not solely the passage in Joshua. Vaughan heads another poem with a quotation from Romans 8:19, where Paul writes *Etenim res Creatae exerto Capite observantes expectant revelationem Filiorum Dei* ("Even the created things lift up their heads and expect the revelation of the sons of God"). The poem accepts this as evidence that so-called inanimate nature is not just responsive to astrological "influence," but alive:

> And do they so? have they a Sense
>   Of ought but Influence?
> Can they their heads lift, and expect,
>   And grone too? why th'Elect
> Can do no more: my volumes sed
>   They were all dull, and dead,
> They judg'd them senslesse, and their state
>   Wholly Inanimate.
> Go, go; Seal up thy looks,
>   And burn thy books.[15]

That natural objects were alive, despite what mechanistic thinkers wrote, also meant for Vaughan that they would be resurrected at the Last Day, just like man. This too was a Hermetic belief. Paracelsus held that each individual flower had its place in eternity: "It is opposed to all true philosophy to say that flowers lack their own eternity. They may perish and die here; but they will re-appear in the restitution of all things. Nothing has been created out of the Great Mystery which will not inhabit a form beyond the aether."[16] Some biblical grounds for this might be found in the prophecy of the new heaven and new earth in Revelations. But orthodox Christians rejected the whole idea. Thomas Aquinas is sure that "animals, plants and mixed bodies, which are entirely corruptible, both in whole and in part, will nowise remain in the state of incorruption."[17] Vaughan's brother Thomas, however, strongly disagreed with this privileged Christian anthropocentrism. "It is not man alone that is to be renewed at the general restoration," he writes in *Euphrates,* "but even the world as well as man."[18] This is the belief that underpins Vaughan's poem "The Book" in which he proclaims that each component of the book—its paper, its leather binding, its wooden cover—is known to God as it was in its original state: the cover as a tree, the binding as a beast's skin, the paper as seed, then as flax, then as linen, then as clothes, then as rags to be made into paper. Further, at the Last Day, the creatures from which the book was made will be restored:

> O knowing, glorious spirit! when
> Thou shalt restore trees, beasts and men,
> When thou shalt make all new again,
> Destroying only death and pain,
> Give him amongst thy works a place,
> Who in them lov'd and sought thy face.[19]

The last line might seem illogical, for if all are to be restored, trees, beasts and men, then Vaughan must be restored too, without praying for it. But his prayer suggests poignantly that nature, which is purer than he is, may be restored, and he may be left out. It is the sense of exile that we find continuously in his poetry—the yearning to end exile, to join, to have a place.

Vaughan's beliefs about man, nature and God were dangerously at odds with orthodox Christianity and linked him, though he seems not to have recognized it, with sectarians on the wilder fringes of the Puritan movement for whom he would have felt, politically, nothing but abhorrence. Under the Blasphemy Act, pantheism, and the belief that God was not transcendent but immanent in his creatures, were punishable heresies. The ranter Jacob Bauthumley wrote in *The Light and Dark Sides of God:*

> Nay, I see that God is in all Creatures, Man and Beast, Fish and Fowle, and every green thing, from the highest Cedar to the Ivey on the wall; and that God is the life and being of them all, and that God doth really dwell, and if you will personally; . . . and hath his Being no where else out of the Creatures.[20]

For writing this Bauthumley was punished by being burned through the tongue with a hot iron.[21]

The strangeness and vagueness of Vaughan's poetic syntax, the disruptions of expected agency and accustomed relationships should be seen, I would argue, as organically related to a worldview that was itself vague, strange, disrupted and unaccustomed. It is not that we can link the syntax and the beliefs in any simple one-to-one way. Why he writes, say, "upon some gloomy grove" cannot be explained by checking through some handbook of Hermetic lore. What we can observe, rather, is a seismic shift in his relation to language consequent upon a set of beliefs that, even for his day, were problematic, deviant, and unsettling.

A further consequence, it seems, of his idiosyncratic vision is that things which we normally think of as opposites, such as height and depth, or warmth and cold, or light and dark, are no longer mutually exclusive. He can be equally drawn to either side of the opposition. This is because he strikes through the mundane reality of these things to a symbolic property that makes them reconcilable. Light, for example, is a persistent—indeed the most persistent—positive in Vaughan's poetry, symbolizing, as we have seen, God's presence in His creatures and the appearance of the glorious dead. But within Vaughan's symbolic mode, darkness can be the equivalent of light, not its opposite. Night, not the sun, becomes the object of desire, and light is a garish distraction:

> Dear night! this worlds defeat;
> The stop of busie fools; cares check and curb;
> The day of Spirits; my souls calm retreat
>   Which none disturb!
>
> *Christs* progress, and his prayer time;
>   The hours to which high Heaven doth chime.
>   Gods silent, searching flight:
> When my Lords head is fill'd with dew, and all
> His locks are wet with the clear drops of night;
>   His still, soft call;
> His knocking time; The souls dumb watch,
> When Spirits their fair kinred catch.
>
> Were all my loud, evil days
> Calm and unhaunted as is thy dark Tent,
> Whose peace but by some *Angels* wing or voice
>   Is seldom rent;
> Then I in Heaven all the long year
> Would keep, and never wander here.[22]

These wonderful stanzas, densely embedded, as Martin's notes show, in scriptural reference, supremely exhibit the fluid, disorienting syntax we have been observing. Night changes, as the lines progress, from a time to a flight to a call to a watch to a tent, and the whole passage becomes an intricate web of only half-decipherable metaphor. But it is the elevation of night to symbolic equivalence with day ("the day of Spirits") that especially calls for comment. God is both light and dark—"A deep, but dazling darkness." The idea was an ancient one, traceable as Martin notes to Dionysius the Areopagite. For Vaughan it conveniently matched the symbolic equivalence of light and dark, which he saw as alternative extremes in which to lose himself.

In the same contradictory way he feels the attractions both of activity and of calm, because both allow escape from the spasmodic irregularity of everyday life. So, in "Regeneration," the stones that dance "quick as light" in the fountain and the "broad-eyed" flowers are favorably contrasted with the stones "more heavy then the night" that are 'Nail'd to the Center" and the flowers still "fast asleepe" at midday.[23] But in "Man," a poem equally concerned with activity and its opposite, lack of movement is presented as the ideal. Man would be better if he were "ty'd" to one place instead of scurrying around the earth.[24]

Within the same symbolic dimension glory and humility, height and lowness, are, for Vaughan, interchangeable ideals. In "They are all gone into the world of light" the blessed walk "in an Air of glory." But in "The Seed growing secretly" glory is disparaged:

> Dear, secret *Greenness!* nurst below
> Tempests and windes, and winter-nights,
> Vex not, that but one sees thee grow,
> That *One* made all these lesser lights.
>
> If those bright joys he singly sheds
> On thee, were all met in one Crown,
> Both Sun and Stars would hide their heads;
> And Moons, though full, would get them down.
>
> Let glory be their bait, whose mindes
> Are all too high for a low Cell:
> Though Hawks can prey through storms and winds,
> The poor Bee in her hive must dwel.
> Glory , the Crouds cheap tinsel still
> To what most takes them, is a drudge;
> And they too oft take good for ill,
> And thriving vice for vertue judge.[25]

The two sets of images that attract Vaughan's longing here are adverse. On the one hand he idealizes lowness, humility, the poor bee, the buried seed, and derides glory. But on the other hand he imagines, with rapture, a glory so dazzling that the sun and stars would hide their heads at it. This paradox is, admittedly, embedded in orthodox Christianity, which worships a crucified God who manifested ultimate humiliation and ultimate triumph in the same moment. However, Vaughan transfers the contraries to his own symbolic landscape, preserving the Christian distinction between real (divine) and false (earthly) glory, but endowing humility with a new set of correlatives, security ("secret"), fostering tenderness ("nurst"), and "*Greenness*," an abstraction (like "magnetisme" in "Cock-Crowing") that here takes the place of an actual, material seed and seems to stand for naturalness, innocence and fertility. As with the other contradictions we have been observing, this alternation between dreams of lowness and dreams of height spreads through all his poetry. It is not confined to this single instance, and it is a sign of his supranormal or supralogical mode.

We find him equating logically opposed entities again when we note how warmth and coolness operate in the poems. He thirsts for coolness—"the cool and shady even," "the cool dew"—but this can quite well co-exist with a desire to be warmed by "immortal heat." Dew as well as sun warms in "The Proffer": "now the dew and Sun have warm' d my bowres."[26] Dew can cool and warm as well because Vaughan reaches beyond the normal physical properties to symbolic essences, and to express what dew means on this symbolic plane requires an imaginative effort to combine things that have been contradictory in the old commonplace world. Dew is one of Vaughan's most powerful images for combining the simple and the ineffable, the vague and the intense. In "The Seed growing secretly" he addresses God as dew, or seems to:

> My dew, my dew! my early love;
> My souls bright food, thy absence kills!
> Hover not long, eternal Dove!
> Life without thee is loose and spills.[27]

The words do not crystallize into distinct meanings. It is not clear what Vaughan is comparing life to when he says it is "loose and spills." "Spills" makes it sound like a liquid, but it would be odd to talk of a liquid as "loose." Yet this vagueness is vital to the line's intensity, evoking as it does the not-quite-expressible that eludes the most strenuous efforts at expression. Similarly the dew Vaughan addresses is both his soul's food and his early love. What is it meant to be? We vaguely think of manna, and Christ's body and blood in the sacrament. We recall that "Duw" in Welsh, Vaughan's first language, means God, and that dew, in Hermetic doctrine, contains star-fire and brings it to earth. But Vaughan's lines cannot be tied to any of these meanings. His yearning, and the indefiniteness of what "dew" means, are intimately linked. It is because the object of his yearning is beyond definition that the sense of loss in the line is so strong. Dew is lost, and lost from meaning. Vagueness calls forth the greatest intensity, because desire for what is vague must always be insatiable.

In Vaughan's mature poetry reference to the actualities of his life and times are rare and questionable—another facet of his vagueness. He looks through the present life to the life beyond. In this respect "The Proffer" is singular, in that it seems to refer, though indistinctly, to an offer of employment or preferment under the Commonwealth which he angrily spurns. It is also arguably his masterpiece, and may serve as a final example of his syntactical strangeness and of the frames of reference—predominantly the bible and George Herbert—within which he operates.

> Be still black Parasites,
>   Flutter no more;
> Were it still winter, as it was before,
>   You'd make no flights;
> But now the dew and Sun have warm'd my bowres,
>   You flie and flock to suck the flowers.
>
>   But you would honey make:
>   These buds will wither,
>   And what you now extract, in harder weather
>   Will serve to take;
>   Wise husbands will (you say) there wants prevent,
>   Who do not so, too late repent.
>
>   O poys'nous, subtile fowls!
>   The flyes of hell
>   That buz in every ear, and blow on souls
>   Until they smell
>   And rot, descend not here, nor think to stay,
>   I've read, who 'twas, drove you away.
>
>   Think you these longing eyes,
>   Though sick and spent,
>   And almost famish'd, ever will consent
>   To leave those skies,

> That glass of souls and spirits, where well drest
>   They shine in white (like stars) and rest.
>
>   Shall my short hour, my inch,
>   My one poor sand,
> And crum of life, now ready to disband
>   Revolt and flinch,
> And having born the burthen all the day,
>   Now cast at night my Crown away?
>
>   No, No; I am not he,
>   Go seek elsewhere.
> I skill not your fine tinsel, and false hair,
>   Your Sorcery
> And smooth seducements: I'le not stuff my story
>   With your Commonwealth and glory.
>
>   There are, that will sow tares
>   And scatter death
> Amongst the quick, selling their souls and breath
>   For any wares;
> But when thy master comes, they'l finde and see
>   There's a reward for them and thee.
>
>   Then keep the antient way!
>   Spit out their phlegm
> And fill thy brest with home; think on thy dream:
>   A calm, bright day!
> A land of flowers and spices! the word given,
>   *If these be fair, O what is Heaven!*[28]

The rapid, elliptical style of this catches glancingly at biblical contexts—the plague of flies from Exodus 8:31 (l. 14), the "burden and heat of the day" from Matthew 20:12 (l. 29), and the parable of the tares from Matthew 13:25 (l. 37). Phrases from Herbert—"My inch of life" from "Complaining," "fictions onely and false hair" from "Jordan I", "Spit out thy flegme, and fill thy brest with glorie" from "The Church-Porch," "man well drest" from "Prayer I"—are adapted and spun into the metaphoric texture. The end of the fourth stanza and the honey in the second suggest that another text passing through Vaughan's mind may have been his translation of Eucherius's *Life of Paulinus:*

> Three daies (saith *Uranius*) before *John* the Bishop of *Naples* departed out of this life, he affirmed that he saw *Paulinus* all clothed with Angeli-

call brightnesse, which shined like the stars, holding in his hand a kind of Heavenly foode in form like a honey-combe, but white as the light, and speaking to him, *brother John, what do you here? pray, that you may be dissolv'd, & come unto us, where we have enough of this provision which you see in my hand.*[29]

These allusions reinforce the poem's detachment and transcendence, its scornful uplift and resolute focus on spaces and texts beyond itself. The syntactical disturbances, of a kind we have by now become used to in Vaughan—"famish'd" eyes (l. 21), "stuff my story / With your Commonwealth" (ll. 35–36), "fill thy brest with home" (l. 45)—compound this sense of a rapidity that cannot stay to translate itself into logical, commonplace terms. In the second stanza, "serve to take" is both vague (which of its many meanings does "take" have here?) and redundant. There are two verbs where, you feel, one should do, and, even with two, the thought remains half-formed, as if the speaker had no time to perfect this bit of argument before hurrying on to the next. Though, at this point, Vaughan is ostensibly relaying what the "Parasites" say, their way of expressing themselves remains suspiciously like his—that rapid, preoccupied, not-fully-meaningful manner is unmistakable (and necessarily so, of course, since the temptations are inside his head). Then again, at the end of the fourth stanza, how are the "skies" the "glass" of souls and spirits? The word contributes transparency, light, and some suggestion of an optical instrument, a sort of spiritual telescope perhaps. But it is impossible to reduce it to anything definite; it will not pale into significance. Though phrases from Herbert help Vaughan to create his effect, Herbert himself never writes in this almost nonchalantly semi-articulate manner.

This manner, and its syntactical bases, are original and distinctive. Vaughan's beliefs, though eclectic, can all be matched, and matched in writers who could never be mistaken for him. It is his stylistic peculiarities that set him apart. His purposeful vagueness, and his refusal to let contraries contradict, are factors that, whatever they may imply about his inner states, give his poetry its unique relation to time, place and logicality. Eliot's outburst, with which I began, seems to have been motivated chiefly by his wish to pillory Blunden. It prevented him from recognizing in Vaughan a poet whose method was no less original and no less dependent on indefiniteness of meaning than his own.

Notes

1. See L. C. Martin, ed., *The Works of Henry Vaughan,* Oxford, Oxford University Press, 1914, second edition 1957 (from which the quotations in this article

are taken, and to which the page and line references apply); "Henry Vaughan and Hermes Trismegistus", *Review of English Studies* 18 (1942): 301–307, and Alan Rudrum, ed., Henry Vaughan, *The Complete Poems,* London, Penguin Books, 1977. Elizabeth Holmes, *Henry Vaughan and the Hermetic Philosophy* (Oxford: Clarendon Press, 1932) was a pioneering study of Vaughan's Hermetic sources. More recent studies such as Ross Garner's *Henry Vaughan: Experience and the Tradition* (Chicago: University of Chicago Press, 1959) and Jonathan F. S. Post, *Henry Vaughan. The Unfolding Vision* (Princeton: Princeton University Press, 1982) downplay Hermeticism.

2. *The Dial*, September 1927, 259–63.
3. T. S. Eliot, "The Waste Land," in *The Complete Poems and Plays 1909–1950* (San Diego: Harcourt Brace Jovanovich, 1950), ll. 71–72.
4. Vaughan, "The Retreat," ll. 21–24.
5. Vaughan, "The Search," ll. 69–71 (italics in Martin).
6. Ibid., ll. 5–16.
7. Rom. 10:15.
8. John Keats, "Hyperion," in *Poetical Works*, ed. H. W. Garrod, 2nd ed. (Oxford: Clarendon Press, 1958), l. 74.
9. Vaughan, "Cock Crowing," ll. 1–12.
10. Vaughan, "The Bird," ll. 14–16.
11. Ibid., ll. 22–24, 37–41.
12. See for example Ross Garner, *Henry Vaughan: Experience and Tradition,* 97–98.
13. Vaughan, "Rules and Lessons," ll. 15–16.
14. Vaughan, "The Night," ll. 19–24.
15. Vaughan, "And do they so? have they a Sense," ll. 1–10.
16. Paracelsus, *The Hermetic and Alchemical Writings of Aureolus Philippus Theophrastus Bombast of Hohenheim, Called Paracelsus the Great*. Edited by A. E. Waite. 3 vols. (London: James Elliott & Co., 1894), 2:269.
17. St. Thomas Aquinas, *Summa Contra Gentiles, literally translated by the English Dominican Fathers* (London: Burns, Oates and Washboume, 1929), 4:320.
18. Thomas Vaughan, *The Works of Thomas Vaughan: Eugenius Philalethes, Edited, Annotated and Introduced by A.E. Waite* (London: Theosophical Publishing House, 1919), 392.
19. Vaughan, "The Book," ll. 25–30.
20. Nigel Smith, *A Collection of Ranter Writings from the Seventeenth Century* (London: Junction Books, 1983), 232.
21. Ibid., 16.
22. Vaughan, "The Night," ll. 25–42.
23. Vaughan, "Regeneration," ll. 56–66.
24. Vaughan, "Man," ll. 15–21.
25. Vaughan, "The Seed growing secretly," ll. 25–40.
26. Vaughan, "The Proffer," l. 5.
27. Vaughan, "The Seed growing secretly," ll. 5–8.
28. Vaughan, "The Proffer," pp. 486–88.
29. Vaughan, translation of Eucherius' *Life of Paulinus*, ll. 35–41.

Shakespeare and Magical Grammar

Linda Woodbridge

> "In its various Medieval forms—*gramarye, gramaire,* and *grimoire*—grammar at once denoted general erudition, literacy, and sorcery."
>
> —William A. Covino

ACTORS' SUPERSTITIONS DICTATE THAT *MACBETH* BE CALLED "THE SCOTtish play." To refer to this demonic tragedy by its true name will supposedly call down fearsome bad luck. It is fitting that such a lexical superstition has attached itself to a play which above all other Shakespearean plays is steeped in magical beliefs and residually magical thinking connected with fear of naming. The witches tell Macbeth they are performing "a deed without a name" (*Macbeth*, 4.1.49). The bloodiest deeds in the play, the Macbeths themselves know, must not be named.

A sizeable body of early modern magical beliefs deals with the danger of drawing attention to somebody, making him or her conspicuous, through praise or even through uttering his or her name. Such attention was thought to attract the evil eye. As Tobin Siebers points out,

> The pronouncing of compliments and curses has always been intimately related to the cause and cure of the evil eye. The custom of addressing children by opprobrious names is one manifestation of the fear of praise.... In southern India, mothers paint black spots on their children's faces, chins, cheeks, and eyelids to deter compliments.... If a misfortune befalls someone who has been praised, he may attribute it to the compliment. His illness is thus explained, while the hostility that must naturally appear in such situations can be dispelled by requiring the admirer to undo the offense through an act of ritual dispraising.[1]

I argued in *The Scythe of Saturn: Shakespeare and Magical Thinking* that a good deal of evil-eye belief attends Shakespeare's representation of the rape of Lucrece, including the fact that Lucrece falls victim to Tarquin's malevolent gaze because her husband has foolishly praised her:

> her husband's shallow tongue,—
> The niggard prodigal that praised her so,—
> In that high task hath done her beauty wrong,
> Which far exceeds his barren skill to show:
> Therefore that praise which Collatine doth woe
> Enchanted Tarquin answers with surmise,
> In silent wonder of still-gazing eyes.
> ("The Rape of Lucrece," ll 78–84)

To attract attention to someone as very beautiful, very chaste, very brave, very eminent in any way often attracts the evil eye, and the person can thereby be blighted and waste away. The very notion of *hubris* as an outstanding individual's attracting the baleful attention of the gods and hence calling down tragedy on him- or herself is related to such beliefs. As Eugene McCartney summarizes, "the blasting effects of praise" come from three sources: "(1) the inadvertence or ignorance of well-meaning people who let slip complimentary remarks; (2) the envy and malevolence of those who have the evil eye; and (3) the jealousy of the gods, who permit no mortal to be supremely beautiful or happy or prosperous without paying for his blessings by counterbalancing woes and adversities".[2] I suggest that the second and third sources are closely allied: dangerous praise awakens the envy of evil-minded humans (endowed by magical belief with the power to harm through the evil eye) and also awakens the jealousy of the gods, as in *hubris*. The centrality of *hubris* to tragedy suggests that related forms of folk belief, such as lore of the evil eye, merit close attention.

Macbeth opens with extravagant praise. Most of the first 45 lines of act I, scene 2 comprise the bleeding captain's fulsome praise of Macbeth' s valor in battle; the captain publicly trumpets Macbeth's exploits, calling him "brave Macbeth" and "valor's minion," and comparing him to eagle and lions (*Macbeth*, 1.2.16, 19, 35). King Duncan chimes in with "O valiant cousin, worthy gentleman!" (1.2.24). Ross too reports that the battle was almost singlehandedly won by Macbeth, whom he dubs "Bellona's bridegroom" (1.2.56), rhetorically elevating him to the celestial pantheon. In the very next scene, witches encounter Macbeth, and to the well-meant but perhaps dangerous praise of the Scottish noblemen, add their own malicious praise, elevating him with "all hail" cries befitting a Roman conqueror. In light of evil-eye belief, it is scarcely surprising that evil comes to Macbeth just after he has been praised to the heavens. His description of the situation to Lady Macbeth emphasizes that the witches appeared at his moment of triumph: "They met me in the day of success" (1.5.1–2). This is the very essence of *hubris*: Macbeth has made himself conspicuous to the gods. It is also the scenario of evil-eye belief, which I think is a specialized form of a more general superstitious belief that happiness and misery alternate in cycles. In evil-eye belief, misery follows upon happiness because conspicuous happiness invites envy and hence retribution.[3]

Beliefs like this were residual in Shakespeare's culture, and traces of them can still be found in ours—which of us has not felt an uneasy sense of impending misfortune at times of unusual happiness? *Macbeth* offers both the genuine supernatural and a realm of magic sublimated into individual psychology, such as another sort of eye magic Lady Macbeth's behavior reveals: the conviction that what one cannot see does not exist. When Lady Macbeth cries, "Come, thick night, / And pall thee in the dunnest smoke of hell, / That my keen knife see not the wound it makes" (1.5.50–52), she first tries to obscure her eyesight with smoke and then displaces her eyesight onto the knife. Similarly with Macbeth: "Stars, hide your fires, / Let not light see my black and deep desires; / The eye wink at the hand; yet let that be / Which the eye fears, when it is done, to see"; "I am afraid to think what I have done; / Look on't again I dare not" (1.4.50–53, 2.2.49–50). Both sorts of magical thinking comprise a kind of linguistic disappearing act: if refraining from naming or praising—or ritual dispraising—can make a person invisible to malevolent forces connected with the evil eye, so one's own evil deeds can be made to disappear through closing one's eyes to them.

This is the other side of the coin from speech acts which conjure the invisible into existence. Lady Macbeth's conjuring of spirits ("Come, you spirits / That tend on mortal thoughts") (1.5.40–41) finds a complement in her efforts to render invisible the evil she plans. Conjuring into existence what had been invisible has its recognized tropes, as Denis Donoghue notes: "De Man, J. Hillis Miller and other rhetoricians have expounded, as a nuance of Speech Act Theory, the figure of *prosopopeia,* the figure that gives a face to the faceless or conjures into a semblance of existence that which otherwise is merely notional."[4]

Conversely, I suggest that there is a grammar for causing unpleasant things to disappear: the use of pronouns rather than directly naming nouns, of passive verbs to evade naming who performed the action, of euphemisms to avoid naming actions or agents, of epithets or praise-names rather than proper names, of synonyms and other substitutive devices. *Macbeth* is Shakespeare's premier exploration of the workings of such "magical grammar."

Both Macbeths suffer from a noun-avoidance syndrome. Their well-known repertoire of euphemisms for murder includes such evasions as the "business" (1.5.68, 1.7.32, 2.1.49, 3.1.126), "his taking-off" (1.7.20), and "the deed."[5] This trick of speech resembles the way, in parts of nineteenth-century India, a tiger was spoken of as "he of the hairy face" or "the striped one" to avoid attracting to the speaker the unwelcome attentions of a tiger by pronouncing its true name.[6] The English proverb "Speak of the Devil and he will appear," or "Talk of the Devil and see his horns" enshrines a magical belief that to speak directly the name of a spirit will cause it to appear. Marlowe's Faustus believes (erroneously, as it turns out) that naming Mephistophilis has caused him to appear; on the same principle Faustus is forbidden by devils to use the names of God or Christ. For the Macbeths to use directly the word "murder" might be in some measure to commit themselves to it, to cause it to happen by mere malevolent thought (2.2.4).[7]

But even "business" and "deed," though having a much higher invisibility quotient than "murder," are still nouns, and the Macbeths greatly prefer pronouns, as in "do it" or "he is about it" (2.2.4). The latter, uttered by Lady Macbeth at the moment Macbeth is killing Duncan, causes "Macbeth" to disappear into "he" as well as "murder" into "it"; the victim disappears entirely. An even higher degree of invisibility is afforded by pronouns whose antecedent is left unspecified, often through the device of beginning a scene in mid-speech, presumably after the utterance of the noun. One such crucial passage beginning with an antecedentless pronoun is Lady Macbeth's opening speech at the beginning of act 1, scene 5: "They met me in the day of success; and I have learned by the perfect'st report they have more in them than mortal knowledge." Here the weird sisters' identity disappears into two "they's" and a "them." (Macbeth has never asked their names, anyway.)

Though she has so far been reading from Macbeth's letter and the pronoun vagueness is his, Lady Macbeth herself soon resorts to an all-purpose "thus" and the generic verb "do," to gesture vaguely toward the homicidal possibility: "'Thus thou must do'." ("Do" and "done" as favored disappearing-act words are prefigured, like other elements of the Macbeth diction, in early witch dialogue—"I'll do, and I'll do, and I'll do" (1.3.10), suggesting that the witches have supernatural affinities with the Macbeths before they even meet Macbeth.)

One of Lady Macbeth's favorite grammatical disappearing devices is the substitution, for a noun, of a noun clause introduced by a relative pronoun. The first time she does this, it is to avoid saying "king": "Glamis thou art, and Cawdor, and shalt be / What thou art promised." (5.15–16). Many cultures provide a repertoire of praise-names and epithets to allow subjects to avoid speaking the dangerous name of a king or even the title "king."[8] Here a vague substitute, the noun clause "what thou art promised," allows Lady Macbeth to avoid saying "king." "Be," indicating a state of being rather than an action, avoids "become" with its implicit act of murder. And the passive verb "art promised" allows elision of who did the promising, namely the evil powers already rendered murky as "they."

Soon Lady Macbeth goes into an orgy of evasive noun clauses substituting for nouns, with the preposition "what" and the relative pronoun "that" performing the magical work of noun-vanishing: "What thou wouldst highly, / That wouldst thou holily"(1.5.19–20) is an invisible way of saying "You want to be king but you'd rather not achieve this by murdering the man who is king now." Next she produces almost a self-parody of her own "its," "dos," "undones," and disappearing-act noun clauses:

> Thou'dst have, great Glamis,
> That which cries, 'Thus thou must do,' if thou have it,
> And that which rather thou dost fear to do
> Than wishest should be undone.
>
> (1.5.21–25)

This passage is hard to follow, and deliberately so: Lady Macbeth's diction is designed to obscure, to cover her tracks. "Thou'dst have" means "you want to have," but in place of the expected object of the verb "have," namely "the crown," we get a noun clause introduced by a relative pronoun, "that which cries, 'Thus thou must do.'" She seems to be saying that the crown itself, representing the office of kingship, cries out to Macbeth that he must commit murder if he is to have it, a neat shifting of responsibility for the murder to a vaguely specified entity, somewhat analogous to her bestowing her eyesight upon a knife. Both of the next two relative clauses, "that which rather thou dost fear to do" and "than [that which thou] wishest should be undone," substitute for the unspoken noun "murder" or "regicide." Does the puzzling "and" indicate that the verb "[would]st have" governs both "that which cries" and "that which . . . thou dost fear to do"? If so, we can make sense—just barely—of the sentence by restoring the disappeared nouns. She means something like "You want to have the crown, an object which itself tells you that you must commit murder to get it, and you want murder, which you are more afraid than unwilling to commit." The way she hurries past "thou wouldest have" by contracting it into "thou'dst have" is one of the sentence's many evasions of willed agency. Trying to understand this sentence only points up the fact that Lady Macbeth does not much want to be understood, even by herself, for all these evasions occur tellingly in a soliloquy.[9]

As Lady Macbeth's soliloquy begins *in medias res,* Macbeth two scenes later begins a closely analogous soliloquy in mid-meditation. Like hers, his soliloquy features a pronoun whose antecedent has been omitted by the mid-utterance opening of the scene: "If it were done when 'tis done, then 'twere well / It were done quickly" (1.7.1–2). Here again the pronoun "it" replaces the noun "murder," and even "it" is contracted to " 't" in "'tis" and "'t were," diminishing the crime almost to invisibility (that tiny " 't") or inaudibility (only a little click of the tongue against the teeth). Again the action is reduced to the vaguest possible verb, "do," and then turned into the passive verb "done" (three times), a magical way of causing the agent to disappear from view. Further evasions follow: "this blow," "these cases" (1.7.4, 1.7.7). Macbeth does not use the word "king" in this speech,[10] preferring the vague phrase "his great office" (l. 18), but he does use the name "Duncan." The king's proper name according to much magical belief is dangerous in a subject's mouth—a loyal subject would not simply fling it around, and "this Duncan" has a further disrespectful tone—it has something of the air of "this fellow," or of someone peripheral to whom Macbeth's attention has just been drawn and to whom Macbeth feels free to refer off-handedly, rather than suggesting that nation's center, the king. The name "Duncan" does not come out right away, though. When Macbeth first brings himself to refer to the object of "this blow," which is not until twelve lines into the speech, he uses the antecedentless pronouns "he" and "his" five times before finally coming out with "Duncan":

> *He*'s here in double trust:
> First, as I am *his* kinsman and *his* subject,
> Strong both against the deed; then as *his* host,
> Who should against *his* murderer shut the door.
> (1.7.12–15)

When the soliloquy is interrupted at the end (as it has been entered in progress at the beginning), it is with an antecedentless pronoun from Lady Macbeth: "*He* has almost supped. Why have you left the chamber?" Replying in kind—"Hath *he* asked for me?", Macbeth is answered with another "he": "Know you not *he* has?" Submerging "murder" again in euphemism, Macbeth declares "We will proceed no further in this business," and gestures again towards that unidentified "he": "He hath honored me of late" (1.7.30–33). His committing of the murder calls forth the invisibility words: "I go, and it is done"; "I have done the deed" (2.1.63; 2.2.15). And under the stress of the occasion, Lady Macbeth's noun aversion and substitution complex grows so intense that she substitutes two relative clauses even for the seemingly innocuous noun "wine": "that which hath made them drunk"; "what hath quenched them" (2.2.1–2).

Lady Macbeth never calls Macbeth by his name, and the play does not even give her a name, beyond "Macbeth's wife." One could regard her namelessness in various ways: as an early modern effacement of the female or as an artistic device to heighten her coldness (the hominess of, say, a Kate Macbeth would definitely not suit the play). But in many cultures, spouses and other close relatives do not call each other by their names.[11] Strong taboos here are sometimes connected with incest rules, sometimes with politeness codes, but probably reflect too the dangerousness of names.[12] In Stith Thompson's *Motif-Index,* classification C435.1 lists English and Irish folk tales containing taboos against uttering a spouse's name.

The spousal taboo is a subtype of the general tendency to protect names. Personal names are among the most magically potent and vulnerable of nouns. Edward Clodd proffers examples from many cultures, including nineteenth-century Scotland and Ireland, of people's great reluctance to give their names, out of fear that whoever knew their name (sorcerer, enemy, or evil spirit) would have power over them. Clodd's 1920 book belongs to a syncretizing, lumping-together period of anthropology, and tends to make haymaking generalizations about "the primitive mind" from geographically farflung evidence, but British examples of this superstition about names appear in more respectable sources too, from the Middle Ages to the twentieth century.

We encounter the superstition about revealing one's name in the folktale *Rumpelstiltskin,* a British variant of which is *Tom-Tit-Tot.*[13] A medieval Welsh legend features a man and a woman who fought at the battle of Cad Goddea who could not be overcome unless their names were known. In other Welsh tales, spinning fairies fall into the power of someone who overhears them muttering their names, very similar to *Rumpelstiltskin*.[14] Stith Thompson's general classification C430, "prohibition against uttering the name of a person or thing," includes English, Irish, Scottish, and Welsh folk tales. The children observed and interviewed by Iona and Peter Opie in English schoolyards in the 1950s attached what the Opies thought to be "an almost primitive significance to people's names, always wanting to find out a stranger's name, yet being correspondingly reluctant to reveal their own."

The danger of giving one's name is sometimes associated with evil-eye belief, and similar tactics avert the evil eye and the danger of revealing a child's name. Just as the evil eye could be averted by ritual dispraising or by painting spots on a child's face or other uglification, so in the Malagasy culture each child is given a second name, "usually referring to some unpleasant item—for example, a small child may be called " 'Garbage Girl,' 'Dung Heap,' 'Dwarf,' . . . Furthermore, this name is usually shared by a number of children. When a speaker refers to a child as 'Dwarf,' he could be talking about any of several children."[15] In British superstition, a child's name should not be revealed before the christening, a notion still current in Cornwall in the 1970s.[16] In no less sophisticated a venue than Cambridge in 1971, a pregnant woman interviewed by a folklorist declined to tell the name chosen for the child, reporting that the parents would refer to the child by a nickname, not revealing to anyone its real name, until it was "safely baptized."[17]

In line with a longstanding tradition wherein warriors are given praise-names in place of their personal name (which might bring ill luck in battle), the early Macbeth is given battle praise names. The captain's pronouncement "brave Macbeth—well he deserves that name" (1.2.16) welds an epithet to a proper name, a way of deflecting such danger, but even this is soon amended to the safer praise-name "Bellona's bridegroom" (1.2.56). Except for the one poignant moment when she refers to him as "my husband" (2.2.14), Lady Macbeth refers to Macbeth by titles ("Glamis," "Cawdor"), formal relationships ("my lord," 3.4.53), or pronouns ("he," "thou"). At one point she deftly avoids both his proper name and any reference to his becoming king, in a carefully self-protective allusion to the witches' prophecy: "Great Glamis! Worthy Cawdor! / Greater than both by the all-hail hereafter!" (1.5.54–55). Macbeth refers to Lady Macbeth by pronouns, by circumlocutions ("dearest partner of greatness") (1.5.11), and by nicknames ("dearest chuck," 3.2.48). The nicknames are usually interpreted as terms of endearment showing that Macbeth's heart has not entirely hardened. But nicknames are a widespread method of avoiding the use of a proper name in cultures that consider such naming dangerous. Despite their superstitious care, however—the caution of those whose conscience is bad—it is clear from the outset that the name "Macbeth" has indeed fallen into the wrong hands. The Third Witch uses Macbeth' s proper name as early as the seventh line of the play, and the first line uttered directly to Macbeth by a witch is "All hail, Macbeth!" (1.3.48).

The witches parody the Macbeths' grammar of invisibility, their terror of naming, and their use of vague euphemisms such as "deed," when Macbeth visits them to demand "How now, you secret, black, and midnight hags? / What is 't you do?" Flinging his weasel-verb "do" and his miniaturized "'t" in his face, they reply in pure Macbeth-speak: "A deed without a name" (4.1.49).

The Macbeths' vague verbs, passive verbs, contractions, antecedentless pronouns, noun avoidance, and name avoidance are in line with common magical beliefs about the dangers of naming, of calling attention to oneself and one's actions. There is a world-upside-down effect in this play, however. Such verbal protection-magic usually functions to ward off malevolent perils such as the evil eye, enemies, evil spirits, or jealous gods. Here, where the protagonists are themselves involved in evil, the protection functions to ward off powers of good. Through verbal subterfuges, the Macbeths close their eyes to the evil they are doing. "To know my deed, 'twere best not know myself," Macbeth realizes (2.2.77). The Macbeths are hiding not from enemy sorcerers but from themselves, and the powers of good they are fending off are their own potentially awakened consciences. What Lady Macbeth is hiding from is not evil spirits—she conjures them to come to her—but heaven and its good spirits:

> Come, thick night,
> And pall thee in the dunnest smoke of hell,
> That my keen knife see not the wound it makes
> Nor heaven peep through the blanket of the dark
> To cry 'Hold, hold'!

(1.5.50–54)

Shakespeare developed such habits of lexico-magical self-protection in other mature plays. Another self-deceiver aided by magical grammar is Brutus. The soliloquy in which he considers murdering Caesar, like Macbeth's soliloquy to which it is homologous, begins in mid-meditation with an antecedentless "it": "It must be by his death" (*Julius Caesar*, 2.1.10). This "it" apparently refers to something like "the removal of the threat of tyranny represented by Caesar's growing ambition," or perhaps "the good accruing to Rome from the restoration of its former republican glories." The dubiousness of this good in Brutus's mind is suggested by its sublimation in an antecedentless pronoun. Brutus does look directly enough at the situation to use the word "death" rather than a Macbethism such as "the deed," but "his death" is still a fairly neutral term, omitting the violence of murder and avoiding the naming of any agent or even the recognition that the death will be accomplished by an agent rather than resulting from natural causes. The state-of-being verb "be" has a Macbethian vagueness. The victim disappears into two pronouns, the "his" of "his death" and the "him" of "I know no personal cause to spurn at him" (2.1.11). Indeed, the victim is referred to by two "he's," three "him's," and two "his's" before Brutus ever gets around to naming him, and then it is by title, "Caesar"——this supposed dear friend never refers to his victim as "Julius" until after he is dead.

In these mature plays, Shakespeare has nearly perfected the technique whereby the fearful and self-deceiving personality makes terrifying objects and ideas disappear semi-magically, through grammatical substitutions.[18] Earlier texts are less sophisticated in technique, but Shakespeare already had the idea as early as *The Rape of Lucrece*, which as I have mentioned exhibits several telltale markers of evil-eye belief. As Macbeth and Brutus mentally revolve, in soliloquy, reasons for and against murder, so Tarquin "lies[s] revolving / The sundry dangers of his will's obtaining" ("The Rape of Lucrece," ll. 127–28). His 174 lines of self-debate have features in common with Macbeth's soliloquy: as Macbeth recalls that he is the kinsman, subject, and host of his intended victim, so Tarquin recalls that Lucrece's husband is "my kinsman, my dear friend" (l. 237). But the most telling resemblance is that Tarquin averts his face from what he is contemplating by refusing to name it. It is not Shakespeare who is squeamish about the word "rape": he frontloads it into his very title. But Tarquin will not use it. As the Macbeths and Brutus substitute "it" or "the deed" for "murder," so Tarquin sidesteps "rape," calling it instead "the deed" (195), "impious act" (199), "my digression" (202), "the thing I seek" (211), "my intent" (218), and "so black a deed" (218). He produces a tangled skein of obscurantist noun clauses, prefiguring Lady Macbeth's:

> Those that much covet are with gain so fond
> That what they have not, that which they possess
> They scatter and unloose it from their bond.
> *(Macbeth,* 134–36)

In *The Scythe of Saturn* I define "magical thinking" as the unconscious residue of a magical mind set that remains after the conscious mind has freed itself from actual magical belief, and it is noteworthy that in all the instances of self-protection through linguistic disappearing acts which I have just discussed, what is being made to disappear is the speaker's own evil. The protection being sought is not against the evil eye of enemy sorcerers but against one's own self-scrutiny. Shakespeare seems quite conscious of his characters' indulgence in magical thinking—here, pure self-deception with no hint of actual magical belief. Such linguistic maneuvers do tend to occur in works with other supernatural elements—*Macbeth, Julius Caesar*—but this is not invariable *(Lucrece* is lacking in witches, soothsayers, and ghosts). Tragedies of Shakespeare's contemporaries, too, offer examples of evasive grammar, often linked with other magical elements: Take, for example, the way Marlowe's Dr. Faustus refers to himself as "Faustus" rather than "I." Inverting the usual evasion by pronoun substitution, this self-splitting operation allows Faustus as speaking subject to distance himself from the Faustus who is selling his soul to the devil.

I have mainly limited myself in this essay to tragedies, with a glance at *The Rape of Lucrece*. I will just mention that one comedy brimming with magic, *The Tempest,* offers traces of word magic: Prospero has enjoined Miranda not to give out her name *(The Tempest,* 3.1.36–37), in this case a sexual protection, and Caliban clearly *wishes* his curses would prove magically effective. When Robert Browning took up Caliban in his poem "Caliban upon Setebos," he gave Caliban's speech a quite Shakespearean evasiveness via pronouns and contractions: we are not even sure Caliban is the speaker of this seeming dramatic monologue, since he refers to himself in the third person, and often elides even the pronoun, reducing "He will sprawl" to "'Will sprawl" in the play's opening words, to evade punishment for dangerous thoughts. But Shakespeare's own Caliban doesn't do this: he refers to himself in the first person and boldly calls Prospero by his name; when he fears he is overheard, his evasion is physical rather than lexical: "I'll fall flat" (2.2.16). Although I have not extensively analyzed Shakespearean comedies for traces of magical grammar, my sense is that even comedies rich in magical elements do not employ what I have called "magical grammar." These complex linguistic maneuvers, to escape notice or evade responsibility, instead typify the mature tragedies.

Of course, Shakespeare was not always careful with pronouns, prepositions, or noun clauses. Take the short but baffling passage at the end of *Antony and Cleopatra*: "I hear him mock / The luck of Caesar, which the gods give men / To excuse their after wrath" (*Antony and Cleopatra*, 5.2.285–87). "Him" at least is clear, since we do have the noun "Antony" just above it, but what is the referent of the relative clause "which the gods give men"? "Luck"? The privilege of mocking? What about "their"? Does it hark back to "gods" or "men"? "After" what? Sometimes, in short, Shakespeare was just plain careless about such stuff. But sometimes the ambiguities created by pronouns, noun clauses, or passive verbs are very calculated indeed, and serve brilliantly to expose the magical mind set of those characters who rely on what Freud called "the omnipotence of thoughts" to save them from the damning recognition of their own evil.

Much remains to be learned about this subject. Linguists and linguistic anthropologists have not plumbed the topic as one might have expected. There is plenty of theory and speculation on "how pronouns signify" (for example, Peter Bosch's *Agreement and Anaphora: A Study of the Role of Pronouns in Syntax and Discourse*), but little that is helpful on the question of why pronouns exist in the first place. It may only be a matter of economy in language to use "he" the second time one refers to someone with a long name like Ebenezer Adamowitz, but that doesn't take us far with why we still substitute "he" for a short name like "Bill." The magical grammar I have been discussing often works by a process of substitution, as does a fair amount of magic more generally—that is, for example, how scapegoating works. When we find a system of elaborate substitutions built into a language, and we know that those grammatical substitution systems date back to a period in the prehistory of the language when its speakers were heavily involved in magical belief and practice, it seems logical to suspect that such substitutive grammatical structures may themselves encode the vestiges of magical belief. The interest of linguists and linguistic anthropologists in the magical side of language seems limited mainly to taboo words, incantations, and spells, rather than the sort of strategic substitutions that intrigue me.[19] Where will further illumination come from—linguistics, anthropology, folklore, history? Literary study? Or perhaps a discipline without a name.

Notes

1. Tobin Siebers, *The Mask of Medusa* (Berkeley: University of California Press, 1983), 41–43; see also Frederick Elworthy, *The Evil Eye: The Origins and Practices of Superstition* (1895; reprint, New York: Collier, 1958). King James showed familiarity with such beliefs in his reference to "such kind of charms, as comely daft wives use for healing forspoken goods, for preserving them from evil eyes" (*Daemonologie* [1597; reprint, New York: Barnes and Noble, 1966], 11). In Shakespeare's day evil eye beliefs were especially strong in Scotland, northern England, and other parts of rural England. Pistol refers to the evil eye when, disguised as a hobgoblin, he tells Falstaff "vile worm, thou wast o'erlook'd even in thy birth" (*Merry Wives of Windsor*, 5.5.87) as does Portia when she tells Bassanio, "Beshrew your eyes,/ They have o'erlook'd me and divided me" (*Merchant of Venice*, 3.2.14–16).

2. Eugene McCartney, "Praise and Dispraise in Folklore," *Papers of the Michigan Academy of Science, Arts, and Letters* 28 (1942): 568.

3. Such beliefs help explain the sudden dread Othello experiences at a moment of extreme happiness: "If it were now to die, / 'Twere now to be most happy; for, I fear, / My soul hath her content so absolute / That not another comfort like to this / Succeeds in unknown fate" (2.1.188–92). Such dangerous and public relishing of happiness draws from Desdemona a nervous disclaimer: "The heavens forbid / But that our loves and comforts should increase, / Even as our days do grow" (2.1.192–94), an utterance resembling apotropaic verbal formulae used to turn away evil after an act of praise or profession of well-being ("touch wood" is the formula most familiar to us). But for her, the protective verbal magic does not work. Immediately after Othello makes himself conspicuous for happiness, evil descends upon him, just as the witches tackle Macbeth "in the day of success." Iago, overhearing Othello's protestation of happiness, declares in an aside, "O, you are well tuned now! / But I'll set down the pegs that make this music" (2.1.200–201). This marks the beginning of his malicious campaign against Othello's happiness, and he appears at this moment to be the very spirit of the sort of malice the evil eye was thought to embody: envy. (For more on the evil eye in *Othello*, see my *Scythe of Saturn*, 65–67.)

4. Denis Donoghue, "Doing Things with Words: Criticism and the Attack on the Subject," *Times Literary Supplement* 4763 (15 July 1994): 6.

5. For the extraordinary permutations of "do 't," "it is done," "do the deed," and so forth, see, for example, 1.7.50, 1.7.77, 2.1.63, 2.2.10, 2.2.13, 2.3.103, 3.1.132, 3.2.14, 3.2.46–47, 4.1.154, 5.1.34, 5.1.66.

6. Edward Clodd, *Magic in Names and in Other Things* (London: Chapman and Hall, 1920), 91. In the Ukraine and in most other Slavic countries, a "bear" is referred to only as a "honey eater," out of fear that to name a bear will be to cause one to appear (Max K. Adler, *Naming and Addressing: A Sociolinguistic Study* [Hamburg: Helmut Buske, 1978], 81). Richard Cavendish maintains that even twentieth-century euphemisms demonstrate to some extent the "continuing hold" of "the magical feeling that to speak the name of something dreaded risks summoning it" (*Man, Myth, and Magic: The Illustrated Encyclopedia of Mythology, Religion, and the Unknown*, 2nd edition, ed. Yvonne Deutch [New York: Marshall Cavendish, 1983], 1940).

7. The Macbeths' linguistic evasions here are not mere circumlocutions but have the quasi-magical force of true euphemism: "Every euphemism is, in a sense, a circumlocution, but not every circumlocution is a euphemism. In order

to be a true euphemism a word or phrase must call an evil thing by a good name, in the hope of thus transforming the evil into good. Euphemism is based upon superstition, whereas circulocution . . . is based upon social custom or desire to escape the commonplace" (Isaac Goldberg, *The Wonder of Words: an Introduction into Language* [London: Owen, 1958], 106). But it is interesting that while English euphemisms have often substituted a Latinate polysyllable for an Anglo-Saxon monosyllable ("perspire" for "sweat," "expectorate" for "spit"), the Macbeths' euphemisms are typically Anglo-Saxon words, and (except for "business") tend to be monsyllabic. The effect is to assimilate the horrific to the everyday and homely, not unlike the Nazi use of the plain word *überstellen*, meaning simply "to send over," to indicate the transporting of a person to another camp to be gassed (Cornelia Berning, *Die Sprache des Nationalsozialismus* [Zeitschrift fur Deutsche Wortforshung, 1962], 113).

   8. See Clodd 110–15, Adler 101, and Edgar H. Sturtevant, *Linguistic Change* (Chicago: University of Chicago Press, 1963), 24.

   9. Later, in another soliloquy—her first appearance as Queen—Lady Macbeth will indulge in another disappearing-act noun clause introduced by relative pronouns: " 'Tis safer to be that which we destroy / Than by destruction dwell in doubtful joy" (3.2.8–9); "that which we destroy" apparently refers to the vulnerable, about-to-be-murdered Duncan, and the very tense of the verbs seems a piece of magical grammar resurrecting the murdered man: The present tense suggests that the murder has not yet taken place. The Macbeths talk uncannily alike, even when apart, and Macbeth too sometimes uses the evasive noun clauses introduced by relative pronouns which are hallmarks of Lady Macbeth's magical thinking. For example, "Let that be / Which the eye fears, when it is done, to see" (1.4.50–53). "That which the eye fears," again, is the murder of Duncan.

   10. This is not his only avoidance of the word "king": The first time we see him as king, he is meditating, with the help of a carefully antecedentless "thus," "To be thus is nothing, / But to be safely thus" (3.3.49–50).

   11. See Clodd, *Magic in Names*, 51–64.

   12. The Renaissance received a double dose of magical belief about names, starting from the broad stream of popular superstition. Irish folklore, for example, abounds in lucky and unlucky names (Seán Ó Suilleabhain, *Irish Folk Custom and Belief* [Dublin: Cultural Relations Committee, n. 79]). Such beliefs stemmed also from the more intellectual body of hermetic and Neoplatonic writings. Henry Cornelius Agrippa, for example, was a keen theorist of name magic. The Renaissance affords many examples of beliefs about unluckiness in names. For example, in the Cinthio tale which was *Othello'* s main source, the only named character is Disdemona, and at the end her father is blamed for having given her an unlucky name meaning "the unfortunate one."

   13. The motif occurs in myths, too, as in the Egyptian myth where Isis takes the power of the sun god by discovering his real name. So widespread is the fear of an enemy gaining power by learning one's name that perhaps it is not farfetched to suspect some magical content behind the many episodes in Greene's cony-catching pamphlets when rogues are able to take advantage of new arrivals to London by learning their names through some clever ruse and then using the names to pretend to be kin or former neighbors.

   14. Gwynne T. Jones, *Welsh Folklore and Folk-Custom* (Woodbridge, Suffolk: D. S. Brewer, 1930), 74.

   15. Elinor Keenan, "Norm-makers, Norm-breakers: Uses of Speech by Men and Women in a Malagasy Community," in *Explorations in the Ethnography of*

Speaking, ed. Richard Bauman and Joel Sherzer (Cambridge: Cambridge University Press, 1974), 72.

16. *Cornish Sayings, Superstitions, and Remedies*, comp. Kathleen Hawke (Penzance: Headland, 1973), 21.

17. Enid Porter, *The Folklore of East Anglia* (London: Batsford, 1974), 22.

18. A soliloquy opening with an antecedentless pronoun and fear of naming also occurs in *Othello*, which begins "It is the cause, it is the cause, my soul. / Let me not name it to you, you chaste stars! / It is the cause" (5.2.1–22). In this case the unfaceable "it" is his wife's supposed unfaithfulness. "The cause" is also evasive, not specifying what is being caused: the murder Othello intends to commit.

19. The sparsity of genuine research throws the investigator back on some dubious sources of information, some from the era of scholars who, like Clodd, acknowledge with reverence the works of Sir James Frazer. This problem dogs the use of regional folklore studies too, and even the use of Stith Thompson's indispensable *Motif-Index of Folk Literature* (6 vols., Rev. ed. Bloomington: Indiana University Press, 1955–58), since Thompson too at times draws on Frazer. To our eyes, Frazer now looks embarrassingly ethnocentric and universalistic; his habit of piling up examples of, say, scapegoating or possible scapegoating or near-scapegoating from around the world has been dismissed by later scholars as "butterfly collecting." Modern insistence on the singularity of cultures runs counter to Frazer's pancultural generalizing.

Shakespeare's Eloquence

Maurice Charney

The *OXFORD ENGLISH DICTIONARY* DEFINES "ELOQUENCE" IN ITS FIRST meaning as "The action, practice, or art of expressing thought with fluency, force, and appropriateness, so as to appeal to the reason or move the feelings."[1] They see it as a word primarily relating to oral utterance, with emphasis on impassioned discourse in its modern usage. Shakespeare's eloquence is intimately connected with dramatic speech, which is quite different from the eloquence of lyric poetry that we read printed on the page. Of course, we do read Shakespeare primarily on the printed page, but we are always trying to reproduce in our reading the words as they may or should be spoken in performance. We are all inherently actors, or, in the popular phrase, "hams." Shakespeare's eloquence can't just apply to the words themselves, *sui generis*, but to the words spoken in their dramatic context. The words in a play can't float free of their place in the text, or their context. I would like to explore some eloquent places in Shakespeare's plays—or at least places that seem eloquent to me, in the sense that the words are endowed with special passion, force, and aptness in the theatrical situation in which they occur.

Let us begin with some relatively simple examples from *Julius Caesar*, a play in which the imaginative resources of language are extremely limited. Written just a few years before *Hamlet*, which has one of the most extensive vocabularies in Shakespeare, *Julius Caesar* has one of the smallest. Shakespeare seems to be trying to create a Roman style for this play that would be appropriate for its Roman theme. The language is relatively simple and so is the syntax, with a very limited use of metaphors, similes, and other figurative devices. The Roman style is sober, direct, and unimpassioned, yet there are occasions of powerful expression. I am thinking particularly of the exciting moment in act 2, scene 5 when Brutus agrees to tell his wife Portia his secrets, especially his decision to join the conspiracy against Caesar. Portia is an early feminist in her insistence on a companionate marriage of equals, something fairly rare in a patriarchal society like Shakespeare's. She argues with her husband that there must be more to marriage than "To keep with you at meals, comfort your bed, / And talk to you sometimes."[2] If that's all there is, then "Portia is Brutus' harlot, not his wife" (2.1.287). Brutus is shocked out of his complacency, and he declares his affection and devotion to his wife with real Roman fervor:

> You are my true and honorable wife,
> As dear to me as are the ruddy drops
> That visit my sad heart.
>
> (2.1.288–90)

This is a powerful example of Shakespeare's eloquence. Brutus speaks in homely, simple, and nonmetaphoric language. His blood is imagined as "ruddy drops," which, by personification, call on his "sad" or serious heart. Brutus is a good Roman husband, devoted to his wife Portia, and, for a man who is not at all passionate by temperament, he speaks with extraordinary feeling. It turns out to be a mistake for him to tell his secrets to his wife, who eventually swallows live coals and dies.

Portia's death is announced in a very moving context in the Quarrel Scene (act 4, scene 3) between Brutus and his friend Cassius. This scene is a wonderful example of Shakespeare's conversational style, as the two friends and coconspirators try to understand each other and the buried affection they feel. As the quarrel abates, Cassius says: "I did not think you could have been so angry," and Brutus explains: "O Cassius, I am sick of many griefs" (4.3.142–43). Cassius reminds Brutus of the Stoic philosophy, which teaches men to resist the petty outrages of this world: "Of your philosophy you make no use, / If you give place to accidental evils" (4.3.144–45). Then Brutus announces his surprising news: "No man bears sorrow better. Portia is dead" (4.3.146). This is a characteristically Stoic utterance, with a large and dramatic pause, or caesura, in the middle of the line. The interlude concludes with a spare Roman expression of deep and sorrowful emotions: Cassius says with surprise "Ha? Portia?" and Brutus answers, "She is dead" (4.3.147–48). This is particularly eloquent in the dramatic context of wild and whirling words between two close friends.

To jump to a different and much more extravagant play, *Hamlet* makes no attempt at all to limit its verbal resources and it involves us in a different sort of eloquence, yet we are still speaking about moments of intensity that are memorably expressed. In the final scene, Hamlet agrees to the fencing match with Laertes, but he has misgivings. Horatio, who seems to suspect the lethal triple plot against Hamlet's life by the King and Laertes, warns his friend: "You will lose this wager, my lord."[3] (5.2.210). But Hamlet persists, even though he has a sense of doom and fatality about what is coming: "But thou wouldst not think how ill all's here about my heart. But it is no matter" (5.2.213–4). Nothing is elaborated and everything is expressed with forceful simplicity. Despite his negative feelings, Hamlet defies "augury," or the prediction of the future based on the flight of birds, and he speaks in New Testament terms with a stoic and eloquent acceptance of whatever fate has in store for him:

> There is special providence in the fall of a sparrow. If it be now, 'tis not to come; if it be not to come, it will be now; if it be not now, yet it will come. The readiness is all.
> (5.2.220–24)

And the final words of this speech are like the sentiments of the Beatles' song: "Let be" (5.2.225).

Hamlet's views of special providence are expressed in a monosyllabic catalogue of the philosophical mood in which one awaits fate to enact his destiny. It's strange hearing Hamlet speaking so simply and religiously when he has been so actively plotting earlier in the play. He is taking cognizance of what he has learned from the sea voyage in which he was supposed to be killed at once by the King of England. Hamlet praises rashness "When our deep plots do pall" (5.2.9) and is convinced that the working out of his fate lies outside his conscious agency: "There's a divinity that shapes our ends, / Rough-hew them how we will" (5.2.10–11). That's probably what Hamlet means by the mysterious and quietistic "Let be" at the end of this speech. "The readiness is all" is matched by "Ripeness is all" in *King Lear*.[4] What does it mean to be ready, or accepting, of whatever may come? The readiness is "all," or everything; nothing else matters. The eloquence of these words in act 5, scene 2 of *Hamlet* lies in their intensity, and there is a certain measure of openness and suspension that the audience is asked to complete. We are speaking, of course, of the words in their dramatic context. "Let be" doesn't mean much outside of the situation and the passage in which it occurs.

Hamlet was first published in the problematic Bad Quarto of 1603, which was followed by the much more authoritative Second

Quarto in 1604. When Shakespeare's collected works were published in 1623 in the First Folio, the text of *Hamlet* was somewhat different from the earlier versions. Perhaps the text of the play was revised in keeping with the play as it was rewritten to represent a changing stage version over about twenty years. In the Folio, Hamlet's last words are

> But I do prophesy th' election lights
> On Fortinbras. He has my dying voice.
> So tell him, with th' occurrents, more and less,
> Which have solicited—the rest is silence. O,o,o,o.
> (*Hamlet*, 5.2.356–59)

Hamlet's O-groans have generally been dismissed by critics as a playhouse interpolation—as if that were bad in and of itself. Yet I claim that these meaningless interjections are full of profound meaning, at least as spoken by a skilled and passionate actor such as Richard Burbage, who could make these O-groans intense and memorable. They are, of course, not eloquent in themselves, but only in the fervent context of Hamlet's death.

The topic of Shakespeare's eloquence extends naturally to effects that lie outside words but are importantly related to the scenes in which they occur. I am thinking particularly of *Coriolanus*, which is not eloquent at all in its language and has an unreflective, martial protagonist. When Coriolanus is exiled from his native city of Rome through the tribunes' manipulation of the plebeians, he suddenly appears "disguised and muffled" in Antium, the city of his enemies. Afterward, he proceeds to attack Rome with the army of the Volscians, and just as he is about to lay the city waste, a Roman deputation appears to him to plead for mercy. It consists of his mother Volumnia, his wife Virgilia, his son Marcius, and Valeria, a friend of his wife. Only Volumnia speaks, and she seems to imply that, before Rome falls, she and her family will seek out their own deaths. In his puzzlement, Coriolanus speaks to himself in an acting image:

> Like a dull actor now,
> I have forgot my part and I am out,
> Even to a full disgrace.[5]

The final words of Volumnia's plea are searing:

> Yet give us our dispatch.
> I am hushed until our city be a-fire,
> And then I'll speak a little.
>
> (3.180–82)

At this point occurs one of those remarkable peripeteias, or changes in fortune, that mark Shakespeare's audacity. Signaling his capitulation, Coriolanus *"Holds her by the hand, silent"* (183 s.d.). As one who flees from words, Coriolanus's gesture is especially eloquent. He knows that his mercy will have a disastrous effect on his present situation:

> O my mother, mother! O!
> You have won a happy victory to Rome;
> But, for your son—believe it, O, believe it!—
> Most dangerously you have with him prevailed,
> If not most mortal to him. But let it come.
>
> (5.3.185–89)

Coriolanus' "let it come" resembles Hamlet's "let be."

To pursue eloquent gestures at the climax of tragedies, we may note the ending of *Antony and Cleopatra*. After Cleopatra applies the poisonous asps to her breast and dies, Charmian, her trusted lady in waiting, has some significant stage business. She shuts her mistress's eyes:

> Downy windows, close;
> And golden Phebus never be beheld
> Of eyes again so royal![6]

Then she straightens Cleopatra's crown: "Your crown's awry; / I'll mend it, and then play" (5.2.318–19). The dead Cleopatra must be a perfect aesthetic object, with nothing amiss. Caesar's Guard then comes *"rustling in,"* and Charmian takes an asp in order to die grandly like her mistress. The Guard questions her, as if in disbelief: "What work is here! Charmian, is this well done?" (5.2.324–25). In her last words, Charmian asserts her nobility:

> It is well done, and fitting for a princess
> Descended of so many royal kings.
> Ah, soldier!
>
> (5.2.326–28)

The "Ah, soldier" is mysterious, as if the guard could not even begin to comprehend Charmian's motives. In her glorious suicide, she places herself in a different world of feeling from mere mortals like the soldier.

This reminds me of another mysteriously eloquent line in *Antony and Cleopatra* that cannot be fully comprehended. This is in the scene where Cleopatra learns the devastating news that the absent Antony is now married to Octavia, the sister of Octavius Caesar. In her final speech in the scene, the distraught Cleopatra speaks to Charmian about Antony:

> Let him forever go!—let him not!—Charmian,
> Though he be painted one way like a Gorgon,
> The other way's a Mars.
>
> (2.5.115–17)

The tricky and undependable Antony is like those contemporary optical toys called perspective glasses, which show different views, depending at what angle the viewer holds the glass. Then she addresses her eunuch Mardian: "Bid you Alexas / Bring me word how tall she is." Her final words are to Charmian: "Pity me, Charmian, / But do not speak to me" (2.5.117–19). Why does Cleopatra want Charmian to pity her but not speak to her? Does Cleopatra feel herself completely separated from all of her confidantes? Does she feel infinitely above and beyond Charmian? For some reason, the line reminds me of Mae West's haughty comment to her servant at a moment of stress: "Beulah, peel me a grape."

I hope you don't think that I am collecting all the lines I like in Shakespeare and giving you a small anthology of dramatically effective moments. Far from it. I am interested in the kind of eloquence that is only minimally carried by words, an eloquence that is energized by the dramatic action and the exact place in the dramatic action where the words or gestures occur. For example, Prince Hal's "I do, I will"[7] in *Henry IV, Part One* doesn't carry much weight outside the play. It is not memorably phrased or in any way epigrammatic, but if you return this curt line to the scene in which it occurs, all kinds of tensions and pressures become evident behind the words. Act 2, scene 4 is one of the most developed Falstaff scenes in the play, in which the fat knight's lies about the robbery at Gadshill are exposed: "I was now a coward on instinct" (2.4.273–74). Falstaff then goes on to play the king with elaborate and self-conscious hyperbole, followed by Hal playing the king in an amusingly censorious way. Hal calls Falstaff "That villainous abominable misleader of youth . . . that old white-bearded Satan" (2.4.460–61). Falstaff defends himself with rhetorical unction, but he is already preoccupied with the traumatic rejection that will inevitably come at the end of *Henry IV, Part Two*:

> No, my good lord: banish Peto, banish Bardolph, banish Poins; but for sweet Jack Falstaff, kind Jack Falstaff, true Jack Falstaff, valiant Jack Falstaff, and therefore more valiant being, as he is, old Jack Falstaff, banish not him thy Harry's company, banish not him thy Harry's company, banish plump Jack, and banish all the world!
> (2.4.474–80)

It is at this point that Hal, entirely shifting the histrionic and expansive style of his earlier speeches, says curtly: "I do, I will" (2.4.81).

Of course, we remember this not only in its immediate context, but in the context of the rejection of Falstaff in the sequel. Prince Hal, now King Henry the Fifth, says cruelly:

> I know thee not, old man. Fall to thy prayers.
> How ill white hairs becomes a fool and jester!
> (5.5.48–49)

Is "I do, I will" predictive of the later speech? Not quite, but its harshly abrasive tone indicates that something is amiss. After all the flowing rhetoric in this scene, and especially in the huffing acting parts of Falstaff and Prince Hal, "I do, I will" comes as a stylistic shock. It is eloquent in the sense that it is aptly phrased and passionate, but it is also eloquent because it carries such a heavy burden of implication for Prince Hal as a dramatic character. We are aware of how cold and circumspect he can be from his early soliloquy at the end of act 1, scene 2:

> I know you all, and will awhile uphold
> The unyoked humor of your idleness.
> (1.2.199–200)

We in the audience know that Hal is just playing at the pleasant role of bosom companion to Falstaff. His surprisingly confessional soliloquy assures us that he knows exactly what he is doing, and that he is only biding his time until his Prodigal Son role will play itself out.

Once we begin to look at verbal effects whose eloquence depends not on the words themselves but on the way they are used in a specific dramatic context, we find many Shakespearean examples. Beatrice's "Kill Claudio"[8] from *Much Ado about Nothing* is the most startling. I think we can all agree that "Kill Claudio" has no figurative or symbolic significance by itself. In act 4, scene 1 of the play, however, it is a shocking and out-of-character statement from the witty and flirtatious Beatrice. This is the scene where Don John's calumniations against Hero take effect, and she is rejected unceremoniously as a "rotten orange" (4.1.31) by her credulous husband-to-be, Claudio. Benedick is properly sympathetic to his own love, Beatrice, who is weeping for her friend Hero's plight. Both of the lovers wittily protest their love for each other, and Benedick dutifully announces, "Come, bid me do anything for thee" (4.1.286). It is at this point that Beatrice astounds her lover by laying upon him a heavy command: "Kill Claudio." Benedick is nonplussed and his immediate reply is to refuse: "Ha! Not for the wide world!" (4.1.288). But he is gradually and hesitantly persuaded that he must demonstrate his manly love for Beatrice on her terms: "Enough, I am engaged. I will challenge him" (4.1.329).

Benedick's "Ha" is an expression of astonishment, among a large group of so-called meaningless interjections or expletives in Shakespeare. These have never been studied as a linguistic group, but I think they have a peculiar dramatic force. We have already spoken of Hamlet's O-groans that are matched by O-groans of Othello and King Lear and O-sighs of the mad Lady Macbeth. The paralinguistic "Ha" figures most importantly in *Othello*, but it is also featured in *King Lear*, *Measure for Measure*, and *Troilus and Cressida*. "Ha" makes an interesting case in point for Shakespeare's eloquence, since it is an emotive, gestural word that can be expressed in many different ways by actors. "Ha, ha, ha" is the conventional sign for laughter, but this is not relevant here.

Let us begin with a striking example from *Othello*. Act 3, scene 3 begins and ends the formal seduction of Othello by Iago, and it is remarkable how quickly Iago's purposes are accomplished. At the beginning of the scene, Cassio is earnestly entreating Desdemona to gain back his lost lieutenancy. Desdemona is eager to oblige such a good friend of her husband's who has lost his place because of what she thinks is a momentary slip. When Othello enters with Iago at line 28, they see Cassio conferring with Desdemona, but he leaves hastily because he is "very ill at ease."[9] Iago, the great improviser, sees a splendid opportunity to poison Othello's mind: "Ha! I like not that" (3.3.35). The credulous Othello is already caught in Iago's web of calumniating hints and suggestions. He asks: "What dost thou say?" and Iago parries with a sardonic half-hint: "Nothing, my lord; or if—I know not what" (3.3.35–36). So it begins, and Iago's piercing "Ha" echoes throughout the play.

It is interesting that the exclamation "Ha" marks the winning over of Othello, who, some hundred and thirty lines further, has caught Iago's "Ha." He is becoming progressively more angry, as the following dialogue indicates:

> Othello: By heaven, I'll know thy thoughts!
> Iago: You cannot, if my heart were in your hand; Nor shall not whilst 'tis in my custody.
> Othello: Ha!
> (3.3.162–65)

Iago's answer is conclusive: "O, beware, my lord, of jealousy!" (3.3.165). Othello's "Ha" is defined by the *Oxford English Dictionary* as an interjectional interrogative, which still persists in modern English in the sense of "What did you just say?" Othello cannot believe either what he is hearing or what is happening to him, and he utters "Ha" not only to express his wild, anarchic frustration, but also to control it. As Othello uses it, "Ha" is a painful, emotive word, whose eloquence depends upon the context in which it is uttered.

I don't want to dwell too long on Shakespeare's meaningless expletives, such as "O," "ha," "pah," "hum," "ho," and others. I only speak about them because they are generally ignored by critics who are searching for eloquence in different places than I am. I'd like to go on to two longer examples from the final scenes of *The Winter's Tale* and *King Lear*. There is no need to argue that these are eloquent scenes in themselves, but certain details that make up their dramatic effects are worth talking about.

The Statue Scene concludes *The Winter's Tale*. It is characteristic of Shakespeare's late romances that magic should be so important. Paulina brings the polychromed statue of Hermione by Julio Romano to life to the accompaniment of solemn music. It is a quasi-religious scene, very ritualistic, as the wife is restored to her husband after seemingly being dead for 16 years, and Perdita and her mother are reunited. The eloquence lies in the way the magical effects are accomplished, with a lyrical merging of the great Renaissance themes of Art and Nature.

Ostensibly, Leontes and his friend Polixenes, along with their children Perdita and Florizel, have come to see a statue of Leontes' "dead" wife that Paulina promises to show them in her gallery. She speaks of the statue as a rarity:

>   prepare
> To see the life as lively mocked, as ever
> Still sleep mocked death.... [10]

This is the heart of the Renaissance doctrine of mimesis, by which art imitates, or "mocks," nature, and the highest aesthetic criterion is that the work of art will be exceedingly lifelike. The statue is imagined to be a real person in a deep, marble sleep. The heart of the scene is that the artificer Paulina will awaken the dead Hermione from her profound slumber. Presumably, Hermione stands on a pedestal and her face is covered with a curtain that has to be opened. The effect of wonder and admiration was something that all of Shakespeare's late romances were aiming at.

Leontes observes that "Hermione was not so much wrinkled, nothing / So *agèd* as this seems," but Paulina sees this as an example of Julio Romano's consummate skill, "Which lets go by some sixteen years, and makes her / As she lived now" (5.3.28–29; 31–32). Part of the imagined interplay of art and life is that the cold, marble statue seems more and more warm to the grieving husband, Leontes. This is the crux of the paradox that art so successfully imitates nature. As Leontes says, "The fixure of her eye has motion in 't, / As we are mocked with art" (5.3.67–68). In his active imagination of bridging the unbridgeable gap between art and nature, Leontes waxes more and more passionate:

> There is an air comes from her. What fine chisel
> Could ever yet cut breath? Let no man mock me,
> For I will kiss her.
>
> (5.3.78–80)

Paulina promises to make the statue move if the onlookers can awaken their "faith" (5.3.95). In lines remarkable for their slow, broken rhythm, full of an unusual number of caesuras (or pauses), Paulina like a goddess commands the statue to come alive:

> Music, awake her: strike.
> 'Tis time; descend; be stone no more; approach;
> Strike all that look upon with marvel; come;
> I'll fill your grave up. Stir; nay, come away;
> Bequeath to death your numbness, for from him
> Dear life redeems you.
>
> (5.3.98–103)

The marveling Leontes can say only: "Oh, she's warm!" (5.3.109) implying that he has already touched his resurrected, dead wife.

The feeling of magic and eloquence go hand in hand, as Paulina executes her supreme work of art.

Act 5, scene 3, the final scene in *King Lear*, is prepared for by act 4, scene 7, where the mad Lear has been discovered by his youngest daughter, Cordelia, who attempts to restore him to reason by music and by "fresh garments" (*King Lear*, 5.3.22). The old king edges slowly to the recognition of his loving daughter, but the actual moment of recognition comes with a sudden flash:

> LEAR: Do not laugh at me,
> For, as I am a man, I think this lady
> To be my child Cordelia.
> CORDELIA: And so I am, I am.
>
> (5.3.68–70)

Cordelia's monosyllables, "And so I am, I am," are among the most moving lines in Shakespeare. There is an anagrammatic jingle on "am" and "man," which echoes, phonetically, Lear's "as I am." "And so I am, I am" is a sudden burst of intensity, which seems to grow out of the emotional pressures that have been building since Cordelia's ravaged "nothings" of act 1, scene 1. The line makes a good case in point about eloquence, since it uses no metaphor, simile, imagery, or any rhetorical device except repetition. It has no inherent, self-sufficient, anthologizable eloquence and, out of context, makes no special claim on our attention. There is a clear difference between lyric poetry on the printed page and dramatic poetry in the theater.

The same argument applies to another line from almost the very end of the old king's part: "Pray you undo this button. Thank you, sir" (5.3.309). If you put the line back in Lear's final speech, at the end of which he dies, we see that it has a peculiar radiance and plangency:

And my poor fool [presumably Cordelia] is hanged: no, no, no, no life?
Why should a dog, a horse, a rat, have life,
And thou no breath at all? Thoul't come no more,
Never, never, never, never, never.
Pray you, undo this button. Thank you, sir.
Do you see this? Look on her. Look, her lips,
Look there, look there.

(5.3.307–13)

Lear dies with the thought that Cordelia's lips are moving and that she is not dead. That is a kind of wild optimism. "Pray you, undo this button. Thank you, sir" balances the five unremitting "never's" of the previous line. I admit that the button line is, out of context, prosaic, if not actually banal, with a suggestion of sick humor. Which button does Lear mean? The theatrical tradition has interpreted the line as referring to the top button on Lear's gown, and the effect is that of suffocation, as if the old king cannot breathe because the button is stopping his breath. It's as if Shakespeare is returning to the theme of clothes that was so important to the mad Lear on the heath: "Off, off, you lendings! Come, unbutton here" (3.4.111). Clothes are the symbol of a corrupt civilization, and the mad Lear wants to strip naked, like Poor Tom, the "unaccomadated man" (3.4.109). Clothes represent the imprisonment of constricting mortality.

Although "Pray you" is a formula of politeness, it has a sweetness unknown to the earlier Lear, who has "ta'en / Too little care of this" (3.4. 32–33). The rhetorical explosion of "never's" in the previous line now gives way to an utter simplicity of expression. We are spectators of Lear's undoing, in the literal sense of undoing clothing, as the old king fumbles with "this button," which one of his followers—traditionally Kent in productions—helps him to unbutton. Again, there is formal politeness for services rendered: "Thank you, sir." "Pray you undo this button" is Lear's acknowledgment of his own death. He divests himself, just as Antony in *Antony and Cleopatra* prepares for suicide by taking off his armor: "No more a soldier. Bruised pieces, go" (*Antony and Cleopatra*, 4.14.42). There is an enactment here that transcends the language in which it is recorded.

The gesture and the words and the dramatic context constitute a single poetic unit that cannot be separated into component parts. The unbuttoning of Lear just before his death is a symbolic act that is performed in full view of the audience and with their tragic participation. It is "Pray you, *undo* this button," as if the button in the buttonhole were the final puzzle Lear must solve, the final lock he must open, before he is ready for death. "Undo" is a gentle, generalized word—much vaguer than the workaday "unbutton"—that suggests grace and an easy accomplishment. "Thank you, sir" is formal and unhurried, and the gesture of undoing a button (or having a button undone) becomes a hieratic act.

Let me recall the definition of "eloquence" from the *Oxford English Dictionary* with which we started: "The action, practice, or art of expressing thought with fluency, force, and appropriateness, so as to appeal to the reason or move the feelings." In discussing Shakespeare, I have tried to move away from lyric poetry on the printed page to something we might call Shakespeare's unpoetic poetry, which occurs in intensely dramatic situations and is energized by its theatrical context. I am trying to direct the discussion to dramatic effects rather than to beautiful language in and for itself. Not that Shakespeare is not a wonderful lyric poet, but my attention is more on the poignant moments that are expressed in plays outside the formal requirements of written poetry. Metaphor, simile, and figurative language aren't what is impressive in Cordelia's ecstatic exclamation when her mad father slowly recognizes her as his daughter: "And so I am, I am." These six monosyllables are a triumphant moment for Cordelia, but they have no independent existence in an anthology of Shakespeare's poetry. They are not lyric at all, but strongly declarative.

If some of you don't agree with me, it doesn't bother me because I don't mean that one kind of poetry will replace the other. The Duke in *A Midsummer Night's Dream* thought that "The lunatic, the lover and the poet / Are of imagination all compact."[11] This is not a very flattering company to put the poet in. But his wife Hippolyta thought that if one takes account of everything that happens in this play—"all the story of the night told over" (15.1.7–8), including the "Pyramus and Thisby" play of the Mechanicals—then that "more witnesseth than fancy's images, / And grows to something of great constancy" (5.1.25–26). So we end with some kind of imaginative stability—"something of great constancy," or consistency. The experience of the play is more important finally than "fancy's images," or any flourish, however brilliant and original, of rhetorical effects.

Notes

1. This paper is a revised version of a talk at the Mercantile Library of New York on April 27, 2000. I am grateful to its gracious director, Harold Augenbraum, for inviting me to give the annual Shakespeare Birthday Lecture. I have profited from the intelligent and ingenious questions of the audience.

2. William Shakespeare, *Julius Caesar*, ed. William Rosen and Barbara Rosen, rev. ed. (New York: Signet Classics, 1998), 2.1.284–85.

3. William Shakespeare, *Hamlet*, ed. Edward Hubler, 2d rev. ed. (New York: Signet Classics, 1998), 5.2.210.

4. William Shakespeare, *King Lear*, ed. Russell A. Fraser, 2d rev. ed. (New York: Signet Classics, 1998), 5.2.11.

5. William Shakespeare, *Coriolanus*, ed. Reuben Arthur Brower, rev. ed. (New York: Signet Classics, 2002), 5.3.40–42.

6. William Shakespeare, *Antony and Cleopatra*, ed. Barbara Everett, rev. ed. (New York: Signet Classics, 1998), 5.2.316–18.

7. William Shakespeare, *Henry IV, Part One*, ed. Maynard Mack, rev. ed. (New York: Signet Classics, 1998), 2.4.481.
8. William Shakespeare, *Much Ado about Nothing*, ed. David L. Stevenson, rev. ed. (New York: Signet Classics, 1998), 4.1.287.
9. William Shakespeare, *Othello*, ed. Alvin B. Kernan, rev. ed. (New York: Signet Classics, 1998), 3.3.32.
10. William Shakespeare, *The Winter's Tale*, ed. Frank Kermode, rev. ed. (New York: Signet Classics, 1998), 5.3.18–20.
11. William Shakespeare, *A Midsummer Night's Dream*, ed. Wolfgang Clemen, rev. ed. (New York: Signet Classics, 1998), 5.1.7–8.

Hamlet's Dramatic Soliloquies
Richard Levin

IT IS A COMMONPLACE OF SHAKESPEARE CRITICISM THAT THE SOLILO-quies in his mature plays, unlike those in his earlier plays or in the plays of his predecessors, are highly "dramatic." This involves two claims that are really distinct (although they may be related): that each soliloquy is integrated into the overall dramatic action, and that each one contains within itself a small dramatic action.[1] I would like to test both these claims in an examination of the soliloquies of Hamlet, which will show that they are also dramatic in another sense, because they serve some very important functions in the play. There are eight of them, which I have numbered for convenient reference:

1. "O that this too too sallied flesh would melt" (1.2.129–59)
2. "My father's spirit—in arms!" (1.2.254–57)
3. "O all you host of heaven" (1.5.92–112)
4. "O, what a rogue and peasant slave am I" (2.2.549–605)
5. "To be, or not to be" (3.1.55–89)
6. "'Tis now the very witching time of night" (3.2.388–99)
7. "Now might I do it pat" (3.3.73–96)
8. "How all occasions do inform against me" (4.4.32–66).[2]

When we apply the first claim—that these soliloquies are integrated into the overall dramatic action—we find that all of them except the fifth easily pass the test. They are all place-specific and cannot be moved, since they follow from the preceding action, or lead into the following action, or both. But if we ratchet up this claim by requiring them to be not only *integrated* parts of the action but also *essential* parts of it, then we find that many do not pass the test. In fact, we can locate them on a kind of continuum ranging from the most to the least dramatic in this sense. Only two of them qualify for placement at the most dramatic pole. The third soliloquy, which comes immediately after Hamlet's encounter with the Ghost, expresses his reaction to that encounter and his determination to obey the Ghost's "commandement" to seek revenge, which precipitates much of the ensuing action; and the sixth, spoken while Hamlet is preparing to meet his mother in the "closet" scene, shows him deciding how he will act when he confronts her.

The seventh soliloquy is less dramatic in this sense. The situation itself, with Hamlet coming upon Claudius at prayer, is certainly dramatic, and it certainly follows from the preceding events, since Claudius is praying as a result of his reaction to the "mousetrap" play, and Hamlet is on his way to his mother's closet as a result of his behavior in the "nunnery" scene; but it is a coincidence that Hamlet should come upon Claudius at this moment. And his decision in this soliloquy to delay his revenge until Claudius is "about some act/ That has no relish of salvation in't" does not lead to any action. It is proleptic in the sense that Hamlet finally does take his revenge, at the end of the play, just when Claudius is engaged in a damnable "act" of this kind that causes the deaths of Gertrude, Laertes, and Hamlet himself, but the revenge is not planned by Hamlet; indeed Shakespeare seems to have arranged the revenge in this way so that Hamlet does *not* have to plan it—a point I will return to later.

The eighth soliloquy has a similar status. It too is generated by the intersection of two lines of action that in this case both stem from Claudius: Fortinbras is marching his army across Denmark to Poland because Claudius granted him permission (2.2.80–82), and Hamlet is proceeding to a port to embark for England because of Claudius's decision, which was initiated by the "nunnery" scene and later reinforced by the "mousetrap" play and the killing of Polonius (3.1.164–70, 3.3.1–4, 4.3.54–68). But the intersection itself is entirely coincidental, like the situation in the seventh soliloquy, since there is no reason why Hamlet should be at this particular place just when Fortinbras's army is passing by. Moreover, again like the seventh soliloquy, Hamlet's decision here does not lead to any action. He declares that "from this time forth,/ My thoughts be bloody, or be nothing worth," but he is going to England, moving *away* from his revenge. In fact, his return to Denmark is not the result of any decision of his, and this is also true, as I just noted, of his revenge on Claudius, which is brought about by the fencing match that he does not plan and that he enters without any "bloody" thoughts. In this case we even have evidence that the soliloquy is not really dramatic in this sense, because it was omitted in the first quarto and the folio without affecting the plot.[3]

I would also place the fourth soliloquy in the middle of this continuum. It is evoked by the First Player's speech about the killing of

Priam during the sack of Troy, but that speech itself is not a necessary part of the preceding action and does not follow from it. Indeed, if we adopt Shakespeare's perspective, it would be more accurate to say, not that the speech caused the soliloquy, but that the soliloquy caused the speech, because the main purpose of the speech is to provide this occasion for Hamlet to contrast his situation to the Player's.[4] It may seem, however, that the soliloquy is a necessary cause of the ensuing action since it concludes with Hamlet's plan to use a play to "catch the conscience of the King"; but the problem here is that he devised this plan before the soliloquy, when he asked the Player to put on *The Murther of Gonzago* and to insert a speech in it that he intends to write (2.2.535–43). I think, therefore, that we would have to say that this soliloquy does not cause the action that follows; it appears, rather, to repeat or explain an action that has already occurred. But since this problem is so closely related to the internal drama within this soliloquy, I will defer a fuller consideration of it until later.

The second soliloquy is not as dramatic in this sense. Like most of the others, it conveys Hamlet's reaction to a specific event that preceded it—the news brought by Horatio, Marcellus, and Barnardo about the Ghost—but it does not lead him to any decision to act (not even a misleading decision), since he has already agreed to watch with them that night (1.2.250–51). The first soliloquy is even less dramatic in this sense. It, too, is place-specific, since it expresses Hamlet's distress at his father's death, his mother's hasty remarriage, and his intolerable situation at court, which we just observed in the preceding episode, but it is not generated by any specific event in that episode. Nor does it generate any further action on his part. It cannot, because it ends with his decision *not* to take any action ("But break my heart, for I must hold my tongue"), and the next event, in which Horatio, Marcellus, and Barnardo come to tell him about the Ghost, marks an abrupt break in the mood established by the soliloquy. Thus the function of this soliloquy is not dramatic but expository, because it serves to explain Hamlet's isolation, his prolonged mourning, and his hostility to Claudius and to Gertrude that were exhibited in the court scene.

The least dramatic of these soliloquies, in this sense of the term, is the fifth, which is also the most famous. It does not follow from anything in the preceding action—indeed, the last time we saw Hamlet, at the end of the fourth soliloquy, he was excited about his plan to "catch the conscience of the King," so that his contemplation of suicide here (unlike his reference to it in the first soliloquy) comes as a complete surprise. Nor does it lead to anything in the ensuing action, since immediately after it, as soon as Hamlet sees Ophelia, his mood changes abruptly, much like the change immediately after the first soliloquy, and we hear no more of suicide. It is, in short, completely detached from the action,[5] and that may help to account for its fame, because teachers could treat it as a self-contained "set piece" of poetry suitable for memorizing and explication (which I think is also true of Polonius's advice to Laertes in 1.3.58–80), and many people who have never seen or read the play know that Hamlet says "To be, or not to be, that is the question," a line that has attained proverbial status. The soliloquy also seems to be detached from Hamlet himself. Several critics have pointed out that most of the specific "ills" of life listed there ("th' oppressor's wrong," "the proud man's contumely," "the law's delay," "the insolence of office," the "spurns" from the "unworthy," and especially the "weary life" grunting and sweating under "fardels") are things that he has never experienced and does not expect to experience.[6] Moreover, the reference to "The undiscover'd country, from whose bourn/ No traveller returns" has been directly contradicted by his meeting with the Ghost; and the conclusion that people refrain from suicide because they are "cowards" is very different from his acknowledgment in the first soliloquy that God has "fix'd/ His canon 'gainst self-slaughter."[7]

We cannot even say that this soliloquy is expository, since it does not shed any light upon Hamlet's actions before or after it, which never turn on the question of suicide. Evidence of its lack of connection to the sequence of action can be found in the first quarto, where it is located before the fourth soliloquy, and also in some modern productions—in the Olivier film, for instance, it comes after the "nunnery" scene, and in Peter Brook's version it comes after Polonius's death.[8] Thus it might be called the wandering soliloquy, since it can be moved to various places without affecting the plot. It could even be removed completely without affecting the plot. It is so well known today that a performance of *Hamlet* without it would be unthinkable (not literally unthinkable, of course, since I just thought of it). Yet if we could find people who never heard of this speech, and presented them with a version of the play that omitted it, they would have no difficulty in following the action and would not be aware that something was missing, just as many early readers of the folio were presumably not aware that the eighth soliloquy was missing. Therefore it is not dramatic in the sense that I am testing now.

Some readers may have noticed that my tests draw on the definition of dramatic unity in Aristotle's *Poetics*, which states that the "several incidents [must be] so closely connected that the transposal or withdrawal of any one of them will disjoin and dislocate the whole. For that which makes no perceptible difference by its presence or absence is no real part of the whole."[9] There are really two criteria here that correspond to the two tests I have applied so far to judge the dramatic quality of each soliloquy: that it cannot be *moved*, and so is integrated into the dramatic action; and that it cannot be *removed*, and so is essential to that action. We saw that all of them except the fifth pass the first test; they cannot be moved because they are what I have been calling "place-specific." But we also saw that many of them fail the second test, since they could be removed without disjoining or dislocating the plot and so are not essential to it. It is clearly not true, however, that their removal would make "no perceptible difference," as Aristotle claims.

The explanation of this lies in the differences between the tragedies that Aristotle based the *Poetics* upon and the tragedies of Shakespeare and his contemporaries. A Greek tragedy has a relatively short, simple plot with a small number of incidents. Sophocles' *Oedipus the King*, for example, which seems to be Aristotle's favorite play,[10] has only six incidents (including the Prologue and Exode), so that each incident is essential to the plot and its removal would disjoin the plot and therefore make a very perceptible difference. But a Shakespearean tragedy is much longer and much more complex, with many more incidents, some of which do not further the plot but serve other kinds of dramatic functions within the plot so that, even though they are not essential in Aristotle's sense, their removal would still make a perceptible difference.

One of these other dramatic functions of Hamlet's soliloquies is to announce and punctuate the breaks between episodes, a function that was important in a theater that did not have a front curtain to do this. Indeed the absence of a curtain is largely responsible for another commonplace of Shakespeare criticism, the claim that the action in his plays is really "continuous," and that the scene divisions in the standard modern editions were inserted arbitrarily by later editors accustomed to a different kind of theater. Like the commonplace about the dramatic nature of the soliloquies, however, this is only partly true. As far as we know, there were no time intervals between episodes in Shakespeare's day, and a few of the scene divisions in modern editions are arbitrary or even misleading.[11] However, most of them correspond to clear indications within the text of breaks in the action, which are sometimes marked by scene divisions in the folio.

The most common way to indicate these breaks was to vacate the stage before the entrance of another character or group of characters, and in all but two of Hamlet's soliloquies everyone else has left just before he begins to speak.[12] The exceptions are the fifth, where Ophelia remains onstage, silently reading a prayer book (and Claudius and Polonius are hiding out of sight); and the seventh, where Claudius remains, engaged in silent prayer. Moreover, after the second, fourth, sixth, seventh, and eighth soliloquies Hamlet himself exits so that the stage is empty before other characters appear to begin a new episode,[13] which is designated as a separate scene in modern editions. It is also significant that all five of these soliloquies conclude in a couplet, since this was another very common way to end an episode in Shakespeare's theater. At the conclusion of the other three soliloquies (which do not have this couplet) Hamlet remains on stage to encounter other characters, but this encounter clearly constitutes a new episode, even though later editors did not mark it as a new scene. After the first soliloquy Horatio, Marcellus, and Barnardo arrive to tell him about the Ghost; after the third, the entrance of Horatio and Marcellus begins what is now called the "cellarage" scene; and after the fifth, he confronts Ophelia, which initiates the "nunnery" scene. It would seem, then, that when Hamlet delivered a soliloquy this was a signal to the audience (not the only one, of course) that an episode was ending and another was about to begin.

Actually each of these soliloquies is itself a kind of pause or interval between episodes during which the action comes to a stop, since while it is spoken there is no other motion on the stage and no interchange between characters, even in the two cases where another person is present. Moreover, each of them is complete in itself and reaches a definite conclusion. Even in the three cases where Hamlet remains onstage and meets other characters, these meetings always occur after he has finished and therefore never interrupt his thinking. In these respects, then, the soliloquies serve a dramatic function roughly analogous to that of the Chorus in Greek tragedy, which was also a poetic statement complete in itself that halted the ongoing action while it was being sung and thus separated the episodes. Indeed, Aristotle might recognize this function, since he defines an episode as "all that comes in between two whole choral songs,"[14] although he does not regard the choral song itself as an incident that must meet his criteria for dramatic unity, whereas I have treated the soliloquies as incidents and tested them by these criteria. The obvious difference is that these soliloquies are not generalized comments by an undifferentiated group of observers as in the Greek Chorus, but are the responses of the protagonist and are intensely personal. Thus they serve another, much more important, function by helping to shape our conception of Hamlet's character. But since this depends on what happens in each soliloquy, I want to move on to test the claim that these soliloquies are dramatic in the second sense—namely, that each one contains within itself an internal action.

Here I believe that the common view is correct; all the soliloquies pass this test and are never limited to the static expression or elaboration of a single idea or emotion that we find in the earlier drama. This is even true of the second soliloquy, which is the shortest (so short that many commentators do not count it and speak of Hamlet's seven soliloquies). It begins with Hamlet's troubled reaction to the news about the Ghost ("My father's spirit—in arms! All is not well,/ I doubt some foul play"), then shifts to his urgent desire to meet it ("Would night were come!"), then to his attempt to calm himself ("Till then sit still, my soul"), and concludes with a reassuring prediction that some important secret will be revealed ("Foul deeds will rise,/ Though all the earth o'erwhelm them, to men's eyes"). I am not suggesting that anything very complicated is going on here, but the soliloquy clearly shows what I will call a "turn" in Hamlet's mood and thought, from apprehension to a kind of optimism, and also an internal conflict between his impatience and his need to control himself. The syntax modulates to reflect this, beginning with a series of five short, hurried sentences or independent clauses, and ending, after the "turn," in a longer periodic sentence (and a couplet) to express his regained self-control and his new hope.

I have examined this soliloquy in such detail because it is so short and therefore constitutes a kind of test case. Obviously I cannot present the same line-by-line analysis of the internal drama within each of the other, much longer soliloquies. Therefore I will discuss them in more general terms by arranging them, again, on a continuum based on their dramatic quality in this second sense, although it will not be as simple as the first continuum because these internal dramas are different in each soliloquy and are conveyed in different ways. In this respect Hamlet (or Shakespeare) never repeats himself. At the least dramatic pole I would have to place the fifth soliloquy, which occupied the same position in the earlier continuum. I do not think this is a coincidence, since it is clearly the most contemplative of the soliloquies and the furthest removed from Hamlet's immediate situation, and therefore from his deepest feelings. It begins with a simple statement of the two options and then elaborates them in a long, complex, and balanced periodic sentence. The next sentence presents the case for suicide, again in relatively calm and measured tones, by envisioning it as a kind of sleep. Then comes the "turn," indicated by a series of very short phrases ("To die, to sleep—/To sleep, perchance to dream—ay, there's the rub"), as if the connection of death to dreaming has just occurred to him. What follows, however, is not a startled reaction to this unsettling connection but a long, measured, and thoughtful elaboration of the idea that we are kept from committing suicide by the "dread of something after death." The idea is stated in several different ways and in some very effective poetry, but it is a rational development of the point with little emotional tension. Even the list of the ills of life ("Th'oppressor's wrong," etc.) seems rather detached because, as I noted, it is not related to Hamlet's own situation. And the highly generalized logical conclusion (signaled by two "Thuses") that "enterprises of great pitch and moment" are forestalled by the "pale cast of thought" is even further removed from Hamlet's thoughts of suicide or his revenge, neither of which seems to qualify as one of those "enterprises." It is a fitting conclusion here, however, because what this soliloquy presents is closer to an abstract intellectual exercise than to an internal action, which is why I believe it is the least dramatic in this second sense.

The first soliloquy could also be called contemplative, but it is more dramatic than the fifth in both senses, which in this case are closely related, because this soliloquy, unlike the fifth, is Hamlet's response to the preceding episode, and it enacts the emotions that were building up in him during that episode but could not be given vent there. He begins with a passionate outburst expressing his longing for death (whereas in the opening of the fifth, death is only one of two options being weighed judiciously), and then he gives an explanation for this longing in terms of a very general dissatisfaction with "the uses of this world" and a very general analogy to "an unweeded garden." But a "turn" to the particular and personal is announced by the exclamation "That it should come to this!" which introduces the real reasons for his dismal view of the world and for his death-wish: the hasty remarriage of his mother and the inferiority of her new husband to her former one. These two complaints are elaborated, for the most part, in rather long and carefully developed clauses and sentences, but his inner turmoil is conveyed by his continually shifting focus, which proceeds from his father to Claudius to his mother and then repeats the sequence, always ending with her. The turmoil is also conveyed by several interruptions of his train of thought that show the emotional pressure breaking through: "nay, not so much, not two," "Frailty, thy name is woman," and "O God, a beast that wants discourse of reason/ Would have mourn'd longer." And two particular interruptions—"Heaven and earth,/ Must I remember?" and "Let me not think on't!"—reveal an internal struggle between two parts or aspects of his mind (like "sit still, my soul" in the second soliloquy). The emotion reaches a climax with "O most wicked speed: to post/ With such dexterity to incestuous sheets," which is directed at his mother (although it also, of course, involves her two husbands) and is his fiercest and most explicitly sexual condemnation of her. Then there is another "turn" at the end when, his emotion spent, he descends to a much simpler style, in which he summarizes the situation in general terms ("It is not, nor it cannot come to good") and retreats into a weary resignation that brings us back full circle to the beginning: "But break, my heart, for I must hold my tongue." He has taken us on an internal journey that gives us our first real access to his thoughts and feelings (as well as some essential information about his family), but nothing actually happens to him on the way.

The sixth soliloquy comes next on this continuum, because it does contain a kind of internal action in which Hamlet undergoes a change. Whereas almost all the other soliloquies are generated by Hamlet's response to an event, here he is anticipating one—his meeting with his mother.[15] At the beginning he seems to be working himself up, by drawing on the sinister imagery of witches, ghosts (emerging from the yawning churchyards), and hell, to the climactic declaration that he could "drink hot blood" and "do such bitter business as the day/ Would quake to look on." But there is an abrupt "turn" when he says, "Soft, now to my mother," as if he has suddenly realized that this bloodthirstiness is not appropriate for her (and perhaps has even been frightened by it). He then tells himself that he must not harm her physically but must limit his cruelty to words. Indeed he has to assert this three times, suggesting his internal conflict and his fear that he will go too far. This is also suggested, I think, by the fact that in this section he keeps referring to parts or aspects of himself ("heart," "bosom," "tongue," "soul") as if they were separate entities that do things and must be dealt with. (We find similar references in some of the other soliloquies, but they are never so densely packed.) The repeated assertions, however, are constructed in a series of neatly balanced antitheses ("cruel" vs. "unnatural," "speak" vs. "use," "tongue" vs. "soul") that show he is growing calmer and so can sum them up at the end with an emphatic and more elaborately balanced couplet expressing his new resolve, in a self-assured tone that is very different from his feeling at the outset.

There is more activity within the third soliloquy, where Hamlet reacts to his meeting with the Ghost. He begins at a very high pitch of nervous excitement—so high that he must try to control himself ("hold, hold, my heart,/ And you, my sinows . . .") much earlier here than in the first or sixth soliloquies. The first section concentrates on his promise to obey the Ghost's parting command to "remember me." The importance he attaches to it (and to his need to reassure the Ghost) is conveyed in the repetition of the exclamation "Remember thee!" and of the word "memory," and in the list of things he will "wipe away" from his mind, which at first comes tumbling out in a series of short phrases ("all trivial fond records,/ All saws of books, all forms, all pressures past") and then slows down to two longer and more carefully crafted clauses that terminate this section. The "turn" is indicated by the exclamation "Yes, by heaven!" that marks a decisive shift from promising to remember to confronting what he will remember—a shift, that is, from the Ghost to Gertrude and Claudius—and also marks a new outburst of passion. Unlike the first soliloquy, when his main target was Gertrude, he now devotes only one line to her ("O most pernicious woman!") and focuses on Claudius. His hatred of Claudius is first expressed in a piling up of epithets—"O villain, villain, smiling, damned villain!"—where his self-control and his syntax seem to break down, but then in another sudden "turn" he decides to write it in his tablet. Some commentators attribute this curious behavior to a kind of hysteria, but it seems to me that Hamlet has become calmer here and takes real satisfaction in his action, as if it were a step in his revenge on Claudius: "So, uncle, there you are." It also allows him to conclude by returning to his promise to the Ghost with a new sense of confidence that he is keeping it.

The seventh soliloquy, spoken when Hamlet comes upon Claudius at prayer, presents an even more striking inner drama. He begins with a largely monosyllabic series of simple clauses: "Now might I do it pat, now 'a is a-praying;/ And now I'll do't—and so 'a goes to heaven,/ And so I am reveng'd." But the mention of "heaven," the consequence of "praying," brings him up short, as if he suddenly realizes what he is saying, and the "turn" is initiated by "That would be scann'd." He then restates the opening lines, in the same flat style, to focus on the discrepancy between taking revenge on Claudius and sending his soul to heaven, and concludes that "this is hire and salary, not revenge." This leads to a more figurative and impassioned account of the fate of his father, who died

"With all his crimes broad blown,"[16] followed by the rhetorical question, "And am I then reveng'd,/ To take [Claudius] in the purging of his soul?" and the very emphatic "No!" that marks the second "turn." He then orders his "sword" (addressed as if it could act on its own volition) to wait for "a more horrid hent." The rest of the soliloquy is an elaboration of this, which dwells with obvious relish on the sinful actions of Claudius that would be better occasions for killing him, since his soul would then "be as damn'd and black/ As hell whereto it goes." Hamlet seems to be very pleased with this decision and with himself, and concludes in the promise (underscored by the couplet) that it "but prolongs" Claudius's "sickly days," so it is viewed as another step in his revenge.

The internal action within the eighth soliloquy is more complicated and more subtle. Hamlet is reacting to the sight of Fortinbras's army marching to Poland, but he begins by generalizing this event to "all occasions" that accuse him and "spur" his "dull revenge," and then he shifts into an even more generalized philosophical inquiry into the nature of man, which concludes that man is "a beast" if he does not use his "godlike reason." The second "turn," announced by "Now," brings him back to his "dull revenge." He first tries to explain his delay in terms of the opposition he just set up between "Bestial oblivion" and "thinking too precisely," but it quickly breaks down in the interjected admission (or suspicion?) that his "thinking" is less wisdom than cowardice. This produces, in another sudden break, his bitter outburst of self-accusation, where the powerful emotion is conveyed by the stark, simple language, in contrast to the more elaborate diction and syntax of the earlier passages: "I do not know/ Why yet I live to say, 'This thing's to do,'/ Sith I have cause, and will, and strength, and means/ To do't." Then comes another distinct "turn" to the "examples" that "exhort" him, which leads to a description of Fortinbras's military adventure, built up in a long, complex, periodic sentence with highly figurative language descending to a very prosaic "egg-shell." In the next "turn" he applies this to his own situation, contrasting his cause (stated again in stark terms—"a father kill'd, a mother stain'd") to that of Fortinbras's army, where the idea of the trivial "egg-shell" is developed at some length as a "plot" that "is not tomb enough and continent/ To hide the slain," and contrasting his inaction ("let all sleep") to their action, seen as a very different kind of sleep (they "Go to their graves like beds"). The final "turn" that this leads to comes as a surprise, since instead of blaming himself again for inaction, he now resolves, not to *act,* but to *think* about acting: "O, from this time forth/ My thoughts be bloody, or be nothing worth!" It is spoken, as I noted earlier, when he is on his way to England, moving further from Claudius, yet the ringing tone of the couplet suggests that he sees this resolve as an achievement and as another step (or "spur") in his revenge.

The fourth soliloquy is the longest and the most dramatic in this sense. The movement of its first part is similar to that of the eighth soliloquy, since here, too, Hamlet is responding to the sight of someone who is able to act even though his cause is trivial, which Hamlet takes as a condemnation of his own failure to act for a much weightier cause. It opens with an outburst of emotion, "O, what a rogue and peasant slave am I!" and then gives the explanation, which begins as a detailed and vivid description of the First Player's portrayal of grief, developed in a long, complex sentence. But this controlled syntax breaks down in a series of short, bitter phrases marking the first "turn": "And all for nothing,/ For Hecuba!/ What's Hecuba to him, or he to Hecuba,/ That he should weep for her?" Then, in another shift he finally comes to the reason for his self-reproach, which is stated as another question: "What would he do/ Had he the motive and the cue for passion/ That I have?" This leads into a description of how the Player would act in that situation, which is also very vivid and detailed but more passionate than the first account. It is also the last we hear of the Player, for in another "turn" (indicated by "Yet I") Hamlet focuses on the contrast to his own inaction and to his much greater cause ("a king,/Upon whose . . . most dear life/ A damn'd defeat was made"). His first explanation for his behavior is stated as yet another question—"Am I a coward?"—which marks a major shift, since he is now finally confronting the charge that apparently was haunting him from the outset and that led him to call himself "a rogue and peasant slave." But he answers this question with a rhetorical question, asking who does the things to him that would be done to a coward, which are enumerated in an extended list of indignities (calling him a villain, breaking his pate, plucking his beard, tweaking his nose, calling him a liar).[17] The obvious answer is that no one dares to do such things to him, and therefore that he cannot be a coward; but instead of taking comfort in this reassurance, he insists that he "should take it" because he *is* a coward, and the proof, voiced with mounting excitement and anger, is that if he were not one he would have "fatted all the region kites/ With this slave's offal."

This is the first direct reference to Claudius in the soliloquy, and it is very significant that in it the epithet "slave," which Hamlet applied to himself in the opening line, is now applied to his enemy.

Clearly the target of his anger has been transferred from his own inaction to Claudius's crime, and this leads to an explosion of passion indicated by the complete breakdown of syntax and logic, in which his words seem to serve as blows that he is raining on Claudius, as a substitute for actually striking him: "Bloody, bawdy villain!/ Remorseless, treacherous, lecherous, kindless villain!"[18] This is a second way out for him, but he refuses it, too, when he stops abruptly, as if he just realized what he is doing, and berates himself—now not as a coward but as a "whore" or "drab"—for cursing instead of acting. This new outburst of self-accusation trails off in "Fie upon't, foh!" and now, his passion drained, he initiates the last major "turn" by commanding his "brains" quite literally to turn "about"—that is, to find another way out of his predicament. What this leads to is a much calmer account, in a much more carefully constructed sentence, of how murderers have been led to confess when they saw a similar crime enacted in a play, followed by his decision to have the actors put on a play that will test Claudius in this manner. Then he explains, with rising excitement, the reason for this test—he fears the Ghost may have been a devil seeking to damn him, and therefore he needs "more relative" evidence of Claudius's guilt. This makes it possible for him to conclude with the triumphant couplet: "the play's the thing/ Wherein I'll catch the conscience of the King."

This final section of the soliloquy raises two serious problems. The more obvious one, which has been noted by many commentators, is that in it Hamlet apparently hits upon this plan to test Claudius for the first time ("Hum—I have heard . . ."), whereas he must have thought of it fifty lines earlier when he asked the First Player to perform *The Murther of Gonzago*.[19] Therefore the soliloquy seems to be out of place, since it really belongs somewhere between line 518, the end of the Player's description of Hecuba that evokes Hamlet's self-reproach (and that presumably gives him the idea of using a play to confirm the Ghost's words), and line 537 where he requests the performance. But then it would be spoken while other characters (the Player, Rosencrantz, and Guildenstern) are still onstage, so that they would have to freeze or mime some action, either of which would be very awkward, especially during such a long soliloquy. (This is another reason that Hamlet is alone in all but two of the soliloquies, as I pointed out above.) Moreover, if it were placed earlier we would lose the powerful sense of closure produced by having Hamlet's couplet end the episode, which, as I also pointed out, is another dramatic function of the soliloquies. Thus the placement of this soliloquy confronted Shakespeare with a choice between logical consistency and theatrical effectiveness, and he opted for the latter at the expense of the former. He usually did.

The second problem is not as obvious, which is probably why it has attracted less critical attention, but it is more relevant to my purpose here. It involves Hamlet's doubt about the Ghost—or, more precisely, the timing of this doubt. The idea that the Ghost may be a demon was introduced by Hamlet when he first addresses it in 1.4.40 ("Be thou a spirit of health, or goblin damned"), and was elaborated by Horatio when he tries to dissuade Hamlet from following it (69–74); but after his meeting with it, Hamlet assures his companions that "It is an honest ghost, that let me tell you" (1.5.138). From then on he never suggests that he has any suspicions about it until this soliloquy, nor does anything occur that might arouse such suspicions. Moreover, in this soliloquy itself, up to the final section, everything that he says is clearly based on an unquestioned belief that the Ghost told the truth. In fact, if we did not assume this belief, we could not make any sense of the thoughts and feelings he expresses there: his bitter self-reproach for not taking revenge; his fear that he is a coward; his savage attack on Claudius; and his reference, just before this final section, to "a dear father murthered." Why then should he suddenly doubt the Ghost now? The best explanation I can think of is that it satisfies his two most pressing needs at this juncture—it justifies his delay in taking revenge, since he cannot proceed without verifying the Ghost's story, which means that the delay was caused not by his cowardice but by his wisdom;[20] and it provides him with an action that he can easily undertake and that has now become an essential step in this revenge. I am not implying that Hamlet consciously makes such a calculation, but it accounts for the fact that this doubt should arise here. It lets him off the hook, so that the soliloquy that began with him feeling disgusted at himself because he is doing nothing to further his revenge can end with him feeling very pleased with himself because he is doing something to further it. But I will return to this point later.

I now want to turn to the relationship of the internal drama within these soliloquies to another important dramatic function that they serve in helping to shape our conception of Hamlet's character. Much of our knowledge of him derives mainly from his soliloquies and would be lost if they were omitted, even though that omission would not affect the plot itself. This knowledge consists not only of essential information about what he is thinking and feeling at the particular moment, but also, more generally, about the quality of his mind and the way it operates, which constitute his unique personality. The proof of this is that it is almost impossible to imagine these soliloquies coming from any other character in the play, or any other character in all of Shakespeare, for they are not only *place*-specific, as I argued, but also *person*-specific. Many of the personal traits that they reveal have been discussed at length by the older commentators, but I will focus on a fundamental trait that has elicited less discussion, although it actually underlies all the others—namely, his personhood itself, our sense (or illusion) that he is a real individual who can *have* a personality. This depends primarily on our impression that he possesses what we now call "interiority," and that in turn depends on the existence within his consciousness of different levels or aspects that are not seamless and can even be in conflict.[21]

In fact, some of the features that were noted in my survey of the internal drama within the soliloquies can be seen as devices for conveying (or creating) this kind of interiority. One of the most obvious of these is the frequent use of what I referred to as "turns," sometimes quite abrupt, from one idea or emotion to another, which suggest the complexity of his mind and the tensions within it. This effect is enhanced by the changes in his speech patterns that often mark these "turns," especially, as we saw, by the descent from a highly wrought "poetic" style to a stark, simple syntax and diction that seem to express a more basic or powerful feeling ("But break, my heart," "that his soul may be as damn'd and black/ As hell," "fatted all the region kites/ With this slave's offal"). Even more striking are the sudden interruptions, usually couched in this simple style ("Must I remember?", "Let me not think on't!", "Yes, by heaven!", "I do not know/ Why yet I live to say," "Am I a coward?"), where we seem to be observing a kind of conflict between two lines of thought or levels of consciousness, with one of them breaking through the other. This sense of internal division is made more explicit when Hamlet addresses "my soul," "my heart," "my bosom," "my tongue," "my sinows," or "my brains," which implies that they are separate parts of his being that he must try to control, and also implies that there *is* a "he"—a real, complex individual—who in some sense underlies these parts and *can* control them. There are also a few places where we witness a partial breakdown of his syntax and rhythm, indicating a temporary loss of composure or of control over the emotions seething within him.[22]

Our sense of Hamlet's internality and personhood is also enhanced by a special kind of "turn" found in four of these soliloquies where he seems to "overhear himself," in Harold Bloom's apt phrase,[23] that is, where he says something that brings him up short, as if he suddenly realizes its real import. In the fourth soliloquy, when he "overhears" his outburst of epithets attacking Claudius, he realizes that he is unpacking his heart with words instead of acting ("Why, what an ass am I!"); in the fifth, he "overhears" the words "perchance to dream" and realizes that "there's the rub"; in the sixth, he "overhears" his murderous intentions ("Now could I drink hot blood") and realizes they must be restrained during his forthcoming meeting ("Soft, now to my mother"); and in the seventh, he "overhears" the prediction "and so 'a goes to heaven" and realizes that "this is hire and salary, not revenge." We have all experienced similar situations in our own lives when we have to explain that "I didn't mean what I said" or "I spoke without thinking." This is literally impossible, of course, because we cannot say anything without a message from our brain, but it shows that there is a deeper level of our consciousness that has "overheard" and rejected what the more superficial level caused us to say. In real life this situation usually occurs during a conversation, when we realize what our words may sound like to other people (perhaps as a result of their reactions). This obviously cannot happen in these soliloquies, where Hamlet is not conversing with anyone. However, since according to the theatrical convention of the time, he is supposed to be "talking to himself" or "thinking out loud,"[24] he can "overhear" what he is thinking/saying and react to it, so the internal mechanism is the same and therefore we are led to attribute this kind of interiority to Hamlet.

There is, finally, another sense in which these soliloquies are dramatic, since they help not only to characterize Hamlet but also to trace his career in the play. Our conception of this career is derived primarily from his interactions with other people, of course, yet the soliloquies contribute to it. The first three form a sequence that generates the tragic action. In the first one we are shown Hamlet's unhappy predicament before the plot proper begins—a predicament that has existed for some time and presumably could continue indefinitely, since he admits in his final line that he can do nothing about it. The crucial change in this static situation is his meeting with the Ghost, who has been walking on the ramparts and presumably could continue to do this indefinitely. It is the intersection of these two lines of action (or inaction) that marks the beginning of the plot proper. This intersection is anticipated by the second soliloquy and concluded by the third, where Hamlet takes the oath of vengeance that initiates much of the ensuing activity and his tragedy.

The remaining soliloquies do not form a temporal sequence of this kind,[25] but they do exhibit a common pattern (except, again, for the anomalous fifth) that helps to shape our conception of Hamlet's tragic career. It is very significant that they all end on an up beat—on a decisive note that allows Hamlet to feel very satisfied with himself and with his progress toward revenge. This pattern first appears at the end of the third soliloquy, where he decides to seek revenge, and where, as I noted, he seems to think that he is furthering it by writing it down in his tablet ("So, uncle, there you are"). The fourth concludes with his decision to "catch the conscience of the King"; the sixth, with his decision about confronting his mother ("I will speak daggers to her, but use none"); the seventh, with his decision about killing Claudius ("This physic but prolongs thy sickly days"); and the eighth, with his decision that "from this time forth,/ My thoughts be bloody." It is obviously not true, therefore, that this is the tragedy of "a man who could not make up his mind," as we are told at the beginning of the Olivier film, since Hamlet makes up his mind five times in these soliloquies.

It is even more significant, however, that the decisions he reaches at the end of each of these soliloquies do *not* bring him any closer to his revenge and even make it more difficult. When he stages the play to test Claudius, this reveals to Claudius that Hamlet knows about the murder and so leads to his two schemes to kill Hamlet. When he begins to "speak daggers" to his mother, she cries out for help, which causes Polonius to call from behind the arras, which causes Hamlet to use a real dagger to kill him, which causes Laertes to seek revenge by plotting with Claudius against Hamlet (it also causes Ophelia's madness and death, which give Laertes another motive). When he decides not to kill Claudius at prayer, he not only forgoes his first opportunity to take revenge but also sets new and much more exacting conditions for it that cannot be created by any action of his; and when he promises to have "bloody" thoughts, he is traveling away from Claudius. I think that "rationalization" is too strong a term to apply to this pattern, since Hamlet always tries to be very honest with himself and his reasoning is always very logical. However, it does reveal an aspect of his personality, or perhaps a syndrome, that accounts for our view that he is delaying his revenge even while he believes that he is pursuing it, and provides an explanation for this part of his tragic career.

That view has to be revised in the fifth act, and one important reason for this is that Hamlet stops soliloquizing. This cessation can itself be regarded as another dramatic function of the soliloquies in this last sense. It may seem paradoxical to claim that the soliloquies can serve a dramatic function by their absence, and of course this would not apply in the case of a less introspective protagonist such as Antony or Coriolanus, but the fact that we have become accustomed to a soliloquizing Hamlet means that the absence of these soliloquies will have an effect on us. Since we saw that the soliloquies mark definite pauses when all activity comes to a halt, their absence contributes to the impression, noted by many commentators, that the action seems to speed up after Hamlet's return from his sea voyage. Moreover, it helps to create the impression, also noted by many commentators, that Hamlet himself has changed. He has become much more explicitly religious than before in affirming the role of "a divinity that shapes our ends" and a "special providence" and the "felicity" of heaven (5.2.10, 219–20, 347), and—closely related to this—he is now willing to let events take their course, without trying to initiate or alter them. Consequently he is no longer planning his revenge or lacerating himself for delaying it, which were the principal concerns of most of the soliloquies. Thus we have what might be called a benign circle, since this change in him accounts for the absence of soliloquies in the final act, and the absence of soliloquies helps us to recognize this change in him.

The result of this change is that Hamlet finally achieves his revenge, not because of any planning on his part to kill Claudius, but because of the plan of Claudius and Laertes to kill him. That is very important since it distinguishes him from the protagonists of the other major revenge tragedies of the period: Hieronimo in Thomas Kyd's *The Spanish Tragedy* (c. 1587); Titus Andronicus in Shakespeare's first effort in this genre (c. 1594); Antonio in John Marston's *Antonio's Revenge* (c. 1600); and Vindici in the anonymous *The Revenger's Tragedy* (c. 1606), now often attributed to Thomas Middleton. Each of these revengers plans an elaborate, deceptive scheme that enables him to trap and destroy those who wronged him, and, as a result, he incurs some guilt himself that must be expiated: Hieronimo commits suicide, Titus is killed, Antonio enters a monastery, and Vindici is sentenced to be executed. But here Claudius and Laertes plan the deceptive scheme (the use of the unbated and poisoned foil) and Hamlet just reacts to it, so he can get his revenge without incurring any guilt or requiring any expiation, and therefore retains our admiration. This outcome also means that the decisions he reached in the soliloquies are finally fulfilled, but in an ironic sense that he never intended. His decisions to test Claudius in the fourth soliloquy and to speak violently to Gertrude in the sixth, lead indirectly to the plot of Claudius and Laertes against him, and this plot in turn makes it possible for him to kill Claudius while he is engaged in a damnable action, which was the decision of the seventh soliloquy. Moreover, this ironic, indirect fulfillment of his decisions made in these soliloquies means that the soliloquies turn out to be essential to the action after all, and therefore are dramatic in the first sense that I tested, as well as in the sense of serving another important dramatic function in tracing this aspect of Hamlet's tragic career.

My treatment of the soliloquies and of the play employs what is now called the formalist approach, and since the proponents of the newer approaches regularly accuse the formalists of not being aware of their critical assumptions, I want to spell them out in my conclusion. I am assuming that *Hamlet* was consciously designed by an author to produce a tragic effect, which means that the parts of the play, including the soliloquies, will have functions that are intended to contribute to this effect. I also assume that this effect depends upon creating the illusion that the play is the representation of a human action, and that this in turn depends upon our accepting Hamlet as an individual with an "interiority" like our own. All three of these assumptions have been rejected by the newer critics, who claim that the concepts of authorship and illusionist drama and the individual did not exist in the Elizabethan (now early modern) period but were created later by the triumphant bourgeoisie.[26] We have a great deal of evidence, however, that proves they are wrong about this, and I hope I have shown that the use of these concepts enables us to understand how Hamlet's soliloquies serve several very important dramatic functions that help to shape our response to him and to his tragedy.

Notes

1. For a typical statement of these two claims, see Wolfgang Clemen, *Shakespeare's Soliloquies*, trans. Charity Scott Stokes (London: Methuen, 1987), 6.

2. *The Riverside Shakespeare*, ed. G. Blakemore Evans et al., 2nd ed. (Boston: Houghton Mifflin, 1997) is used for all quotations and citations. Evans's text of *Hamlet* is based on the second quarto.

3. Frank Kermode suggests that it was cut from the text on which the folio is based because of the "puzzling inappropriateness of the speech at this moment in

the action" (*Shakespeare's Language* [New York: Farrar, Straus and Giroux, 2000], 99, 124).

4. Some critics argue that the speech is relevant because Pyrrhus is driven to kill Priam by a "roused vengeance" for Achilles's death (2.2.488) and so is another father-avenger. But Hamlet does not notice any parallel to his own cause (as he does when he speaks of Laertes in 5.2.75–78); he is only struck by the Player's description of Hecuba's reaction to her husband's death.

5. For an ingenious attempt to relate this soliloquy to the action, see James Hirsh, "Shakespeare and the History of Soliloquies," *Modern Language Quarterly* 58 (1997): 1–26.

6. It can be compared to the list in Sonnet 66 ("Tir'd with all these, for restful death I cry"), which belongs to a minor poetic genre called the *Enueg* (the Provencal word for "vexation")—see my "A Second English *Enueg*," *Philological Quarterly* 53 (1974): 428–30, which cites some studies of this form in Provencal, Catalan, Portuguese, Italian, and French poetry. It shows Hamlet's awareness of and sympathy for the sufferings of those lower on the social scale, and so can also be compared to Lear's speech on "Poor naked wretches" (3.4.28–36), which is much longer and more impassioned because Lear, unlike Hamlet, feels responsible for this suffering ("O, I have ta'en/ Too little care of this!").

7. In the first quarto, however, the fifth soliloquy has Hamlet speak of being "borne before an everlasting judge" after death, when "the happy" will be rewarded and "the accursed damn'd."

8. See Samuel Crowl, "*The Tragedy of Hamlet*," *Shakespeare Bulletin* 19 (2001): 32; Marguerite Tassi, "*The Tragedy of Hamlet*: Peter Brook's Adaptation of Shakespeare's *Hamlet*," *Shakespeare Newsletter* 15 (2001): 40; and Mary Z. Maher, *Modern Hamlets and Their Soliloquies* (Iowa City: University of Iowa Press, 1992), 10.

9. Aristotle, *Poetics*, trans. Ingram Bywater, in *The Basic Works of Aristotle*, ed. Richard McKeon (New York: Random House, 1941), 8.1451^{a}32–35.

10. See *Poetics* 11.1452^{a}24–34, 14.1453^{b}7, 1453^{b}31, 15.1454^{b}8, 16.1455^{a}18, 24.1660^{a}30, and 26.1462^{b}2.

11. One of the worst examples is the division in *Romeo and Juliet* between 2.1 and 2.2, which breaks up a couplet. The only questionable scene divisions in standard modern editions of *Hamlet* are between 1.4 and 1.5 (where Hamlet follows the Ghost) and 4.2 and 4.3 (where Rosencrantz, Guildenstern, and Claudius are trying to find Polonius's body). The folio text only marks the divisions between 1.1, 1.2, and 1.3, and 2.1 and 2.2.

12. The dialogue always makes this explicit: the fourth soliloquy is introduced by Hamlet's comment, "Now I am alone" (2.2.549); the sixth, by his request, "Leave me, friends" (3.2.387); and the eighth, by a similar request, "go a little before" (4.4.31). Just before the first, Claudius orders the members of the court to "Come away" (1.2.128); just before the second, Hamlet bids his companions "farewell" (1.2.253); just before the third, the Ghost bids Hamlet "Adieu" (1.5.91); just before the seventh, Polonius bids Claudius "Fare you well" (3.3.33), leaving Claudius alone when Hamlet comes upon him; and just before the fifth, Polonius asks Claudius to "Withdraw" to their hiding place (3.1.54), leaving Ophelia alone when Hamlet enters.

13. This is not quite accurate for the seventh soliloquy, since after Hamlet exits Claudius remains to speak two lines—also forming a couplet—that end the episode (and the modern scene).

14. *Poetics* 12.1452^{b}22.

15. The fifth soliloquy is the only one in which Hamlet is neither reacting nor anticipating, which is why I said it is the least dramatic in the first sense and why it is so movable.

16. The Ghost complained that he died without receiving the sacraments (1.5.76–79). These two passages are usually overlooked by commentators who argue that Hamlet must be a Protestant because he went to Wittenberg.

17. Compare the rhetorical question (about killing Claudius at prayer) in the seventh soliloquy that also calls for a negative answer. But there Hamlet gives the answer—a decisive "No!"—and moves on to another option.

18. Compare the lines in Sonnet 129, "perjur'd, murd'rous, bloody, full of blame,/ Savage, extreme, rude, cruel, not to trust," where the speaker is also giving vent to his anger in a barrage of abuse and displacing its object from himself to an external target (here, to a personified "lust"). In the folio Hamlet's list of epithets terminates in "Oh Vengeance!", which presumably would be bellowed out, and which serves as a more effective climax to this buildup of emotion and also, because of its very excess, as a more probable cause of his sudden "turn." (The third soliloquy contains a similar list—"O villain, villain, smiling, damned villain!"—but it is shorter and less frantic since there Hamlet is not reproaching himself for anything.)

19. There have been attempts to explain away this inconsistency—see, for example, Joseph Hunter, *New Illustrations of the Life, Studies, and Writings of Shakespeare*, 2 vols. (London: Nichols, 1845), 2.235; John Dover Wilson, *What Happens in "Hamlet"* (Cambridge: Cambridge University Press, 1959), 142; and Harley Granville-Barker, *Prefaces to Shakespeare*, 2 vols. (Princeton: Princeton University Press, 1947), 1.76—but I do not find any of them convincing. (The word "Hum," which suggests a thinking process, is not present in the first quarto or the folio, but that does not seem to make much difference.)

20. Compare the eighth soliloquy, where he suspects that his delay may be the result of "thinking too precisely on th' event—/ A thought which quarter'd hath but one part wisdom/ And ever three parts coward." There may be a kind of corroboration of my hypothesis in the curious sequence of Hamlet's logic in this section, since he first works out his plan to trap Claudius and only then states the reason for it—his doubt about the Ghost—almost as if it were an afterthought.

21. I hope it is clear that I am not taking the Freudian route that hypostatizes these levels or aspects as separate psychic entities that have different purposes, operate by different laws, etc.

22. Of course, Shakespeare does not confine these effects to soliloquies—compare, for example, the powerful simple style in Lear's "Didst thou give all to thy daughters? And art thou come to this?" (3.4.49–50), which is analyzed in Norman Maclean, "Episode, Scene, Speech, and Word: The Madness of Lear," in *Critics and Criticism Ancient and Modern*, ed. R. S. Crane (Chicago: University of Chicago Press, 1952), 612–15, or the collapse of syntax and rhythm at the end of Othello's speech in 5.2.259–82. There is a very perceptive account of the changes in Hamlet's style, in both the dialogue and soliloquies, in Maurice Charney, *Style in "Hamlet"* (Princeton: Princeton University Press, 1969), 258–313.

23. Harold Bloom, *Shakespeare: The Invention of the Human* (New York: Riverhead, 1998), xvii.

24. The evidence for this convention is assembled in Hirsh's article cited in note 5. This kind of self-overhearing also occurs in some Shakespearean dialogue, where it is an example of what William Dodd calls the "metacommunicative dimension of verbal intercourse" that leads us to "confer personhood" or "inner

being" on a character ("Destined Livery? Character and Person in Shakespeare," *Shakespeare Survey* 51 (1998): 148–49). He does not mention its use in soliloquies.

25. For a very different attempt to find a sequence in the soliloquies, see Leon Howard, *The Logic of Hamlet's Soliloquies* (Lone Pine, Calif.: Lone Pine Press, 1964).

26. Thus Francis Barker tells us that "the text" (not Shakespeare, who is never mentioned) is trying to give Hamlet the "interior subjectivity" of an "individual" but fails because of the "historical prematurity of this subjectivity," so that "at the centre of Hamlet, in the interior of his mystery, there is, in short, nothing," although this is "doubtless unknown to him" ("Hamlet's Unfulfilled Interiority," in *New Historicism and Renaissance Drama*, ed. Richard Wilson and Richard Dutton [London: Longman, 1992], 163–64). For refutations of the claims that these three concepts did not exist then, see Barbara A. Mowat, "Constructing the Author," in *Elizabethan Theater: Essays in Honor of S. Schoenbaum*, ed. R. B. Parker and S. P. Zitner (Newark: University of Delaware Press, 1996), 93–110, on the author; David Aers, "A Whisper in the Ear of Early Modernists; or, Reflections on Literary Critics Writing the 'History of the Subject,'" in *Culture and History 1350–1600: Essays on English Communities, Identities, and Writing*, ed. David Aers (Detroit: Wayne State University Press, 1992), 177–202, on the individual; and my "Unthinkable Thoughts in the New Historicizing of English Renaissance Drama," *New Literary History* 21 (1990): 433–47, 463–70, on illusionist drama.

Denzil Holles and the Stylistic Development of the Early English Memoir

Martine Watson Brownley

SOMETIME BEFORE FEBRUARY 14, 1648, DENZIL HOLLES LOST HIS TEMper. His anger in itself was not unusual; Holles was a choleric man known to contemporaries for his irascibility. But this particular eruption was different in one way. This time his rage impelled him to write, and the result was a powerfully vitriolic narrative discussing selected events in England during the period from 1641 to 1648. The piece smoldered in manuscript for just over half a century. Then, in 1699, John Toland prepared an edition of it, which was published as the *Memoirs of Denzil Lord Holles*.

Holles himself had never used the title *Memoirs*; within the manuscript he twice describes it as "this Discourse."[1] Patricia Crawford's biography of Holles calls the title "misleading," arguing that "Holles was not writing his memoirs or a history, but a political pamphlet justifying himself and his party."[2] Toland, ever the astute publicist, undoubtedly added the title of Holles's work to capitalize on public interest aroused by the spate of civil war memoirs pouring from the presses in England during the 1690s. But in addition to his marketing savvy, Toland possessed considerable literary abilities and an excellent sense of genre, revealed most clearly in his elaborate reworking of Edmund Ludlow's wildly meandering *Voyce from the Watchtower* into the more sober and politically effective *Memoirs of Edmund Ludlow*.[3]

Toland's literary expertise served him well in the case of Holles's manuscript, for his appended title was actually quite appropriate, whatever the origin of the work. Holles's "Discourse" exhibits all of the primary literary qualities of the English memoir as it had developed by the end of the seventeenth century. In particular, its style shows various characteristics of the early English memoir as a genre that highlight its uneasy relationship to historical discourse during the period, while presaging its ultimate usefulness to the emerging English novel. Holles's language reflects the conflicted relationship to historical discourse that rapidly destabilized the memoir over the relatively brief course of its development.

Significantly, in the later 1640s when Holles was writing, no published work existed in England with the title *Memoirs*. A few English memoirs were written during the Elizabethan period, but the first one actually published, Francis Osborne's *Historical Memoires on the Reigns of Queen Elizabeth, and King James*, did not appear until 1658. Scattered examples of the form surfaced during the 1660s and 1670s, and by 1677 Gilbert Burnet noted of memoirs that "this way of Writing takes now more in the World than any sort of History ever did."[4] By the 1680s the genre was well enough established for polemicists to adapt it for their arsenals.[5]

The 1690s and the opening years of the eighteenth century were the brief golden age of the historical memoir in England. The example of Holles reflects the popularity of the form, for his was one of a number of earlier pieces unearthed and presented to the public as "memoirs" during the period. Although the opening years of the eighteenth century began auspiciously with two of the finest examples of the form, memoirs about Charles I from Sir Philip Warwick (1701) and Sir Thomas Herbert (1702),[6] by the middle years of the first decade the historical memoir was in generic trouble. In 1705 Daniel Defoe, who was to do so much in developing the memoir as a polemical and a fictional form, first used the word "memoirs" in a title, and two years later, the notorious Edmund Curll entered the market for memoirs with four different titles.[7] By 1709 its increasingly fictional connotations were clear when *Tatler 84* explained that "the Word *Memoir* is *French* for a Novel," and in 1711 Shaftesbury proclaimed, albeit somewhat prematurely, that "already the world begins to sicken with the kind."[8]

Although in subsequent decades contemporaries continued to write historical memoirs, after the middle years of the first decade of the century, the bulk of putative historical memoirs written and published in England were fictional. By 1735, when Thomas Dyche's *New General English Dictionary* defined memoirs as "properly such Histories of Facts" written by participants or eyewitnesses, it added the caveat that "many Books go under this Name that are not so qualified."[9] J. C. Major cites 1737 as the date marking "the period of the decline and almost complete disappearance of English historical memoirs as a distinct literary genre," because he includes fictional memoirs.[10] For the historical memoir, however, the disabling damage had been inflicted much earlier. Thus as a form of historical discourse, the memoir takes root in England in the 1650s and 1660s, develops in the 1670s and flourishes in the

1680s, reaches its high point in the 1690s and the early years of the eighteenth century, and begins to decline slowly after about 1705.

There are of course many reasons for the metamorphosis of the memoir into a predominantly fictional form. From a stylistic perspective, however, Holles's *Memoir* offers a convenient case study of three central features that can succinctly highlight the problematic status of the memoir as a form of historical discourse: the parodic rhetoric of authentication, the range of language, and the fictional elements.

Marcus Billson has noted the close connection of the memoir with periods of crisis,[11] and Holles was among many Englishmen who turned to the genre during and after the tumultuous period of the civil wars. Situated uneasily in the shifting generic ground between history and autobiography, as a form of historical discourse the memoir is an account of events of public concern narrated from some kind of limited perspective, usually a personal one. The limitations in perspective result in omissions in the texts and pervasive biases. Holles's work is typical in these respects; thus Crawford's claims that his work cannot be classified as a memoir because of its elements of apologia and polemic are not generically convincing. The memoir is almost always a defensive genre, and Holles's is no exception.

By the time the memoir began to emerge in England, William Camden, John Selden, and other English historiographical pioneers had established the new kinds of historical methods and procedures that later antiquarians continued to develop and refine throughout the century. Elements of fable and legend that had embellished the chronicles and other earlier historical forms gradually disappeared as English historians became increasingly concerned with more careful documentation and identification of sources. Richard Brathwait in his *Survey of History* (1638) is typical in finding "nothing more beneficiall" for historical writing than "the exact scrutinie of ancient Records."[12] By mid-century, documentation was considered important enough in any writing that made historical claims that even aspiring memoirists felt the pressure of such expectations.

One of the memoirists' stylistic responses was a rhetoric of authentication, which emphasized their historical knowledge, authority, and sources. But this discourse, inserted to enhance their historical credibility, created its own difficulties in their texts, frequently ending up undermining their authority. In many cases the explanations they added to support their claims read like inadvertent parodies of various processes of historical authentication. Holles's undercutting of his own authority assumes various stylistic forms.

The narrators in memoirs tend to show a good deal of self-consciousness, undoubtedly generated in part by the tensions between their public perspectives and private biases. In addition, with so much of the authority of any memoir resting on assertions of the writer's privileged knowledge, major elements in their rhetoric of authentication were always self-reflexive. Such discourse repeatedly functions—or malfunctions—to reveal historical limitations in their texts. Memoirs could not be written without the clause "I think" and assorted associated expressions. Holles's variants, however, suggest the textual problems that tended to arise. As "I remember" becomes "I have heard," which then leads to "if I misremember not," which in its turn gives way to "if I be not deceiv'd,"[13] the vagaries of the human memory become inscribed in Holles's form and content.

One telling sequence shows how the rhetoric of authentication in memoirs undermines itself. Detailing the gifts and offices that the Independents bestowed on their supporters, Holles writes: "The Speaker had Money given him, I know not how much, *6000 l.* at one time (as I remember) . . ." (133). His painstaking specificity, characteristic of memoirists, undercuts the very historical authority that it is deployed to establish:

> Sir *Philip Stapleton* . . . [lost the profits from] his whole Estate during all the Wars, which *Hastlerig* did not, if his Neighbours in *Leicestershire* say true, that his Grounds have continu'd full stock'd all this while, better than ever they were before, so safe and well protected (as I have heard) that his Neighbours when there was danger, would send their Cattel thither; I confess, I understand not the mystery. (139–40)

The quasi-parodic rhetoric of authentication characteristic of the memoir as a genre is particularly clear in attempts to specify sources. Many witnesses are identified only by surnames or titles. Unidentified sources abound, along with dead ones. After writing that certain letters were seen by "my Lord *Willoughby* and Mr. *Whitlock*, who are yet alive, and can testifie it, and by the Earl of *Essex*, Sir *Philip Stapleton*, and Sir *Christopher Wray*, who are dead," Holles proceeds to explain that some of the letters "were written by *Savil's* own hand, some copy'd out by a person of Honour, who was employ'd by him, and is yet alive to make it good . . ."

(40). Even when names are given, the sources are often dubious. After reading Holles's *Memoirs*, Horace Walpole was outraged by his "weak attempt to blast Cromwell for a coward," particularly the citation of "such witnesses as a Major-General Crawford and a Colonel Dalbier!"[14]

The way that this rhetoric of authentication undercuts itself is typical of the functioning of many stylistic elements in the memoir. By definition the memoir is a genre marked by incompleteness, a natural result of its biases, gaps, and personal perspectives. As the examples quoted above show, in memoirs the texts themselves usually disclose their own limitations as historical writing, in style as well as content. The tendency of memoirs to be internally self-correcting, even in small formal details, can be seen stylistically in Holles's treatment of parentheses.

Discussing how actions taken by any Parliament threatened by armed forces can be reviewed and either confirmed or nullified later by a free Parliament, Holles writes that despite anything that occurs while a Parliament is under duress, "when that force is over, and the Spirits recollected, it returns to it self to do the functions of life, move and act as formerly. It is but like a Parenthesis in a Sentence, and remains one and the same as if the Parenthesis were not at all" (167). This remark becomes particularly interesting in view of Holles's own copious employment of parentheses throughout his narrative.

Directly reflecting the temper and personality of their writer, Holles's *Memoirs* are unruly and impetuous, with a narrative that careens ahead at breakneck speed and seldom slows for reflection. Parenthetical organization makes such a style easier to read. In 1815 when Francis Maseres edited Holles's *Memoirs* for his *Select Tracts*, he frequently added parentheses.[15] In doing so he was replicating features already prominent in the original text. Holles himself had used parentheses for many different kinds of information, including personal opinions and asides, additional details, and corrections of his characteristic overstatements.[16] These kinds of additions validate his claim that the sentences themselves remain substantively the same, with or without the parenthetical insertions.

However, other parenthetical material in Holles's text could not be removed without more serious historiographical consequences. Sometimes parentheses establish the progression of the events described: "They had likewise (upon occasion of the Order of Summons) written of the uncertain report . . ." (198–99). In addition to clarifying time, obviously a basic unit of any historical narrative, other parentheses offer essential historical information. For example, Holles writes that the House of Commons "prostitu[ted] their honor" when they obeyed certain demands put on them by the Army: "And when the Parliament had done it (as they did [in] all but suspending their Members) . . ." (122–23). Preparations for the Irish campaign were "faithfully perform'd by the Committee (that is, by part of it) . . ." (82). Parentheses like these are necessary for historical precision in the account.

Similarly, a number of parentheses involve identification of sources, whether Holles himself—"as I have heard" and "as I remember" often appear parenthetically—or others: "(as Sir *Thomas Fairfax* wrote up from *Cambridg*)" (139, 48, 74, 101). Equally useful in a different way for assessing the validity of Holles's statements are the parenthetical materials that contrast the rhetoric of his opponents to actual historical circumstances: "They require further, That the Officers who had deserted the Army (as they call'd it, but in truth who had left them for their Rebellion, and engag'd for *Ireland*) should have no more of their Arrears paid them . . ." (115).

Thus Holles's textual practice deconstructs his own contention in the *Memoirs* that a sentence containing parenthetical material "remains one and the same as if the Parenthesis were not at all" (167). Some of his parentheses, such as those clarifying time, offer essential information to the reader, while in the cases of source identification and of the rhetoric/reality distinctions, the parentheses are essential for historical assessment. This small but telling stylistic deconstruction on Holles's part microcosmically reflects the kinds of dissociations or deferrals of historical authority that are characteristic of early English memoirs.

Obviously, it would be foolish to hold these early memoirs to the more exacting historiographical standards of later periods. But even by the standards of his own era, Holles's deconstructions, whether of his rhetoric of authentication or his parenthetical insertions, suggest some of the limitations of the memoir that hastened its decline as a historical form. Moreover, this kind of discourse, which was prominent in most of the memoirs of the period, is actually a good textual indication of the growing historical sophistication of the mid-seventeenth century. For instance, in the case of the quasi-parodic rhetoric of authentication, obviously no parody can exist without widespread understanding of the established conventions of a form.

From classical times, memoirists had generally been considered historians, and the association of the two continued throughout the seventeenth century. For example, although commentators from Cicero to Rapin had on occasion differentiated Caesar's *Commentaries* from actual histories, in the seventeenth century the *Commentaries*, along with Commines's *Memoirs*, were constantly termed "histories" and were praised as such by Brathwait, Burnet, John Dryden, and other writers.[17] The ultimate separation of memoirists from historians developed in response to the practices of early writers of memoirs, in part because their styles themselves vividly revealed the distance between the methods and approaches of the two kinds of discourse.

Most of the characteristics of the memoir noted so far—the pervasive bias, the incompleteness, and the limited historical authority—involve constrictions of point of view. But with the memoir, as often happens in cases of self-imposed limitations, the result was certain kinds of freedom within the given parameters. One stylistic ramification of these freedoms was an openness in expression that characterizes the genre.

The antiquarian movement, while significantly advancing historiographical analysis and methods over the seventeenth century, did not exert a similar positive influence on historical prose. Brathwait commented that the antiquarians' "great Volumes" produced "small benefit to the Reader,"[18] and one reason for the minimal readerly profit was undoubtedly the difficulty of perusing such material. Similarly, in the early eighteenth century, John Hughes complained of the "cold and barren Stile" that too often resulted from the antiquarians' "laborious Plunder of Libraries, Manuscripts, publick Rolls and Records."[19]

In contrast to the antiquarians, memoirists expanded the stylistic range of early modern English historical writing. Dryden pointed out that lives or biographies were "more extensive in the style" than annals and histories, in part because they employed more informal expression suitable for the private and domestic elements they incorporated.[20] Reflecting this feature of the old lives and new biographies, memoirists usually avoided the elevated and dignified expression associated with the historian. James Wellwood, for example, proclaims: "As to the Stile, I have taken very little pains about it; and all I have aim'd at, is to be understood."[21] In this respect memoirists reflect the tendency to neglect literary art characteristic of most seventeenth-century historians. However, while the memoirists' loose and informal writing contributed to the general diminution of stylistic standards for histories, it simultaneously widened the range of expression available for historical discourse.

As a new form for the English, the memoir encouraged experimentation. Some memoirists developed distinctive narrative voices in their works, and many incorporated a diversity of tones unusual in the historical prose of the time. Holles's caustically dramatic rhetoric, sweeping from magisterial denunciation to homely colloquialism, is an excellent example. From his opening dedication to the "Unparallel'd Couple" Oliver St. John and Oliver Cromwell, whom he credits as "principal in ministring the matter of this Discourse, and giving me the leisure of making it, by banishing me from my Country and Business" (xiii), he deploys a range of literary styles and references to mold a powerful case.

In his prefatory address to readers, Toland noted Holles's "vehemence" of style (xi), and his mastery of invective sears the *Memoirs*. Biting sarcasm is a major linguistic weapon. Among supporters of the Independents, Colonel Thompson was rewarded with "2000 *l*. for his wooden Leg, which nothing but a Cannon could have helpt him to, for he would never come within Musket shot" (136–37). Another stylistic specialty is negative superlatives. In its treatment of Parliament the Army exhibited "the most transcending presumption that ever was heard of," while the Parliament itself "set up the Star Chamber, the High Commission, the Spanish Inquisition, in one Committee of ten Lords and twenty Commoners" (121, 169). One denunciatory tour de force is his description of Captain Massey's seizing and reading the Scots Commissioners' letters as "the highest affront, the greatest violation of the publick faith, the greatest scandal to all Princes, States, and even Societies of Men, the basest unworthiest dealing with a Nation to whom we were engag'd . . . that ever was heard of, or read in any Story, or I think ever will be again" (55–56).

Holles's stylistic ingenuity in skewering his enemies is inexhaustible. Animal imagery runs throughout the *Memoirs*. Those he opposes are "Vipers," "Whelps," "Northern Beagles," "Drones," and "Bloodhounds" (2, 8, 65, 70, 129). On the Army in particular he lavishes a range of denigratory classical and Biblical references. The military and its leaders are compared to Hannibal, Anak, Jehu, Haman, Caesar and Antony, Rabshekah, Achitophel, and of course Judas (105, 114, 123, 151, 159, 165, 158). These "Men of Belial" and "Children of Darkness" are Egyptians, Philistines, the elders of Jazreel, Ahab's prophets, and, picking up on the animal imagery, "*Pharaoh*'s lean Kine [who ate the others]" (205, 75, 123, 124, 134–35, 106, 79).

Throughout the *Memoirs*, classical references from Homer, Virgil, Juvenal, Tacitus, and Roman history add depth to the analysis, alongside a plethora of Biblical quotations and allusions, from Genesis to Job and the Psalms, and from Sampson to St. Paul (with whom Holles, not surprisingly, associates himself). Among the English poets, Chaucer and Milton are cited.[22] This range of learned literary references is complemented in the *Memoirs* by a more direct, even homespun, style that offers a different kind of rhetorical immediacy and appeal than the lofty invective. For example, the Committee of Examinations operated as "a continual Horse Fair" (130). Trying ineffectually to negotiate with the Army, "The poor Parliament all this while is sitting upon addle Eggs, take a great deal of pains, like Children, to build Castles of Cards, a puff from their faithful Army blows it all down" (104). Proverbial expressions anchor the text in everyday experience. Often Holles juxtaposes classical with proverbial references to enhance the stylistic impact. When various Members of the House of Lords and the House of Commons abandon the Parliament in London to go out to the Army, "they were really under a force, and under a fear, they did *vitare Charibdim incidere in Scyllam*, and leap (as the old Proverb is) out of the Fryingpan into the Fire" (152). The Army's charges that the Eleven Members corresponded with the King and his Party were "a *Decimo sexto* to their Folio, a Mole-hill to their Mountain" (127).

Holles was among the early memoirists who were able to manipulate both formal and informal expression to break the stylistic boredom too often induced by the bland and impersonal writing in other historical forms during the period. At times the openness of style in the memoir allowed writers to render experiences with compelling immediacy. A commonplace in classical discussions of effective historical style, echoed by English commentators from Roger Ascham to Hugh Blair, is that the writing should make the reader become a spectator of the events depicted.[23] Such writing is often characteristic of memoirs.

Holles's active style renders a sense of immediacy through both word choice and sentence structure. Strong verbs and verbals predominate. Instead of supporting Parliament, the citizens of London "prostitute all to the Lust of heady and violent Men, suffer Mr. *Cromwel* to saddle, ride, switch, and spur them at his pleasure" (107). The Army "interrupt[s] Ministers as they were preaching, miscalling, reviling them, sometimes pulling them down by violence, beating and abusing them, getting into the Pulpits themselves, and venting either ridiculous or scandalous things" (71).

Holles often switches from past tense to present to add dramatic immediacy: "One would think now these had bid fair for an absolute breach with *Scotland*, but they are not satisfy'd yet; one thing more they will do which they are confident will do the feat" (56). Breaks into present tense frequently combine with colloquial expression to produce a strong forward propulsion in the narrative: "Well, they carried it, and to work they go" (15; see also 31, 42). Sentence structure, too, contributes to textual immediacy. Exclamations of outrage dot the text: "O the impudence!" (132); "O the wickedness of these Men, that thirsted after nothing but to see the two Kingdoms weltering in that blood which they must let out of one another's Veins!" (58–59) Rhetorical questions, often rolling in series, demand the reader's evaluative engagement:

> How many Ministers were pull'd out of their Livings for very small faults? [H]ow many Persons made Delinquents, their Estates torn in pieces, themselves, their Wives and Children turn'd to beggery, and ready to starve for no great offences, at least that for which they did not deserve so severe a punishment? What Committees were set up? (129)

The sense of activity, of incessant movement, produced by the style of the *Memoirs* works well with its theme, which is the destruction of all social and political order in England after Holles's own class loses governmental and military control in the 1640s. That focus is established in the opening sentence: "The wisest of Men saw it to be a great Evil, that Servants should ride on Horses, and Princes walk as Servants on the Earth: An Evil now both seen and felt in our unhappy Kingdom" (1). In the penultimate section Holles summarizes his text as a proof that "*England* is become, by the actings of these Men, that Monster whose shape is perverted, the head standing where the feet, and the feet where the head should be, mean Men mounted aloft, and all that is or should be great, Lacqueying it after them. . . ." (207–08). Throughout the *Memoirs* the designations "Masters" and "Servants," along with "Lords" and "Subjects," are deployed as sarcastic metaphors, with each element of the binary bitterly redefined as the political situation increasingly deteriorates.

The role of the memoir as a genre in providing the effective style lacking in most English historical writing of the period should not be overemphasized, mainly because too few memoirists consistently took advantage of their stylistic options. As a whole the literary quality of historical memoirs was seldom distinguished; the average memoirist tended to be mute and inglorious rather than a

Milton. But stylistic developments that from a strictly belletristic point of view might seem rudimentary could in this period be extremely important in historiography. As the case of Holles suggests, at a time when dull and desiccated antiquarian styles were making many English histories almost unreadable, the memoir offered opportunities for an expanded stylistic range, a linguistic breath of fresh air sorely needed in the historiography of the later seventeenth century.

Both Holles's quasi-parodic rhetoric of authentication and his colorfully vigorous language reflect the instability of the memoir as a genre of purely historical discourse. Simultaneously conveying certain kinds of historical truth and deconstructing that truth in the ways it was presented, the memoir maintained a conflicted relationship to history as traditionally understood. One result was a vulnerability to fictional elements, which more than any other characteristic eventually sabotaged the genre for historical discourse.

Judith H. Anderson has traced the deliberate "convergence of fiction and historical truth in Tudor-Stuart *Lives*," showing in detail how Renaissance life-writing always included "a considerable element, not of untruth, but of fiction."[24] Similar points could be made about the seventeenth-century historical memoir, which was always a volatile mixture of public and private elements, of objective and subjective components. Ultimately, the private and the subjective prevailed. As a historical genre, the memoir is a good example of Alistair Fowler's contention that later generic developments often "interiorize the earlier kind."[25]

As the memoir steadily became more autobiographical, by the early eighteenth century Major points out its "loss of historical weight."[26] As the century progressed, the memoir became the province of autobiographers and particularly biographers. Before midcentury the increasingly loose employment of the title is shown in the *Apology for the Life of Colley Cibber* (1740), where Cibber first describes his work as the "Memoirs of my own Life," then calls it "my History" and the "History of my private Life," and finally terms himself "my own Biographer."[27] The affinities of the memoir had by the end of the century moved away from the autobiographical apology toward the confession.

As the memoir developed toward a more personal focus, it simultaneously moved toward a fictional one. Traces of this development can be seen in Holles's work. A good example is his striking description of Hasilrig's return to Parliament to report on military matters. Holles uses many of his characteristic stylistic techniques, including sarcasm, colloquialism, dramatic immediacy, Biblical allusion, and manipulation of verb tenses:

> Sir *Arthur Haslerig* could come up to *London*, and into the House of Commons, all in beaten Buff, cross girt with Sword and Pistols as if he had been killing his thousands, when 'tis more probable, if there was any danger, that he had been crying under a Hedg, as he did at *Cherrington* Fight, bellowing out, *Ah wo is me, all is lost! we are all undone!"* (27)

This picture of Holles's longtime enemy, one of the dedicatees of the *Memoirs*, is vividly unforgettable, both entertaining and damning. Unfortunately, it has no basis whatsoever in historical fact. Military historians actually give Haselrig major credit for the victory at Cheriton.[28] Moreover, in assessing Haselrig's valor, Sir Charles Firth emphasizes that "His fault throughout his life was overboldness rather than want of courage."[29]

Similarly, in the prefatory letter to the *Memoirs*, Toland questions Holles's depiction of his other dedicatee Cromwell, leaving it to the reader to determine whether Holles had not drawn *"the lines of* Cromwel's *Face too strong, and the shadows too many."* Toland's comments are couched in terms of Holles's style: *"I think him bad enough painted in his own true Colours, without standing in need of exaggerating Rhetoric to make him look more odious or deform'd"* (xi). In Toland's view, Holles's style also leads him generically and historically astray when his treatment of the Scots becomes a *"long Panegyric on that Nation,"* containing *"more in their behalf than their own Historians have ever been able to offer"* (xii).

Obviously, in these particular cases Holles's biases were particularly virulent. But even in less inflammatory instances, the instability of the rhetoric of authentication and the direct and informal expression that mark the memoir highlights the susceptibility of the genre to incursions of fictional discourse. As a formal attempt to expand the boundaries of historical writing, the memoir ultimately failed. The stylistic range that added directness and immediacy to memoirs was finally inadequate for maintaining the dignity traditionally demanded in historical writing. In addition, a number of elements made the genre inadequate to meet the new standards for historical research and writing that evolved over the seventeenth century. Claiming some historical authority without meeting these stricter standards became less and less satisfactory; the memoir finally emerged as an overextension of history. But in the process, it resituated the boundaries of historical writing in ways that were positive for the development of other genres. Although the memoir made vital contributions to the emergence of autobiography and biography during the period, its major beneficiary was the novel.

French influence of course played a major role in the increasing fictionalization of the memoirs. However, several basic stylistic characteristics of the English historical memoir that are reflected in Holles's work suggest the genre's vulnerability to intentional or inadvertent fiction. Memoirists had made certain historical claims without taking full historical responsibility. The step to making the claims without assuming any historical responsibility at all required almost half a century, but it was basically a matter of rhetoric, and that rhetoric was already available in the works of the memoirists. Aphra Behn, Daniel Defoe, and their peers would skillfully adapt the rhetoric of authentication, the colloquial and dramatic immediacy, and other stylistic techniques characteristic of the early English memoir for their own very different purposes.

NOTES

Original spelling, capitalization, punctuation and italics have been reproduced in quotations, with the exception of the seventeenth century printed "f" replaced by "s."

1. Denzil Holles, *Memoirs of Denzil Lord Holles* (London: T. Goodwin, 1699) xiii, 3. Subsequent references will appear within the text.

2. Patricia Crawford, *Denzil Holles, 1598–1680: A Study of his Political Career* (London: Royal Historical Society, 1979) 167–68.

3. Blair Worden's excellent introduction traces Toland's manipulations of Ludlow in *A Voyce from the Watch Tower; Part Five: 1660–1662*, Camden 4th ser., 21 (London: Royal Historical Society, 1978) 1–80.

4. Burnet, "The Preface," *Memoires of the Lives and Actions of James and William Dukes of Hamilton and Castlehearld, &c.* (London, 1677) a^v.

5. During the Popish Plot and the Exclusion Crisis, typical productions were hostile memoirs of both the Duke of York (*Memoirs of the Most Remarkable Enterprises and Actions of James Duke of York, Albany and Ulster* [London, 1681]), and the Earl of Shaftesbury (*Memoires of the Life of Anthony Late Earl of Shaftesbury* [London,1682/3]). A few years later it was Titus Oates's turn for a scathing memoir (*The Memoires of Titus Oates* [London,1685]).

6. Warwick, *Memoirs of the Reign of King Charles the First* (Edinburgh: Ballantyne, 1813); Herbert, *Memoirs of the Two Last Years of the Reign of King Charles I* (London, 1813).

7. Defoe's work was *The Consolidator, or Memoirs of Sundry Transactions from the World in the Moon*, an allegorical and satirical treatment of the civil wars and the Glorious Revolution. Maximillian E. Novak notes "the memoir of political

or military life" as "the form which had the greatest appeal to Defoe" ("Defoe's Theory of Fiction," *Studies in Philology* 61 [1964]: 656). Information on Curll is from Ralph Straus, *The Unspeakable Curll* (London: Chapman, 1927), 205–206; however, Straus admits his bibliography is incomplete.

8. *The Tatler*, ed. Donald F. Bond (Oxford: Clarendon Press, 1987) 2: 36; Anthony Ashley Cooper, Earl of Shaftesbury, *Characteristics of Men, Manners, Opinions, Times* [1711], ed. John M. Robertson (Indianapolis: Bobbs-Merrill, 1964) 1:146.

9. T[homas]. Dyche, *A New General English Dictionary* (1735).

10. John Campbell Major, *The Role of Personal Memoirs in English Biography and Novel* (Philadelphia: University of Pennsylvania Press, 1935) 93. Major points out Horace Walpole as the "one notable exception," with his *Reminiscences of the Courts of George I and George II, and Memoirs of the Reign of George III from 1771 to 1783*.

11. Billson, "The Memoir: New Perspectives on a Forgotten Genre," *Genre* 10 (1977): 280. He also comments on the "peculiar suitability of the memoir for recreating periods of historical uncertainty and turmoil" (261).

12. Brathwait, *A Survey of History: Or, a Nursery for Gentry* (London, 1638) 277.

13. *Memoirs* 30, 147, 162; 123, 139, 145, 146; 162–63; 137.

14. *A Catalogue of the Royal and Noble Authors of England*, new ed. (Edinburgh, 1796) 196.

15. See for example, pp. 242–43, 275, 290, 294–95, 305, in *Select Tracts Relating to the Civil Wars in England*, ed. Francis Maseres (London, 1815). Maseres also inserted additional dashes into Holles's text (for example, 260, 274, 296).

16. For personal opinions and asides, see *Memoirs* 32, 55, 108, 145; for additional details, see 45, 53, 89, 154; for corrections of overstatements, see 9, 19, 149.

17. On Cicero and Rapin, see Thomas Hearne, *Ductor Historicus*, 3rd ed. (London, 1714) 147–48, 149; Braithwait 32, 67; Burnet a^r; Dryden, *Life of Plutarch*, in *Of Dramatic Poesy and Other Critical Essays* (London: Dent, 1968) 2: 5, 6. Burnet ranked Caesar first, followed by Commines, an order reversed by Dryden. See also Degoraeus Wheare, *The Method and Order of Reading Both Civil and Ecclesiastical Histories*, trans. Edmund Bohun (London, 1685) 201.

18. *Survey of History* 271.

19. Hughes, "Preface," *A Complete History of England*, 2nd ed. (London, 1719) 1: n.p.

20. Dryden, 2: 8–9.

21. "To the Reader," *Memoirs of the Most Material Transactions in England* (London, 1700) n.p.

22. Classical references from *Memoirs* 184, 75, 169, 78, 151; Biblical, 190, 206, 208, 87, 138; English poets, 21, 196.

23. Ascham, *A Report and Discourse . . . of Germany*, in *The Whole Works of Roger Ascham* (London, 1864) 3, 6; James Amyot, "Amiot to the Readers," in Plutarch, *Lives of the Noble Greeks and Romanes*, trans. Thomas North (London: Nonesuch Press, 1929) xx; Brathwait 101, 107; Thomas Hobbes, "Of the Life and History of Thucydides," *Hobbes's Thucydides*, ed. Richard Schlatter (New Brunswick: Rutgers University Press, 1975) 18; Hughes 1: n.p.; Blair, *Lectures on Rhetoric and Belles Lettres*, ed. J. C. Bryce, 1983 (Indianapolis: Liberty Classics, 1985) 86–87, 111–12.

24. Anderson, *Biographical Truth: The Representation of Historical Persons in Tudor-Stuart Writing* (New Haven: Yale University Press, 1984) 70, 79.

25. Fowler, *Kinds of Literature: An Introduction to the Theory of Genres and Modes* (Cambridge: Harvard University Press, 1982) 163.

26. Major, 94.

27. *An Apology for the Life of Colley Cibber*, ed. B. R. S. Fone (Ann Arbor: University of Michigan Press, 1968) 5, 7, 8.

28. For example, Anthony Baker, *A Battlefield Atlas of the English Civil War* (London: Allen, 1986) 53; Peter Newman, *Atlas of the English Civil War* (London: Croom Helm, 1985) 49.

29. *Dictionary of National Biography*, 9: 744.

"New Philosophy Calls All in Doubt": Chaos Theory and the Fractal Poetics of John Donne

Allen Michie

ONE OF THE FEW UNBROKEN THREADS IN JOHN DONNE'S CRITICAL REception history is the attempt to find inconsistency in his biography and consistency in his poetry.[1] It is a weary truism by now that the religious imagery of holiness and spirituality pervades the love poetry of "Jack" Donne, while the erotic imagery of rapture and physicality pervades the religious poetry and sermons of "Dr. John" Donne, Dean of St. Paul's. To read Donne for consistency of style is to simultaneously read against the grain of the radical inconsistency in his life. Donne's is an example of a creative mind that continually identifies opposites and the alternates that lie between them—sometimes pulling the opposites together into unity, but more often simply exploring the ironies and surprises of difference. Perhaps Donne's own life provided the template. "Is it not, we may ask, an indictment of Donne's historical period that a genius was forced to abase himself before the rabble of idlers, confidence men and pederasts who ruled the country?" asks John Carey. "Might we not have had more *Songs and Sonnets*? An equally cogent question, perhaps, is whether we should have the *Songs and Sonnets* at all were it not for the thwarted, grasping, parasitic life that Donne was forced to lead."[2] In form, content, and biography, Donne remains our preeminent poet of coexisting contradictions and of making peace with one's life in a world of chance.

There is a new mirror that scientists and forward-looking humanities scholars have been holding up to nature, and it is providing bizarre and paradoxical views of what we have long taken for granted as "common sense." Donne, I believe, would have been intuitively drawn to it. In Harriett Hawkins's last and most boldly interdisciplinary book, *Strange Attractors: Literature, Culture, and Chaos Theory*, she reminds us that the impact of this evolving branch of math and physics "on the creative arts and the global village of modern popular culture is by now so widespread that it shouldn't be ignored by critical or cultural theorists, students and teachers of literature."[3] The fact that nonlinear dynamical systems theory (much more evocatively known as chaos theory) has only emerged since the 1960s should in no way impede us from applying its insights to literature written hundreds of years before. "Indeed," Hawkins writes, "one could argue that in seeing a deterministic order ordaining as well as containing chaos, art got there before science did."[4]

Introduction to Chaos Theory

This article is hardly the place for an in-depth history, account, and critical evaluation of chaos theory.[5] I will summarize specific aspects of it as they come in my analysis of Donne, but it may nevertheless be helpful to provide a general overview here for readers coming to these concepts for the first time in order to fully appreciate from the outset why *this* theory is so appropriate to *this* author.

Chaos theory provides a scientifically quantifiable, but simultaneously poetically suggestive, way of looking at how almost everything in life is connected with everything else. Anything that has definition and coherence—such as a single-celled organism, a war, a novel, or a flock of birds—is a *system*. Anything that changes, grows, deepens, or expands is *dynamic*. Anything that depends upon subtle chains of cause and effect, such as fender-bender leading to a conversation leading to a date leading to a marriage leading to a family, is *deterministic*. Perhaps most importantly, any system that is open to rapid and unpredictable change, not moving in a straight and unbroken trajectory, is *nonlinear*. The most interesting, intriguing, challenging, and exciting things in life tend to be dynamic, deterministic, nonlinear systems.

Chaos theory is radical for its challenge to the *certainty* of traditional science. It freely confesses, and persuasively demonstrates, what science has been desperately denying ever since the Enlightenment (which Donne, of course, predated): we cannot know all of the answers. Although chaos theory does not displace Enlightenment ideas of scientific determinism, it makes clear that even with an infinite amount of data and information, we cannot ever be 100% certain about the behavior of any system, even the simplest of systems like a swinging pendulum, as long as it interacts with other systems and is open to the influence of small changes. Simple systems can rapidly cascade into disorder, as any child who has ever built a house of cards or a sand castle knows, but what may come as a surprise are the ways in which highly disordered and chaotic systems exhibit surprising patterns of simplicity.

Chaotic systems tend to fall into certain stable pathways over time as they wind their charted ways through the "phase space" in which they operate. They are influenced by the magnetic pull of "attractors." The "strange attractor" of Hawkins's title is a particular kind of attractor unique to nonlinear systems that shows both long-term stability and short-term unpredictability when the system is mapped out in its phase space. The simple lines of these attractors, when examined closely, reveal unending layers upon layers of unfolding complexity. Patterns, like the individual scales which make up the sinuous line of a snake, repeat themselves into infinity. This "self-similarity across scale," which you can see in natural systems ranging from snowflakes to fern leaves to mountain ranges, is called *fractal* geometry.

Fractal objects have a number of distinct properties, each of which is immediately relevant to aspects of Donne's imagery, religious philosophy, and poetic form. The first of these is a sophisticated new way of looking at what a much older scientific vocabulary used to call the "microcosms" and "macrocosms" found in Mother Earth and Father Donne. The word "fractal" was coined by the mathematician Benoit Mandelbrot to mean the "fraction" that can exist between dimensions. For example, if a two-dimensional plane (think of a sheet of paper) fills the space of a three-dimensional object (think of that sheet of paper crumpled into a ball), then the plane essentially has a dimension somewhere between two and three (in the case of our crumpled paper, the fractal dimension would be higher the tighter it is crumpled and the more wrinkles it has). The fractal dimension corresponds to the degree of irregularity in the system, and it will remain constant across scale. In a natural system such as an Alpine mountain range, for example, the degree of jaggedness across a single mountaintop tends to remain constant for the degree of jaggedness across the entire range spread across the horizon.

Fractal Dimension

What fractal geometry teaches us to look for in Donne's works is an understanding of how self-similarity across scale is a product of, and leads to, the "in-between" nature of dimension, be it physical, spiritual, or emotional. In the Holy Sonnet "I am a little world made cunningly," for example, Donne makes the familiar comparison between a single human body and the larger "body" of land that God sees when he looks down on Earth:

> I am a little world made cunningly
> Of Elements, and an Angelike spright,
> But black sinne hath betraid to endlesse night
> My world's both parts, and (oh) both parts must die.[6]

It is not enough that Donne's body is a fractal of the earth, a "little world"—the purpose of the image is to establish that being a microcosm of something larger than yourself means that you share the same *essence* of the macrocosm, only on a smaller scale. The image is a conventional one until Donne adds the essential element that places him in-between the dimensions of the physical body and the planet as a whole: he has an "Angelike spright" that has no limitations on size. This opens up the fractal image to several scales. The physical body is made of both physical "elements" and metaphysical "spright," both of which are vulnerable to the corruption of sin. Insofar as the speaker is a "little world," the microcosm reflects back onto the macrocosm, suggesting that the entire "body" of mankind somehow has the same two-level pattern of physicality and spirit. The accompanying implication in this poem is that the death that comes to the speaker will likewise come to all of mankind on judgment day.

Often it is chaotic images of destruction, fluctuation, and fluidity that mediate these conflicting states of body and spirit. Donne continues:

> You which beyond that heaven which was most high
> Have found new sphears, and of new lands can write,
> Powre new seas in mine eyes, that so I might
> Drowne my world with my weeping earnestly,
> Or wash it, if it must be drown'd no more:
> But oh it must be burnt; alas the fire
> Of lust and envie'have burnt it heretofore,
> And made it fouler; Let their flames retire,
> And burne me ô Lord, with a fiery zeale
> Of thee'and thy house, which doth in eating heale.[7]

Like an explorer with a telescope, God sees new lands with the creation of every new human being. What is destroyed on one dimension or scale is renewed on another: the new seas that fit the scale of the earth drown the world of the speaker's scale. But since the "world" of the speaker corresponds to the world at large, he takes

God's promise that the world will be destroyed with fire and not water to apply across scale to his own "little world." The metaphysical forces of lust and envy cross dimensions to affect the speaker's physical body as a literal and symbolic fire, only to be extinguished with the fire of the soul in the form of God's "fiery zeale." The parallels exist across scale, from the large "world" of the small Donne to the small "house" of the large God, but it is only because Donne poises the speaker *between* the dimensions of the physical and the spiritual that the mortal destiny of the one can become the redemptive promise of the other.

In fractal geometry, the importance of size is replaced with the importance of scale. Even the simple measurements we have come to take for granted become problematic. Mathematicians get a taste, perhaps, of what readers of poetry have long known with Christopher Marlowe: there are "infinite riches in a little room" (or, as Donne writes more piously of the pregnant Mary, she has "*Immensity cloysterd in thy deare wombe*").[8] Hawkins summarizes the ideas of Mandelbrot:

> The coastline of Britain is a case in point. Seen on a large scale from far above it has an irregular outline; looked at more closely, more details of the same irregular coastline-outline will emerge, and so on down to the smallest scale. Its length seems finite and measurable, easily mapped, but followed through to a microscopic scale it becomes virtually infinite: its promontories and crannies contain their own promontories and crannies, symmetries and asymmetries, and so do these, and so on.

Now to Donne:

> No man is an *Iland*, intire of it selfe; every man is a peece of the *Continent*, a part of the *maine*; if a *Clod* be washed away by the *Sea*, *Europe* is the lesse; as well as if a *Promontorie* were, as well as if a *Mannor* of thy *friends* or of *thine owne* were; any man's *death* diminshes *me*, because I am involved in *Mankinde*; And therefore never send to know for whom the *bell* tolls; it tolls for *thee*. . . .[9]

The value of complexity across small scales over simplicity in large measurable size is consistent throughout meditation 17 and the *Devotions upon Emergent Occasions* in general. Revisiting his fractal image from the Holy Sonnet quoted above, Donne writes in meditation four, It is too little to call *Man* a *little World*; Except *God*, Man is a *diminutive* to nothing. Man consistes of more pieces, more parts, then the world; then the world doeth, nay then the world is. And if those pieces were extended, and stretched out in Man, as they are in the world, Man would bee the *Gyant*, and the world the *Dwarfe*, the world but the *Map*, and the Man the *World*."[10] Donne continues: "If all the *Veines* in our bodies, were extented to *Rivers*, and all the *Sinewes*, to *vaines of Mines*, and all the *Muscles*, that lye upon one another, to *Hilles*, and all the *Bones* to *Quarries* of stones, and all the other pieces, to the proportion of those which correspond to them in the *world*, the *aire* would be too litle for this *Orbe* of Man to move in . . ."[11] As it turns out, we now know that the combined length of the veins in the average human body totals over sixty thousand miles! It is possible to contain all of this in a five-to-six-foot frame only because a bifurcating fractal pattern is shared from the largest arteries down to the smallest capillaries, something akin to the measureless coastline of Britain or the infinite boundary of the Mandelbrot set (easily reproduced on a small sheet of paper).

In Donne's hands, there is a characteristic theological and poetical significance attached to the value of scale over size. No sin is too small to catch the attention of the Almighty; no object is too tiny (e.g., a reflection in a single teardrop) to carry deep feeling. As he memorably puts it in an Easter sermon from 1628, "The Cedar is no better a glasse to see God in, than the Hyssope upon the wall; all things that are, are equally removed from being nothing . . ."[12] From his fractal position between dimensions, viewing the 3-D human scale somewhere between the 2-D miniscule and the 4-D infinite, Donne makes us aware of how repetition and circularity give us a zone of comfort and stability within the spiraling chaos of what the mind finds difficult to grasp. Be it parting from a lover, facing illness and death, or working through grief over the loss of a family member, feelings that threaten to push us into the uncontrollable are often countered with fractal images that pull us back into the disciplined. To value scale over size is to reduce the threat of imposing emotions or realities that we cannot, or will not, face.

Death is often overcome in Donne's works by images of life stubbornly enduring as fragments, atoms, or recycled cells. As Donne writes in "The Dissolution,"

> Shee'is dead; And all which die
> To their first Elements resolve;
> And wee were mutuall Elements to us,
> And made of one another,
> My body then doth hers involve,
> And those things whereof I consist, hereby
> In me abundant grow, and burdenous,
> And nourish not, but smother.[13]

To live inside another is a metaphysical state—between the dimensions of the self and the other—and the size of the shared particles is meaningless compared to the scale of what it represents. The concept appears most famously in "The Flea": "Oh stay, three lives in one flea spare, / Where wee almost, nay more then maryed are: / This flea is you and I, and this / Our mariage bed, and mariage temple is."[14] Most powerful, however, is Donne's macabre Easter day sermon of 1626 on the re-compacting of atoms scheduled for judgment day. No amount of randomness and unpredictable trajectory from an initial condition will matter to God on the day when chaos falls into order:

> [W]here mans buried flesh hath brought forth grasse, and that grasse fed beasts, and those beasts fed men, and those men fed other men, God that knowes in which Boxe of his Cabinet all this seed Pearle lies, in what corner of the world every atome, every graine of every mans dust sleeps, shall recollect that dust, and then recompact that body, and then re-inanimate that man, and that is the accomplishment of all.[15]

As in a pure fractal, size does not matter, just the pattern of the whole that emerges from the essence contained with each atom. In an earlier sermon Donne writes that despite the elements of his decayed body being scattered to the four winds over time,

> I, I the same body, and the same soul, shall be recompact again, and be identically, numerically, individually the same man. The same integrity of body, and soul, and the same integrity in the Organs of my body, and in the faculties of my soul too; I shall be all there, my body, and my soul, and all my body, and all my soul.[16]

What is fractal is, again, what is somehow between dimensions. To have the essence of the larger whole contained within the infinitely small multitude of the parts is to have the mortal share, across scale, a pattern with the divine:

> But when after all this, when *after my skinne worms shall destroy my body, I shall see God*, I shall see him in my flesh, which shall be mine inseparably, (in the *effect*, though not in the *manner*) as the *Hypostaticall union* of God, and man, in Christ, makes our nature and the godhead one person in him. My flesh shall no more be none of mine, then Christ shall not be man, as well as God.[17]

STRANGE ATTRACTORS

In each of these passages from the sermons, and many more could just as easily be cited, Donne contrasts his images of fragmentation and order. Donne of course makes effective use of contrasts for their own poetic sake, but a chaos theorist would immediately recognize that there is more than a casual or coincidental connection between the two. Fractal order is a unique and surprising byproduct of chaos. This is the difference between the "chaotic" and the simply "random": chaotic systems never repeat themselves while remaining an identifiable system, whereas random systems can fall into repetitive cycles because they are free to end back at a point where they once began. (For example, five fish swimming in a tank is a chaotic system because all five will never be in exactly the same position with the same direction and momentum twice; rolling five dice is random because it is perfectly possible to roll the exact same combination several times.) Each chaotic system exists within the borders of its own phase space, so if the system never exactly repeats itself, then a graph of the system's movement (for example, a dot on a piece of graph paper representing the X and Y axis of position and velocity for each of our five fish inside their bounded tank, with samples taken at regular intervals) will necessarily have an infinite number of dots with no two ever taking up exactly the same space. One would expect the dots to appear randomly on the paper and, for a while, they do.

After many iterations, however, a shape starts to take place. ("And as, though all doe know, that quantities / Are made of lines, and lines from Points arise."[18]) This particular kind of shape, only recently identifiable with the help of increasingly powerful computers, is called a "strange attractor." The name represents any force that pulls a chaotic system into a patterned order (such as gravity), as well as a graph of that system that shows its identifiable shape. As we have seen, the only way for an infinity of points to be contained within a finite space is for the lines connecting those dots to take a fractal shape: "its promontories and crannies contain their own promontories and crannies, symmetries and asymmetries, and so do these, and so on." In other words, all strange attractors are by definition fractal.

This is the profound and elusive connection between chaos and order. "It is equally interesting and, I believe, theoretically crucial, that in art and in very different theologies, as in history itself, the positive and negative forces of order and chaos incessantly interact in ways so strikingly cognate to the interactions chaos scientists observe in the dynamics of nature itself," writes Hawkins. What she claims for Milton is, it seems to me, equally true of Donne's *oeuvre*: "Looked at from this angle, the range and variety, the continuous spectrum, of *interactions* between order and chaos, harmony and discord, on every conceivable scale, are what create the enduring power as well as the strangely musical, symphonic beauty of *Paradise Lost* as a whole."[19] The interactions between order and chaos in Donne are scientific, theological, and metaphysical, but they remain ultimately and resolutely *aesthetic*. Strange attractors, for all of their dry mathematical precision, are often stunningly beautiful.

The simplest kind of attractor, such as gravity, simply pulls the dynamic system down to a boring standstill. When there are two or more attractors at work, however, the system will often swing between them in an unpredictable manner, producing the data that could be measured in a strange attractor. Poetically and intellectually, a parallel can be found in the works of Donne since his fractal order is often the direct result of the push-and-pull competition of conflicting ideas. Achsah Guibbory is one of the many critics who have noted how Donne's poetry is marked by paradox and a vacillation between alternatives: "It is appropriate that the state of being vexed by unresolved contraries would be expressed by paradox . . . since paradox is self-contradicting, asserting that mutually contradictory statements are simultaneously true. If Donne felt vexed by contraries, it should not be surprising to find that his poetry is too."

As a result of this complexity, an unexpected simplicity appears, like an attractor emerging from the haze of seemingly random iterations: "Although the canon of his poetry is of a piece—it has a consistency or identity that allows us to recognize a poem as Donne's—it is also varied, full of complex poems exploring his sense of the contradictions at the heart of human experience and desire."[20] Donne, at turns, both longs for and resists both change and permanence. "Several poems bring together the attraction to change and the desire for stability, exploring whether it is possible to have both in love," writes Guibbory. "For though Donne dislikes mutability as it is a sign of mortality, he also seems to dislike stasis, which he identifies with stagnation."[21] What Guibbory and others don't see, but which chaos theory allows us to see, is that Donne intuits rightly that the very chaos of change paradoxically *creates* the long-term stability. It is the voice of Boethius's Philosophia once again, in the accent of twenty-first-century theoretical physicists.

Examples of specific competing attractors in Donne's poems are easy to come by. Sensuality and spirituality are perhaps the two most obvious, exerting their influence on almost all of his lyrics and much of his religious poetry. As much recent scholarship on Donne has been at pains to point out, the two cannot be as neatly divided at Izaak Walton tried to make them in his tidy distinction between pre-conversion "Jack" Donne and the post-conversion "Dean John" Donne. The two forces have been intertwined throughout Donne's life in a complex, interdependent, mutually engendering way. "When we think of Donne as the author of the *Songs and Sonnets*, then, the images which come to mind should include not only the young libertine and apostate but also the disgraced courtier hunched in a damp study at Mitcham," writes Carey.[22] Perhaps as a result of his own paradoxical life, there are several dichotomies that act as pulling attractors for Donne. Carey writes about many of them throughout *John Donne: Life, Mind, and Art* and in the introduction to his edition of Donne's *Major Works*. Carey finds a pattern in many poems "which combines private self-assertion with a public display of submission and conformity,"[23] which Carey connects to the necessities brought on by his Catholic upbringing. "Donne's ambitious nature contained within it, then, contradictory seeds: of self-assertion and of self-negation. Both elements—the wish to make his way in the world, and the wish to be integrated into it—inclined him to an active rather than a contemplative life. As an intellectual, however, he inevitably felt torn between thought and action."[24]

No single attractor works its way through both Donne's "self-assertion" and "self-negation" like the twin concepts of sin and redemption. In a sermon preached at Essex House in December 1618, plants are used as a conceit for the dynamic processes of growth and decay: "And as in the bringing forth, and bringing up, of the best, and most precious, and most delicate plants, men employ most dung, so the greatest persons . . . there is more dung, more uncleanness, more sin in the conception."[25] From the initial condition of Adam and Eve's original sin (discussed brilliantly in Hawkins's chapter "Paradigms Lost"), a complex, unpredictable, and nonlinear chain of events has created an attractor of corruption that pulls us inevitably into the shape of sin, which remains constant across scales of class, race, gender, and nationality: "The body, being without sin, and the soul being without sin, yet in the first minute, that this body and soul meet, and are united, we become in that instant, guilty of Adam's sin, committed six thousand years before."[26] We are caught between the metaphorical attractors of gold and dung, each one feeding on its opposite in a feedback loop, like a positive and negative charge creating a vacuum between them. "If it be a vessel of gold, it is but a vessel of excrements, if it be a bed of curious plants, it is but a bed of dung; as their tombs hereafter shall be but glorious covers of rotten carcases, so their bodies now, but pampered covers of rotten souls . . ."[27]

In the kind of paradoxical twist relished by chaos theorists and literary critics alike, instability itself often seems to work as an attractor in Donne's work. "Donne's imaginative commitment to instability, which seems the most potent single impulse behind his poems, expresses itself in the sermons in many different ways," Carey claims. "It generates, for example, rhapsodies upon the destructive power of supernatural agents."[28] As a result, *movement* is highly characteristic of Donne's dialectic style. The poems have the feel of truly dynamic non-linear systems, partially because of the way Donne's own conflicted personality took shape under the influence of his own personal attractors. The satires in particular, Carey writes, are remarkable less for their social insight than for their impatient physical movement: "This is apparent as much in the vehement, bludgeoning rhythms as in the way the syntax and subject matter are fractured and pushed about. They are hives of energy. In Satire I the verbs describing the actions of the tiresome companion keep the poem mobile. He creeps, skips, grins, smacks, shrugs, stoops, leaps, jogs, drops behind, overtakes, and finally: 'flings from mee / Violently ravish'd to his lechery.' This frantically animated 'humorist' is a facet of Donne himself, though one which he strives to externalize and condemn. His 'humorous' (i.e., changeable, mercurial) disposition, in love, studies and religion, was something he endlessly and unavailingly deplored . . ."[29]

The force of competing attractors creating an ironic permanence of impermanence, or in chaos theory terms a fractal order self-similar across scale emerging from the unpredictability of single iterations, is of course a central theme in "Elegy 5: Change." Disorder is the *natural* state, associated with the random flight of birds and the untamed animal nature of the beasts, and what order there is that emerges from the "attraction" of sexual conquest is itself contained within the larger context of freedom:

> Another fouler using these meanes, as I,
> May catch the same bird; and, as these things bee,
> Women are made for men, not him, nor mee.
> Foxes and goats; all beasts change when they please,
> Shall women, more hot, wily, wild then these,
> Be bound to one man, and did Nature then
> Idly make them apter to'endure then men?
> They'are our clogges, and their owne; if a man bee
> Chain'd to a gallery, yet the galley'is free . . .[30]

Change, women's constancy, and sin are prevailing attractors in much of Donne's poetry. There is one thing that all three have in common: Eve. "What could be called 'the apple effect' in *Paradise Lost* perfectly illustrates what chaos theorists metaphorically term 'the butterfly effect'," writes Hawkins. A "small change in one variable can have a disproportional effect on other variables—the flapping of a single butterfly's wing today may produce a change that affects other variables so that what the global atmosphere actually does diverges from what it otherwise would have done."[31] If fractals and attractors are how order lurks deep within the dark heart of chaos, then what chaologists refer to, prosaically, as "sensitive dependence on initial conditions" is how chaos lurks like a moving clot in the otherwise stable and regular heart of order. Just as no one can confidently predict whether or not it will be sunny or wet past three or four days' time because too many interlocking variables are at work in the nonlinear dynamic system of the weather, no one can confidently predict what the near future will bring in most other aspects of life. All we have are patterns and attractors (e.g., Wednesday is Bridge night), but as we have seen, the strange attractors of chaotic systems show patterns without ever exactly repeating themselves (no Bridge night ever has the same exact deal of cards twice). Historical hindsight can therefore be dizzying: "What, for example, if Cleopatra's nose had been an inch longer?" asks Hawkins. "And what might *not* have happened if the Viennese Academy of Art had sent a letter of acceptance, rather than twice rejecting, the eighteen-year-old Adolph Hitler, who had consequently taken over the chairmanship of an Austrian architectural firm . . . and so on."[32] Our most innocuous acts can have global consequences, or as Charles Coffin puts it, "the individual fact or experience" can participate "in the universal."

Sensitive Dependence on Initial Conditions

The words above are Coffin's definition of "metaphysical." The metaphysical is not so much the juxtaposition of otherwise unrelated ideas or objects as it is a realization that all objects are, somehow, connected in physical and spiritual chains of cause and effect that we cannot clearly see. "This is an attitude that takes its rise from the unified personality, which, while realizing the contradiction involved in its position, nevertheless, refuses to relax hold on the idea that the very nature of things in essence is an interpenetration of mind and matter," writes Coffin. "When cast into its most general and comprehensive terms, the metaphysical problem with which the poet is concerned, as stated above in other words, is the relation of the Many to the One."[33] Indeed, the title of chaos theorist Edward Lorenz's seminal paper in 1972, "Does the Flap of a Butterfly's Wings in Brazil Set Off a Tornado in Texas?" seems as appropriate a title for a metaphysical conceit as for a talk at a scientific conference.[34] "And what at first was call'd a gust, the same / Hath now a stormes, anon a tempests name," Donne writes in "The Storme."[35]

For Donne, sensitive dependence on initial conditions takes many forms. In its simplest sense, the closing of one door is the satiric opening of another: in "Cales and Guyana," "one things end doth still beginne a new."[36] In his theology, however, sensitive dependence strikes a more ominous tone. We have already seen how God alone is able to trace back the unknowable origins of worm meat back to its origins in our human flesh. Like the Greek gods before them, the Christian angels and devils can not only thoroughly know our world, but also alter it for better and for worse, in a trice. They can do so because they exist in a "middle Condition," that fractal space between dimensions, affecting our world but also detached from it, their actions having real consequences in our time line but themselves existing apart from time. In a sermon from November 19, 1627, Donne argues that angels

> are Creatures, that have not so much of a Body as *flesh* is, as *froth* is, as a *vapor* is, as a *sigh* is, and yet with a touch they shall molder a rocke into lesse Atomes, then the sand that it stands upon; and a milstone into smaller flower, then it grinds. They are Creatures *made*, and yet not a minute elder now, then when they were first made. . . . They are super-elementary meteors, they hang between the nature of God, and the nature of man, and are of middle Condition.[37]

These "Riddles of Heaven" are nevertheless associated with us, despite their distance, in the same fractal way that all things are associated with one another in God's creation: We share a universal essence in Coffin's sense of the "metaphysical," a pattern that runs deeper than the local iterations of surface appearances. "If by being *like* the Angels, we shall *know* the Angels, we are more then *like* our selves, why doe we not know our selves?" Donne asks, which brings him back to the paradox of spiritual unity of physical individuation.

> Why did not *Adam* know, that he had a Body, that might have been preserved in an immortality, and yet submitted his body, and mine, and thine, and theirs, who by this union are to be made one, and all, that by Gods goodnesse shall be drived from them, to certaine, to inevitable

Death? . . . How little we know our selves, which is the end of all knowledge![38]

Change and Transition

Sensitivity to the "butterfly effect" makes a dynamic system open to radical change, usually as rapid as it is transformative. A favorite example of complexity theorists is the sand pile—one grain of sand is unlikely to make a difference at any single moment in time, but sooner or later, one of those single grains of sand will inevitably trigger a collapsing landslide. These are called "phase transitions," and chaos theorists have identified unexpected stabilities in the ways one state of matter exponentially bifurcates into another. Systems that are most receptive to phase transitions are those that live on the "edge of chaos." As Mitchell Waldrop explains it,

> It's a lot like the difference between solids, where the atoms are locked into place, and fluids, where the atoms tumble over one another at random. But right in between the two extremes . . . at a kind of abstract phase transition called 'the edge of chaos,' you also find *complexity*: a class of behaviors in which the components of the system never quite lock into place, yet never quite dissolve into turbulence, either. . . . These are the systems that can be organized to perform complex computations, to react to the world, to be spontaneous, adaptive, and alive.[39]

Living, writing, and reading on the "edge of chaos" is all undeniably relevant to art, according to Hawkins: "Order and chaos arising together may resonate beyond their artistic confines. Pure disorder does not. And neither does pure order."[40]

This essay is not the place to survey the vast body of criticism and numerous examples from Donne's biography, poetry, and theology which make him our preeminent writer of *change*. The pervasive imagery of fluidity, melting, and the transformation of the physical into the spiritual and back again creates the dominant impression that Donne's imagination is attracted first to those regions where matter exists on the edge of chaos and where reality exists as a fraction between the whole numbers of strictly defined dimension. "The 'metaphysical conceit' is usually thought of as a device for establishing similarity between incongruous objects," writes Carey. "But Donne is not ultimately interested in similarity. He uses the conceit, rather, as a means of generating change, in both the materials and the structure of his poems. In "A Valediction: of Weeping," for example, the development of thought follows the changing identities suggested for the tears—coins, fruits, seas, mirrors, globes. By means of the conceit, the poem projects instability."[41]

Instability, yes, but also a kind of paradoxical stability that emerges precisely *because* of the edge-of-chaos state of physical matter in "A Valediction: of Weeping." The world of the two lovers is fragile and open to change by random forces beyond their control: the sea may or may not drown the speaker on the journey that parts them, and "Since thou and I sigh one anothers breath, / Who e'r sighes most, is cruellest, and hasts the others death."[42] The famous opening image of transformation is essentially fractal, insofar as the pattern (here, the lover's face) remains constant across the scales of a tear, a coin, the face itself, a globe, and ultimately the world. In Donne's treatment, therefore, the significance of the pattern takes on a greater rather than a lesser meaning for its imaginative extension. A fractal exists between dimensions, the exclusive property of neither one physical state or another. The face of the lover is just as "pregnant" with hope of a reunion and the promise of new life on the coin as it is on the map of the world. As the speaker travels at sea, each of the images in the poem would be available to him on a daily basis: tears, coins, fruits, maps, the moon. By finding the essence of his lover in all of these things, he keeps her with him, even in the very air he breathes and exhales. Because of the fractal positioning of the microcosm/macrocosm imagery, transitional states of matter keep the lovers closer, not further apart; they preserve more than they destroy. As Donne expresses it in "The Exstasie,"

> But as all severall soules containe
> Mixture of things, they know not what,
> Love, these mixt soules, doth mixe againe,
> And makes both one, each this and that.[43]

CIRCLES AND ARROWS OF TIME

One way in which Donne does *not* always seem to follow the prescripts of chaos theory is in his circular conception of time. When physical systems make phase transitions from state to state, or when they break down into chaos because of their sensitivity to some influential initial condition, they are speeding down a one-way street. Even when water turns to steam and condenses back into water again, it never has quite the same volume and molecular makeup that it once had. As Tom Stoppard puts it in his play "Arcadia," there is no un-stirring the jam in the rice pudding to turn it back into its original lump—"Indeed, the pudding does not notice and continues to turn pink just as before."[44]

Similarly, chaos theorists Ilya Prigogine and Isabelle Stengers, in their authoritative and comprehensive book on the implications of nonlinear science on questions of time and causality, *Order out of Chaos*, close the question on time travel. It may be theoretically possible to move forward in time by slowing your own aging in relationship to those around you (see Einstein's theory of relativity), but it is not possible to move backwards. Simply put, how would we know where exactly to find the past? Where is all the information about the past stored? What supercomputer could ever hold enough information to completely recreate even one instant in the life of one square inch of space? The further back you go, the data would simply multiply exponentially. Every choice in every millisecond is a fork in the road, and no one is keeping a road map to trace our way backward. If every dynamic system on earth (or even in the universe) is delicately linked to every other one, then the simple act of reappearing in the past makes it null and void. It is then no longer the "past" as we think of it, just an alternative present. "There is both one time and infinite times. Time is the great arrow which couples all systems together and a multitude of arrows which constitute the bifurcations and changes of each individual system," write John Briggs and F. David Peat. "Each of us has his or her own autonomous irreversible arrow but that arrow is intertwined with the irreversible arrow of the universe."[45]

There is a circularity at work in much of Donne's imagery that belies modern science, but Donne was working from the context of a pre-Newtonian paradigm that usually privileged theology over raw experimental data. There is nothing in Donne's imaginative sense of circular time that ultimately contradicts his basic notions of the fractal nature of life and art, however. At times it even strengthens it. We have already seen how God exists as exactly the kind of supercomputer described above, pulling together the scattered atoms from every moment of the past to reconstruct the physical bodies of all people on the final day. Nothing ever seems to be completely lost in Donne's poems: stretched, expanded, transformed, melted, or etherealized, perhaps, but never *lost*.

The protective "circle of time" is an image found throughout the sermons. "The principle of participating likeness between God and man, in the pattern of Christ's life developing circularly in time, is the central notion," writes Terry Sherwood in his subtle consideration of Donne's theological use of time, *Fulfilling the Circle*.[46] Sherwood argues that the paradox of the necessarily linear experience of the individual Christian in time and the necessarily nonlinear promise of God throughout time is resolved in Donne's thought as a matter of "the individual's conscious and willing participation in God through the Spirit's recreative motions. It follows that the fruition of time, its fullness, becomes a function of human epistemology and psychology."[47] The incessant attractor of time, in other words, is managed through the unstable and variable initial conditions of each individual's unique consciousness. Although Sherwood does not discuss chaos theory, much of what he writes endorses the fractal logic I am claiming is found throughout Donne's work. Donne's theology of time, according to Sherwood, relies upon a fractal self-similarity that resolves the paradox of time's one-directional flow on the small scale and circular flow on the cosmic scale:

> Just as man's likeness to God is renewed through the Spirit's internal and external motions, time is fulfilled simultaneously by the Spirit moving within the believer. . . . The principle of participating likeness between God and man, in the pattern of Christ's life developing circularly in time, is the central notion. Like Christ's life, Christian history is an irreversible circle of sequential events from beginning to end, ever informed by God who 'fills every place' as the circles' omnipresent centre. . . . Christ, his life, the Church, man's soul, man's life, and the history of salvation—all are 'circles.' Thus, like man's soul, time is God's creature made in his likeness, for God himself is an unending circle containing both a beginning and end in himself.[48]

Time, in other words, starts to look a bit like the graph of a strange attractor. It repeats itself in circular loops, but since it is different in the consciousness of each individual believer's psychology, it will never take exactly the same path twice. The fractal pattern it makes, therefore, goes to infinity even as it is readily identifiable within its defined limits. When the timeless God enters into the timebound world of human history through Christ, Sherwood claims, "Time is fulfilled thereby. . . . However, fullness does not contradict time's own continuing, developing sequentiality, which follows Christ's pattern." This "pattern" has its set of pulling attractors, its self-similar fractal dimension, and even its element of "strangeness." In Sherwood's words, "Although Christ's own fullness was contained in each moment, his life paradoxically developed in a pattern of birth, suffering, death, and resurrection. That pattern itself will be completed in the spiritual lives of erected, conforming believers. The Spirit will fill these members of Christ's Body, the Church, according to Christ's pattern."[49] As in the love poetry found in the *Songs and Sonnets*, Donne will sometimes create his Möbius-strip circles by using word play that moves in two different directions simultaneously, creating the "between dimensions" effect of his recurring dialectic of the physical and the spiritual. In the Easter sermon of 1622, Donne plays on the word "end," using it to point both to a single moment in the temporal flow of lived experience (e.g., the "end" of the story) and the promises of God that exist for all eternity (e.g., means and "ends"). The result is a sense of timelessness contained within time, like the infinite line drawn on a single page of paper:

> *When I begin*, says God to *Eli, I will make an end;* not onely that all Gods purposes shall have their certain end, but that even then, when he begins, he makes an end: from the very beginning, imprints an infallible assurance, that whom he loves, he loves to the end: as a Circle is printed all at once, so his beginning and ending is all one.[50]

As readers of Renaissance poetry know better than Einstein, time is experienced by all lovers on a relative scale. "Me thinkes I lyed all winter, when I swore, / My love was infinite, if spring make'it more," writes Donne in "Loves Growth."[51] Love, from its initial condition of a chance meeting, snowballs into an exponentially increasing force, "As princes doe in times of action get / New taxes, and remit them not in peace, / No winter shall abate the springs encrease."[52] The infinity of passion is nevertheless fractal. It is recursive, circling back upon itself, moving both inward and outward to trace the kind of infinity that lives between dimensions and is self-similar across scale, like the ever-expanding coastline of Britain. Using the geometric image of concentric circles and the one-way chronological image of stirred water, the speaker's love begins locally, stretches to the infinity of the heavens, and then finds the heavens themselves grounded in the woman standing before him:

> If, as in water stir'd more circles bee
> Produc'd by one, love such additions take,
> Those like to many spheares, but one heaven make,
> For, they are all concentrique unto thee . . .[53]

In "The Computation," the infinity which defies rational conception is again immediately contrasted with a logical sense of the grounded and precise. Love, it seems, demands both ways of thinking. What binds the two competing attractors of infinity and finitude, as in so many of Donne's other poems based on a dialectic or dichotomy, are the *emotions*. "Its feelings are not mathematical, but measureless," writes Carey. "It tosses its vast chronological periods about with wry abandon, to indicate that time and number belong to a different and less serious realm of reality than the experience of loss. . . . He confronts the linguistic problem, original, challenging and ambitious. Number is used to defeat numerability; quantity, to annihilate quantification."[54] The effect of chaos theory has been the same on many mathematicians—number is used to defeat quantification, and calculation gives way to a sense of wonder. James Gleick's best-seller *Chaos: Making a New Science*, largely consisting of often-ecstatic interviews with chaos theory's founders, sometimes reads more like an anthology of spiritual autobiographies than a book about advanced mathematics.

An Integrated System: *Devotions upon Emergent Occasions*

In conclusion, I will summarize ways to apply chaos theory to Donne by looking very briefly at a single work that embodies them both as the integrated systems that they are, not just as an assortment of decontextualized correspondences between selected fragments of science and selected fragments of literature (as has sometimes been the case when chaos theory is imported for the purposes of literary criticism and theory). The *Devotions upon Emergent Occasions* are Donne's most movingly personal and subtly reasoned considerations of fate, willpower, and plain bad luck. Just as chaos theory describes how deterministic systems governed by sensitive dependence find themselves organizing into strange attractors, so does Donne describe how the illness that overtakes him in the *Devotions* creates a chaos in his individual life that nevertheless falls into stable patterns of fractal correspondence between the microcosm of the self and the macrocosms of the entire human family and the "body" of Christ.

The first and second devotions emphasize how disorder can interrupt the most ordered and well-managed system with no warning:

> Variable, and therfore miserable condition of Man; this minute I was well, and am ill, this minute. I am surpriz'd with a sodaine change, & alteration to worse, and can impute it to no cause, nor call it by any name. We study *Health*, and we deliberate upon our *meats*, and *drink*, and *Ayre*, and *exercises*, and we hew, and wee polish every stone, that

goes to that building; and so our *Health* is a long & a regular work; But in a minute a Cannon batters all, overthrowes all, demolishes all; a *Sicknes* unprevented for all our diligence, unsuspected for all our curiositie; nay, undeserved, if we consider only *disorder*, summons us, seizes us, possesses us, destroyes us in an instant.[55]

Donne's conception of the sudden violence of this unwelcomed sensitive dependence is drawn from the highly dynamic imagery of fluidity, disruption, and nonlinearity. The *"little world"* of Man has "*earthquakes* in him selfe, sodaine shakings; these *lightnings*, sodaine flashes; these *thunders*, sodaine noises; these *Eclypses*, sodain fiery exhalations, these *rivers of blood*, sodaine red waters."[56] Yet it is the inherent nonlinearity of life that best draws us into the phase space of a shared experience with others. It is the very dissipative nature of man that links us with the eternal, since the only constancy in life is change itself:

> The *Heavens* are not the lesse constant, because they move continually, because they move continually one and the same way. The *Earth* is not the more constant, because it lyes stil continually, because continually it changes, and melts in al the parts thereof. *Man*, who is the noblest part of the *Earth*, melts so away, as if he were a *statue*, not of *Earth*, but of *Snowe*.[57]

The third devotion introduces the contradictory nature of God's nontemporal logic. As God's eternal plan intersects with Donne's impatient desire to return to health, paradoxes pull us into the zone between dimensions where time and timelessness meet in a desperate and delirious fever. "As yet God suspends mee betweene *Heaven* and *Earth*, as a *Meteor*; and I am not in Heaven, because an earthly bodie clogges me, and I am not in the Earth, because a heavenly *Soule* sustaines mee."[58] Time is also the subject of devotion 14, where it too becomes fractal, existing in layers and concentric circles operating across various scales rather than as an uninterrupted one-way trajectory:

> If we consider *Eternity*, into that, *tyme* never Entered; *Eternity* is not an everlasting flux of *Tyme*; but Tyme is as a short *parenthesis* in a longe *period*; and *Eternity* had bin the same, as it is, though time had never beene; If we consider, not *Eternity*, but *Perpetuity*, not that which had no *tyme* to beginne in, but which shall out-live *Tyme* and be, when *Tyme shall be no more*, what *A Minute* is the life of the Durablest *Creature*, compared to that?[59]

The circles reappear in the twenty-first devotion, where the paradox of stillness contained within a shell of constant motion introduces something akin to Einstein's relativity: a man in a rocket moving close to the speed of light for a year will have aged less than his family back on earth. For Donne, the larger patterns that exist in an eternal physical and spiritual space keep coming back to the personal pain that he cannot escape in every moment of his present. Wheels within spinning wheels, pendulums hanging from swinging pendulums, all trace out the patterns of strange attractors within the defined limits of their round phase space—the very repetition of Donne's language suggests the feedback loop of the future collapsing back on the past and present:

> Man hath no *center*, but *misery*; *there* and onely *there*, hee is *fixt*, and sure to finde himselfe. How little soever he bee *raised*, he *moves*, and moves in a *circle*, giddily; and as in the *Heavens*, there are but a few *Circles*, that goe about the whole world, but many *Epicicles*, and other lesser *Circles*, but yet *Circles*, so of those men, which are *raised*, and put into *Circles*; few of them move from *place* to *place*, and passe through many and beneficiall places, but fall into little *Circles*, and within a step or two, are at their *end*, and not so well, as they were in the *Center*, from which they were *raised*. Every thing serves to *exemplifie*, to *illustrate* mans *misery* . . .[60]

What grounds us within the chaos of time and mitigates to an extent "mans *misery*" is, as with other dynamic systems, the stabilizing force of attractors. "*Honors, Pleasures, Possessions*" are undeniably attractive, but they are meaningless free of the phase space of *time* which gives them their relative value. "We rejoyce in the comfort of *fire*," Donne writes, "but does any Man cleave to it at *Midsomer* . . . ?"[61]

Devotion 17 is of course one of literature's most famous expressions of human empathy. Seen in the full context of the *Devotions*, its impact is even greater. Sensitive dependence on initial conditions brings Donne an illness that could just have easily struck another man, or struck him at another time—"a *pinne*, a *combe*, a *haire*, pulled, hath gangred, & killd," he writes in meditation 12. Yet precisely because death can come ungracefully to any man at any time or place, we are bound together in the collective patterns of our own randomness. Each chapter of a book says something different, yet all are bound together in a single volume (e.g., the phase space of our single iterations). The tolling of the funeral bell is an image of regularity, consistency, repetition, and the inevitable progress of linear time. Again, however, *because* of the linearity of time and the regularity of the ultimate attractor (death) that the tolling bell represents, the dissipation and phase transitions that keep us all from ever remaining the quite the same person from moment to moment are the sources of our continual renewal. Theologically, Donne finds this renewal in the larger community of God's people; *emotionally*, however, the renewal takes the form of an awareness that all people (and by implication in his choice of similes, all objects) are, and will always be, connected:

> Another Man may be *sicke* too, and sicke to *death*, and this *affliction* may lie in his *bowels*, as *gold* in a *Mine*, and be of no use to him; but this *bell* that tels mee of his *affliction*, digs out, and applies that *gold* to *mee*: if by this consideration of anothers danger, I take mine owne into Contemplation, and so secure my selfe, by making my recourse to my *God*, who is our onely securitie.[62]

Finally, as the disease runs its course and the physicians give him hope for recovery, Donne does what many other chaos theorists will do after him: he looks through the lens of his own experience into the full complexity of Nature and finds it delicately balanced on the edge of chaos and order. When the doctors in devotion 19 look for the stability they need to find in the disease before they can safely purge it, Donne seizes the irony and recognizes the inherent irregularity of anything that operates as randomly and spreads as uncontrollably as an illness: "Why should wee looke for it in a *disease*, which is the *disorder*, the *discord*, the *irregularitie*, the *commotion*, and *rebellion* of the *body*? It were scarce a *disease*, if it could bee *ordered*, and made obedient to our *times*."[63] Nature as a whole, however, has the stability that is missing in the chaos of its individual parts. "Why should wee looke for that in *disorder*, in a *disease*, when we cannot have it in *Nature*, who is so *regular*, and so *pregnant*, so forward to bring her worke to perfection, and to light?"[64]

There is no better image from Nature to represent *fractal order* than a tree. Each part is connected to every other part, the forking of the smallest twigs shares an identical fractal dimension with the forking of the largest branches, and no two leaves are exactly alike even though they can be simulated with a simple mathematical algorithm. In devotion 19, man is joined in a metaphysical conceit with a tree to show how no two grow the same way under the same conditions, yet each obeys laws that prevent them from breaking their prescribed boundaries and escaping their phase space of ripeness in time. There is no better image from Nature to represent a *chaotic* system than a cloud. A cloud exists as a link in an endless chain of cause-and-effect, touching and touched by water, temperature, sunlight, air pressure, tides, etc. It has discernible shape, but as you get closer to it, you realize that its precise edges can never be measured. Each cloud will have the same fractal dimension as every cloud in the system of which it is a part, and each mountain-shaped peak of the cloud has smaller mountain-shaped peaks within it, as far as anyone can get close enough to see. A cloud can be a source of renewal, cleansing, and refreshment, but a random variation somewhere along the chain of events can just as easily make it a source of violence, destruction, and gloom. In devotion 19, the cloud is (typically for Donne) both. The physicians look for the telltale clouding of the sick man's eyes or blood as indications of his improving or worsening illness. At a low point, Donne considers God's assurance to be nothing but a cloud, something insubstantial and transient.[65] But the winds of the dialectic soon blow the other way, and the chaotic cloud becomes the stable attractor of God's promises: "Thy *great Seale* to all the world, the *raine-bow*, that secured the *world* for ever, from *drowning*, was but a *reflexion upon a cloud*. A *cloud* it selfe was a *pillar* which guided the *church*, and *the glory of God*, not only *was*, but *appeared in a cloud*."[66] Donne concludes in his prayer to God, "none of thy *Indications* are *frivolous* . . ."[67] In 1972, Edward Lorenz would write something quite similar, in his own way, about butterflies.

Donne's difficult and complex poetry has resulted in a critical reception history that has agreed on little else besides the fact that Donne's poetry is difficult and complex. A. J. Smith's *John Donne: the Critical Heritage* combined with Deborah Larson's *John Donne and Twentieth-Century Criticism* provide ample testimony that "evidence for both acceptance and rejection of a variety of beliefs, theories, and observations exists, and emphasizing one side over the other, here as in other areas of Donne scholarship, has made that scholarship at once illuminating and problematic."[68] This is partially a result, of course, of the way in which dialectical and dichotomized argumentation is built into the poems themselves. Donne's poetry is regularly characterized by a vacillation between alternatives, like opposing currents following the same attractor, or a single current pulled between two attractors. This makes his rhetoric paradoxically ordered and chaotic at the same time: "It is appropriate that the state of being vexed by unresolved contraries would be expressed by paradox," writes Guibbory. "If Donne felt vexed by contraries, it should not be surprising to find that his poetry is too. Although the canon of his poetry is of a piece—it has a consistency or identity that allows us to recognize a poem as Donne's—it is also varied, full of complex poems exploring his sense of the contradictions at the heart of human experience and desire."[69]

It is useful here to make the connection between Donne's life and his dialectical method, as Guibbory implies. For example, the notorious difficulties of dating Donne's poems prevent us from constructing a convincing and consistent narrative that accounts for the linear trajectory or "progression" of his ideas. At any one time, we can find Donne's poetry drawing from scholastic philosophy, Ptolemaic astronomy, Paracelsian medicine, Calvinist theology, or simple hedonism ("Full nakedness, all joyes are due to thee"[70],) in no particular order and with little discernible consistency. What is the biographer's loss can be the critic's gain, however. "Rather than constructing a progression in Donne's various treatments of love, perhaps we should see the variations and contradictions as expressing conflicting attitudes and contrary impulses that might characterize a full range of experience and desire," Guibbory suggests.[71] The poetry, then, begins to look less like "a life" and more like *life*. Since Donne thinks of his poetry as a process rather than as a collection of static objects, our own experience as readers perforce takes on something of the same nonlinear pattern. "Literary study is, after all, the analysis of complex systems that cannot be well-defined by linear models," writes Allen W. Grove. "Chaos theory provides us with not just a metaphor, but a methodology for better understanding this complexity."[72]

Donne lived in a time of profound change in the sciences, not unlike what relativity, quantum physics, and chaos theory have created in our own time. In Donne's time, as now, there are some who embrace the new science, others who reject or avoid it by returning to fundamentalist readings of scripture, and still others who forge their own hybrids of science and religion. There is a general consensus that Donne explored the New Science of Copernicus and others, overturning the old Ptolemaic certainties, but he ultimately remained on the side of a non-rational faith. This provided a chaotic critical situation that suggest the oppositional dialectics in Donne's own poetry. "In some studies, evidence about Donne's attitude toward the New Science is used to support a particular theory about his beliefs, but since this evidence is sketchy and often contradictory, it can be used to support almost any other hypothesis," writes Larson. "Those believing Donne is essentially medieval can maintain that he rejected the New Science, while those believing he is akin to the moderns show that he embraced it with open arms."[73] In "The First Anniversarie," Donne associated the New

Science with the rising chaos of the world, ultimately leading to the end of everything stable and worthwhile about life. Donne fought against the irrationality of chaos by ironically turning to nonrational intuitive faith. The death of a young girl by the accident of a fever and the shifting of a global scientific paradigm are linked in Donne's associative imagination—both portend the darkness of chaos.

> And new Philosophy cals all in doubt,
> The Element of fire is quite put out;
> The Sunne is lost, and th'earth, and no mans wit
> Can well direct him, where to looke for it.
> And freely men confesse, that this world's spent,
> When in the Planets, and the Firmament
> They seeke so many new; they see that this
> Is crumbled out againe t'his Atomis.[74]

The attractors are missing ("She that had all Magnetique force alone, / To draw, and fasten sundred parts in one"[75],) and the reassuring symmetries of the universe seem nonlinear and irregular. The sentiments are not dissimilar, one suspects, to the faculty comments written on the dissertation proposals of the first generation of chaos theorists:

> We thinke the heavens enjoy their Sphericall
> Their round proportion embracing all.
> But yet their various and perplexed course,
> Observ'd in divers ages doth enforce
> Men to finde out so many'Eccentrique parts,
> Such divers downe-right lines, such overthwarts,
> As disproportion that pure forme.[76]

Still, as we have seen, Donne was able to consider both sides of most every issue, finding correspondences between the most dissimilar ideas and objects. Between the knowable three dimensions of lived experience in time and the fourth dimension of faith in things spiritual, he found a vocabulary that let him articulate in poetry the equivalent of a fractional number somewhere between three and four. This combination opened a door for him into a clear and focused vision of how, and why, all things in Heaven and Earth are wheels within wheels in cascades of concentric circles.

Notes

1. I would like to thank John Carey for serving as guest editor for this essay. Thanks also to the members of the Project on the Rhetoric of Inquiry at the University of Iowa for their suggestions and input.

2. John Carey, *John Donne: Life, Mind and Art* (New York: Oxford University Press, 1981), 90–91.
3. Harriett Hawkins, *Strange Attractors: Literature, Culture and Chaos Theory* (New York: Prentice Hall/Harvester Wheatsheaf, 1995), 10.
4. Ibid., 4.
5. Readers wishing good general introductions to chaos and complexity theory are directed to James Gleick, *Chaos: Making a New Science*; Edward Lorenz, *The Essence of Chaos*; John Briggs, *Turbulent Mirror: an Illustrated Guide to Chaos Theory and the Science of Wholeness*, and Mitchell Waldrop, *Complexity: the Emerging Science at the Edge of Order and Chaos*. For those particularly interested in literary applications, see N. Katherine Hayles, *Chaos Bound: Orderly Disorder in Contemporary Literature and Science*; Alexander Argyros, *A Blessed Rage for Order: Deconstruction, Evolution, and Chaos*; and of course Harriett Hawkins, *Strange Attractors: Literature, Culture, and Chaos Theory*.
6. John Donne, *The Divine Poems*, 2d ed., edited by Helen Gardner (Oxford: Clarendon Press, 1978), 13.
7. Ibid.
8. Ibid., 2.
9. John Donne, "Selected Prose," in *Selected Prose*, edited by Helen Gardner Evelyn Simpson, and Timothy Healy (Oxford: Clarendon Press, 1967), 101.
10. John Donne, *Devotions Upon Emergent Occasions*, edited by Anthony Raspa (Montreal and London: McGill-Queen's University Press, 1975), 19.
11. Ibid.
12. Donne, "Selected Prose," 335.
13. John Donne, *The Elegies and the Songs and Sonnets*, edited by Helen Gardner (Oxford: Clarendon Press, 1965), 86.
14. Ibid., 53.
15. John Donne, *The Sermons of John Donne*, ed. Evelyn M. Simpson and George R. Potter (Berkeley and Los Angeles: University of California Press, 1953–62), 10.115.
16. Ibid., 3.109–10.
17. Ibid., 3.113.
18. John Donne, *The Epithalamions, Anniversaries and Epicedes*, ed. W. Milgate (Oxford: Clarendon Press, 1978), 44.
19. Hawkins, *Strange Attractors*, 52.
20. Achsah Guibbory, "John Donne," in *The Cambridge Companion to English Poetry: Donne to Marvell*, edited by Thomas N. Corns (Cambridge: Cambridge University Press, 1993), 124.
21. Ibid., 144.
22. Carey, *John Donne*, 93.
23. John Carey, "Introduction," in *John Donne: The Major Works* (Oxford: Oxford University Press, 1990), xx.
24. Carey, *John Donne*, 62.
25. John Donne, *The Major Works*, edited by John Carey, Oxford World's Classics (Oxford: Oxford University Press, 1990), 279.
26. Ibid., 280.
27. Ibid.
28. Carey, "Introduction," xxxi.
29. Carey, *John Donne*, 62–63.
30. Donne, *The Elegies*, 19–20.
31. Hawkins, *Strange Attractors*, 41.

32. Ibid., 42–43.
33. Charles Monroe Coffin, *John Donne and the New Philosophy* (Morningside Heights, NY: Columbia University Press, 1937), 16.
34. The paper is reprinted in Edward Lorenz, *The Essence of Chaos* (Seattle: University of Washington Press, 1993).
35. John Donne, *The Satires, Epigrams and Verse Letters*, edited by W. Milgate (Oxford: Clarendon Press, 1967), 56.
36. Ibid., 51.
37. Donne, *Sermons*, 8.106.
38. Ibid., 8.106–07.
39. M. Mitchell Waldrop, *Complexity: The Emerging Science at the Edge of Order and Chaos* (London: Penguin, 1992), 293.
40. Hawkins, *Strange Attractors*, 164.
41. Carey, "Introduction," xxiv–xxv.
42. Donne, *The Elegies*, 70.
43. Ibid., 60.
44. Tom Stoppard, *Arcadia* (London: Faber & Faber, 1993), 5.
45. John and F. David Peat Briggs, *Turbulent Mirror: An Illustrated Guide to Chaos Theory and the Science of Wholeness* (New York: Harper & Row, 1989), 148.
46. Terry G. Sherwood, *Fulfilling the Circle: A Study of John Donne's Thought* (Toronto: University of Toronto Press, 1984), 13.
47. Ibid., 10.
48. Ibid., 11–13.
49. Ibid., 13.
50. Donne, *Sermons*, 4.96.
51. Donne, *The Elegies*, 76.
52. Ibid., 77.
53. Ibid.
54. Carey, *John Donne*, 127.
55. Donne, *Devotions*, 7.
56. Ibid., 7–8.
57. Ibid., 11.
58. Ibid., 17.
59. Ibid., 71–72.
60. Ibid., 111.
61. Ibid., 72.
62. Ibid., 87.
63. Ibid., 97.
64. Ibid.
65. Ibid., 102.
66. Ibid., 103.
67. Ibid.
68. Deborah Aldrich Larson, *John Donne and Twentieth-Century Criticism* (Rutherford, N.J.: Fairleigh Dickinson, 1989), 160.
69. Guibbory, "John Donne," 124.
70. Donne, *The Elegies*, 15.
71. Guibbory, "John Donne," 139.
72. Allen W. Grove, "Sexual Chaos: The Gothic 'Formula' and the Politics of Complexity," in *Disrupted Patterns: On Chaos and Order in the Enlightenment*,

edited by Theodore E. D. Brown and John A. McCarthy (Amsterdam and Atlanta: Rodopi, 2000), 116.
73. Larson, *John Donne*, 159.
74. Donne, *The Epithalamions*, 27–28.
75. Ibid., 28.
76. Ibid., 29.

III
Fashion, Culture, and Politics

"An artificiall following of nature": Dryden, Etherege, and the Perfection of Art

Michael Neill

> *But I, imagining my selfe often times how this grace commeth ... finde one rule that is most generall ... And that is to eschue as much as a man may ... too much curiousnesse, and (to speake a new word) to use in everye thing a certaine disgracing to cover arte withall, and seeme whatsoever he doth and saith, to cover it without paine, and (as it were) not minding it .... Therefore that may bee saide to be verie arte, that appeareth not to be arte, neither ought a man to put more diligence in any thing than in covering it: for in case it be open, it looseth credite cleane and maketh a man little set by.*
>
> —Baldassare Castiglione

IN THE BEST KNOWN PORTRAIT OF JOHN WILMOT, EARL OF ROCHESTER, the Restoration courtier-poet is shown crowning a monkey with a wreath of bays. The painting is generally attributed to Jacob Huysmans, but its witty conceit was surely of Rochester's own devising. On the personal level, it can be read as a statement of aristocratic disdain for the fame that most poets notoriously desire, but it is also capable of a more philosophic interpretation as an ironic allegory of the vexed relationship between art and nature. The monkey itself is charged with ambiguous significance: a representative of the animal nature from which humankind vainly seeks to distance itself, its anthropoid appearance nevertheless suggests a burlesque of humanity, a type of sterile mimicry whose behavior seems deliberately to ape our own. In Rochester's own poetry, the monkey features both as a beast whose obedience to natural instinct is contrasted with the "forc'd disguise" of human culture in the "Satyr [against Reason and Mankind]" (lines 5, 150), and as the "curious miniature of Man" in "A Letter from Artimiza in the Towne to Chloe in the Countrey"—a "dirty chatt'ring Monster" that serves as a kind of parodic mirror for the garrulous Fine Lady and for the social artifice and affectation of her urban world (lines 135–70).[1] The monkey of the portrait performs both of these roles.

At first sight the naked grimacing primate could hardly contrast more starkly with the elegantly poised figure of the courtier, with his artificial trappings of full-bottom wig, rich satins, and lace. Yet the two opposites are also distorted mirror images of one another: in his left hand the poet holds what appears to be a sheaf of verses, while in the same hand his simian rival grasps a blank page torn from one of the books on the table. The creature seems to offer this ragged leaf as an ironic tribute to the poet, even as Rochester extends his own accolade in recognition of the superior artistry constituted by this spontaneous act of literary vandalism. The two are not, however, locked in a closed circle of reflection—for just as the grinning gaze of the laureate monkey is fixed upon the poet, so Rochester's own level, slightly mocking stare seems directed at his portraitist, as if in contemptuous challenge to the very art that has immortalized him upon the canvas. Looked at from this point of view the portrait becomes an ingeniously artful celebration of nature's resistance to art, and a satire of artificiality that arrogantly parades its own witty artifice.

In this recessive play with aesthetic paradox, the Rochester portrait exploits a characteristic Restoration ambivalence about the rivalry of art and nature—one that surfaces in numerous works of the period, but which is given particular prominence in the two key texts I wish to examine here: John Dryden's great critical manifesto, the *Essay of Dramatic Poesy*, and George Etherege's definitive comedy of manners, *The Man of Mode*. Though one is concerned with poetry and the other with the arts of social conversation, each is constructed as an extended (though deliberately inconclusive) debate on the allowable limits of artifice and the means by which it is best made conformable with nature.

In the *Essay of Dramatic Poesy*, written just eight years after the return of Charles II, Dryden offered to chart the literary future of a nation whose muses, buried for twenty years "under the ruins of a monarchy," could now again achieve their proper eminence through the general "restoration of our happiness" promised by the restoration of the King: already, he declared, "we see revived poesy lifting up its head, and . . . shaking off the rubbish which lay so heavy on it."[2] But, for all this nostalgic gesturing, what Dryden had in mind was no mere return to prewar achievements, since art now faced new challenges. This, he believed, was a time in which, thanks to extraordinary advances in natural science, "almost a new nature has been revealed to us"; if poetry was to respond to this philosophic revelation, it would have to move beyond the raw achievements of what Crites dismisses as "those credulous and doting ages from Aristotle to us."[3] The "genius" of the new age, Dryden insisted, would ensure that the arts and sciences together, "being pushed on by many hands, must of necessity go forward. . . . for if natural causes be more known now than in the time of Aristotle, it follows that poesy and the other arts may, with the same pains, arrive still nearer to perfection."[4]

Despite the brash self-assurance of its rhetorical stance, however, the *Essay* is a work notoriously riven by uncertainty, and Dryden's doubts about his own most cherished principles are implicit in the decision to cast his argument in a dialectical form. The dialogue is a device that seeks to contain intellectual contradictions within the bounds of polite conversation, but in the notably unresolved ending of Dryden's debate, the effort of containment is abandoned. The cultural anxieties that inform the *Essay*, and that ultimately frustrate its promised resolution, are particularly evident in its approach to the two key terms of its argument—*art* and *nature*. Dryden's conflicted ideas as to how the first could best represent the second are revealed in the participants' disagreements about the merits of ancient rules and models, in their diverging views of classicising French practice versus English pragmatism, and in their extended dispute over the advantages and disadvantages of rhyme.

But it is in his attitudes towards Shakespeare and Jonson that Dryden comes closest to an open admission of his own ambivalence. Through his mouthpiece Neander, the writer sets up Jonson—"the most learned and judicious writer which any theatre ever had"—as the English author whose work (in the example of *The Silent Woman*) offers "the pattern of a perfect play."[5] But Dryden remains haunted by the disturbing recollection that in the previous age Shakespeare's reputation had been so far above Jonson's that even "Sir John Suckling, and with him the greater part of the courtiers, set our Shakespeare far above him,"[6] and this chimes with his own uncomfortable awareness that Shakespeare's practice somehow threatens to confound all the best precepts about the decorum of dramatic poetry. Elaborating a comparison that can be traced back through Milton to Jonson's own verses in the First Folio, Dryden balances Shakespeare's "natural" genius against Jonson's meticulous "art": if Jonson was "the more correct poet," then Shakespeare, Neander concedes, was "the greater wit"; if "Jonson was the Virgil, the pattern of elaborate writing," then "Shakespeare was the Homer, or father of our dramatic poets; I admire [Jonson], but I love Shakespeare."⁷ It is this instinctive attraction to the seemingly artless genius of his predecessor that Dryden acknowledges in the prologue to *Aureng-Zebe* (1675), where his increasingly frustrated sense that "Nature flies him like enchanted ground" makes him confess to the experience of a "secret shame . . . at Shakespeare's sacred name."⁸

Announcing a growing weariness with the restrictive fetters of "his long-lov'd mistress, rhyme," the prologue anticipates Dryden's abandonment of this cornerstone of his poetic practice in his next tragedy, *All for Love* (1677).⁹ But it was surely the poet's already gathering doubts about the practical sustainability of his own theories that led to the abrupt and inconclusive termination of the *Essay's* debate, just at the point where his surrogate, Neander, is in full flight on the virtues of rhyme:

> Neander was pursuing this discourse so eagerly, that Eugenius had called to him twice or thrice, ere he took notice that the barge stood still, and that they were at the foot of Somerset Stairs, where they had appointed it to land.¹⁰

With this wryly managed anticlimax, Dryden returns us to the outer framework of his dialogue, which he introduced in such dramatic fashion with an evocation of the distant sea-battle of Lowestoft (June 13, 1665)—a detail to which I now want to give some attention.

The obvious model both for the dialectical design of Dryden's essay and for the conspicuously unfinished form of its debate was Castiglione's *The Courtier* (1528). Castiglione's conduct book, though it is concerned with courtly manners rather than with the art of poetry, nevertheless adumbrates a similar aesthetic, discovering in the courtier's cultivation of "grace" something close to the poet's or the painter's "artificiall following of nature."¹¹ However, Dryden's construction of a dramatic frame, contrasting the violence of an offstage battle with the civilised restraint of the intellectual combat on the Thames, was his own addition. Surprisingly little critical attention has been applied to this device, but it does, I believe, have an important relationship to the essay's treatment of art and nature. In the first place, it establishes an ironic context for the literary broadsides of Neander and his friends. The irony, which is playful rather than destructive, is activated as soon as Crites imagines their debate as a battle of civilisations:

> If confidence presage a *victory*, Eugenius, in his opinion, has already *triumphed over* the ancients: nothing seems more easy to him, than to *overcome* those whom it is our greatest praise to have imitated . . .¹²

This benign irony surfaces again through the defiant cultural nationalism of Neander, when he imagines the struggle with the French for literary supremacy as a heroic contest, in which English poesy throws off the confusion of the interregnum years to assert itself against the foreign enemy, rather as on the political stage war against the Dutch has replaced the confusion of internecine strife:

> If this comedy [Ben Jonson's *The Silent Woman*] and some others of his were translated into French prose . . . I believe the controversy would soon be decided betwixt the two nations. . . . But we need not call our *heroes* to our aid. Be it spoke to the *honour of the English*, our nation can never want in any age such who are able to dispute *an empire of wit* with any people in the universe. And though *the fury of a civil war*. . . . had buried the muses under the ruin of a monarchy; yet, with the restoration of our happiness, we see revived poetry lifting up its head, already shaking off the rubbish which lay so heavy on it. We have seen since his majesty's return many dramatic poems *which yield not to those of any foreign nation*, and which deserve all laurels but the English.[13]

To begin with, the *mise-en-scène* seems to place the text at a disconcerting distance from its nominal subject, as the "vast floating bodies" of the English and Dutch fleets "[move] against each other in parallel lines," and the sound of their cannonades alarms the citizens of London "in a dreadful suspense of the event." Sharing in the general consternation, the four participants in Dryden's narrative (Eugenius, Crites, Lisideius, and Neander) are anxious to get closer to the uncertain noise of battle—muted as it is by the sound of the "great fall of waters" under London Bridge. As they move down the Thames, however, the noise of fighting recedes in what they quickly recognize as a "happy omen of our nation's victory." At this point, a relieved Crites drily contemplates the awful "price" of the battle, which turns out not to be the great cost in men and treasure, but the fearful effects wrought upon the combatants by "those eternal rhymers, who watch a battle with more diligence than the ravens and birds of prey; and the worst of them surest to be first upon the quarry."[14] It is this alarming prospect that launches the four critical rivals into their own great contest upon the river.

An additional irony is set up, of course, by the way in which Dryden's evocation of the far-off battle has itself already begun the process of literary transformation that Crites anticipates. In a passage of singularly beautiful prose, the clamor of gunfire is metamorphosed first into "distant thunder," and then (with an oddly domestic touch) into the rustle of nesting birds in a chimney:

> having disengaged themselves from many vessels which rode at anchor in the Thames, and almost blocked up the passage towards Greenwich, they ordered the watermen to let fall their oars more gently; and then, every one favouring his own curiosity with a strict silence, it was not long ere they perceived the air to break about them like the noise of distant thunder, or of swallows in a chimney—those little undulations of sound, though almost vanishing before they reached them, yet still seeming to retain somewhat of their first horror, which they had betwixt the fleets.[15]

The strange alchemy of the movement from the conspicuously formal images of battle to their remote and delicate aftermath in those "little undulations of sound" might almost be taken for an allegory of the process through which poetry, in Neander's words, seeks to "[make] art and order appear as loose and free as nature"[16]—the process which it is the main business of the ensuing dialogue to regulate and define.

Neander pronounces this formula for reconciling art with nature in the course of his debate with Crites about the appropriateness of rhymed verse in dramatic compositions; it amounts to a restatement of the famous Latin formula that Crites, declaring that in rhyme "the hand of art will be too visible," has himself deployed: "*Ars est celare artem* . . . it is the greatest perfection of art to keep itself undiscovered."[17] There is a teasingly recessive paradox in this apparently simple prescription, since for the work to have its full effect as "an artificiall following of nature" (in Castiglione's phrase),[18] the audience must have a sense of the exquisite artfulness by which they are persuaded to think it so artlessly natural. Neander seeks to address this paradox in terms of an elaborate and somewhat contorted theory of art as "nature wrought up to a higher pitch." Plays, he argues, are like statues on tall buildings that are "made greater than the life, that they may descend to the sight in their just proportion";[19] by the same token, the use of rhyme can be justified as "an art which appears"—but only like the shadows that are used to create three dimensional effects in painting,

> which being to cause the rounding of it cannot be absent; but while that is considered, they are lost: so while we attend to the other beauties of the matter, the care and labour of the rhyme is carried from us, or at least drowned in its own sweetness, as bees are sometimes buried in their own honey.[20]

Crites has been arguing that because "a play is an imitation of nature," rhymed dialogue can only violate probability, "since no man without premeditation speaks in rhyme"; the deployment of rhyme to point and ornament repartee is especially absurd, since "it will look rather like the design of two, than the answer of one: it will appear that your actors hold intelligence together; that they perform their tricks like fortune-tellers, by confederacy."[21] But Neander responds with a particularly telling analogy: there is no more reason, he argues, for such devices to appear distractingly artificial than for the patterns of a "well contrived" dance to seem forced and unnatural.

> You see there the united design of many persons to make up one figure: after they have separated themselves in many petty divisions, they rejoin one by one into a gross: the confederacy is plain amongst them, for chance could never produce anything so beautiful; and yet there is nothing in it that shocks your sight.[22]

It is, I think, no accident that only a few pages later the essay, its arguments still unresolved, should draw to a close with just such an exhibition of dancing, in a passage that returns to the note of refined lyricism first sounded in the opening sequence:

> The company were all sorry to separate so soon, though a great part of the evening was already spent; and stood awhile looking back on the water, upon which the moonbeams played, and made it appear like floating quicksilver: at last they went up through a crowd of French people, who were merrily dancing in the open air, and nothing concerned for the noise of guns which had alarmed the town that afternoon.[23]

The exquisitely elegiac tone of this passage is directly related to the subtlety with which it associates the flickering play of moonbeams on the water with the carefree dancing of the French crowd. The dancers' supreme unconcern for the noise of guns at sea implicitly extends to the momentous critical battle upon the Thames, placing it in a doubly ironic light—even as the elusiveness of "floating quicksilver" now seems to mock the clumsy efforts of art to capture the looseness and freedom of nature. Yet of course we cannot be unaware that (like the artful figures produced by the "confederacy" of the dancers themselves) the whole thing is an effect of art, a brilliantly self-consuming artefact that perfectly captures the ambiguities of Dryden's aesthetic—albeit by an odd kind of epiphany that gestures at perfections which elude the most refined reaches of artifice.

Something very similar, I want to argue, happens in that most finished exemplar of Restoration dramatic art, George Etherege's *The Man of Mode* (1676)—a play whose title suggests a self-conscious tribute to Dryden's pioneering comedy of manners, *Marriage à la Mode*, but whose aesthetic preoccupations make it in many ways a theatrical counterpart of the *Essay of Dramatic Poesy*. Like the *Essay*, *The Man of Mode* pays homage to the aesthetic ideals of *The Courtier* in its efforts to reconcile the contradictory imperatives of art and nature, and it too contrasts the exaggerated artifice of French preciosity with the more natural easiness of English practice—though where Dryden's approach is charged with a sometimes painful anxiety, Etherege elaborates his tissue of paradox with a cool detachment reminiscent of the Rochester portrait. Like the *Essay*, *The Man of Mode* is equipped with a frame that at once ironizes the agonistics of its action, and bathes its ending in a peculiar nostalgia, while the "petty divisions" of its civil warfare are once again resolved in the fragile confederacy of a dance.

There can be little doubt that Etherege was well acquainted with Dryden's criticism,[24] and, read with the *Essay of Dramatic Poesy* in mind, *The Man of Mode* might almost be construed as an elaborate metacommentary on Dryden's aesthetic arguments. It is not necessary to suppose that the *Essay* was consciously in Etherege's mind when he wrote the play, however: it is rather that the symmetry between the two works, despite the generic difference that separates them, reveals something important about the structures of thought and feeling in Restoration culture.

At the beginning of *The Man of Mode*, the play's infamously libertine protagonist, Dorimant, entering *"in his gown and slippers, with a note in his hand made up,"* recites the opening couplet from Edmund Waller's poem "Of a War with Spain, and a Fight at Sea":

> Now, for some ages, had the pride of Spain
> Made the sun shine on half the world in vain.
>
> (1.1.1–2)[25]

Were it not for the conspicuously domestic setting and the hero's incongruously casual undress, the tone of these lines might for a moment tempt the audience with the notion that they are about to witness the performance of a tragedy.[26] As it is, like the description of the naval battle at the beginning of Dryden's *Essay*, this invocation of a world of martial heroism outside the play suggests an ironic counterpart to the social combat of the plot—the erotic warfare and battles of wit in which (as his shoemaker predicts) Dorimant will emerge as a conquering Caesar of the boudoir.[27] Waller's elegant verses find their sordid domestic equivalent in the "dull, insipid . . . billet-doux" that Dorimant has prepared for Mrs. Loveit: "written in cold blood," this missive is dismissed as a piece of labored artifice by its self-deprecating author, who disdainfully labels it "a tax upon good nature" (3–5), but "heighten[ed] with a little invention" by Medley (185) and with the assistance of Belinda's "genius," it will successfully set in motion the histrionic plot in which Dorimant engages to play his triumphant part (185, 212).

By drawing immediate attention to the hero's self-conscious artistry, the Waller quotation serves to initiate the complex set of reflections on the rivalry of art and nature that lies at the heart of Etherege's comedy, even as it supplies a kind of wryly inflated motto for the action that ensues. The device will be repeated at a number of key points in the play, where Dorimant and his equally witty mistress Harriet decorate their encounters with verses culled from Waller, Cowley, and Suckling. According to the critic John Dennis, Dorimant's fondness for such tags was one of the details that encouraged contemporaries to identify the hero with Rochester, whose famous idiosyncrasies included a penchant for quoting Waller.[28] But these quotations have a much more important function in relation to the play's aesthetic debate. On the one hand (as Congreve's Millamant, with her admiration for "natural, easy Suckling," reminds us),[29] the air of artless insouciance cultivated by the Cavalier lyricists made them a touchstone for the style of effortless elegance to which both Dorimant and Harriet aspire. But, at the same time, the trick of citation, heightened by the artificiality of rhyme, has the effect of drawing attention to the artifice of the characters' performance—placing their actions in quotation marks, as it were, or functioning as a species of caption that arrests the action and turns it into an exemplary tableau. At the same time, the highly self-conscious deployment of rhyme subtly modifies the audience's response to the couplets that conclude each act—especially because the first of them actually takes the form of another literary quotation, when Dorimant accompanies his exit at the end of act I with verses sung from Shadwell's operatic version of *The Tempest*. Their artificiality made conspicuous in this way, the closing couplets cease to function as the mere dramatic punctuation marks prescribed by theatrical convention, and work like Dorimant's quotations as metadramatic captions, drawing attention to the elegant symmetries of Etherege's design.

Perhaps the most conspicuous example of this captioning effect occurs near the end of the play, at the celebrated moment when the pairing of Dorimant and Harriet is symbolically confirmed through the open "confederacy" of a shared couplet from Waller:

> *Dorimant.* "Music so softens and disarms the mind—"
> *Harriet.* "That not one arrow does resistance find."
> (5.2.88–89)

This is Dorimant's last entrance in the play, and (with the recollection of the Spanish war now transmuted into the pretty skirmishing of Cupid) it is like a reprise of his first entry—except that here the initiative is wrested from the rake-hero by the designed victim of his erotic stratagems. The entry is perfectly cued by the performance of a song, supposedly of Dorimant's own composition, that celebrates the "strange . . . art" of seduction; the shared couplet acts both as a commentary on the seductive artistry of the song itself ("Music so softens and disarms the mind") and as a kind of coda to its rhyming quatrains. Dorimant himself draws attention to the shimmeringly self-reflexive artifice of the moment by proposing a further caption for the scene, freezing it into a painted tableau—only for Harriet to cap him once again by relocating the histrionics of the encounter back into the theater where they belong:

> *Dorimant.* What have we here—the picture of a celebrated beauty giving audience to a declared lover?
> *Harriet.* Play the dying fop and make the piece complete, sir.
> (5.2.93–95)

Not to be outdone, Dorimant proposes to "improve the hint" by incorporating the pathetic tableau into a set of tapestries designed to illustrate "the whole mystery of making love" in the fashion of Ovid's *Ars Amatoria*.[30] But Harriet wins the exchange with the acid observation that no artifice is required to expose a folly so naturally conspicuous that it constitutes its own punishment: "'Twere needless to execute fools in effigy who suffer daily in their own persons" (99–100).

In her wonderful essay on *The Man of Mode,* Harriett Hawkins was among the first to explore the characters' fascination with their own highly wrought theatricality, observing how "the art of love and the art of the theatre . . . merge in a play where the characters are so conscious of behaving artificially."[31] Indeed, it is patently the report of Harriet's talent for satiric mimicry, as much as the accounts of her wealth and beauty, that first arouses Dorimant's interest (1.18–9), and their mutual pleasure in role playing is exhibited both in the lovers' mimicking of each other's style of flirtation (3.3.83–92) and in their public rehearsal of looks and gestures at Lady Townley's soirée (4.1.96–154). The same histrionic delight in what Harriet calls "the dear pleasure of dissembling" (3.1.106) is apparent in her mime of courtship with Young Bellair in act 3 (101–62), in Dorimant's pretence of jealousy over Mrs Loveit's flirtation with Sir Fopling in 2.2, in his adoption of the ludicrous guise of "Mr. Courage" (that lover of bygone "forms and ceremonies," 4.1.11), and in his burlesque mimicry of Fopling (5.1.78–96).

These are not simply exercises in metatheatrical wit, however. Like the meticulous assembling of Dorimant's public "person" at the hands of his valet and shoemaker that occupies the whole of act I, they belong to a world whose systematic aestheticization of social behavior is signalled by the "mode" of the title. Thus the whole point of Dorimant's levee is to display the innate "genius" of the truewit's fancy, as opposed to the mechanical, rulebound imitation that governs the affected style of his Francophile rival, that "great critic . . . in these matters," Sir Fopling Flutter (1.316–28). Fopling is in effect the Lisideius of Etherege's comedy, as firmly wedded to Gallic fashion and to what Harriet dismisses as the "rules of charming" (4.1.106) as Dryden's speaker is impressed by French observation of the "rules of the stage."[32] Dorimant's superiority is systematically affirmed by appeal to the seemingly effortless naturalness of his performance, expressed by his offhand show of disdain for Handy's "unnecessary fiddling," his impatient dismissal of the notion "that a man's excellency should lie in neatly tying of a ribbon or cravat," and his insistence upon "smell[ing] as I do today" (1.303–12). "All that he does and says," the admiring Young Bellair declares, "is so easy and natural" (3.3.22).

Sir Fopling, by contrast, is mocked for the exaggerated artifice of his performance, and for the studious observation of the rules derived from his practice as a pedantic critic rather than a true poet of the mode (3.2.169–70): with the aid of such rules this "bashful English blockhead" has sought to transform himself into "a fine, undertaking French fop" (4.1.365–66), but the regular exercise of his art is persistently frustrated by the presence of another "damned English blockhead"—John Trott, Fopling's lumbering *alter ego*—among his retinue of French dancers (3.3.243; 4.1.274, 287–90). The hopelessness of the entire enterprise is registered in the fop's plaintively expressed hope for the footman that "imitation in time may bring him to something" (4.1.291–92).

Dorimant's exquisitely managed negligence is a version of the *sprezzatura* advocated by the great theorist of courtly manners, Castiglione, who turned the familiar requirement for art to conceal its own artifice to social ends by celebrating the Courtier's performance as an "arte, that appeareth not to be arte."[33] Castiglione's English translator, Sir Thomas Hoby, had rendered *sprezzatura* as "Recklessnesse,"[34] but Etherege's preferred equivalent is "wildness"—another key term (as Virginia Ogden Birdsall recognised in *Wild Civility*) for the understanding of Restoration values.[35] Traditionally the "wild" had been a powerfully negative concept: Standing for all that belonged outside the world of culture in that region of unregenerate nature known as the wilderness, it denoted all that was rude, uncultivated, disordered, barbarous, savage, cruel and destructive.[36] In the playful iconoclasm of Cavalier literature, however, with its fondness for turning familiar pieties on their head, wildness had acquired an unexpectedly positive valency—exemplified in the baroque elegance of lyrics such as Herrick's "Delight in Disorder," from which Birdsall took her title:

> A winning wave, deserving note,
> In the tempestuous petticoat;
> A careless shoe-string, in whose tie
> I see a wild civility:
> Do more bewitch me than when art
> Is too precise in every part.

Even Dryden—despite his high regard for neoclassical rules and his conviction that the imagination (or fancy) was a "Wild and Lawless" faculty that needed to be "Bound[ed] and Circumscrib[ed]" by the regularity of rhyme[37]—manifests something of this suspicious attitude toward excessive artistic precision: the *Essay* defends English writers against the complaint that they fall short of the "regular" perfection of French drama, by arguing that "in most of the irregular plays of Shakespeare or Fletcher . . . there is a more masculine fancy and greater spirit in the writing than there is in any of the French."[38] Translated into social terms, spirit and masculine fancy are precisely the qualities we might associate not only with the more attractive side of Dorimant, but with Harriet too; in them the aesthetic sketched in by Herrick carries courtly *sprezzatura* to an oxymoronic extreme that locates the perfection of urbane artifice in the cultivation of an extravagance that (as Dryden's prologue for the revival of *The Wild Gallant* suggested) would once have been considered "monstrous."[39]

It was in *The Man of Mode*, then, that the preromantic aestheticization of wildness reached its apogee.[40] Preeminent among those whom Foggy Nan the pandering Orange-Woman describes, with mock horror, as "the wild young men o' the town" (1.1.100), is the rake-hero himself. Denounced by Lady Woodvill as "a wild, extravagant fellow of the times" (4.1.301), Dorimant is seen as a kind of civil wild man whose "barbarous" behavior at once bewitches, appalls, and infuriates his rival mistresses, Belinda and Loveit (2.2.93–94, 136). In keeping with the traditional theology that identified wild nature as a consequence of the Fall, Dorimant's wildness is repeatedly associated with the diabolic role in which he is cast by his enemies as "prince of all the devils in the town" (3.3.105–6). But such precisian judgments are destabilized by the carefully developed parallel between Dorimant's aesthetic and that of his sharp-tongued but scarcely vicious inamorata, Harriet. Described by Medley as "wild as you would wish her," and by Dorimant himself as "wild, witty, lovesome, beautiful and young" (1.1.130, 4.3.312–13), Harriet selfconsciously shows off her wildness from the moment of her first appearance in the play. In an episode that exactly matches Dorimant's mock irritation with Handy's "unnecessary fiddling," Harriet bridles against the ministrations of her maid, her reckless impatience contrasting with Mrs Loveit's careful self-inspection the previous scene (2.2.1–5):

> *Busy.* Dear madam, let me set that curl in order.
> *Harriet.* Let me alone. I will shake 'em all out of order!
> *Busy.* Will you never leave this wildness?
> (3.1.1–3)

Her eyes, Harriet teasingly informs Dorimant at their second encounter, "are wild and wandering like [her] passions, and cannot yet be tied to rules of charming"; disingenuously insisting on her own "want of art" even as her prose slips into iambic pentameter,[41] she proclaims that everything about her comes "from nature," even as she accuses her wooer of a contagious "affectation" (3.1.23–24, 38; 4.1.98–106).

Affectation is the social vice that provides the irregular wildness of the witty couple with its aesthetic justification. As Medley's burlesque description of a popular new conduct book entitled *The Art of Affectation* reminds us (2.1.128–36), it stands for a mode of art that, by failing to hide itself, fatally discloses its own unnatural artifice. This manual, Medley claims (in a speech that clearly invites the actor to engage in his own burlesque performance) will teach how to draw up your breasts, stretch up your neck, to thrust out your breech, to play with your head, to toss up your nose, to bite your lips, to turn up you eyes, to speak in a silly soft tone of voice that will infallibly make your person and conversation charming. (2.1.129–33)

With these elaborately codified rules of charming, *The Art of Affectation* represents the bourgeois decadence of Castiglione's social aesthetic. It is the kind of text from which Sir Fopling Flutter, assembled as he ostentatiously is from "originals of the most famous hands in France" (3.2.195–96), has fashioned himself; Dorimant, by contrast, prides himself on his ability never to "mistake art for nature," implicitly comparing the relaxed spontaneity of his own "good nature" (2.2.177–80) with both Loveit's cosmetic arts and the studiously "acquired follies" of that slavish apostle of imitation, Sir Fopling (1.1.333, 4.1.291). If Fopling, in his abject devotion to French originals, resembles Lisideius, the Francophile critic of Dryden's essay, then Dorimant, with his defiant irregularity, love of "variety," and spiritedly "masculine fancy," shares Neander's disdain for the "narrowness of imagination" that results from the "servile observation" of the Gallic rules.[42]

The opposition between affectation and wildness restates, in extreme terms, the familiar contest between art and nature. But it is part of the wit of Etherege's design to confuse this seemingly absolute distinction. When Busy dismisses the "powdering, painting, and . . . patching" of Lady Dapper as "a little *too* pretending" (3.1.14–16; emphasis added), she acknowledges the extent to which pretense, masquerade, and dissembling are an indissoluble part of what it means to have a social identity of any kind in the modish world. However "wild" Dorimant and Harriet may wish to appear, they nevertheless cultivate "an artificiall following of nature" that sets their behavior apart from the raw nature exposed in Loveit when Dorimant successfully "pluck[s] off [her] mask and show[s] the passion that lies panting under" (3.3.294–95). Dorimant's suggestive eating of Foggy Nan's peach (1.1.45 ff.) may invite us to read his amours as the mere satisfaction of natural appetite—the cure of "an irregular fit" by the kind work of Nature, as he himself characterizes his conquest of Belinda (4.2.64–68)— but the theatrical metaphor with which he distinguishes between the pleasures of his new mistress and the tedium of his old ("'Tis not likely a man should be fond of seeing a damned old play when there is a new one acted," 4.2.32–33) complicates that straightforward reading.

No wonder, then, that the erotic combat between the play's central couple should conducted as a teasing debate over the allowable limits of art in the conduct of social relations. Thus when Young Bellair, invoking the ease or grace that distinguishes Castiglione's perfect courtier, insists on the "easy and natural" qualities of Dorimant's wit and person, Harriet (to his astonishment) instantly contradicts him: "Some men's verses seem so to the unskilful; but labour i'the one and affectation in the other to the judicious plainly appear" (3.1.23–24). Dorimant's wildness, she will suggest to Emilia, itself constitutes a mode of self-conscious performance whose artifice is only too apparent to the judicious eye:

> *Emilia.* Mr Dorimant has a great deal of wit.
> *Harriet.* And takes a great deal of pains to show it.
> *Emilia.* He's extremely well-fashioned.
> *Harriet.* Affectedly grave, or ridiculously wild and apish.
> (5.2.53–56)

The ape (as the "dirty chatt'ring monster" of Rochester's *Artemiza to Chloe* reminds us) is a wild creature whose nature is corrupted by senseless mimicry, and apishness—ironically enough—is exactly the vice of which Loveit has accused Dorimant in the previous scene: "Is there a thing so hateful as a senseless mimic? . . . A ridiculous animal, who has more of the ape than the ape has of the man in him" (5.1.89–93). Their quarrel has been provoked by Dorimant's satiric imitation of Sir Fopling, but Loveit makes it plain that her critique extends to his whole habit of artificial dissimulation (lines 105–6)—the same habit to which Harriet refers when she professes to have learned affectation from the histrionics of her admirer's "grave bow" (4.1.98), or when she insists that the truth of his feelings will be corrupted the moment he utters them by the "art" of his "counterfeit" sighs: "Do not speak if you would have me believe it. Your tongue is so famed for falsehood, 'twill do the truth an injury" (5.2.115–16, 118–27). These shafts are accurately aimed, given that Dorimant expressly manages his affairs through the adoption of self-consciously performed roles (1.1.212; 3.2.62, 95–98).[43] But, as her elaborate charade of courtship with young Bellair (3.1.104–61) reveals, Harriet herself is the play's most accomplished actor, willing to "play [her] part" only for "the dear pleasure of dissembling" (3.1.106–7); if it is the genius of her artificial invention that makes Belinda worthy of the hero's attentions when she casts him as Loveit's injured admirer (1.1.208–18), it is equally the wit of Harriet's contrivance that delights his admiration when she casts him as the pompous "Mr Courtage" (3.3.311).

Indeed it is their mutual fascination with "the pleasure of play" (3.3.42–43) that draws the central couple together. The Orange-Woman first piques Dorimant's interest by describing how Harriet has mockingly imitated his own demeanour ("she told me twenty things you said . . . and acted with her head and with her body so like you," 1.1.58–59), and their first encounter climaxes in a piece of mutual mimicry that might have been choreographed directly from the pages of *The Art of Affectation*:

> *Dorimant.* As I followed you, I observed how you were pleased when the fops cried "She's handsome, very handsome, by God she is! and whispered aloud your name – the thousand several forms you put your face into; then, to make yourself more agreeable, how wantonly you played with your head, flung back your locks, and looked smilingly over your shoulder at 'em.
> *Harriet.* I do not go begging the men's, as you do the ladies' good liking, with a sly softness in your looks and a gentle slowness in your bows as you pass by 'em. As thus, sir – (*Acts him*) Is not this like you?
> (3.3.83–92)

Each of their subsequent encounters is marked by the same self-delighting theatricality: their lovemaking at Lady Townley's soirée is orchestrated as a second public display of the art of courtship in which the lovers deliberately assume the expressions and gestures dictated by the very "rules of charming" they privately repudiate (4.1.115):

> *Harriet.* I will put on my serious look, turn my head carelessly from you, drop my lip, let my eyelids fall and hand half o'er my eyes – thus, while you buzz a speech of an hour long in my ear and I answer never a word. Why do you not begin?
> *Dorimant.* That the company may take notice how passionately I make advances of love and how disdainfully you receive 'em.
> (4.1.149–54)

Once again, as in the mock courtship of Harriet and Young Bellair, the characters invoke an expressive regime whose conventions are those of contemporary acting,[44] but whose choreography of feelings also bears an uncomfortable resemblance to that outlined in Medley's *Art of Affectation*.

Something more than aesthetic self-indulgence is involved in their histrionic cultivation, however: the function of social art, after all, is to exercise a necessary formal restraint upon the dangerous extravagance of natural feeling. It is precisely Mrs Loveit's inability to preserve her social mask that renders her vulnerable to the cruelty of Dorimant and Harriet, and exposes her to the laughter of the audience, for whom her passionate rants constitute a gross violation of comic decorum. More than that, Etherege contrives to suggest that the "violence of . . . nature" revealed in Loveit's all too naked emotions (5.2.245–46) constitutes a hazard to the artificial order of society itself, as in her fury she threatens a bizarre apocalypse that will "bring universal ruin and misery on mankind" (2.2.251–52). Thus, even while they celebrate the "wildness" that distinguishes them from the rule-bound dullness of lesser mortals, the witty couple are repeatedly forced to admit the fierce necessity of masking their deepest feelings:

> *Harriet (aside)*. I feel as great a change within, but he shall never know it. (3.3.57)
> *Dorimant (aside)*. He guesses the secret of my heart. I am concerned but dare not show it . . . (3.3.267–68)
> *Dorimant (aside)*. I love her and dare not let her know it. (4.1.132)
> *Harriet (aside, turning from Dorimant)*. My love springs with my blood into my face. I dare not look upon him yet. (5.2.91–92)
> *Dorimant*. . . . I will open my heart and receive you where none yet did enter. You have filled it with a secret, might I but let you know it—
> *Harriet*. Do not speak it if you would have me believe it.
> (5.2.112–15)

The problem with such artificial restraint, of course, is that there is in principle no way of safely breaching it—especially since Dorimant's habit of dissimulation and their mutual fondness for parody render every gesture of sincerity liable to sceptical construction. Frustrated by the recessive ironies of their performance, Busy urges the lovers to abandon artifice: "Faith, madam, now I perceive the gentleman loves you too. E'en let him know your mind, and torment yourselves no longer" (5.2.151–52). But even for Harriet such a violation of the artificial "*rules* of decency and honour" (5.2.151–52; emphasis added) is inconceivable; consequently the love plot can be wound up only by a further reach of irony that leaves it as conspicuously unresolved as the debate in Dryden's *Essay*.

For, even as the marriage of Emilia and Young Bellair is celebrated in the elaborate confederacy of a wedding dance, Harriet and her mother are preparing for their departure to the dismal rusticity of their "great, rambling lone house" in the country—a place whose wintry "desert" condition and "hateful noise of rooks" identify it as the domain of nature, unredeemed by social art (5.2.138,

368–78). It is at this precise moment that Harriet, her ears already filled with the rooks' harsh kawing, indulges in a moment of anticipatory nostalgia: "There's music in the worst cry in London—'My dill and cucumbers to pickle'" (1.379). The wry humour of this line only intensifies its strange pathos, and Harriet's longing for the rough "music" of the streets (set against the stilted harmonies of the ensuing dance) produces a sort of comic epiphany that is the play's equivalent of Dryden's elegiac retrospect, when his company, "sorry to separate so soon," stand for a moment looking back on the "floating quicksilver" of the moonlit Thames. Harriet's affectionate imitation of that London cry suddenly reminds us of a vigorous and unaffected world of urban commerce that is otherwise almost wholly excluded from the fashionable confines of Etherege's play (as indeed from the theater in which it was staged)—except perhaps through the luscious peach that Dorimant receives from the Orange-Woman during his levee, and the fresh nectarines and nosegays that Belinda pretends to have sought in the morning market near the Strand (5.1.27–28, 40). By contrast with the "essences and sweet waters" with which the fashionable world conceals "the stinks of the town" (5.1.30–32), those fruits and flowers might seem to invoke an uncontaminated natural domain, were they not co-opted and corrupted by the artifice of erotic innuendo. Harriet's "dill and cucumbers," however, are something else: they belong to a world in which art, divorced from affectation, appears innocently allied with nature, and where the quotidian is infused with unexpected music. But, like Dryden's evanescent play of moonbeams, this teasing glimpse of the ineffable lies beyond the reach of any language available to the denizens of the mode: as imaginary, perhaps, as the love between Harriet and Dorimant itself may be—sustained as that is solely by the pressure of comic convention and the sentimental desires of the audience—it is apprehensible only as an elusive flicker on the mirrored surface of Etherege's irony.

In the end *The Man of Mode* is no more able than the *Essay of Dramatic Poesy* to resolve its conflicted attitudes toward those expressions of human ingenuity (or perversity) that it variously characterizes as art, artifice, and affectation. But it regards even its own ambivalence with wry amusement. Etherege presents a world where knowledge of the social arts comprehended in "the mode" is the crucial determinant of power. Yet in a society sustained by the studious observation of manners, the relaxed grace commended by the courtly ideal requires the cultivation of "a certain disgracing"; if it is not to seem like affectation, Etherege suggests, the easy and natural must show itself off in a charade of wild spontaneity. The play's archly ambiguous title seems to point impartially toward either the "modish man" Dorimant (2.2.29) or "this man of mode" Fopling (5.2.357) as the principal object of its satire. Between the contradictory imperatives represented by these rivals, the one ludicrously affected and the other dangerously extravagant, there is no viable middle way, with the result that the difference between them is always threatened with collapse.

The unalloyed affectation of Sir Fopling [for whom "a room is the dullest thing without [a mirror]" and "no . . . woman is worth the loss of a cut in a caper" (42.80–81; 5.2.332)] results in antisocial narcissism, but wildness (as Dorimant's cruelty reminds us) always threatens to topple into a barbarous extravagance capable of undoing the social order altogether. Moreover the selfconsciousness with which the true man of mode endeavors to distance himself from his false opponent renders even his wildness liable to the charge of affectation. When Harriet accuses Dorimant of counterfeiting his passions with the same suspicious "ease" that women employ in painting and patching, the rake responds with a defense whose straight-faced irony is exquisitely impenetrable: "the inimitable color in your cheeks is not more free from art than are the sighs I offer" (5.2.124–25). With the absolute poise of that artfully offered "truth" we are back in the recessive ironies and graceful insolence of Rochester's enigmatic portrait, in a world where, if is not quite the case that (as Polixenes has it in *The Winter's Tale*) "The art itself is nature" (4.4.96), at least for one "lucky minute" it can seem to be so.

Notes

This quotation is taken from Baldassare Castiglione, *The Book of the Courtier*, trans. Sir Thomas Hoby, intr. W. H. D. Rouse (London: Dent, 1928), 45–46.

1. Cited from Keith Walker, ed., *The Poems of John Wilmot, Earl of Rochester* (Oxford: Shakespeare Head Press / Basil Blackwell, 1984), 86–87. For a conjecture that the monkey may be intended to satirize Dryden, see Keith Walker, "Lord Rochester's Monkey (Again)," in Nicholas Fisher (ed.), *That Second Bottle: Essays on John Wilmot, Earl of Rochester* (Manchester: Manchester University Press, 2000), 81–87.

2. John Dryden, *An Essay of Dramatic Poesy*, in Edmund D. Jones (ed.), *English Critical Essays: Sixteenth, Seventeenth, and Eighteenth Centuries* (London: Oxford University Press, 1947), 157. All quotations are from this edition; emphases are my own.

3. Ibid., 111.
4. Ibid., 111, 118.
5. Ibid., 151, 149.

6. Ibid., 150.
7. Ibid., 152.
8. Cited from Keith Walker and Frank Kermode, eds., *John Dryden* (Oxford: Oxford University Press, 1987), 139. Unless otherwise indicated, all citations from Dryden's poems are to this edition.
9. Ibid.
10. Dryden, *Essay*, 174.
11. Castiglione, pp. 43, 79.
12. *Essay*, 111 (emphasis added). Dryden works the same analogy in reverse in his *Annus Mirabilis* when, at the opening of the *Fourth Day's Battle*, Prince Rupert's guns "speak thick like angry men" (line 47).
13. Ibid., 157.
14. Ibid., 104, 105.
15. Ibid., 104–5.
16. Ibid., 165.
17. Ibid., 160.
18. Castiglione, 79.
19. *Essay*, 170.
20. Ibid., 171.
21. Ibid., 159–60.
22. Ibid., 171.
23. Ibid., 174.
24. Not only did Dryden and Etherege move in the same literary circles, but one of the four participants in his debate, Lisideius, is even thought to be modeled on Etherege's friend Sir Charles Sedley.
25. All quotations from *The Man of Mode* are from the New Mermaid edition, ed. John Barnard (London: Ernest Benn, 1979).
26. This impression would have been reinforced if the lines were spoken (as they were surely meant to be) within the scenic stage behind the proscenium arch—a space that Restoration convention dedicated principally to tragic action.
27. See Swearing Tom's suggestion at 1.1.243–45 that Dorimant's lampoons constitute the scandalous equivalent of Julius Caesar's commentaries on his triumphant campaigns in Gaul.
28. See his *Defence of Sir Fopling Flutter* in *Critical Works,* ed. E. N. Hooker, vol. 2 (Baltimore: Johns Hopkins University Press, 1939–42), 248.
29. William Congreve, *The Way of the World* , 4.1, in Eric S. Rump (ed.), *The Comedies of William Congreve* (Harmondsworth: Penguin, 1985), 377; appropriately enough for a heroine in whom the "natural" and the "artful" appear indistinguishable (line 1, p. 328), Millamant demonstrates Suckling's naturalness with a couplet about amatory art.
30. For the Ovidian influence on the play, see Harriett Hawkins, *Likenesses of Truth in Elizabethan and Restoration Drama* (Oxford: Clarendon Press, 1972), 84.
31. Hawkins, *Likenesses of Truth*, 89.
32. *Essay*, 129.
33. Castiglione, 46.
34. Ibid., 48.
35. Virginia Ogden Birdsall, *Wild Civility: the English Comic Spirit on the Restoration Stage* (Bloomington: Indiana University Press, 1970).
36. For traditional constructions of wildness, see Edward Dudley and Maximilian E. Novak, *The Wild Man Within: An Image in Western Thought from the Re-*

naissance to Romanticism (Pittsburgh: University of Pittsburgh Press, 1972), esp. Hayden White, "The Forms of Wildness," 3–38. Earl Miner's essay, "The Wild Man through the Looking Glass" in the same volume (87–114) explores the relationship between wildness and the libertine tradition. Arguably the rehabilitation of wildness as a natural corrective to the corruptions of artifice begins with the primitivism of Montaigne's influential essay "Of the Cannibals" (*Essays* I, xxx), where his Brazilian indigenes are described as "even savage, as we call those fruit those fruits are *wilde*, which *nature* her selfe, and of her ordinarie progresse hath produced: whereas indeed they are those which our selves have altered by our *artificiall* devices. . . . there is no reason, art should gaine the point of honour of our great and puissant mother *Nature*."; cited from John Florio (trans.), *Montaigne's Essays*, 3 vols. (London: Dent, 1910), pp. 219–20 (emphasis added).

37. Preface to John Dryden, *The Rival Ladies* (1664), cited from John Harrington Smith, Dougald MacMillan et al. (eds), *The Works of John Dryden*, 9 vols. (Berkeley: University of California Press, 1962), vol. 8, 99. Cf. also *Essay*, 173: "[Rhyming] verse is a rule and line by which he keeps his building compact and even, which otherwise lawless imagination would raise either irregularly or loosely." There was, of course a politics to this Restoration preference for the "rule" and "law" of rhyme, which Milton brought out clearly in his prefatory note to the second edition of *Paradise Lost* (1674), where, scorning French theory and contemporary fashion, he offered his epic as "a example set, the first in English, of *ancient liberty recovered* to heroic poem from the troublesome and modern *bondage of rhyming*"—cited from John Carey and Alistair Fowler (eds.), *The Poems of John Milton* (London: Longmans, 1968), 457. Dorimant's professed scorn for rules is one aspect of his (pseudo-)revolutionary persona—see my "'Heroic Heads and Humble Tails': Sex, Politics, and the Restoration Comic Rake," *The Eighteenth Century: Theory and Interpretation*, 24 (1983), 115–39.

38. *Essay*, 148.

39. In this prologue, written in 1667, four years after the comedy's first appearance, Dryden affected a mock-astonishment at the transformation whereby his "monstrous lewd" protagonist would now appear to "the town" as "a very civil man" (Walker, *John Dryden*, 65, lines 15–18).

40. For some perceptive comments on the significance of wildness in the play, see John Barnard's introduction to the New Mermaid edition, xxix–xxxi.

41. On this point, see Birdsall, *Wild Civility*: "at the very moment when [Harriet] is impudently apologizing for her 'want of art', she is speaking in blank verse and thus at once parodying such 'art' and suggesting the special quality of her own artistic control, organic to her essentially poetic nature" (96–97).

42. *Essay*, 146, 148.

43. Cf. Robert Markley, *Two-Edg'd Weapons: Style and Ideology in the Comedies of Etherege, Wycherley and Congreve* (Oxford: Clarendon Press, 1988): "Dorimant's 'Nature' is his 'Art'; he takes Loveit's 'damn'd dissembler' as a compliment" (128).

44. On the emerging eighteenth-century rules for external representation of emotion, see George Taylor, "'The Just Representation of the Passions: Theories of Acting in the Age of Garrick," in Kenneth Richards and Peter Thomson (eds.), *The Eighteenth Century Stage* (London: Methuen, 1972), 51–72; and Joseph R. Roach, "Power's Body: The Inscription of Morality as Style," in Thomas Postlewait and Bruce A. McConachie (eds.), *Interpreting the Theatrical Past; Essays in the Historiography of Performance* (Iowa City: University of Iowa Press, 1989). Roach notes how Augustan culture encouraged such externalization as a means to regulate the activity of the emotions: "They transform Passions into manners, for if Passions may not be controlled, style can" (99–118).

Discourses on Health and Leisure and Modern Constructions of Holidays at the Restoration Spas

Manuel J. Gómez-Lara

For the treasures of Thracia
In Memoriam Harriett Hawkins

THE CONCEPT OF PLACE—THE SYMBOLIC INTERACTION BETWEEN ENVIronments and humans—has been used in the fields of cultural geography and anthropology as a repository of information about social behavior.[1] This concept will help us approach a series of Restoration works focusing on life at the spas in the late seventeenth century. Medical treatises, travelogs, and literary pieces draw an iconography of the wells based upon several stereotypes: the confusion of social rank, the purging effects of the waters, and sexual promiscuity. I will argue that it is this constructed picture of the spas, rather than a naturalistic environmental record, that designates these fashionable natural spaces as contact zones, suitable for an appealing display of nontraditional attitudes towards class and gender. Eventually all these discourses contributed to the cultural understanding of the spas as places of mirth and fun in which everyday conflicts were to be set aside, thus helping to redefine, in a way that was more appropriate to London citizens, the boundaries between productive and leisure time.

I

The complex interplay of courtship and adulterous relations in a play like Thomas Shadwell's *Epsom Wells* (1673)[2] seems to demand an appropriate urban scenario. In Epsom, the visitors organize the day going from the wells to their lodgings, meeting in gardens where there are walks where one can see and be seen. Nevertheless there is an asymmetry between this evoked scenario and contemporary topographical descriptions of Epsom, thereby challenging any realistic interpretation of the literary locale.

William Schellinks's detailed drawing of Epsom in 1662 does not show the village but the Downs, a plot of barren land with a hut in the middle, which housed the well and shrubs interspersed with people.[3] Schellinks had to stay at a guesthouse because inns could not be found at Epsom, and he explained that many visitors had to lodge at nearby villages. Samuel Pepys also had problems finding accommodation. He visited Epsom twice in the 1660s and noted that he slept "in a little hole we could not stand upright in" (25 July 1663) and again in an "ill room" (14 July 1667). This situation could not have changed drastically by the time Shadwell wrote his play and it only seems to have improved towards the turn of the century. In 1690, Celia Fiennes still complained after her arrival to Epsom that the wells were dirty, with no basin or pavement, and the town unsophisticated.[4] However, during her second stay in 1712, she noticed major rebuilding and a new series of amusements and enterprises that were making the town flourish.[5] A year later, Toland's description of Epsom[6] ratifies Fiennes's impression, and so does Defoe's in his *Tour* (1724–26).

The style of life portrayed in the spa plays and poems produced during the period 1663–1700 seemed to publicize certain forms of leisure that took time to materialize as actual commodities. Osborne and Weaver have characterized the years 1663–1700 as a period of transition at the spas in which previous investments that appear "to have been demand led" are replaced rather by "catering for expanded tourism through innovation."[7] As one of the female leads in *Epsom Wells* asserts, "London is so empty, 'tis a very wilderness this vacation" (1.2.14–15). Is she just quoting a familiar image to the audiences about the spas as holiday resorts or projecting an enticing offer for future clients?[8]

It is my contention that the literary spas provided a mental picture, a specialized imaginary landscape,[9] in which the well-to-do urbanized populace of the Restoration could construe and explore certain social practices outside the formal decorum of everyday city life. The relation between the spas as natural spaces and spas as literary constructions can be obscure and puzzling, so a conceptual model encompassing both real and signified place may help us toward a better understanding of its cultural significance.

II

Several works have addressed the relations between the Restoration spas and their literary constructions. Reginald Lennard's chapter on wells, "Watering-places," draws evidence mainly from travelogs, natural histories, diaries, and medical treatises rather than from literary works. The analysis of special literary topographies was Richard H. Perkinson's target in his "Topographical Comedy in the Seventeenth Century." Perkinson focused on comedy to assert that "the effect of locale . . . may be seen in the treatment of manners, in the plot and in the Dramatis Personae of a comedy" and argued for the value of locale as one of the strategies of realistic comedy: "Locale then performs a double and somewhat contradictory function: the particular place contributes to realism or credibility; its characteristic atmosphere or reputation, by extension and exaggeration, to improbability."[10]

Perkinson assumes the existence of fixed public images for the places he lists—walks, fairs, markets, wells—without further considerations of their changing cultural value during the second half of the seventeenth century. J. Douglas Canfield's discussion of *Epsom Wells* addresses the sociological implications of the phenomena; he argues against an idealized interpretation of Epsom as a privileged "site of freedom" and prefers to see it as a microcosm: "a state of apparent suspension of the order of society and at least partial subversion of its official discourse, it serves at the same time to reveal the interconnectedness of the levels of society and to reaffirm the power of the class at the top of its hierarchy."[11] But Canfield's enlightening reading of Shadwell's play proves somehow defective if we try to expand his conclusions to other works on the same topic; besides, it ignores the physical status of these places and the diversity of discursive realms engaged in their presentation.

In order to articulate those questions concerning both the natural and the literary spas as part of one single reality created by its signifying practices,[12] I will borrow the conceptual model of "place/territoriality" developed by David Sack in two of his books: *Human Territoriality* and *Homo Geographicus*. For Sack, a certain natural space becomes a place as the result of the intervention of human agency in three interconnected realms: meaning, social relations, and nature. The construction of a place demands the interaction between the natural realm of space and the cultural realms of meaning and social relations. This interaction may be visualized as a loop-movement between the three realms. This loop-movement can originate at any of them, although when the three realms are at work, each full movement along the realms determines a new stage in the cultural construction of that place.[13] Sack frames social relations within the so-called "in/out loop," that is, what place includes and excludes (territorial rules); these rules of place require social power to stipulate and enforce them. As it overlaps the other realms, it socializes parts of nature and meaning, making them adhere to social norms.[14] The physical aspects of nature, which condition the cultural construction of place, are visualized in the "spatial interaction loop." Territorial rules originate to control and reorient spatial relations; but the information flow may help to challenge those same rules and, consequently, the power system they support.[15] Finally, the realm of meaning is framed within the "surface/depth loop," as reading a landscape always involves the issue of appearance and reality. Cultural landscapes may help to reify a hegemonic set of beliefs and disguise gender inequality or social injustice, but meaning also engenders its own problematization, and by doing so it may replace a surface or appearance with another that was formerly its subordinate; this new appearance in its turn will activate a new loop movement by altering spatial relation and rules of "in/out place," and so the circuit continues.[16] Reading the spas as cultural landscapes "in the making" may help us to focus upon the lifestyle associated with them: leisure and fashion, social mobility, or even the presentation of male and female desire.

III

Some of the wells had been known since Classical times and others came into use during the Middle Ages, but it was during the sixteenth and seventeenth centuries that a large number of them were rediscovered or newly found.[17] The pamphlet *A True and Exact Account of Sadlers Well* tells how this spot "was famed before the Reformation for several extraordinary cures"—hence its old name "Holywell." At the time the friars from the Priory of Clarkenwell who frequented the place "made the people believe that the virtues of the Waters proceeded from the efficacy of their Prayers."[18] The well was closed following the Reformation and gradually "grew out of remembrance."[19] Accidentally, the place was rescued from oblivion and the medicinal properties of the mineralized waters discovered; the friars were then replaced by an army of doctors, quacks, and chemists. Other authors provide similar examples of such transference of meaning. James Brome's *Travels over England, Scotland and Wales* (1700) confirms that the old practices still held among the visitors to certain wells. For instance, he reports that at St. Winnifred's, "Some we saw kneeling about the Well, mumbling over their Beads with such profound Murmurs, as the Conjurers did of old . . . and kissing the Stones on which they kneeled with as great Reverence as if the sacred Feet of St. Winefrid, or the Pope's Toe had been there present before."[20]

The "Devout Fancy" about "the Sanctity of Waters" brings into focus another relevant aspect in the development of the spas: their accessibility to people of all ages and degrees, including "the Lame and the Blind" or "impotent and decrepit Persons and little Children too."[21] Visits to the medieval religious sites had been justified by the faith of the believers, hence the universal extent of their benefits; but when scientific discourse resignified the wells as places for the recovery of the sick, the material benefits led to serious competition for their control. From the late sixteenth century one of the main aspects highlighted by the first medical treatises is the convenience—or rather inconvenience—of the free use of the waters and open access to the spas. The Poor Law of 1572 already tried to stop "the concourse of poor people at Buxton, as well as Bath";[22] but these measures were hard to enforce as the waters, so efficiently sanctioned by empiric science, had the advantage for most city dwellers of being cheap: "For those obstructions being stubborne . . . which in their owne nature are not incurable; but onely remaine uncured, either because the Patient is not able to willing undergoe such a course of Physicke . . . or because hee loveth his purse too well. But these Waters bring no charges, and after one hath beene used a little while to them, the taking of them is not troublesome at all."[23]

Several descriptions had helped to construct the spas as spaces in which God's designs upon England were shown in the gift of a medicinal panacea.[24] Rowzee's *The Queenes Welles. That is, A Treatise of the nature and vertues of Tunbridge Water* (1632), probably the best guide to seventeenth-century medical interpretations of mineral waters, opens with the classical precedents and explains how Pliny had listed a whole set of wells whose waters had wondrous effects: the fountain Crathis procured whiteness; Sibaris, blackness. He also talks of two Springs in Baeotia by the river Orchomenus, the first of which strengthened memory, the second caused oblivion; and later "A fountaine in Arcadia called Linus preserveth conception and hindreth aborsement, and on the other side, the river called Amphrisus maketh women barren."[25] After these references, the general idea is that mineral waters show Nature's paradoxical workings, its contradictions and diversity: "Diverse springs draw sometimes contrary faculties . . . and from hence it happeneth that oftentimes one & the same medicinable spring cureth diverses diseases, which are either contrary one to another, or at least have but small affinitie together."[26] This paradoxical effect was attributed to the fermentation of the mineral components and "maketh it excellent for most diseases, and as it were a generall Panpharmacon."[27] In spite of this reasoning, Rowzee warns the reader not "make it a Panpharmacon, or a Panacea, a medicine for all diseases."[28] This warning becomes a threat in a later treatise: "This Medicine being unskilfully Administered proves most often more formidable than the Disease."[29] By conjuring the image of the panpharmacon and then denying free access to the curative waters, the medical profession tried to ensure control of both the remedy and the clientele of the wells.

The emphasis on medical supervision and the proliferation of scientific publications about the wells, however, also generated a stream of criticism. Although it is always considered beneficial "to apply proper Agents [of the waters] to the Patient,"[30] we also find accusations of abuses from the same doctors. In this vein, Byfield congratulates the proprietors of the fountains found at Hoxdon [Hoxton] because they were "Trustees by the Providence of GOD, for the PUBLIQUE GOOD, in this Affair" and the wells were not in the "Hands of Physicians . . . who are too apt to Monopolize, and make Arcana."[31] Likewise, for John Peter the "impertinent superfluity" of treatises had to do with the benefit of the practitioners at the wells, mainly the "Metropolitan Luminaries."[32] Obviously, some resident physicians regarded parvenus as a threat to their potential business.[33] Since the lack of intrinsic monetary value of the waters could result in a diminishing of their appeal for those who could actually pay for the commodity—"what nothing costs, at under-rate is"[34]—medical supervision was a way to feed back value into the product. Hence medical treatises recommended professional attention even before getting to the wells and insisted on the preparation of the body for drinking the waters.

In the section devoted to the "Preparation of the body," Rowzee exhorts "all such as come to the Water, to compose and frame themselves to mirth, and to leave all cares and melancholy at home."[35] This advice connects the effects of the water to one of the traditional cures for melancholy and adds another imaginary quality to the wells: they are a place of mirth and fun.[36] Medical treatises emphasize the need to make the visit to the wells in a special state of mind in order to obtain the benefits of the waters. Dr. Madan's essay about Tunbridge Wells explains this humoral interpretation of the effects of the waters upon the passions of the mind: "Those who drink these Waters, must be Facetious, Merry, Cheerful, Gay, Jovial, free from Melancholy, Jealousy, Suspicion, Discontent, Peevishness, etc, because such Passions as these corrode both Soul and Body: impede the benefit they may reap by the Waters . . . Wherefore the way to have *mens sana in corpore sano*, or to be every way sound, is to leave pinching cares behind when you come to Tunbridge . . . It's an Antidote against the spleen."[37] Medical texts, too, construct fantasies of place in which cares, contrary passions and melancholy can undoubtedly be left behind.

By publicizing the spas, medical texts, like the plays and poems, worked as an invitation to a visit but also naturalized a modern concept of leisure; that is, the idea that the holiday resorts might help to cure melancholy by breaking the rhythms of everyday life in the city. In this way, traditional discourses about the miraculous wells merged with the new scientific discourse to describe a full movement within the realm of meaning. We should now try to consider how these meanings affected the geographical perception of the wells in their relation to London.

IV

The nodal relation of the spas to London not only enabled an entire repertoire of social images to circulate among them, but also promoted their use according to both mechanical and symbolic perceptions of distance and accessibility. For the sake of our discussion, the distance between Epsom and London and the possibility of covering that distance by public transportation emerge as two of the essential attributes of Epsom. From a social perspective Tunbridge was close enough to Epsom and Bath to become a social alternative to both of them. Medical reasons recommended this transition since the strong waters of Epsom helped to purge the body and so prepared it for the treatment at Tunbridge.[38] But in *Epsom Wells*, Carolina proposes to Lucia that they move to Tunbridge because of her disgust with the "scurvy company" of citizens (1.2 3–15).[39] From this perspective, a relative short distance to London could be regarded both as a positive attribute of these places but also as a potential danger for their reputation. Thus Hoxdon's Wells and Sadler's Wells at Islington were recommended by comparing the quality of their waters to those of Tunbridge with a warning against discriminations upon distance and not the medical effects of the waters: "'Tis true, They are not Farfetch'd, therefore may be disesteem'd by some."[40]

The anonymous *An Exclamation From Tunbridge And Epsom Against The Newfound Wells At Islington* (1684) provides a clue to this cultural value of distance. The two spa-towns, in the first person, argue against the new well found on the outskirts of London, voicing their advantages as

> staying out a Month or two, without being troubled with the peivish Yoak-fellow, save only on Saturday and Sunday Nights (on which you are sure to be very Sick) and all the rest of the Week as blyth as Batchellors, and free and uncontrouled as the most absolute Monarches of the East, having nothing to doe, but Cajole the beleiving Fopp at Home with a few kind Lines, for a Supply of Cash, dictated by the obliging Miss or Gallant, to make the Sport more divertive. Consider well all these Advantages of a remoter distance, consult your Interest, and abandon this upstart Haeresy of Flocking to Islington.[41]

The "advantages of a remoter distance" indicate the complex relationship between London and its surrounding areas. For instance, Bath and Tunbridge Wells had managed to attract the nobility and the more powerful groups in trade and commerce respectively. Transferring from one place to the other favored contacts between none-too-distant social groups and it was a sign of belonging to the fashionable world. Their physical distance from the capital posed an important obstacle to their accessibility, as they demanded from their visitors longer stays and considerable wealth to face the expense of the social and private life at the spa. For example, D'Urfey's comedy *The Bath* (1701) is peopled by country lords, rich knights, high-ranking militia, and ladies. Similarly, the Dramatis Personae of the two plays that have Tunbridge as their setting—*Tunbridge-Wells* (Thomas Rawlins, 1678) and *Tunbridge-Walks* (Thomas Baker, 1703)—present a social entourage full of gentlemen, squires, aldermen, rich merchants, parsons, and doctors; as Defoe states, "without money a man is no-body at Tunbridge."[42] Hence Epsom, where the company seemed "to be a degree or two" lower in rank,[43] received the lesser middle classes because it was an easy transfer from the capital (approximately four hours by coach). The offer was to be completed by the wells in the London suburbs—Sadler's Wells at Islington, Hoxdon, or Lewisham—and if we are to believe their literary manifestations, the proximity to the capital allowed an even greater social confusion.

But the individualized perception of each spa and its physical and social distance from the capital was linked to the changes taking place in the metropolis. London by 1675 was not just the City or the Town, since its most immediate liberties had already been engulfed in the London conurbation. King James had already predicted in 1616 that "With time England will onely be London and the whole countrey be left waste."[44] In 1724, Defoe perceived the capital as a "vast mass of buildings" without boundaries: "Whither will this monstrous city then extend? And where must a circumvallation or communication line be placed?".[45] This unnatural growth led to the assimilation of larger parts of its surrounding areas to its economic and symbolic concerns and to favor the interactive relation between city images and the spa fashion. In *Epsom Wells*, when Clodpate, "an immoderate hater of London," lists the vices of the City, he advances the actions and characters we are to discover at Epsom:

> CLODPATE: There's pride, popery, folly, lust, prodigality, cheating knaves, and jilting whores . . . Ay, and cards and false dice, and quarrels, hectors and reform'd officers to borrow a crown, and beat a man that refuses it, or asks for't again.
>
> (1.1, 213–30)

As Lawrence Manley has argued, the image of London changed drastically during the seventeenth century "as the cultural facts of urban life began to be conceptually opposed to nature."[46] The overcrowded city was regarded as a source of contagion and a disease in itself. The experience and memories of the plague in 1665 drastically redefined the relationship between the city and the country as it helped to publicize the healthy atmosphere of the latter. For the first time, large numbers of citizens followed the advice that "the surest preservative is to change the air, according to that trite Distich: Flee quick, Go far, and Slow return."[47] This "confortlesse desertion" affected all social groups (excluding the poor) but it was specially resented in the case of the middle class who "sit in the Countrey secure, and thank God they are there."[48]

Those sections in the medical treatises dealing with diet[49] also ratified the spas as privileged places for displaying new concerns about health and mirth that only made sense in the fashionable world of London. The fact that the air at the wells was "pure and wholesome" connected them to an ongoing discussion about the effects of air on human health and also to the perception of the capital itself as disease.[50] Through this ambivalent association, the pastoral value of the spas[51] was, paradoxically, linked to their status as a distorted version of city life.[52] Hence, London's bad air makes Clodpate roar,

> CLODPATE: Ud's bud, I go to London! I am almost sick at Epsom, when the wind sits to bring any of the smoke this way, and by my good

will would not talk with a man that comes from thence till he hath air'd himself a day or two.

(1.1, 208–11)

Together with this cultural redefinition of physical distance, the seasonal circumstances of the visit changed accordingly. Although medical discourses explained this aspect according to the hot or cold nature of the waters, they lack coherence. For Rowzee, "Concerning the season of the yeare, Sommer is the fittest . . . and the chiefest moneths June, July, August, and September," but the relationship between "summer time" and "fittest time" is not particularly clear, since he adds that "whensoever the weather is cleare and dry, the water is then best, as well in Winter as in Summer, yea in hard frostie whether the Water is commonly strongest."[53] Another treatise gives advice that adds a note of common sense: "for the season of the year, Summer is the best, when the weather is commonly settled, warm and dry."[54]

But Matthew Mackaile in his *Topographical-Spagyricall description of the Mineral Wells, at Moffet*, favors "the autumnal months . . . for, in the winter and spring time times, it is debilitat and vitiat by rain."[55] Autumn and Spring were also the favorite seasons for visiting Bath,[56] although as early as 1628, Thomas Venner had already dismissed such a calendar and argued for the summer season.[57] John Peter—speaking about the suburban Lewisham Wells—rejected the superiority of any specific time: "As to the Season of the Year, I prefer neither Summer, nor Winter, Spring nor Fall, but as Occasions, and every Ones particular Circumstances shall require."[58] It seems that the recommendations publicizing the summer season—and not spring or autumn—depended on the distance from London and the availability of free time on the part of the visitors rather than on specific medical recommendations.

The literary texts offer some clearer hints that explain the specific cultural notions about work and rest time attached to the summer vacation. In *An Exclamation*, Epsom and Tunbridge remember the good old days when they were always crowded:

Loretto was scarce haunted with such swarms of Pilgrims as our Health-restoring Plains, nor Rome more crowded in a Jubilee, than we were, from merry May till after the Dog-starr had done Barking, and the more important Negotiations of Bartoldom-Fair, called home our customers.[59]

Bartholomew Fair took place at the end of August, when autumn started according to traditional calendars. If we compare this to those quoted in the medical treatises, we notice that the temporal frame here is modeled on business time; that is, leisure is made dependent on the working schedule of the citizens.[60] Unlike the annual work and rest cycle of rural societies which were controlled by the rhythms of nature, life at Epsom or Tunbridge was ruled by the rhythms of trade and commerce. This utilitarian philosophy of time regulated personal duties to a fixed temporal schedule based on principles of efficiency.[61] Simultaneously the mercantile calendar also gave room to the idea of leisure time: a fixed period of the year fit to encompass those activities which were not essential for economic welfare. When Edward Ward opens *A Walk to Islington* (1699) with "In Holiday Time, when the Ladies of London/ Walk out with their Spouses,"[62] he is naturalizing the idea that "Holiday time" is not one single day appointed by the liturgical calendar but rather a larger span of private time in summer that could be used for personal purposes.

From a place for the sick (a none-too-distant image from pilgrims' visits to holy places) to the spas as described by Defoe, we can attest the consolidation of an emerging fashion: "This place seems adapted wholly to pleasure, so the town is suited to it . . . that the people who come out of their confined dwellings in London, may have air and liberty, suited to the design of country lodgings."[63] Probably the plays and poems written during the period prior to Defoe's account played an essential role in popularizing the connections between the body-healing effects of the waters and the enjoyment of leisure time. There was nothing new in leaving the city behind, only the fact that the number of those who could do it had changed drastically, and in so doing, had begun to blur another symbolic line of discrimination.

V

The potential transformation of the English spas from centers of health to leisure resorts was foregrounded in the medical treatises as part of the cure for melancholy, but the portrayal of social relations at the wells was the essential image in the lifestyle publicized in the literary works. The link I would suggest between medical discourse and the social environment referred to in the plays and poems is the purging effects of the waters, an aspect that can be read in connection with the social medley and the display of female and male desire at the wells.

According to Rowzee, activity started early in the morning:

"When the Sunne is an houre more or lesse, high, is the fittest time to drinke the water." The reason was that "when the Sunne beginneth to be of force, it doth attract some of the minerall spirits, and the water looseth some of its strength"(53–54).[64] Another important aspect was the procedure for water ingestion: it should take place within a short space of time, and demanded that "their naturall heate should be something awaked and excited, because then the water will be the better attracted, and have the more speedie passage."[65] Hence while one is drinking, after every glass, or every two or three glasses, Rowzee—and most medical treatises—recommend the taking of caraway comfits, coriander seed, and other herbs to help the digestion and passage of the waters. "A Glass of Rhenish, White-wine or Clarret" and a pipe or two of tobacco were also considered beneficial. He also recommends exercise, although "I utterly dislike it if it be too violent, as running, leaping, jumping, as some in wantonnes use to doe."[66] Once more, medical directions did not prevent people from doing just the opposite. *Epsom Wells* opens with a scene in which one of the bullies asserts, "How the white aprons scuttle, and leap, and dance yonder; some of 'em are dancing the hey."[67] This opening would evoke in the audience not only an ideal of freedom and joy, but also "wantonness," an association that would be even more obvious when reporting or portraying the passing effect of the waters. At this point we must consider what Gail Kern Paster has called "a semiology of excretion," that is a way to implicate "an ostensibly natural behavior [like bodily functions of evacuation] . . . in a complex structure of class and gender differences."[68] The purging effect of the waters and their usage as a panpharmacon introduced several images of democratic leveling in the spas.

The most outstanding is probably the public performance of evacuation. The desired effect of the water was that "the greater part of those that drinke of it, are purged by stoole, and some by vomit, as well as by urine."[69] This gave the wells a rather peculiar quality. Schellinks reported that the waters "work extraordinary well, with various funny results—*probatum est*. Gentlemen and ladies have here separate meeting places, putting down sentinels in the shrub in every direction."[70] Schellinks's account seems to agree with several other seventeenth-century reports that confirm the method employed at Epsom and other spas: People drank as many glasses—rather, pints—of mineral water as possible, after which they had to do some exercise, so that the waters might "pass well," leading to vomiting—especially if the person had been drunk the previous night—or simply "evacuating."[71] Epsom wells were over half a mile away from the town, which meant that the company had to walk for 15 to 20 minutes in order to reach their lodgings. This would have been somewhat difficult for those with urgent bodily needs, so the purgative effect of the waters was usually achieved among the bushes near the wells; hence the separate areas for men and women, and the convenience of those "sentinels in the shrub."

The literary texts naturalize this sight by stressing the lack of prudery in talking about the purge:

> Here you may see Spewing by your side,
> A City Coxcomb by his Country Bride.
> How does your Waters pass to Day? says Jenny,
> I've drank six Pints that are well worth a Guiney;
> They come so freely from me, and so Cool,
> I vow to you this is the seventh Stool.
> With this Discourse they pass'd away the time,
> And wash away their nasty Filth and Slime.[72]

The "changing threshold of embarrassment and shame," in Gail Paster's words, varies from text to text. The pamphlet *Flos Ingenii vel Evacuatio Discriptionis. Being an Exact Description of Epsam, and Epsam Wells* (1674), for instance, uses scatology as a rhetorical device for burlesque:

> The Heath or Common on which the Well stands, is a place contra di stinkt to Hide-Park, for here many secrets are disclosed . . . When the water drinkers are in a Body on the Common as sometimes they are postur'd you would take them to be the Representatives of the Rump Parliament. How different soever they are in their judgements they meet there with one Consent. There are none idle there, but all at their Business . . . And as the silly Bustard . . . thinks if his head be hid in a bush or brake, his whole body is invisible too, thus these water drinkers, so their Tayles be hid they care not if their heads, and all the rest of their bodies be seen.[73]

If we agree with Stanley Cavell that shame is "the specific discomfort produced by the sense of being looked at" and the response to shame "as the desire to cover up not your deed but yourself,"[74] then we have also to agree that the evacuating practices at Epsom were regarded as perfectly shameless. This contradicted the new rules of privacy that were beginning to influence the behavior of upper- and middle-class men and women,[75] hence showing the liminality of the spas regarding the construction of new social manners.

However, in spite of the proclaimed universal effect of the waters, it is generally female purging that comes under the scrutiny of the male poetic "I" in the literary texts. This literary persona likens himself to an "incognito" peripatetic philosopher,[76] only to pry upon the appearances of the visitors and, eventually, to end up in the ladies' private areas:

> But walking on with gentle pace,
> And musing thoughts that oft do clog us,
> I stepped into the women's boghouse:
> Where four or five together sat
> Like Hunted Hares upon the squat.[77]

Women react violently—"Never was Man so bawl'd at by such Curs,/Nor Dogs Bark more at Beasts in Lions Furs";[78] but this reaction from the incontinent females, far from deterring the gallants, seems to incite them to rhetorical incontinency. In a rather peculiar example of mock heroic, they even adorn with mythological attributes a lady's miscalculations in her hasty run to the wells:

> With that she Curs't the fatal Hour,
> And trudg'd away to Secret Bower . . .
> And e're she reach't the place design'd,
> As Cotton of his Dido feigned,
> A Yellow Aromatick Matter,
> Dropt down her Heels comix't with Water.[79]

This type of scene abounds in spa literature and mirrors common beliefs about women's incontinency. According to the humoral theory, the female body is colder in temperature, hence female urine was lighter in color and greater in quantity than that of healthy male adults.[80] This excess of fluid was even more obvious in the spas, and its depiction was another form of enhancing curiosity and desire in the audience.[81] The purging effects of the wells allowed visual pleasure to enter by locating the male gaze on the narrow realm of privacy permitted in the wells.[82] This voyeurism accounts in many cases for the lack of success in the sexual adventures undertaken by the male characters:

> By this time it happen'd, without Pill or Potion,
> Or help of the Waters, my Breech had a motion;
> Left Doxie alone, and the Place chanc'd to chuse,
> Assign'd for the Laxative Ladies to use;
> Not knowing my Error, I shut to the Door,

> In order to do what I hinted before;
> And who should come running immediately after,
> But a pretty young Damsel to scatter her water;
> Who being in haste, had the scurvie mishap
> To thrust open the door, and clap Arse in my Lap:
> Ads-wounds, said I, Lady Fair, as I am a Christian,
> I never deservd from your Sex to be pissed on.[83]

The lady runs out and then, when he recalls the situation, the scatological-erotic connection comes into focus:

> A curse on the Hovel, if lighter't had been,
> Bless my Eyes! What a delicate sight had I seen?
> Her person denoted her on such a Genus,
> I dare to engage she'd a Bum like a Venus:
> So soft, that I thought, I for ever cou'd feed-on
> Such forbidden fruit, like an Adam in Eden.[84]

Although the literary spas are presented as a feminized landscape open to male scrutiny—"like a bare Buttock to be lasht by the Describer of it"[85]—women are something other than the objects of gendered gaze in the wells. Scientific discourse on medicinal waters substantiated the idea that paradox stands at the heart of nature, and this was particularly evident in the female body. Of all the diseases listed in the medical treatises, the only ones relevant to the literary authors were related to women: "irregularities which chiefly either proceed from the obstructions of the Matrix . . . or proceed from the debilitude of the Womb."[86] Rowzee, as every other doctor, gives special advice to women that "there is nothing better against barrennesse and to make them fruitfull."[87] In fact, the popularity of the wells at certain periods during the century coincides with the presence of female members of royalty in search of an heir. The medical reasons lay in the waters' ability to "Cleanse, Strengthen, and Contract the Womb, which must be of great use to such as are subject to Miscarriages, Weakness in those parts, and are unapt to breed."[88]

But there were other potential effects derived from the paradoxical nature of the mineralized waters. If it was "the propertie of all equivocall agents to varie their operations according to the varietie of their objects,"[89] then the waters could also aid contraception: "Medicament [mineral waters] are not convenient for Sound and Healthy Persons. Moreover, they are Judged not proper for Women with Child: Because whatever provokes Urine, as these Water do, provokes also the Terms, and whatever provokes 'em in Women causes Miscarriage; therefore not fit for them in this circumstance."[90] Hence the spas were places in which unwanted pregnancies could easily be dealt with, and this was due, among other reasons, to the presence of midwives at the wells. In both cases female control of their reproductive lives figures as a threat more imaginary than real.

The literary texts also scrutinized the procreative/abortive effects of the waters and portrayed the wells as places for female regularities-irregularities:

> KICK: Many a London strumpet comes to jump and wash down her unlawful issue, to prevent shame; but more especially charges.
> CUFF: Others come hither to procure conception.
> KICK: Ay pox, that's not from the waters, but something else that shall be nameless.[91]

As Kick points out, lust provides a rather more credible interpretation of the medical paradox.[92] Sexual wantonness seems to be the practical consequence of not only the publicized procreative/abortive effect of the waters in every spa, but also the result of the poor condition of the lodgings. Pepys, Schellinks, and the fictional works point out the lack of convenient accommodation at Epsom and how visitors had to share rooms in the few existing houses.[93] This physical closeness stands as a visual signpost to social and sexual accessibility, one of the main features of this cultural landscape. Women enjoyed at Epsom the freedom of receiving male visits in their lodgings, as this was the "Place in the World the freest from Censure and Observation."[94] Their access was more restricted at Tunbridge, although "anything that looks like a gentleman, has an address agreeable, and behaves with decency and good manners, may single out whom he pleases . . . may talk, rally, be merry."[95] It was only a matter of social decorum as to how much of the sexual play could be made open.[96]

VI

Medical treatises regarded the gatherings at the wells as an undesired effect of their popularity, and they were also the main target of satire for the literary authors. Both the purging effect of the waters and the social medley introduced images of leveling that endangered social hierarchy and became a transformed version of the "grotesque company" of the Middle Ages and the Renaissance. For

Rochester, the wells are "The rendezvous of fools, buffoons, and praters, / Cuckolds, whores, citizens, their wives and daughters." But, in spite of their differences, the social types that flocked to take the waters are in fact mixed, showing in this way another paradoxical aspect of the wells:

> But ne'er could conventicle, play, or fair
> For a true medley, with this herd compare.
> Here lords, knights, squires, ladies and countesses,
> Chandlers, mum-bacon women, semptresses
> Were mixed together, nor did they agree
> More in their humors than their quality. [97]

Other texts present a different perspective as they publicize the leveling effect of a visit to the wells by explicitly commenting on the sexual, social and ideological differences among the visitors:

> We have been frequented by the Noble and the Gay, the fine and the fair, the roaring Fopps and the still, sly formall Coxcombs; the Swaggerers in Buff, the venerables in Satin; the Flaming Lasses and the simpering Dames, those that help others; and those that help themselves, the wits and the jilts, the fond Husbands and the more foolish maintainers, the miserly Fathers and the generous Sons, and the free sporting Daughters, and the procuring Cozens, the Hectoring Bullies, and the snuffling Precisians; the long Hair and the overgrown Ears; Whigg and Tory, Trimmer and all, were every Mothers son, our constant Customers.[98]

The wells accepted everybody as customers as far as they were ready to engage in the strategies of negotiation that made coexistence possible. Defoe presents a schematic version of the social variety gathered at the spas: "namely, that as the nobility and the gentry go to Tunbridge, the merchants and rich citizens to Epsome; so the common people go chiefly to Dullwich and Stretham . . . which makes the better sort also decline the place; the crowd on those days being both unruly and unmannerly."[99] But the comedies and poems display nothing of this clearcut division and stress instead the fluid interplay of people and social practices.[100] The interactive and improvisational dimensions of the encounters at the spas make possible the copresence of individuals previously separated by geographical and social disjunctions and whose trajectories intersect because of the specific attributes of place.

Courtship proves the most efficient tool for social intercourse, and consequently the potential dangers of its control by women's will are also foregrounded. The hegemonic position of women is somehow naturalized since the wells are places devoted to mitigating the concerns of everyday life—among other aspects, married life. But the danger may also come not simply from their irresponsible appeal to pleasure, but from an even more dangerous inclination to think and to act. In the three comedies dealing with Epsom and Tunbridge this is quite obvious: in *Epsom Wells*, Carolina and Lucia control courtship both by actively seeking suitable social and cultural partners and also by delaying their potential marriage. Courtwit manages to engage her rakish brother to the wealthy Alinda and stop Squire Fop's unsuitable marriage to the whore Brag in *Tunbridge-Wells*. Hillaria makes clear in *Tunbridge-Walks* her prospects for finding a suitable match at the wells and her conditions for doing so:

> HILLARIA: Love is a stupid Passion that betrays the weakness of our minds; Who that has Reason wou'd Sacrifice the Pride of Life to a momentary Joy? which ev'n in the Name of Marriage extinguishes; but a Man that wou'd maintain me in all the Pomp of Quality, to out-shine the Court, and be the Envy of the vying World, I swear, were he Old, Diseas'd, Perverse, were he any thing, I cou'd Love him, Caress him, and dote on him to Death.[101]

But the most radical version of female dominion at the wells appears in the short prose narrative *The Revengeful Lady* (Poor-Robin, 1679). The story opens at the wells with the introduction of a Gentleman who "wanted the government of the Tongue." There he meets a "young Lady, beautiful in her Person, and pleasant in her Conversation." After a first meeting and a failed attempt at her virtue, he accepts the rules fixed by the lady. Once he has gained her trust, he invites her to play a game in which he ties her hands with ribbons, and then "the Story says she cryed out Murder, but withal, that she Died only in the phrase of modern Poets." After copulation he runs to tell a friend his adventure; but this friend, being secretly in love with the lady, reveals the whole story to her. Then the lady starts planning her revenge "after pretending a greater fondness to her Gallant for the sake of what had past."

One day she proposes a game: she will tie him this time, but instead of using ribbons, she uses garters to bind him soundly to a bush: "The Fellow all this while pleased with the Conceptions he had of the amorous Stratagem, lay stock still." Once she has placed him in this position she talks to him "in a more unpleasant dialect than perhaps became either her Sex or Quality." Then she becomes the avenger for all her sex: after withdrawing "a very sharp Pen-knife," she tells him "I should make a Capon of you."[102] Once she has emasculated the gentleman, she sends for the doctor as a final act of humiliation. This "Ironical Baggage" manages to get her revenge, and neither law nor man seems to be able to stop her. This popular romance presents an extreme picture of the potential threats for male desire when confronted by female will, and it certainly exemplifies some of the male fabrications about the dangers of gender equality.

VII

The literary and medical texts present a wide range of images in which gender and social conflict are reinterpreted in light of the special conditions of accessibility created in the wells. From the semiotically safe grounds of medical discourse, the spas emerged during the Restoration as particular sites in which concepts of healing and leisure time could be resignified in terms of wider concerns about lifestyle and manners.

The emergent consumerism promoted new rituals directly connected to bourgeois practices of time and space. The visit to the wells was one of these new rituals, and the conditions of "being there," as they are shown in the plays and poems, were an uneasy truce in which each social or sexual party respected, in so far as possible, the position of the other. This seems a necessary requirement for the existence of both commodity exchange and a culturally mediated version of the war of the sexes, such as we find in the literary texts. The consolidation of the spa as a contact zone can also be connected to the new symbolic and economic relation between the metropolis and its surrounding areas. I have argued that the spa made possible the scrutiny of city-life practices characterized by their liminality, either in terms of gender or social rank. As these varied realms of meaning and social relations associated with the spas throughout the final decades of the seventeenth century, contemporary ideas about the individual's use of free time started to take shape.

The concept of vacation time observed in the wells differed from the perception of continued leisure of the powerful and the Sunday rest of both the bourgeoisie and the manufacturing classes. Although it retained some of the cyclical characteristics of other festive periods of the year, the people visiting the spas traveled there for individual reasons.[103] Health care may have been their original concern, but soon some particular aspects of the scientific and literary discourse about the waters caught people's imagination, particularly the sex-purge homology and the social medley. The waters enhanced men's sexual appetite; for women, they helped barrenness, chlorosis, and other related problems; for both, they might be a practical treatment for venereal diseases.

Moreover, the literary spas procured images of class and gender confusion between the visitors which made them a privileged site for projecting nonthreatening but unsettling images of social merging.[104] Affectation, social transvestism, and the whole casuistry of marriage targeted conflicts which engaged both the upper classes and the emerging citizenship in new and surprising ways. According to John S. Pipkin, during the Restoration period "the vanguard of an emerging nonaristocratic urban elite had to develop mores to deal with their betters at Court, in theaters, and in the places of public displays in which they were increasingly tolerated."[105] This awareness of the new central position of the citizens' agency in the spas can be perceived in Sedley's prologue to *Epsom Wells*, when following the conventional request for a positive reaction from the audience, he sketches the ambiguous position of the elite towards the citizens' symbolic appropriation of the wells—or the theatre pit: "But you kind burghers who had never yet, / Either your heads or bellies full of wit, / Our poet hopes to please."[106]

The gallant's superior role as a detached consumer is nevertheless challenged when the literary generic convention demands a change in the persona of the poetic "I." In such cases, in spite of his privileged position, a gallant must acknowledge and come to terms with two traditional affected patients of his gaze: women and social inferiors. If comedy works to uncover the metaphoric and symbolic undertones of this consumption, we can understand better the relevance of the purging effect of the waters and the presentation of sexual and social promiscuity as part of the new concept of leisure time displayed at the wells. The popularization of the spa and its interpretation as a place for renewal, an imaginary site to escape from everyday conflicts—two favorite topics in the dialectics of vacation—installed them progressively in the citizens' imagination as a privileged site for social and gender levelling. As this idea took hold, a new stage in its spatial configuration emerged. In the remodeled spas of the eighteenth century, architectural design tried to fulfil the different requirements of leisure and health care providing a suitable urban frame for enjoying the advantages of personal accessibility, without the conflicting ambiguities that the poor conditions of the spas had favored during the Restoration.

Notes

1. A version of this paper was delivered at the XI SEDERI Conference (Huelva, February 2000).
2. All references to Shadwell's *Epsom Wells* are to the edition by J. A. Prieto-Pablos et al. (Sevilla: Secretariado de Publicaciones de la Universidad de Sevilla, 2000).
3. Schellinks's sketch is kept in the Archives of the National Library of Austria (Vienna); for a reproduction see Shadwell (xlvii).
4. *The Journeys of Celia Fiennes*, ed. Christopher Morris (London: The Cresset Press, 1949), 337–38.
5. Ibid., 349–50.
6. Toland's *The Description of Epsom, with the Humours and Politicks of the Place, in a Letter to Eudoxa* was appropriated by J. Macky in his *A Journey through England in Familiar Letters from a Gentleman Here to his Friend Abroad* (London: 1732), 141–57.
7. B. Osborne and C. Weaver, *Aquae Britaniae: Rediscovering Seventeenth-Century Springs and Spas in the Footsteps of Celia Fiennes* (Malvern: Aldine Press, 1996), 39.
8. Reginald Lennard, in *Englishmen at Rest and Play: Some Phases of English Leisure (1558–1714)*, also notices this lack of realism in Shadwell's play as he comments that the popularity of the weekend visits to Epsom "was hardly reached during the Stuart period: it is Defoe's description of the spa in the reign of George I which shows us this side of the life at Epsom" (Oxford: Clarendon, 1931), 60.
9. For Steve Pile, "the mental map of the city is not a product but a process", the result of "the psychodynamics of place" [*The Body and the City* (London: Routledge, 1996), 236]. On the concept of mind maps and urban landscapes see also K. Lynch, *The Image of the City* (Cambridge: Massachusetts Institute of Technology Press, 1960); R. M. Downs and D. Stea, eds., *Image and Environment: Cognitive Mapping and Spatial Behaviour* (Chicago: Aldine, 1973); Y. F. Tuan, *Space and Place: The Perspective of Experience* (Minneapolis: University of Minnesota Press, 1997), D. Ley and M. S. Samuels, eds., *Humanistic Geography: Prospect and Problems* (London: Croom Helm, 1978); D. Cosgrove, "Towards a Radical Cultural Geography: Problems of Theory," *Antipode* 15 (1983): 1–11; J. Gold and B. Goody, "Behavioural Geography and Perceptual Geography: Criticisms and Responses," *Progress in Human Geography* 8 (1984): 544–50; and Lester B. Rowntree, "The Cultural Landscape Concept in American Human Geography," in *Concepts in Human Geography*, ed. C. Earle, K. Mathewson, and M. S. Kenzer (Lanham: Rowman & Littlefield, 1996).
10. Richard H. Perkinson, "Topographical Comedy in the Seventeenth Century," *English Literary History* 3 (1936): 277.
11. J. Douglas Canfield, "Shadwell at the Crossroads of Power: Spa as Microcosm in Epsom-Wells," *Restoration* 20 (1996): 142–43.
12. Pile, *The Body and the City*, 53.
13. Robert David Sack, *Homo Geographicus: A Framework for Action, Awareness, and Moral Concern* (Baltimore and London: The Johns Hopkins University Press, 1997), 27–30. The principles that hold the model could be summarized as it follows: Firstly, all our knowledge of physical reality comes in the form of language. Meaning then molds or influences other realms because we do not have any other form to apprehend either social relations or nature, unless we vehicle our knowledge into a symbolic system of communication. Secondly, places affect

each other because they are connected in physical space. Places, as nodes, draw upon and weave together elements that move from place to place (85). Hence, places become cultural sites that favor the circulation and redistribution of meanings about natural spaces and social relations (88).

14. Ibid., 90–91.
15. Ibid., 92–94.
16. Ibid., 97.
17. W. Turner's *A Booke of the natures and properties as well of the bathes in England as of other bathes in Germany and Italy* . . . (1562) is the first attempt to publicize the benefits of this practice. Travelogs and descriptions of the late decades of the century will start listing the wells as a treasure of the country (Lennard, *Englishmen at Rest and Play,* 1–17).
18. Thomas Guidott, *A True and Exact Account of Sadlers Well: or The New Mineral-Waters Lately Found out at Islington* (London, 1684), 1.
19. Ibid.
20. Brome, James. *Travels over England, Scotland and Wales* (London, 1700), 224–25.
21. Ibid., 18, 213
22. Lennard, *Englishmen at Rest and Play,* 4.
23. Lodwick Rowzee, *The Queenes Welles. That is, A Treatise of the nature and vertues of Tunbridge Water* (London, 1632), 40–41.
24. This belief was grounded upon a providential interpretation of the wells, as it was "God that must first heal the Waters, before they can have any virtue to heal you" [Thomas Ken, *Prayers for the Use of all Persons Who come to the Baths for Cure* (London, 1692), 5]; but also on an understanding of physical disease as a "picture" of moral ill (23, 33). See also the sermons by Anthony Walker, *Fax Fonte Accensa,* conveniently commented on as "An endeavour to kindle devotion from the consideration of the fountains God hath made . . ." [*Fax Fonte Accensa . . . Two Sermons Preached at New Chappel by Tunbridge . . . Also some Form of Meditations, Prayers and Thanksgivings Suited to the Occasion* (London, 1684), title page].
25. Rowzee, *The Queenes Welles,* 23–24.
26. Ibid., 29.
27. Ibid., 30.
28. Ibid., 38.
29. E. Prat, *A Short Treatise of Metal and Mineral Waters, wherein is described their bad as well as good qualities, with the dangers of Peoples too frequent and unadvisedly Drinking them. Mirabilis in Aquis Dominus* (London, 1684), 11. Ken's *Prayers* warns that the dangers of an uncontrolled use of the waters are not only physical, but also moral: "Do not abuse the Bath, by any Lasciviousness, or Impurity, which may defile your selves, or others: for this the way to turn the means of your cure, into an occasion of the more outragious sin: and to provoke God to send you away with a dreadful Curse, instead of a Blessing" (59).
30. John Peter, "To the Reader," in *A Treatise of Lewisham (But Vulgarly called Dulwich) Wells In Kent* . . . *with Directions for the Use of them* (London, 1681).
31. T. Byfield, "Epistle Dedicatory," in *A Short and Plain Account of the Late-Found Balsamich Wells at Hoxdon* (London, 1687).
32. John Peter, "To the Reader," in *A Treatise of Lewisham.*
33. Venner, a resident doctor at the wells, recommends as the only means to ensure a correct use of the waters "the counsell and direction of some learned

Physitian resident at the Baths" [*The Baths of Bathe* (London, 1628), 7], and he argues against any "practicall Minister, Parish Clarke, Apothecary, Chirurgeon or the like" (16) and "Empericks" whose help is sought "because it is cheape" (15).

34. Richard Ames, *Islington-Wells, or, The threepenny-academy, a poem* (London, 1691), 260.

35. Rowzee, *The Queenes Welles*, 65–66.

36. Robert Burton writes: "No better physic for a melancholy man than change of variety of places, to travel abroad and see fashions" [*The Anatomy of Melancholy*, ed. Holbrook Jackson (London: Dent, 1975), 2.67]. He also devotes a whole subsection of "The Cure of Melancholy" to "Mirth and merry company, fair objects, Remedies" (2.119–26).

37. Pat Madan, *A Philosophical and Medicinal Essay of the Waters of Tunbridge* (London, 1687), 17–19.

38. Ibid., 10.

39. The burlesque *Mundus Muliebris: or The ladies Dressing-Room Unlock'd and her Toilette Spread Mundus Muliebris* by Mary Evelyn (London, 1690) warns the gallant that in order to court his mistress according to the "Forms and Decencies of making Love in Fashion," he must be ready to "follow her to Tunbridge at the season of drinking the Waters, though you have no need of them your self" (Preface).

40. Byfield, *A Short and Plain Account*, 29.

41. *An Exclamation From Tunbridge And Epsom Against The Newfound Wells At Islington* (London: 1684), 2.

42. Daniel Defoe, *A Tour through the Whole Island of Great Britain*, ed. Pat Rogers (Harmondsworth: Penguin, 1971), 142.

43. Ibid.

44. James I, speech in the Star Chamber, 20 June 1616; quoted in Lawrence Manley, "From Matron to Monster: Tudor-Stuart London and the Languages of Urban Description," in *The Historical Renaissance. New Essays on Tudor and Stuart Literature and Culture*, ed. Heather Dubron and Richard Strier (Chicago: University of Chicago Press, 1988), 349.

45. Defoe, *A Tour through the Whole Island of Great Britain*, 288.

46. Lawrence Manley, "From Matron to Monster," 350.

47. Gideon Harvey, *A Discourse of the Plague . . . With several waies for purifying the air in houses, streets, &c.* (London: 1665), 16.

48. *Lamentatio Civitatis or, Londons Complaint Against her Children in the Countrey* (London: 1665), 22.

49. Rowzee explains the special meaning of the term "diet." It includes, "besides meate and drinke, ayre, motion, and quiet, things retained and voyded, sleeping and watching and the passions of the minde" (*The Queenes Welles*, 65).

50. Burton addesses the topic in "Air rectified. With a digression of the Air" (2. 34–69). Prat prescribes that there is nothing more healthful for the body of man than to live in an air "pure and not corrupted" (*A Short Treatise of Metal and Mineral Waters*, 46).

51. At Tunbridge, Burr describes the newly laid out fish ponds as having "a pretty rural taste" (Lennard, *Englishmen at Rest and Play*, 59). Private gardens also deserve detailed descriptions in Fiennes's or Toland's reports of Epsom, but the aesthetic pleasure this rural ambiance could provide was subordinated to its mercantile purpose of attracting guests to the lodging houses, as "such as neglect their Gardens, find their Error in the Emptiness of their Rooms" (Macky, *Journey through England*, 145).

52. In Henry Peacham's *Minnerva Britanna* (1612), the emblem *Rura Mihi et Silentium* shows a rural landscape. The commentary, after identifying the city with infection, "Chaos and Confusion," expands upon the benefits of natural life. But the final stanza redefines the relation between desire and reality: "Yet love the Citie, as the kindly Nurse/Of all good Artes, and faire Civilitie: Where though with good, be intermix't the worse,/That most disturbe our sweet Tranquilitie:/Content thyselfe, till thine Abillitie,/And better hap, shall answere thy desire,/But Muse beware, least we too high aspire" (Leeds: The Scolar Press, 1966), 187.

53. Rowzee, *The Queenes Welles*, 50–51.

54. Prat, *A Short Treatise of Metal and Mineral Waters*, 41.

55. Matthew Mackaile, *Moffet-Well: Or, A Topographical-Spagyricall description of the Mineral Wells, at Moffet in Annandale of Scotland* (Edinburgh: 1664), 83.

56. Humoral theory with its homologized version of the evacuatory processes did not recommend purging during "the months of greatest heat and cold," hence Bath's double season (spring-autumn); see Gail Kern Paster, *The Body Embarrassed: Drama and the Disciplines of Shame in Early Modern England* (Ithaca: Cornell University Press, 1993), 134.

57. Thomas Venner, *The Baths of Bathe* (London: 1628), 6–7.

58. John Peter, *A Treatise of Lewisham (But Vulgarly called Dulwich) Wells In Kent . . . with Directions for the Use of them* (London: 1681), 91.

59. *An Exclamation From Tunbridge And Epsom*, 1.

60. A precedent for the separation of resting time and sacred days appeared in the parliamentary proceedings of "Die Martis 8. Iunii 1647" in which traditional holidays like the Nativity of Christ, Easter and Whitsunday "and other festivals commonly called Holy-dayes" were abolished and a system of regular vacations for schools proposed.

61. On the utilitarian philosophy of time see Eviatar Zerubavel, *Hidden Rhythms: Schedules and Calendars in Social Life* (Berkeley: University of California Press, 1981), 54–64; on the connection time/place, see Tuan, *Space and Place*, 179 ff.

62. Edward Ward, *A Walk to Islington: with a Description of New Tunbridge-Wells and Sadler's Music-House* (London, 1699), 3.

63. Defoe, *Tour through the Whole Island of Great Britain*, 169.

64. Rowzee, *The Queenes Welles*, 53–54. In the literary texts the reasons are normally quite different as, for both women and men, this was a rare opportunity to see each other "Drest Dishabillee" in public (Ames, *Islington-Wells*, 68). This casual outfit was nevertheless an occasion for extravagant exhibitions: "Then a Young Semptress of th' Exchange/In an Undress so loose and Strange,/ She was thought by every Man,/ To come from China or Japan" (113–16). For gallants such as Tom Fairlove in Thomas Rawlins's *Tunbridge-Wells*, Bevil and Raines in Shadwell's *Epsom Wells*, or the poetic "I" of most poems, a bad night was normally the cause for trotting to the waters.

65. Rowzee, *The Queenes Welles*, 54.

66. Byfield, *A Short and Plain Account*, 52, 55.

67. Shadwell, *Epsom Wells*, 1.1.20–21.

68. Gail Kern Paster, *The Body Embarrassed: Drama and the Disciplines of Shame in Early Modern England* (Ithaca: Cornell University Press, 1993), 34–35.

69. Rowzee, *The Queenes Welles*, 35–6.

70. William Schellinks, *The Journal of William Schellinks: Travels in England 1661–1663*, ed. M. Exwood and H. L. Lehman (London: Royal Historical Society, 1993), 88.

71. Pepys, who visited Epsom in 1663, wrote in his diary that "we drunk each of us two pots and walked away—it being very pleasant to see how everybody turns up his tail, here one and there another, in a bush, and the women in their Quarters the like" (July 26).

72. *A Poem on the New Wells at Islington* (London: 1684), 2.

73. *Flos Ingenii vel Evacuatio Discriptionis. Being an Exact Description of Epsam, and Epsam Wells* (London: 1674), 165.

74. Qtd. in Paster, *The Body Embarrassed*, 123.

75. See Paster's discussion of Sir John Harington's *A New Discourse of a Stale Subject, Called the Metamorphosis of Ajax* (1596) and the development during the sixteenth century of both books of conduct and utensils that fostered privacy during the act of evacuation as a sign of civility (*The Body Embarrassed*, 23–29).

76. Ames, *Islington-Wells*, 251.

77. *A Mornings Ramble, or, Islington Wells Burlesq't* (London: 1684), 1. The comparison reveals the unconscious levels of desire at stake in the poems. Hares evoked not only shyness, but also lust and fecundity. Nevertheless they could also suggest more threatening images: in Gothic sculpture, a knight who flees in terror from a hare was the iconography of Cowardice [James Hall, *Dictionary of Subjects and Symbols in Art* (London: John Murray, 1974), 127], and Whitney's version of Alciato's *Cum Larvis Non Luctandum*—a warning against taking advantage of inferiors—shows a pack of hares pulling the hairs of a dead lion [Geffrey Whitney, *A Choice of Emblems And Other Devises* (1586), ed. Henry Green (London: Lovell Reeve, 1867), 127]. In spite of the superiority assumed by the male gaze, the view of female genitalia is, nevertheless, disturbing.

78. *A Poem on the New Wells at Islington*, 2.

79. *A Mornings Ramble*, 1.

80. Paster, *The Body Embarrassed*, 44.

81. Freudian interpretations of the development of sexuality emphasize that any one of its stages is exclusively linked to one single erogenous area; however, in the literature of spas and spa culture, these areas are continuously resignified to provide substance for new fantasies: the orifice—the anus, the mouth, the vagina—is self-referential and any of the stages may be evoked by one of them. For Freud's theory on the development of erotogenic zones, see "Fragment of an Analysis of a Case of Hysteria [Dora]" [*The Freud Reader*, ed. Peter Gay (New York: Norton, 1995), 172–238.]; *Three Essays on the Theory of Sexuality and Other Works* (Harmondsworth: Penguin, 1977), 7:39–169; and "Character and Anal Eroticism" (*The Freud Reader*, 293–96); also Paster, *The Body Embarrassed*, 132–33.

82. Pat Gill's analysis of female bodily discharges in works by Rochester and Swift concludes that "women, class and filth are often in metonymical relation to one another in the satires of these writers" ["'Filth of All Hues and Odors': Public Parks, City Showers and

Promiscuous Acquaintance in Rochester and Swift," *Genre* 27 (1994): 345].

83. Ward, *A Walk to Islington*, 10.

84. Ibid.

85. *Flos Ingenii*, 164.

86. W. Sympson, *The History of Scarbrough-Spaw* (London: 1679), 102. Not only medical advice and literary satires paid special attention to female irregularities. In Ken's *Prayers*, the only one specially addressed to a specific disease is "A Prayer for a Wife" in which we can read: "Deliver me, O my God, from either a barren, or from a miscarrying womb, and from dry Breasts" (77).

87. Rowzee, *The Queenes Welles*, 47–48.
88. Byfield, *A Short and Plain Account*, 39–40.
89. Rowzee, *The Queenes Welles*, 41.
90. Madan, A Philosophical and Medicinal Essay, 9.
91. Shadwell, *Epsom Wells*, 1.1.22–27.
92. Even doctors acknowledged the erotic quality of the waters at Tunbridge. According to Madan's *A Philosophical and Medicinal Essay*, this was due to its "Spirituous Ferment," which "incites and inspires men and women to Amorous Emotions and Titillations, being previous Dispositions, enabling them to Procreation." This *Aitiology* is completed with a poetical explanation of the waters' effect as the result of an amorous encounter between Venus (the waters) and her "beloved Mars" (the minerals): "Mars gives the strength, Venus the Grace" (6–8). In Rochester's "Tunbridge Wells" (ca. 1675), Cuff and Kick themselves are the instrument of the procreative miracle: "For here walk *Cuff* and *Kick*, / With brawny back and legs and potent prick, / Who more substantially will cure thy wife [Fribble's], / And on her half-dead womb bestow new life. / From these the waters got the reputation / Of good assistants unto generation" [*Complete Poems*, ed. David M. Vieth (New Haven: Yale University Press, 1968), 143–48].
93. In *An Exclamation*, we find a burlesque of these lodgings: "Happy were they that could get shelter in our Illustrious Pallaces, covered with immortal thatch and delicately hung with the spinstry of Arachne, Vulgarly called Cloath of Cob-web. Three Families not seldom dwelt in one Chamber scarce so big as a Taffity Tart; and without any superstitious witness about difference of Sex, lovingly pigg'd in together" (1).
94. Macky, *A Journey through England*, 139.
95. Defoe, *A Tour*, 142.
96. Bath, "a Valley of Pleasure, yet a sink of Iniquity" (Ward, *A Walk to Islington*, 16), kept sexual flimsiness away from the critical public eye. Or, as Defoe puts it, "Here, the ladies and the gentlemen pretend to keep some distance" (*A Tour*, 360).
97. Rochester, "Tunbridge Wells," 4–5, 80–85.
98. *An Exclamation*, 1.
99. Defoe, *A Tour*, 166.
100. Pepys, for instance, comments upon Epsom, "But Lord, to see how many I met there of Citizens that I could not have thought to have seen there, or that they had ever had it in their heads or purses to go down thither" (July 26, 1663).
101. Thomas Baker, *Tunbridge-Walks: or The Yeoman of Kent* (London: 1703), 1.11–12.
102. Poor-Robin, *News from Epsom: Or, The Revengeful Lady . . . A Novell . . . In imitation of Monsieur Scarron* (1679), 1, 3, 5–6.
103. For a historical discussion on the individual motivations for a journey, see Valene L. Smith, "The Quest in Guest," *Annals of Tourism Research* 19 (1992): 1–17.
104. In *Merry Newes from Epsom-Wells* (1663), the cuckolding of the cit ends with a warning to the visiting gentlemen: "They flout and fleer, they jest and jear / the Town is full of laughter, / But many of them were there, / had padled in such water" (in Shadwell, *Epsom Wells*, 161–64, lines 93–96).
105. John S. Pipkin, "Space and the Social Order in Pepy's Diary," *Urban Geography* 11 (1990): 155.
106. Shadwell, *Epsom Wells*, 25–30.

Jewish History and Christian Providence in Elizabethan England: The Contexts of Thomas Legge's *Solymitana Clades* (*The Destruction of Jerusalem*), c. 1579–88

Paulina Kewes

> ... As these Tragicke Poets flourished in Greece ... and these among the Latines ... so these are our best for Tragedie, the Lorde Buckhurst, doctor Leg of Cambridge, Doctor Edes of Oxforde, maister Edward Ferris, the Author of the Mirrour for Magistrates, Marlow, Peele, Watson, Kid, Shakespeare, Drayton, Chapman, Decker, and Beniamin Iohnson.
>
> As M. Anneus Lucanus writ two excellent Tragedies, one called Medea, the other de Incendio Troiæ cum Priami calamitate: so Doctor Leg hath penned two famous tragedies, ye one of Richard the 3. the other of the destruction of Ierusalem.
> —Francis Meres, *Palladis Tamia* (1598)

> ... I suppose it shal not be amisse to write something of mourning, for *London* to harken counsaile of her great Grand-mother, *Ierusalem*.
> —Thomas Nashe, *Christs Teares over Ierusalem* (1593)

RANKED ALONGSIDE SHAKESPEARE, AND COMPARED TO LUCAN, IN FRANcis Meres's *Palladis Tamia*, Thomas Legge is best known today for his neo-Latin three-part, fifteen-act, theatrical extravaganza *Richardus Tertius*. It was lavishly produced, with music by William Byrd, on three successive nights at St. John's College Cambridge during the Commencement Act in March 1579. Copies of Legge's tragedy circulated in manuscript, and his adaptation of Hall and More may have inspired Shakespeare's *Richard III*.[1] Yet the Cambridge don's reputation as a dramatist did not rest solely on *Richardus Tertius*. As *Palladis Tamia* shows, Legge, who from 1574 served as Master of Gonville and Caius College and, in 1587–88 and again in 1592–93, as Vice-Chancellor of the University, was also known to have produced a neo-Latin trilogy about foreign history.[2] *Solymitana Clades* chronicled the Jewish uprising against Rome from its outbreak in A.D. 66, through the destruction of Jerusalem in A.D. 70, to the capture of Massada in A.D. 73. Written some time after 1579 and, as its ample and sophisticated stage directions and production notes indicate, designed for performance, the play was never staged. The manuscript of the trilogy, however, must have been accessible to at least some of Legge's contemporaries: the extant copy, not in Legge's hand, is preceded by a prose Argument that suggests intended readership. *Solymitana Clades* had been presumed lost until a copy came to light in a manuscript miscellany (once the property of another Cambridge man, Joseph Diggins) at a Christie's sale in 1973 and was acquired by the Cambridge University Library. Although a facsimile edition has been available since 1989 and a parallel text Latin-English edition since 1993,[3] the trilogy has been ignored by modern scholars.

In *Richardus Tertius*, the first dramatization of fifteenth-century English history and an important model for later history plays, Legge exploited the topical potential of the chronicle material. He drew a parallel between the conclusion of the Wars of the Roses by Henry VII and Elizabeth's peaceful accession after the turbulence of Mary's reign.[4] Legge's Jewish play was no less attuned to contemporary concerns. It shows a dizzying succession of military conflicts, political machinations, and religious controversies, foreign wars and civil wars. Are the Jews justified in rebelling against their oppressors or should they submit to the Roman yoke? Should we sympathize with the Zealots who urge resistance to the Romans or with King Agrippa and the Jewish elders who advocate submission? Is the destruction of Jerusalem to be seen as providential punishment for deicide or the tragic end of a brave if hopelessly divided people? Dana F. Sutton, editor and translator of Legge's plays, has cautioned prospective students: "There is an obvious possible interpretation of *Solymitana Clades*, but one from which the reader ought to be warned away. For once the equation Zealot-Puritan parallel is drawn, one can easily go to work on a vigorous job of Puritan-bashing . . . But such an interpretation would contradict everything we know of Legge."[5] Contrary to Sutton, I shall contend that Legge does suggest an affinity between Jewish Zealots and English Puritans. But I shall also contend that his preoccupation with sectarian division is far subtler and more complex than mere "Puritan-bashing."

Solymitana Clades does not offer a transparent religious or political allegory. The Jewish elders cannot be simply equated with the hierarchy of the Church of England or the Zealots with the Puritans, even if such connections are implied at certain points in the play. Far from anticipating the negative stereotypes of the Jew constructed in the 1590s in such public theatre offerings as Marlowe's *The Jew of Malta* and Shakespeare's *The Merchant of Venice*, Legge challenges his audience to recognize themselves among stage Jews and Romans. According to Sutton, *Solymitana Clades* "present[s] the catastrophe as God's vengeance for the Jews' rejection of Christ and for the crucifixion."[6] Yet Legge's prefatory statements, manipulation of sources, and emphasis on the political repercussions of the war undermine the providential reading of the fall of Jerusalem. By including among the *dramatis personae* the historian Josephus, on whose account the play is founded, Legge holds up to scrutiny the process of making, narrating, and transmitting history.

Jewish History in Post-Reformation England

Legge wrote *Solymitana Clades* when knowledge of the ancient Jewish past, based both on the Bible and on classical, Hebrew and Christian historiography, was growing rapidly.[7] Protestant preachers and pamphleteers regularly cited the destruction of Jerusalem as an example of divine vengeance on the Jews (hitherto God's chosen people) to terrify, edify, and reform His new elect nation—the English.[8] So we must ask in what ways Legge's treatment of this critical episode in the Jewish—and Christian—pasts departs from the providential approach propagated by the pulpit and the press.

As Patrick Collinson, Margaret Aston, and others have taught us, the general typology casting post-Reformation England as the new Israel was supplemented by a range of specific parallels that were invoked in sermons, pamphlets, civic pageants, plays, and parliamentary speeches.[9] Queen Elizabeth had been hailed as Deborah in the coronation entry mounted for her by the City of London on 14 January 1559. The analogy continued to be exploited by preachers and politicians as well as being rendered visually—for instance in the queen's entry into Norwich during her progress through East Anglia in August 1578.[10] From the beginning of her reign, Elizabeth had also been seen as a type of the biblical King Hezekiah—or Ezechias as his name was rendered in sixteenth-century England—who had abolished idol-worship and repulsed the Assyrian invasion. "And for your better encouraginge to runne this right and straite course," spoke the Lord Keeper, Sir Nicholas Bacon, addressing Elizabeth in the opening speech of her first parliament, "I thinke I may affirme that the good king Ezechias had noe greater desire to amende that was amisse in his tyme."[11] Five years later, in August 1564, Elizabeth saw a performance of Nicholas Udall's *Ezechias* during her visit to Cambridge, and we know that Legge was involved in the production of this and other dramatic entertainments for the royal guest.[12] In the early years of her reign the Hezekiah parallel was used to compliment the queen for her extirpation of popery and to urge her to carry out a more thoroughgoing reformation; after the providential dispersal of Philip II's Armada, Hezekiah's divinely assured victory over the Assyrian Sennacherib was readily seized upon as an apposite precedent. The old trope gained fresh currency.[13]

The Bible was a source of admonitory as well as laudatory figures. The English needed to be reminded not only of their special status and the benefits the covenant had conferred on them, but also of their responsibilities and the punishment that would inevitably ensue should they falter in their commitment to God.[14] At times of natural disaster or impending foreign invasion, preachers sought to awaken the hardened English hearts and minds. Among dozens of tropes of warning, none was more potent and more frequently invoked than the destruction of Jerusalem.[15] Christ's lamentation over the city, recounted in Luke 19.41–44, was the standard text. Its exegesis and application were routinely supplemented with details from Flavius Josephus and the Latin offshoots of the so-called *Sefer Yosippon*. Josephus had by then received a near-canonical status; his history was accepted as a bridging narrative between the Old Testament and the New. More accessible to the English public, however, were the Christianized versions of the *Sefer Yosippon*, a tenth-century Hebrew chronicle that had itself drawn on a Latin abridgement of Josephus's classic account.[16]

Homiletic tradition spawned and was in turn influenced by images of the fall of Jerusalem in ballads, poems, pamphlets, and prefaces to translations of Jewish histories.[17] In all of them, the defeat of the Jews was regarded as providential. Undertaken at the suggestion of a London publisher, Peter Morwyng's *A Compendious and most marveilous History of the latter tymes of the Jewes commune weale* (1558) was a translation of Sebastian Münster's Latin version of Abraham Ibn Daud's twelfth-century abstract of *Yosippon*. The aim of the translation, Morwyng says in the preface, was not merely to make available post-Biblical history of the Jews "to al men in the English tong," but also to illustrate the workings of divine providence and so encourage readers to apply the Jewish example to the present: "As when thou seest the Jewes here afflicted with divers kinds of misery, because they fell from God: then maist thou be admonished hereby to see the better to thine owne waies, least the like calamities light upon thee."[18] In this scenario, the Romans serve as tools of divine retribution. "Consider over and marke well," Morwyng continues,

> the Jewes were counted Gods people, the Romaines contrary his enemies . . . yet for all this, God wold they should prevaile against the Jewes, and subdue them under their yoke. Wherbi we mai learn how greatly God is incensed against iniquitie, in so much that he will rather bring in upon his own children a nation more wicked: then to leave them unpunished, to run forward in their wicked race . . . (sig. π6ᵛ)

Morwyng's approach to Jewish history was enthusiastically adopted by John Stockwood, minister from Tunbridge Wells, who more than once addressed the congregations at St Paul's Cross in London and whose sermons exerted further imfluence in print. "They [the Jews] cry, his bloud be vppon vs and our children," Stockwood reminded his Paul's Cross audience in 1578, "and they hadde their desire at the full, when their Cittie was taken," for "These horrible vices, deserued thys fearefull reiection."[19] Six years later Stockwood devoted a complete Paul's Cross sermon to the theme of Christ's lament over Jerusalem and the city's dreadful punishment. Drawing extensively on Morwyng's translation, which he recommended to his auditors, *A Very Fruitful and Necessary Sermon of the most Lamentable Destruction of Jerusalem* reiterated the justice of God's judgment upon the Jews: "And thus were the wicked Jewes worthily vexed with warre, that refused Jesus Christ."[20]

Providential exegesis of Jewish history readily migrated from sermon to pamphlet and ballad. Indebted to both Stockwood and Morwyng, Thomas Nashe's plague pamphlet *Christs Teares over Jerusalem* (1593) ventriloquized Christ's address to the seditious city:

> O *Ierusalem*, not the Infidell-Romaines, which shall inuade thee, and make thy Citty (now cleped a Citty of peace) a shambles of dead bodies, teare down thy Temple, and sette vp a brothel-house in thy Sanctuarie, not they (I say) shall haue one droppe of thy blood layde to theyr charge; not one stone of thy Temple or Sanctuarie testificatory against them: Thy blood shal be vppon thine owne head, whose transgressions violently thrust swords into theyr hands . . .[21]

Lodowick Lloyd's *Stratagems of Jerusalem* (1602), a miscellaneous compilation of military lore, ancient history, and political maxims, characteristically explained the fall of Jerusalem in terms of Jewish ingratitude and betrayal of God: "The cause wherof was the sinne of *Ierusalem*, which would neuer acknowledge the goodnesse of God towards them, nor his myracles and his mercy wrought amongst them, they refused his grace offered, and persecuted him most violently to death."[22]

The object of these rehearsals of the condign punishment visited on the Jews was to root out the abuses and sins rife among the English lest the new elect nation suffer the fate of the old. "And to thee I say, O London . . . see that thy liuing be answerable to thy knowledge, and thy manners agreeable to thy teaching," warned Stockwood, "otherwise I assure thee, it shall fall out vnto thee, as it did vnto these Jewes."[23] "As great a *desolation* as *Ierusalem*, hath *London* deserued," Nashe lashed out in a by now familiar diatribe, "Whatsoeuer of *Ierusalem* I haue written, was but to lend her a Looking-glasse," for "No image or likenes of thy *Ierusalem* on earth is there left, but *London*."[24] A bestselling ballad version of Nashe's tract composed some time in 1593, *Christs Teares over Jerusalem. Or, A Caveat for England, to call to God for Mercy, lest we be plagued for our contempt and wickednesse*, dwelt on the lurid episodes of the siege of Jerusalem—"Yea, Dogs and Cats they ate, / Mice, Rats and euery thing: / For want of food, their Infants young, / unto the Pot they bring"—before scolding the native public: "Awake, *England*, I say, / rise from the sleep of sinne."[25]

Legge's *Solymitana Clades* differs from the English jeremiads in three signal respects. It was not intended for popular consumption; it did not unambiguously subscribe to the providential reading of Jewish history; and it did not condemn outright the Jewish rebellion against Rome. In contrast to ballads, sermons, and pamphlets for heterogeneous audiences, composed in English and delivered *viva voce* or printed as cheap broadsides, quartos, or octavos, Legge's was a Latin play to be staged by and for academics.[26] Whereas "the literature of warning" (MacKerness's phrase) drew mainly on the Bible and Christianized accounts of Jewish history, *Solymitana Clades* dramatized the most authoritative historical account, that of Josephus, which it supplemented with information from humanist treatises and, in one or two instances, from a recension of *Yosippon*. Stockwood claimed that his source was Josephus, but his reference to the book's availability in English makes it clear that he had in fact relied on Morwyng's translation of the Latin abridgement of *Yosippon*.[27] (Until the publication of Thomas Lodge's impressive folio version in 1602, Josephus had been accessible only to those conversant with Latin, Greek, or French.)[28] By contrast, Legge rightly stresses the historical accuracy and authenticity not only of his narrative, but also of his presentation of Jewish ceremonies, religious rituals, and dress. He cites ancient and modern authorities—Josephus, Justus Lipsius, Carlo Sigonio, Petrus Ciaconnius—in marginal annotations that anticipate Ben Jonson's elaborate marginalia in the quarto of *Sejanus* (1605).

The audience Legge aimed at was both more exalted and more sophisticated than the recipients of the popular jeremiads. He could count on the scholars' familiarity with the story and its historical context as described by Josephus and others. In Elizabethan grammar schools and universities, the study of Latin and rhetoric involved reading, translation, and paraphrase of classical writings, above all historiography. Academic disputations in a variety of disciplines further fostered the knowledge and critical appreciation of ancient history, political thought, and religion. Legge's audience was therefore well placed to make informed connections that would have escaped most consumers of popular fare. Courtesy of Tacitus, Suetonius, Dio Cassius, they had a good understanding of imperial Roman politics that serves as a backdrop to Legge's play.[29] They knew that the Jewish rebellion against Rome had coincided with the uprisings by the Britons and the Batavians in A.D. 60–61 and A.D. 69–70, respectively. Given the circulation of Continental books in England and given the strong ties between foreign and native intellectuals, some Cambridge men may have been aware of the topical applications of the destruction of Jerusalem that were made elsewhere in Europe, especially in France and the Netherlands. During the turmoil of the Wars of Religion both Huguenots and Catholic Leaguers drew parallels between Jewish and French civil wars. The Dutch revolt against Spain prompted literary and iconographic comparisons of heroic Dutchmen and their legendary and spiritual forbears, the Batavians and the Jews, respectively.[30] The great Dutch scholar Justus Lipsius, editor of Tacitus and admirer of Josephus, had sought to arrange a meeting with Legge, whose mastery of Latin he highly esteemed, during a planned trip to England in 1585.[31] Had Lipsius come to Cambridge, Legge might well have shown him a draft of his dramatization of Josephus.

Yet however steeped Cambridge scholars may have been in classical or continental historiography and political writings, their interpretation of the fall of Jerusalem need not have been any less providential than that of their not-so-erudite contemporaries. Late sixteenth-century Cambridge was torn by religious controversies such as the surplice dispute of the mid-1560s or the showdown, in 1570, between John Whitgift, Master of Trinity College, and the

Puritan Thomas Cartwright, Lady Margaret Professor of Divinity, that resulted in Cartwright's expulsion from his chair and prohibition from preaching in the university. (The Cartwright affair led to the imposition of the new, more repressive University Statutes that Whitgift himself had helped to draft.)[32] Puritan members, for their part, often castigated the allegedly popish proclivities of their heads of houses: both Legge and his predecessor as master of Gonville and Caius College, John Caius (who had endowed and re-founded the college), had been targets of their attacks. The complaint filed against Legge in 1581 stigmatized his papist leanings, ungodly pastimes, and mismanagement of college affairs, and it nearly cost him the mastership.[33] As Christopher Brooke has pointed out, Legge must have genuinely believed in religious tolerance: he could not have presided over the election of so many ardently Protestant fellows, some of whom later became his accusers, while harboring equally ardent Catholics otherwise. The strength of Puritan opposition not only in his own college but the university at large may have persuaded Legge not to mount another high-profile amateur production in the vein of *Richardus Tertius*. He nonetheless continued to work on his adaptation of Josephus that remained unfinished, or rather unrevised, at his death.[34]

In dramatizing this key episode in both secular and ecclesiastical history, Legge had to deal with the contradictory demands of his theme. *Solymitana Clades* is a neoclassical play: its historical subject matter has been cast into quasi-Senecan dramatic form. Yet the classicism of Legge's play is undermined by the awkward importation of the Protestant perspective. *Solymitana Clades* registers and intermittently resists the pressure to conform to the providential reading of Jewish history.

Providence and Politics

On the evidence of the prefatory arguments and the structure and tone of the first several acts, Legge did not set out to illustrate divine vengeance against the Jews. He emphasized, instead, the political and historical dimension of the end of the Hebrew commonwealth, concentrating on the clash with Rome and the sectarian dissension with which the Jewish uprising was closely enmeshed. Yet more than halfway into the trilogy, one of the Jews abruptly confesses to a sense of shame for his part in the crucifixion of the Son of God. This theme is then taken up and elaborated in the Prologue to the Third Action. How does this change of tack affect the overall impact of the play?

Original to Legge, the prose arguments that precede the text of the trilogy are revealing of his aims. The general Argument stresses God's special care of the Jews but makes no connection between ancient Israel and Elizabethan England (though the audience might readily infer one). Nor does it adopt an anti-Jewish stance. Nashe's *Christs Teares* does both. The equivalence between Jerusalem and London is the organizing principle of the pamphlet that opens with a bitter invective: "This gorgious strumpet *Ierusalem*, too-to much presuming of the promises of old, went a whoring after her own inuentions."[35] Legge's summary avoids the gloating attitude of Nashe and his ilk. Instead, it evokes compassion for the fallen city: "urbs miseranda exhausta rapini, homicidio, ruina toto campo prostrata iacet" ["this pitiable city, worn out by pillage and murder, collapsed and was laid prostrate"] (p. 6). There is no hint that the Jews are responsible for deicide or that they are being punished for it. Speaking in the first person, Legge explains that his goal is to show how the Jews were provoked to rise up by the tyrannical conduct of the Roman governor. He certainly does not criticize them for resisting the foreign yoke, but he does condemn their turning against one another. Legge's introduction of Eleazar, the original leader of the rebellion and chief of the Zealots, who will later emerge as one of the villains, is neutral in tone. Since Eleazer is said to be the city's military commander for the year, one might reasonably assume that it fell to him to lead his people against the Romans because he was in office when the oppression became intolerable.

At the heart of the Argument to the First Action are Roman failure and Jewish triumph. Legge emphasizes the Machiavellian machinations of Florus, the Roman Procurator, who seeks to incite rebellion in order to conceal his own misconduct. Newly returned from Rome, King Agrippa advocates patience and forbearance. His pacific stance incenses the Jews, who drive him out of the city. Yet rather than reviling the mob, the author dispassionately relates the expulsion of the king, and he notes that the Jewish elders have managed to calm the people. Eventually, fresh Roman outrages prove unbearable and the Jews follow Eleazer's audacious call to arms. So formidable is the Jewish threat that it intimidates Nero into sending an embassy of peace. The emperor proposes remarkably favorable conditions that the citizens reject. In retaliation, Cestius, the Roman Proconsul of Syria, attacks Jerusalem; but when victory is within reach, he panics and abandons the siege. The Jews who pursued the retreating Romans return home laden with spoils and celebrate a triumph. The Argument thus juxtaposes Florus's misgovernment and corruption, Nero's despondency, and Cestius's lack of nerve with Jewish suffering, rebellion, and victory. Although in a couple of instances Legge refers to Jewish sedition, it would be misleading to attribute an anti-Jewish outlook to the Argument.

Legge's focus on politics rather than providence is further emphasized: first, by a series of framing devices; secondly, by his choice and manipulation of sources; and, thirdly, by his use of spectacle. Beginnings and endings of the three parts, and of individual acts, shape the perception of the Roman-Jewish conflict. In dire distress when the First Action opens, the Jews are triumphant at its end. The overarching frame of the trilogy attests to the ascendancy of Rome. Whereas the first play closes with Jewish triumph, the third one closes with Roman one. Since the First Action started with an account of Roman atrocities, the concluding spectacle of the maimed and defeated Jews might indicate that we are back to where we started. But this is not so. With their city in ruins, the Jews are now a landless and stateless people.

Legge seems to have wanted above all else to demonstrate his massive erudition, and never missed an opportunity to do so. His preference of Josephus over the Latin abridgement suggests that he prized the completeness and accuracy of the former. It may also indicate that he wished to avoid the providential drift inherent in the latter.[36] With one or two exceptions, Legge's departures from the historical record are designed to place Jewish-Roman relations in the context of imperial politics, not to vindicate Christian providence. Nor is the spectacle of Jewish suffering at the hands of the Romans a tendentious illustration of divine justice. Stockwood, Nashe, and others systematically catalogued the omens of impending disaster and affirmed that Christ himself had prophesized every single affliction the city had to endure prior to its ultimate collapse: sacrilegious murders, cannibalism, famine, plague. In *Solymitana Clades*, omens and prophecies, and scenes of Jewish tribulations and crimes they foreshadow, serve a different purpose. They are a warning against civil war and sectarian division.

The Prologue to the third part does bring providential perspective to the fore. Spoken by Vastitas (Devastation), it provides a familiar recounting of Jewish crimes. To punish the impious city ("urbs impia," l. 5113), Devastation summons Vengeance: "Solymas novis vexate tormentis. statim / delere quid cessatis invisum genus?" ["Torment Jerusalem with novel agonies. Why do you hesitate to exterminate this hateful nation immediately?"] (ll. 5134–

35). No amount of suffering will be enough for the reprobate Jews: "fata, quaeso, parcite / si Vastitas ulciscar Hebraeos parum" ["Fates, I pray you grant me pardon if I, Devastation, wreak insufficient vengeance on the Jews"] (ll. 5164–65). Yet Devastation's harangue sits oddly with the thrust of the final play. There are no references to Christianity or the Messiah in the Third Action. Instead it is relentless in its stress on Jewish factionalism and the city's resulting inability to defend itself. The war against Rome is lost because Jews fight each other when they should unite to meet the common enemy. Although nominally wreaked by the Romans, the destruction of Jerusalem amounts to a collective Jewish suicide.

THE JEWISH REBELLION

Had he wished to draw the viewer's attention to Jewish apostasy, Legge could have easily inserted more allusions to Christ, such as Jehoshue's unexpected admission of guilt for the crucifixion.[37] Or he could have introduced a choric figure such as the biblical prophet Hosea in Thomas Lodge and Robert Greene's *A Looking Glass for London and England* (c. 1590), a sensational but also heavily moralistic play about the reformation of Niniveh. Instead, Legge chose to focus unremittingly on politics.

Albeit for divergent reasons, Josephus and the Elizabethan Jeremiahs all condemned the Jewish revolt against Rome. *Solymitana Clades* partly justifies it. Josephus had been commander of Jewish forces in Galilee. With defeat imminent, Josephus, rather than committing suicide together with his fellow soldiers, saved himself by a trick and surrendered to the Romans who employed him as interpreter. After the war, he became a Roman citizen and recipient of Flavian patronage.[38] In *The Jewish War*, Josephus set out to exonerate the upper class to which he himself belonged by attributing responsibility for the failed uprising to the seditious element among the Jews. For all his pride in Jewish bravery and military muscle, Josephus sided with the Romans whom he hailed as the nation destined to rule the world.

In post-Reformation English writings, the Jews' rebellion against their Roman masters was seen as a type of rebellion against their ultimate master, God. "Thou shalt read here," Morwyng warned his readers, "of terrible and horrible events of sedicion and rebellion."[39] According to Stockwood, the Jews' taking "armour agaynste *Cestius Florus* theyr ruler . . . was in deede the verye cause of theyr utter ruine and decay."⁴⁰ Nashe castigated the rebellion as a sign of Jewish conceit and arrogance: "Forty yeeres were expired after our Lordes lifting vp into Heauen, when the Temple-boasting Iewes (elate in theyr owne strength) began to pretend a wearines of the Romaine regiment, and coueted to raigne intire Lords, ouer the Lords that raignd ouer them." Appealing to the rules of "humaine policie," he rebuked the Jews for disobeying the Romans:

> Thou lets *Eleazer*, a priuate man, take the sword of thy freedome into his hands vnauthorized; Thou sufferedst him (vnpunished) to resist the Romaine Prouinciall *Florus*. Ill didst thou therein, for in gouernment (though it be to resist publique violence) it is not safe to suffer a priuate man to vnder-take Armes as generall. The reasons hereafter I wil open in some other discourse treating wholly of those matters.⁴¹

The promised discourse never materialized; however, the implicit comparison between legitimate and illegitimate forms of resistance indicates that Nashe's concerns were similar, although he dealt with them differently, to those aired in the explosive Huguenot resistance tract, *Vindiciae, contra Tyrannos* (1579). Anticipating the objection that it authorized popular sedition, the *Vindiciae* distinguished spontaneous actions of the mob from resistance coordinated by elected public officers, citing the example of "the princes and elders of Israel."⁴² Other writers did not bother about such nice distinctions. Lloyd was typically blunt: "the Iewes . . . could not be quiet, but rebelled euer against the Romanes . . . they would not be brought to subiection."⁴³ The charge of sedition was repeated over and over.

In the first part of his trilogy, Legge tries, if not wholly to vindicate, at least to explain the grounds for the Jewish rebellion against Rome. He diverges from his sources and devises powerful scenic emblems to engage our sympathy for the Jews by appealing to our sense of *Realpolitik* and our emotions. The received historical record is distorted to blacken the Romans. In Josephus, Florus is certainly a corrupt administrator, prone to bribery and extortion, but nothing there prepares us for Legge's despotic and lustful plotter.⁴⁴ Legge's Florus brazenly admits that his goal is to ignite the Jewish rebellion in order to cover up his own wrongdoing, and he condemns their loyalty and restraint in failing, despite repeated provocations, to fight back. Far from upholding the law, he cynically insists that it can be dispensed with at will (the First Action, I.ii.551). Aside from having the procurator incriminate himself in asides and soliloquies, Legge invents a confrontation between

Florus and Salamuth, a married Jewess, who resists his advances but whom the tyrant is nonetheless determined to enjoy. Another original scene illustrates the damage Florus's ruthless drive to satisfy his sexual appetite inflicts on an ordinary Jewish family: in spite of his wife's tearful entreaties, the father of a young woman who has caught Florus's eye resolves to yield his daughter to the monster's lust (the First Action, II.i.407–55 and II.iii. 583–92).

Far from being civil and civilized, Roman soldiers appear cruel, even sadistic. As they carry out Florus's criminal orders, the soldiers mock their Jewish prey, instinctively relishing the role of executioners. When a Jew asks a Roman soldier what crime he has committed, the latter jeeringly replies "ferrum quod imo non vorasti pectore" ["You refused to take my sword into your breast"] (the First Action, I.ii.580). In addition to making the Romans more vicious than warranted by his source, Legge uses visual means to demonize them. Throughout *Solymitana Clades*, violence is enacted before our eyes, not just reported by messenger or chorus. In the First Action, onstage brutality serves to excite pity for the Jews as innocent and helpless victims of Roman depredations. Possibly most poignant is the massacre of unarmed Jewish civilians who, in accordance with Florus's command, have issued out of the city to welcome the returning legions with music and song: *"Let the Souldiers set upon the Citizens and drive them awaye"* (p. 50).[45] In Josephus the assault is a response to anti-Florus jeers; in Legge it is entirely unprovoked.[46] There are also reports of a sacrilegious attack on the Temple whose treasury is the object of Florus's greed.

The play subtly steers the response of the audience. Our initial impression that in rallying his countrymen Eleazer is unselfish and patriotic is quickly dispelled.[47] This does not mean, however, that Jewish resistance is wholly illegitimate or that Zealots are the only Jews ready to fight the Roman oppressors. Rapes, killings, and expropriations are not Eleazer's fabrication. They are a fact, as we ourselves have been made to witness. Nor is the anti-Roman stance associated exclusively with the mob. The trilogy opens with a prayer by Manasche, a respectable and wealthy citizen ("princeps populi"), who is indignant that the chosen people should have submitted to gentile yoke ("nunc (horreo dicere) Abrahae electum genus / ingens superbis praeda facta gentibus / collum grave servili submittit iugo" ["Now (I shudder to say it) the chosen race of Abraham has been made great prey for the arrogant gentiles and has lamentably submitted its neck to the yoke of servitude"] (the First Action, I.i.16–18). That someone of such exalted standing is the first Jewish character to denounce Rome and her past and present officials and to paint a harrowing picture of Florus's crimes proves that Jewish grievances must be taken seriously. Manasche's recounting of the complaint submitted to Cestius effectively demonstrates that the Jews cannot hope for redress from the metropolis whose officers are either corrupt or indifferent. King Agrippa makes a case for obedience to the Romans irrespective of the personal shortcomings of the current governor. Yet contrary to Sutton's assessment, Agrippa is not an unproblematic character. A smooth politician, the king preaches submission to Rome not only or not primarily because he thinks this is the right thing to do, but because he realizes the awkwardness of his own position should his people revolt against the power that has licensed his rule.[48] Agrippa's advocacy of subjection does not endear him either to his compatriots or to the viewer. True, at one point his appeal for calm brings tears to the eyes of the auditors; but elsewhere he is shown to scold his countrymen harshly. They are the guilty party, he says, and yet we have seen them being treated inhumanely by the Romans: in fighting back, the Jews have acted in self-defense and to protect from pillage the most sacred of sites, the Temple. Overall, Legge's complex presentation of character alerts us to the conflicting demands of national interest and political allegiance, public duty and private ends.

Solymitana Clades is a long and messy play, so to examine all the twists and turns of the plot is not feasible. But we must ask how the Jewish-Roman war is presented in the Second and Third Actions. Legge strikingly departs from his chief source, *The Jewish War*, in assigning to the High Priest Anani a pro-war attitude. In answer to Josephus's enquiry whether he ought to continue fighting or enter into peace negotiations with the Romans, Anani says: "pacem dedisse maior urbis laus erit . . . talia Iosepho mandata rediens nuncia. / noli ferire indigna Solymis foedera. iniqua bello corrigenda pax erit, dux arma sancti numinis sancta geras. magnam dei potentis auge gloriam" ["It is more praiseworthy for our city to grant peace than to ask for it . . . So return and transmit these orders to Josephus: you must not enter into a truce shameful to Jerusalem. An unfair peace must be remedied by fighting. You are a leader who bears the weapons of our sacred God"] (the Second Action, II.ii.2866, 2883–87).[49] With supreme dramatic irony, Legge then interrupts the spectacle of the mourning procession for Josephus with the news that, rather than sacrificing his life for the cause, Josephus has ignobly saved himself by a ruse that has led to the death of all but one of his co-defenders. The erstwhile mourners greet the report of Josephus's baseness with derision; and they reassert the patriotic duty of each Jew to continue fighting. Throughout the trilogy the Romans, whose own courage and military discipline are not what they were wont to be, acknowledge Jewish bravery even as they pour scorn on Jewish guile.[50] Albeit weakened by internal divisions and beset by plague and famine, the Jews long defy Roman attempts to re-conquer Jerusalem.

Repeatedly exasperated by the insubordination of their troops, Roman commanders are themselves far from perfect. Even Titus, ostensibly a paragon of prudence and clemency, foolishly exposes himself to danger and is almost caught in an enemy trap. More damningly, he alternates between mercy and brutality. Legge takes considerable liberties with history by having Titus command that crosses, with bodies of Jewish captives stretched on them, be displayed before the walls of Jerusalem to dampen the spirits of the defenders. This is psychological warfare with a macabre twist: "metum tam maesta gignunt mentibus spectacula" ["Such a sad sight will terrorize their minds"] (the Third Action, III.v.7004–8).[51] The corresponding stage direction calls for *"bodyes hanged on Crosses* [to] *bee sett up against the Cittye"* (p. 426). The play highlights Titus's greed (he accepts gifts from fugitive Jewish priests whom he despises) and his authorization of looting. Legge further blurs the distinction between Romans and Jews, which various characters insist on, in his account of the collective suicide of the Jews at Massada. With its exaltation of constancy, liberty, virtue, and personal courage, Eleazer's speech urging the Jews to kill themselves rather than endure foreign bondage sounds more Roman than Jewish.[52] Titus's offhand dismissal of the Jewish act as "furor" (lunacy) implicitly questions his own Roman values.[53] Throughout *Solymitana Clades* Legge juxtaposes *romanitas* and Jewishness. That juxtaposition, we shall now see, invites a critical examination of the concept of national ethos. Legge encourages his viewers to assess their notions of Englishness vis-à-vis the Jewish and the Roman models.

Liberty and Empire

In Elizabethan England, the sense of nationhood was commonly expressed through historical analogies. The analogy with Celtic Britain emphasized, by way of contrast, contemporary England's independence from foreign influence and, especially in the aftermath of the Armada, her impregnability against invasion; the analogy with ancient Rome highlighted, by way of similitude, the country's imperial ambitions. Both the British and the Roman examples, moreover, were readily cited as warnings against internecine strife.

Elizabethan accounts of the Roman conquest of Britain offer a useful frame of reference for Legge's treatment of Roman-Jewish relations. Having been conquered by Caesar and subjected to Rome by Claudius, Britain, like Judea, was a tributary province. In *Solymitana Clades* the parallel between them, of which Legge's audience needed little reminding, is invoked both verbally and visually. Legge recalls Vespasian's service in the Claudian campaign of A.D. 43 (Nero puts Vespasian in charge of suppressing the unrest in Judea on the strength of his exploits in Britain);[54] and he includes Britons among the troops besieging Jerusalem: "*Let the Souldiers be Moores, Africans, Aramites, Chaldeans, Persians, Burgundians, Brittons, Kederans. Ioseph de bello Iudaico*" (p. 372). Had the play been performed, Legge's Britons would have been identifiable through distinctive costume, most likely based on descriptions in current historical and antiquarian writings such as Camden's *Britannia* (1586). In fact, Josephus is one of the principal sources quoted by Camden in his account of the Roman conquest: "And Iosephus in the person of Titus, speaketh thus to the Iewes: *What greater wall and barre than the Ocean? Wherewith the Britans being fensed and inclosed, doe yet adore the Romans forces.*"[55]

Public discussion of the prospects for a Protestant empire gained momentum with the union of English and Scottish crowns under James I and VI and the creation of Great Britain in 1603. Yet already in the closing decades of the sixteenth century we find both a strong interest in England's historic subjection to foreign dominance (Roman, Danish, Saxon, Norman) and an articulation of her current aspirations to empire through expansion within the British Isles (chiefly in Ireland) and in the New World.[56] Camden's *Britannia* documented the island's past as a Roman province. The *Britannia* and several Jacobean plays—Shakespeare's *Cymbeline* (1608–11), Fletcher's *Bonduca* (1611–14), and R. A.'s *The Valiant Welshman* (1610–15)—used the Roman conquest to compare the values of the Romans and of the Britons, and assess the price of Rome's military triumph and its civilizing mission.[57] So whatever the religious implications of his theme, in pitting Rome's claim to empire against the Jewish claim to liberty, Legge was addressing a serious contemporary concern.[58] If preachers and pamphleteers pressed Englishmen to identify with biblical Hebrews (the new chosen nation with the old), *Solymitana Clades* invited them to view imperial expansion through the lens of ancient British and ancient Jewish subjection to Roman rule.

Legge does not adjudicate between the competing claims of liberty and empire. Or at least he does not do so at the outset of the trilogy. If anything, the First Action seems to sanction the Jewish bid for freedom by dwelling on the Roman governor's corruption and injustice; it is only when radical elements among the Jews take over, and when internecine strife divides defenders of Jerusalem and leads to bloodshed, pillage, and treachery that our sympathy is alienated. One could argue that the outcome of the drama— Rome's crushing victory and annihilation of the Jewish state— endorses the claims of empire. But the intimation of the wretched fate of the Jews in the play's final visual emblem militates against this conclusion, just as the staging of Roman atrocities in the First Action worked to excuse the Jewish rising. "THE SONG OF THE CAPTIVED JEWES IN THE TRIUMPH *having one hand wrapt in a bloudy clout as cutt off*," with its reproving refrain, "Hierusalem gemenda o Hierusalem, / tandem deum conversa cognoscas tuum," ["Jerusalem, lamentable Jerusalem, at length repent and acknowledge your God"] (the Third Action, V.ix.9142–43), focuses squarely on Jewish apostasy, not their uprising against Rome, which is not even mentioned. "The shew in the end of the Tragedy," with its procession of "Soldiers Burgundians, Brittaines, Persians, Chaldaeans, Aramites, Africans, Moores, Kedarians, Romans, Italians," followed by a display of spoils and captives, testifies to the might and territorial extent of imperial Rome.

And yet, for all its visual splendor, this is not a Roman but divine triumph. When the Jews chant their ultimate *mea culpa*—"proles scelesta cum scelestis patribus / errore ducimur rebelles devio. / iniqua proni multa perpetravimus / dum mens libidine concita effraeni furit" ["Wicked children with our wicked fathers, we went astray as rebels. Headlong, we worked many iniquities as our unbridled minds raged with desire"] (ibid, ll. 9162–65)—they acknowledge themselves guilty of revolt against God rather than secular authority. There is a substantial difference, moreover, between Josephus's espousal of Rome's imperial destiny in his history and the expression of similar sentiments by Legge's *dramatis personae*. Josephus was writing when the Roman empire was at its zenith; Legge long after its demise. Early modern nations aspiring to universal dominion sought to understand why the Roman model had failed. In depicting the Roman mistreatment of the Jews, in giving voice to Jewish sense of nationhood, and in alluding to the turbulence of A.D. 69, the year of the four emperors (Galba, Otho, Vitellius, and Vespasian), Legge's play offered tentative answers: corrupt administration, cruelty towards the conquered peoples, and internal division.

Published two years before the presumed date when Legge began composition of *Solymitana Clades*, Holinshed's *Chronicle* (1577, 2nd edn 1587) adopted a similar position. The chronicle provided an account of the Roman conquest of Britain and of British resistance to the Roman yoke. Holinshed's sympathetic narrative of Voadicia's (Boudicca's, Boadicea's) rebellion of A.D. 60–61 could serve, with little adjustment, to underwrite Jewish rebellion against Rome as depicted by Legge:

> the Britains began to conferre togither of theyr great and importable miseries, of their grieuous state of seruitude, of their iniuries and wrongs, which they dailie susteined: how that by sufferance they profited nothing, but still were oppressed with more heauie burthens. Ech counrie in times past had onelie one king to rule them: now had they two, the lieutenant by his capteins and souldiers spilling their bloud, and the procurator or receiuer . . . bereauing them of their goods and substance. The concord or discord betwixt those that were appointed to rule ouer them, was all alike hurtfull vnto the subiects, the lieutenant oppressing them by his capteins and men of warre, and the procurator or receiuer by force and reprochfull demenaours, polling them by insufferable exactions.[59]

Where the two rebellions differ is in their leadership: the factionalism of the Jews contrasts sharply with the royal-led British uprising. To apply the distinction made in the *Vindiciae*, the native queen's leadership lent a legitimacy to the British rebellion that the Jewish uprising lacked. Recounting the withdrawal of the Romans from Britain and the collapse of their empire, Holinshed highlighted the despotism of provincial administrators that alienated the local population; he also pointed to the adverse effect of Rome's domestic turmoil on her ability to maintain imperial outposts:

> They possessed it [Britain] almost fiue hudreth yeares, and longer might haue doone, if either their insufferable tyrannie had not taken awaie from them the loue of the people as well here as else-where; either that their ciuill discord about the chopping and changing of their emperours had not so weakened the forces of their empire, that they were not able to defend the same against the irruption of barbarous nations. (ibid, II: ii)

The patriotic approach to ancient British history coexisted with a providential one. The tension between the two can be discerned in

Nashe's *Christs Teares over Jerusalem*. Nashe's reference to Julius Caesar's conquest of "Gallia, Belgia, thys our poore Albion, and the better part of Europe" hinted at a resentment of the Roman yoke. However, later in the pamphlet he interpreted the various conquests of Britain as meet punishment for the nation's sins: *"England*, thou needst not be ambitious, thou needst not be vaineglorious, for ere this hast thou been bowed and burdned till thy backe crackt. As the Israelites were tenne times led into captiuity, so seauen times hast thou beene ouer-runne and conquered."[60]

If England's remote past suggested affinities with ancient Judea, her present position fostered comparisons, however wishful or inflated, with ancient Rome. Holinshed likened the English conquest of Ireland under Henry II to the Roman and Saxon conquests of Britain. He attributed the success of the English campaign to Irish factionalism that, in his view, mirrored the factionalism of ancient Britons making the task of foreign invaders easier:

> ... nothing more hindred the fierce and vnquiet nation [the Irish] from making resistance, than that they could not agree to take councell togither for defending of their liberties, and entier state of the commonwelth. Wherevpon, whilest euerie of them apart by himselfe was in doubt to attempt the hazard of war against so mightie a king, they were all ouercome, as were the Britons likewise in the time of Cesar and the Saxons.[61]

In the last decade of the sixteenth century, Richard Beacon explicitly applied the Roman example to the situation in Ireland in *Solon his Follie, or A Politique discourse, Touching the Reformation of common-weales conquered, declined or corrupted* (1594).[62] Beacon's dialogue paralleled England and Ireland with Athens and the Athenian colony Salamina, respectively. Yet, as Markku Peltonen has shown, Beacon's model for the reformation of the English government in Ireland was not Athens but the early Roman republic as refracted through Machiavelli's *Discourses upon Livy*.[63] Addressed to Queen Elizabeth whom he likened to the founder of the Roman republic, Lucius Junius Brutus, Beacon's tract proposed "the sound & universall reformation of this your Realme of Ireland."[64]

Legge made no reference to Ireland, whether explicit or implicit. Yet given his political justification of the Jewish uprising and his ambivalent picture of Roman imperial administration, we are entitled to ask how far his audience might have related those to England's involvement in Ireland. By setting the Jewish struggle for national liberation against the background of internecine strife and religious tension, Legge not only alluded to confessional divisions within late Elizabethan society, but also raised the question of the rights and wrongs of imperialism. At the time he composed his play, Ireland was the site of continued unrest: the Pope and Philip II of Spain sponsored a revolt in 1579, and the Earl of Tyrone's rebellion (nine years' war) lasted from 1594 until 1603. Spain intervened again in 1601. England, for her part, had aided the rebel Dutch provinces in their struggle against the Spanish yoke.[65] (Among the Elizabethans, the revolt of the Netherlands was the great topic of debate about native revolt against foreign tyranny.)

In many respects *Solymitana Clades* was irrelevant to the Irish problem: rather than being aided by foreign powers such as Spain and the papacy, both of whom assisted the Catholic Irish, the Jews are besieged by the Romans who head a multinational force, and they are persecuted elsewhere. In terms of religion, there is hardly a correspondence between the pagan Romans fighting the Jews and the Protestant English fighting the Catholic Irish. Besides, England was aiming for subjection of Ireland, not total extinction or dispersal of her people. Legge certainly did not set out to write *Solymitana Clades* as a covert commentary on Ireland, but I suspect that his assessment of imperial administration and of the clash in national ethos between the conquerors and the conquered might have led his audience to reflect on England's expansion in Ireland and the New World.[66]

Legge exaggerated the Roman misconduct in order to make the Jewish uprising more excusable. He also departed from his main source, Josephus, in depicting Nero's embassy to the Jews. Dana Sutton has supposed that the embassy was Legge's invention. In fact, it is based on a version of *Yosippon*. The scene strengthens the political dimension of the play. Rome acknowledges the misconduct of her officers and is ready to grant self-government to her tributary province:

> . . . hoc Caesar . . . edixit . . .
> edixit et populi potestas altera.
> nunquam minas metuet Latini militis
> Iudaea, gentis fraena tractabit suae,
> regetque Solymas iuris aequi vinculis
> praefectus Hebreus, patrum qui firmiter
> mores avitos servet exteris.
>   (the First Action, IV.ii.1766–72)

[Thus says Caesar . . . Thus also says the Roman people on its independent authority: let Judaea never fear any Roman military threat; let it

> hold the reins of its own government; let a Jewish governor rule Jerusalem with the bonds of fair law, who will firmly defend the ancestral ways of your forefathers against foreign influence.]⁶⁷

For Legge to have deviated from Josephus on this score is significant: he shows a way in which Roman domination could have been maintained without riling the Jewish national feeling. The Jewish elders wish to accept Nero's offer; but the armed intervention of the Zealots, aimed at both the Jewish elders and the Romans, prevents the conclusion of a treaty. This scene, which marks the effective beginning of the Jewish civil war, is also the turning point in the presentation of the Jewish revolt. However justified the Jews may have been in taking up arms, their rejection of so favorable a settlement means that they have now lost the moral high ground: no longer victims of Roman oppression, they become their own oppressors.

Rome's preeminence was based on her military might. Having absorbed and transvalued the superior culture of Greece, the Romans became agents of civilization for the nations they conquered. Their civilizing mission was not seen as an unmixed blessing. "Agricola," we are told by Holinshed's *Chronicle*,

> tooke paines to reduce the Britains from their rude manners and customs, vnto a more ciuill sort and trade of liuing, that changing their naturall fiercenesse and apt disposition to warre, they might through tasting pleasures be so inured therewith, that they should desire to liue in rest and quietnesse . . .⁶⁸

As a result Britons acquired a propensity for servitude and thralldom.

To vindicate their policy in Ireland, Elizabethan commentators stressed the barbarity of the native population. The contrast between civilization and barbarism is at the heart of Legge's play. The word "barbarian" and its cognates recur throughout the trilogy. Contrary to what we might expect, barbarity is not associated exclusively with the Jews. In the First Action it is the Romans who are persistently denounced as barbaric. Yet as the Jewish in-fighting escalates, the implied evaluation of the two sides alters. By the end of the play, not only the Romans but also the Jews condemn as barbaric the instances of infanticide and cannibalism that are the product of bloody internal schism as much as of siege conditions. The Romans are hardly torchbearers of enlightenment and civility, but they cannot be blamed for the worst atrocities: those the Jews inflict on themselves.

Legge's presentation of Jewish history is not allegorical. His Jews are Jews and his Romans are Romans. The responsibility for deducing contemporary relevance, if any, rests squarely with the reader or spectator. In a variety of public contexts, late sixteenth-century Englishmen were urged to think of themselves alternatively as latter-day Romans and as latter-day Jews. During the closing decades of the century, England faced attack from Spain, chief modern aspirant to universal dominion. England also had to contend with unrest, often fomented and abetted by the Spaniards, in her own colony: Ireland. By staging a confrontation between an imperial power and a rebellious people, Legge's trilogy might have provoked, whether designedly or not, a meditation on the rights and wrongs of empire. The play makes possible a double identification for the audience. They might well side with the triumphant Romans: first, because England is now the colonial power ruling the conquered peoples; secondly, because of her emergent sense of identity as a modern and civil nation innately superior to the wild and barbarous Irish. But the allusions to the Roman conquest of Britain remind the audience that, like the Jews, their ancestors had once been subject to Roman rule against which they too had rebelled.

The Jewish Civil War

If, ultimately, resistance to Rome is condemned by virtually every Jewish character with whom we have been invited to sympathize, this is because the tyranny of domestic faction has come to outweigh the real or imagined menace of the Roman yoke. In the first part of the trilogy, Legge demonized the Roman governor Florus to justify the Jewish revolt against Rome; now he demonizes the Jewish rebels to show the disastrous effects of religious dissension and factionalism. Power hungry, devious, and unscrupulous, the three rebel leaders, Eleazer, Jechochanan, and Schimeon, terrorize the city. The crimes visited by Jew upon Jew exceed anything we have seen Florus and his minions perpetrate in the First Action. Civil war proves more destructive than foreign war.

To drive the point home, Legge subtly Anglicizes the Jewish civil war. First, he heightens the social dimension of the conflict through characters and episodes, some invented and some adapted from Josephus, that bring to mind the peasant uprisings of medieval England. Secondly, he uses visual means to suggest correspondences between members of the Sanhedrin and English judges; and, thirdly, he highlights the danger of religious innovation masquerading as reformist zeal. In a scene that has no counterpart in Josephus although it is loosely inspired by his account, a robber chief and a peasant chief declare their intention to profit from the war by looting the war-torn metropolis. With its distinctly English rural flavor conjured up by references to leeks, garlic, black bread, pitchforks, whips, and clubs, the peasant leader's threatening speech raises the spectre of Jack Straw's rebellion of 1381.[69] Legge's account of the Zealot mob assaulting royal palaces, burning public archives, and slaughtering upper-class citizens too evokes memories of popular unrest at home. Like the followers of Straw who, according to Holinshed, "purposed to burne and destroie all records, euidences, court-rolles, and other minuments, that the remembrance of ancient matters being remooued out of mind, their landlords might not haue whereby to chalenge anie right at their hands" (II: 737), Legge's Jewish rebels "documenta quaque creditorum perdere / illi studebant, crediti ne ratio / exstaret ulla debiti seu memoria ut iungerent suas rebelles copias / potentiam faciunt egenis liberam / ut creditores in potentes saeviant" ["wanted to destroy all documents pertaining to loans, so that there would be no records of credit or debt. So that the rebels could gather them to the fold, they gave the poor the opportunity of freely committing violence against their wealthy creditors" (the First Action, III.iv.1616–21).

If Zealot rabble are reminiscent of seditious English crowds that would be brought on to the public stage in later history plays such as the anonymous *Jack Straw* and Shakespeare's *2 Henry VI*, the Sanhedrin is rendered familiar through analogy with an English court of law. Whereas elsewhere in the play Legge aims to recreate local color via historically accurate costume, in a remarkable scene depicting the reception of Nero's embassy by the Sanhedrin, he insists on contemporary dress—Aldermen's gowns—for the Jewish elders. For all his apparent concern about the historicity of the Sanhedrin, Legge's elaborate stage direction, part English, part Latin, effectively naturalizes and modernizes the ancient Jewish institution. In performance, that translation into contemporary reality would have been apparent to the eye:

> Then let the Curtaines bee drawen that these sitting may appeire. Anani in the middest, on the right side Iosephus a Pharisee, Amittai a docter of the Law, Iehoshue another Dr. of L. on the other side Manasche., Jehochanann bar Sakkai, Rashbagg. under them a company in Aldermens gownes representing 70 Seniors in consistorio Gaith et hoc iudiucum erat 70 Iudicum et decebatur Sanhedre ghedola, id est con-

silium magnum. Sanhedrim id est Iudicum sive Seniorum Israel. dicebantur Nehotekim id est Scribae sive Legum latores; hi errant quos ordinaries Iudics dicimus. Galat. De Arcanis Cathol. Veritatits lib. 4. hi sedebant in consistorio Gazith, Galat. ibidem, Sigonis de Repub. Hebr. Cap. 7 lib. 6. (p. 108)[70]

Rather than drawing a parallel with the English Parliament, however, Legge settles for a more innocuous if less apposite model of the Aldermanic Court.[71]

For an academic audience reared on sermons replete with analogies between England and Judea, and ever on the alert for potentially controversial undertones of such analogies, any theatrical representation of sectarian conflict, but especially of religious dissension within the Hebrew Commonwealth, was an open invitation to exercise their exegetical skills. Legge need not even have departed from the historical record to provoke a topical application: it was enough to show the Zealots—religious fanatics par excellence—in action. Nor need he have built a sustained parallel. The appellation was itself suggestive: in his 1582 tract, *A Briefe Discourse of Certaine Pointes of the Religion, whiche is among the Common Sorte of Christians: which may bee termed the "Countrie diuinitie,"* the Puritan George Gifford made the Puritan "Zelotes" his mouthpiece.[72] With their insistence on restoring pristine forms of worship beyond what the Elizabethan settlement had secured, Puritans were typically castigated as innovators.[73] They were also disparaged as misguided appropriators of Jewish lore: "you *Judaizare*, 'play the Jew,'" Whitgift told Thomas Cartwright in 1572. (Cartwright's offence was to argue for the strict observance of Jewish "ceremonial laws.")[74] In February 1586, Legge himself sat on a university tribunal, presided over by Vice-Chancellor Andrew Perne, that tried one John Smyth whose Lent sermon *ad clerum* had not only berated all those acting in and watching plays on Sunday as destined for eternal damnation, but also fervently upheld a twenty-four-hour Jewish "sabbath by divine law." To the question "Whether the length of time of the Lord's Day must by divine law extend for the period of twenty-four hours," Smyth answered "Yes," members of the court "No." However, when asked "Whether Christians are as strictly bound to the observance of the Lord's Day with respect to works as the Jews are to the observance of the Sabbath," both he and his interrogators replied "No."[75] The upshot of the case was that Smyth was required to deliver another sermon to clarify (read: recant) his earlier misguided opinions; the new sermon was to be vetted and approved by the Vice-Chancellor.

In such a climate Eleazer's call for abolition of gentile sacrifice as an impious accretion would have immediately struck a chord: it sounds very like the attacks on the Church of England for retaining what militants saw as popish rites.[76] Tellingly, the verdict issued in the play by the experts in Mosaic law is that gentile sacrifices, which have been accepted since time immemorial, are not an infringement of the law and ought to continue; hence Zealot arguments are exposed as hollow and self-serving. Their abolition of hereditary priesthood—the Zealots mastermind an election, by lot, of the peasant Phani to the position of the High Priest—also could have suggested the anti-prelatical zest of the Puritans.[77] Even so, it is important to recognize, first, that Legge does nothing to strengthen the link between Zealots and Puritans by altering Josephus's account, and, secondly, that the link dissolves altogether in the Second and Third Actions as factional warfare intensifies.

The Zealot call for liberation might seem devoid of topical significance. But given that in Protestant thought ancient Rome was continuous with papal Rome, the notion of a Jewish campaign may have suggested a contemporary application. In the Third Action, Schimeon, temporarily allied with Eleazer and Jechochanan, imagines not only the overthrow of the Roman yoke but the Jewish conquest of Rome itself: "si vicimus, statis Romae ante moenia" ["If we win, we shall stand before the very walls of Rome"] (I.iii.5370). This rhetorical flourish, which has no precedent in Josephus, is consistent with militant Protestant perspective. A severe blow to papal Rome, the Henrician Reformation was often likened to military victory. For instance, in a welcome speech with which Gurgunt, the legendary founder of Norwich, was to have greeted Elizabeth outside the city walls in August 1578, that analogy was made explicit. The mythic expedition of two ancient British worthies Belinus and Brennus was presented as a forerunner of King Henry's break with Rome. According to Gurgunt, his father King Belinus, and his uncle Brennus, "Old Rome did rase and sacke, and halfe consume with fire." So did Henry VIII, who "new Rome that purple whore / Did sacke and spoile hir neere, of all hir glittering tire."[78] In 1589, animated by the recent routing of the Armada, George Peele mapped a bold route of conquest for English Protestants in a poem dedicated to commanders Norris and Drake on the eve of their launch of the Portuguese mission. "[H]ewe a passage with your conquering swords," urged Peele, "Even to the Gulfe that leades to loftie Rome, / There to deface the pryde of Antechrist, / And pull his Paper walles and popery downe."[79] In Legge's play such militancy is thoroughly discredited.

If we discern an inconsistency in Legge's treatment of the Jewish-Roman conflict, this is because initially we are drawn to sympathize with the Jews as victims of Roman depredations. But when Jewish sedition leads to mass slaughter of innocent citizens and compromises war effort, we are steered in the direction of a providential interpretation, supplemented by a severe indictment of civil war, that was a staple of pulpit oratory and that became pervasive in the history plays of the 1580s and 1590s: *The Troublesome Reign of King John*, *The True Tragedy of Richard III*, *1–3 Henry VI*, *1–2 Henry IV*, and many others.[80] Yet although *Solymitana Clades* imparts a lesson against civil discord and the pitfalls of religious fanaticism, Legge never wholeheartedly condemns the Jewish rebellion against the rule of the Caesars.

Legge and the Jews

Solymitana Clades is the earliest, and the only extant, Elizabethan play to present the non-biblical Jewish past and to analyze that past predominantly in political rather than religious terms.[81] Although it remained unperformed, Legge's trilogy was known to at least some contemporaries. The first staging of the fall of Jerusalem occurred not at one of the universities or in London but in a provincial town. In response to pressures from the local community who wanted civic drama to continue, and from the Puritan preachers who clamoured for its suppression, the City Fathers of Coventry resolved on a compromise. They commissioned one John Smith, a native of Coventry and now an Oxford scholar, to write a play about *The Destruction of Jerusalem* as a replacement for popish cycle drama. Smith had been given a generous payment, and his historical pageant show was lavishly produced by the Coventry guilds in 1584 (when Legge was still at work on his play). It was possibly revived at the request of the Commons in 1591.[82]

Within a year, a professional company may have put forward its own version of the overthrow of Jerusalem in the lost *Titus and Vespasian*.[83] It is difficult to speculate on the content of these lost plays. Whereas the Lord Strange's Men's play is a complete unknown, the Coventry records give some indication of characters (the rebels Simon, Eliazar, and John, the High Priest Ananus, soldiers, the Chorus); the set (the Temple); props (beards for the Jews); costumes (red coats for the soldiers, a couple of green cloaks); and special effects (the storm). However, that is not sufficient evidence from which to infer how the fall of Jerusalem was interpreted. What makes *Solymitana Clades* uniquely valuable is that, as the only surviving late sixteenth-century play about the destruction of Jerusalem, it tells us what a Cambridge academic, administrator, and civil lawyer made of Jewish history. We do not know whether, and if so how, Legge's play influenced the others—a contemporary report that it was plagiarized has been discredited by modern scholars.[84] The trilogy is significant as a testimony to the perception of the Jews in Elizabethan high culture. Legge's preoccupation with the political ramifications of Jewish war of liberation and civil war puts in perspective popular jeremiads, with their incessant harping on Jewish culpability for deicide. It demonstrates that, shortly before the appearance of evil stage Jews in public plays by Marlowe, Shakespeare, Greene, and others, an attitude of qualified empathy and historical understanding could coexist with a nod toward providential reading.[85]

Elizabethan commentators who dwelt on the ingratitude and disobedience of the Jews to God typically complemented their narratives of divine vengeance with an *excursus* on the deservedly dismal situation of contemporary Jews. "[T]hey themselues are nowe driuen and banished from those places," Stockwood told his congregation in 1578, "and are become a byworde and reproche in those places where they in small number dwell, carrying a note of reproche on theyr garments, that they may be knowen from other people."[86] In a sermon delivered seven years later, in 1585, Bishop Edwin Sandys (who had accused Legge of harboring popishly inclined youth in his college) insisted that "the remnant of that elect and chosen people . . . doth live in all contempt, hatred, and slavery; marked like Cain to be known as a murdering vagabond upon the earth, to be a bye-word, and an example of God's justice to all the world, throughout all succeeding ages."[87] Anti-Jewish invective was omnipresent in sermons and pamphlets: Stockwood speaks of the Jews as the "most abhominable wicked creatures;" "Not *Abrahams* sonnes are you," Nashe rejoins, "but the sonnes of blood."[88]

Given the prevalent anti-Semitism, reflected in Elizabethan pronouncements on ancient Jews (Christ-killers) and modern Jews (contemptible vagabonds), Legge's depiction would have been something of a surprise. Throughout the play the distinctness of Jews as a nation is emphasized via modes of address, sometimes scornful and debasing but mostly proud and flattering: "genus," Abraham's offspring, seed, sons. What is particularly striking about Legge's presentation of the Jewish people is his determination to expose his audience to elaborate spectacle of religious rites, customs, and ceremonies. He achieves this through his extraordinary depiction of the celebration of the Feast of the Tabernacles, which he combined with elements of the Passover (the First Action,V.i.). Another example is the scene of sacrifice in the Temple, complete with the killing of a real lamb on stage, with music and psalm-singing brutally interrupted by the rebel troops who slaughter the worshipping civilians (the Second Action, III.iv).[89]

Legge is certainly more concerned to historicize the Jews than the Romans. There is no indication that he gave much thought to the appearance of Titus and his soldiers but he took pains to describe the appropriate—and historically authentic—costumes for the Jews. His production notes include, for example, a remarkable diagram detailing the order of the *Processio Lugubris* in the Third Action: "Lictor templi," "Janitores templi," "Nazarei sive Gabaonitae," "Nazarei," Hemerobaptistae," "Gaulonitae," "Herodiani," "Saducei," "Essei," "Pharisei," "Scribae sive legum doctores," "Cantores sive Levitae," "Sacerdotes . . . some priests, some Pharises, some Docters of the Law," "Summuys Sacerdos," and "Milites Templi." This is accompanied by a description of "The attire of such as be in the shew in the beginning of the third Action."[90] Of the "Pharisei" Legge says: "A long linen gowne somthing strait against their body. the undergowne sleeves turned up at the hands. on their shoulders Philacteres; that is a litle short cloake of linnen like a Womans cloake, mantelwise laied on their shoulders. which Philacteries are now also used of the Jews with a fringe about them and tenn knottes hanging downe signifying the tenn commandements. . . . on their forehead also and about their left arme a scroll with the tenn commandements."[91]

In post-Reformation England rabid antisemitism was no obstacle to Puritan emulation of Jewish traditions in ways that pitted them against the hierarchy of the Church of England.[92] By the 1590s, attempts were being made by middle-of-the road Anglicans to reclaim Old Testament Jews from Puritan propagandists: Hooker's *Laws of Ecclesiastical Polity* sought to do just that. One of his ploys was to annex Jewish customs and religious rituals in defense of Anglican liturgy that was so often charged with retaining elements of popish ceremony.[93] Would it be too farfetched to suggest that, in devising elaborate scenes of Jewish ritual and ceremony, Legge was intent on familiarizing his audience with ancient rites that could be seen as symbolic precedents for the ceremonial worship of their own church?

Solymitana Clades raises questions about Christian perceptions of Judaism and the Jews, about religious ceremony and sectarian division, about secular power and internecine strife, about the politics of empire, and about the terms of allegiance of province to metropolis. By modifying his sources and exploiting to the full the visual potential of his medium, Legge is able to engage the audience at an intellectual and emotional level without imposing on them the providential view of Jewish rebellion and Jerusalem's fall.[94]

NOTES

This was published in Francis Meres, *Palladis Tania* (London, 1598), sig. Oo5[r-v].

In full, *Christs Teares over Ierusalem. Wherunto is annexed, a comparatiue admonition to London*, in *The Works of Thomas Nashe*, ed. R. B. McKerrow, 5 vols. (London: A. H. Bullen, 1904), II: 15.

1. *Records of Early English Drama: Cambridge*, ed. Alan Nelson, 2 vols (Toronto: University of Toronto Press, 1989), I: 282–84, 286; II: 713, 720–22, 754, 769, 918–19; 943–46, 1024, 1220. On the Shakespeare connection, see G. B. Churchill, *Richard the Third up to Shakespeare* (Berlin: Mayer & Müller, 1900), 265–395.

2. For biographical information on Legge, see Christopher Brooke's article in the New *DNB* and his "Thomas Legge and the Elizabethan College," in idem, *A History of Gonville and Caius College* (Woodbridge: Boydell, 1985, repr. with addenda 1996), 79–93; Peter Stein, "Thomas Legge, a Sixteenth-Century English Civilian and His Books," in idem, *The Character and Influence of the Roman Civil Law: Historical Essays* (London and Ronceverte: Hambledon Press, 1988), 197–208; John Venn, *Caius College* (London: F. E. Robinson & Co, 1901, repr. 1923), 76–92.

3. *Richardus Tertius*, prepared with an introduction by Robert J. Lordi, and *Solymitana Clades*, prepared with an introduction by Robert J. Lordi and Robert Ketterer, in *Renaissance Latin Drama in England*, general editors Marvin Spevack, J. W. Binns, Hans-Jürgen Weckermann, Second Series: 8 (Hildesheim: Georg Olms Verlag, 1989); *Thomas Legge: The Complete Plays* (vol. I: *Richardus Tertius*; vol. II: *Solymitana Clades*), edited, with a translation and commentary, by Dana F. Sutton, 2 vols (New York: Peter Lang, 1993). All references will be to Sutton's edition.

4. The analogy was first articulated in Elizabeth's coronation entry, with its elaborate pageant of "The uniting of... Lancaster and Yorke" (*The Passage of our most drad Soveraigne Lady Quene ELYZABETH through the Citie of LONDON to WESTMINSTER, the daye before her Coronation, Anno 1558–9*, in *The Progresses and Public Processions of Queen Elizabeth*, ed. John Nichols, 3 vols (London, 1823), I). Legge made the parallel explicit in *"an Epilogue... where in lett* [sic] *be declared the happy uniteinge of both houses, of whome the Queenes majesties came, and is undoubted heyr, wishinge her a prosperous raigne"* (320).

5. Introduction to *Solymitana Clades*, in Legge's *Works*, op. cit., II: xi.

6. Ibid, II: ix.

7. On the expansion of Hebrew learning in England and Continental Europe, see C. Lloyd-Jones, *The Discovery of Hebrew in Tudor England: A Third Language* (Manchester: Manchester University Press, 1983); Jerome Friedman, *The Most Ancient Testimony: Sixteenth-Century Christian-Hebraica in the Age of Renais-*

sance Nostalgia (Athens Ohio: Ohio University Press, 1983); and idem, "Sebastian Münster, the Jewish Mission, and Protestant Anti-Semitism," *Archive for Reformation History*, 70 (1979), 238–59; "Sixteenth-Century Christian Hebraica: Scripture and the Renaissance Myth of the Past," *Sixteenth-Century Journal*, 11 (1980), 65–85; "Protestants, Jews and Jewish Sources," in *Piety, Politics, and Ethics: Reformation Studies in Honor of George Wolfgang Forell*, ed. Carter Lindberg (Kirksville: Sixteenth-Century Journal Publishers, 1984), 139–56; "The Myth of Jewish Antiquity: New Christians and Christian-Hebraica in Early Modern Europe," in *Jewish Christians and Christian Jews from the Renaissance to the Enlightenment*, ed. Richard H. Popkin and Gordon M. Weiner (Dordrecht, The Netherlands: Kluwer Academic Publishers, 1994), 35–55.

8. E. D. MacKerness, "'Christ's Teares' and the Literature of Warning," *English Studies*, 33 (1952), 251–54; Michael McGiffert, "God's Controversy with Jacobean England," *American Historical Review*, 88 (1983), 1151–76; Patrick Collinson, "Biblical Rhetoric: The English Nation and National Sentiment in the Prophetic Mode," in *Religion and Culture in Renaissance England*, ed. Claire McEachern and Debora Shuger (Cambridge: Cambridge University Press, 1997), 15–45; Alexandra Walsham, *Providence in Early Modern England* (Oxford: Oxford University Press, 1999), esp. chapter 6: "'England's Warning by Israel': Paul's Cross Prophecy," 280–325; Peter Lake with Michael Questier, *The Antichrist's Lewd Hat: Protestants, Papists and Players in Post-Reformation England* (New Haven and London: Yale University Press, 2002), esp. 335–61; Mary Morrissey, "Elect Nations and Prophetic Preaching: *Types* and *Examples* in the Paul's Cross Jeremiad," in *The English Sermon Revised*, ed. Lori Anne Ferrell and Peter McCullough (Manchester and New York: Manchester University Press, 2000), 43–58; Tessa Watt, *Cheap Print and Popular Piety, 1550–1640* (Cambridge: Cambridge University Press, 1991). Contrary to William Haller's *Foxe's Book of Martyrs and the Elect Nation* (London: Jonathan Cape, 1963), Collinson and others have shown that the English thought of themselves as "an" not "the" elect nation.

9. Margaret Aston, *The King's Bedpost: Reformation and Iconography in a Tudor Group Portrait* (Cambridge: Cambridge University Press, 1994); Collinson, "Biblical Rhetoric," op. cit. For discussions of biblical drama, see Ruth Blackburn, *Biblical Drama Under the Tudors*, Studies in English Literature 65 (The Hague: Mouton, 1971); Lily B. Campbell, *Divine Poetry and Drama in Sixteenth-Century England* (Cambridge: Cambridge University Press, 1959); Murray Roston, *Biblical Drama in England: From the Middle Ages to the Present Day* (London: Faber & Faber, 1968); Paul Whitfield, *Theatre and Reformation: Protestantism, Patronage, and Playing in Tudor England* (Cambridge: Cambridge University Press, 1993).

10. See Thomas Churchyard's *A Discourse of the Queenes Majestie's Entertainment in Suffolk and Norfolk* (1578), reprinted in *Progresses and Public Processions of Queen Elizabeth*, op. cit., II: 179 ff.

11. T. E. Hartley, ed., *Proceedings in the Parliaments of Elizabeth I*, 3 vols (London and New York: Leicester University Press, 1981–95), I: 35.

12. Legge had been involved in amateur theatricals since his student days in Cambridge in 1558–59, 1560–61, 1562–63, 1563–64, 1564–65, 1565–66, and 1566–67. See REED: Cambridge, op. cit., II: 968–71. On the heated religious disputation, also staged before the queen during that visit, in which Catholic and Calvinist viewpoints clashed, see Patrick Collinson, "Andrew Perne and his Times," in *Andrew Perne: Quatercentenary Studies*, Cambridge Bibliographical Society Monograph No. 11, ed. David McKitterick (Cambridge: Cambridge Bibliographical Society, 1991), 1–34.

13. Aston, op. cit., 97–127. The analogy was used by Stockwood in his sermon of 1578 and persisted after the queen's death, for instance in William Leigh's *Queene Elizabeth, Paraleld in her princely virtues, with David, Iosua and Hezekia* (London, 1612). Yet another trope likened Elizabeth to Solomon: see, for example, the engraved frontispiece representing Elizabeth as "Reg. Pacis" and Solomon as "Rex. Pacis," accompanied by the lion of Juda and the branch of the tree of Jesse, prefaced to Thomas Morton of Berwick, *Salomon or A treatise declaring the state of the kingdome of Israel, as it was in the daies of Salomon. Whereunto is annexed another treatise, of the Church: or more particularly, Of the right constitution of a Church* (London, 1596). Morton uses the example of the Kingdom of Israel to shore up divine-right monarchy; later commentators, first in the Netherlands and afterwards in England, will cite the example of the Hebrew Commonwealth to legitimate a republican model. On Elizabethan image-making more generally, see Susan Frye, *Elizabeth I: The Competition for Representation* (New York and Oxford: Oxford University Press, 1993); John N. King, *Tudor Royal Iconography: Literature and Art in an Age of Religious Crisis* (Princeton, NJ: Princeton University Press, 1989); and idem, "Queen Elizabeth I: Representations of the Virgin Queen," *Renaissance Quarterly*, 43 (1990), 30–74.

14. The Israelite paradigm rested on the assumption that God's covenant with Abraham (the covenant of grace) applied to the English nation. On the emergent distinction between the covenant of grace and the covenant of nature or works, see McGiffert, "God's Controversy with Jacobean England," op. cit., pp. 1163 ff.

15. Walsham notes the popularity of ballads on the subject, but she incorrectly assumes that "Jerusalem [was] besieged by Titus and Vespasian in AD 74" (*Providence*, op. cit., 311).

16. On Josephus, see Louis H. Feldman, *Josephus and Modern Scholarship (1937–1980)* (Berlin and New York: Walter de Gruyter, 1984) and Louis H. Feldman and Gohei Hata (eds.), *Josephus, Judaism, and Christianity* (Detroit: Wayne State University Press, 1987).

17. On sermons, ballads, plays, and pamphlets, see MacKerness, "'Christ's Teares' and the Literature of Warning;" Patrick Collinson, "Biblical Rhetoric;" Walsham, *Providence in Early Modern England*, op. cit., 280–325; Lake and Questier, *Antichrist's Lewd Hat*, op. cit., 335–61; Watt, *Cheap Print and Popular Piety*, op. cit., 96–98.

18. *A Compendious and most marveilous History of the latter tymes of the Jewes commune weale, beginnynge where the Bible or Scriptures leave, and continuing to the utter subversion and laste destruction of that countrey and people: Written in Hebrew by* Ioseph Ben Gorion, *a noble man of the same countrey, who sawe the most thinges him selfe, and was auctour and doer of a great part of the same. Translated into Englishe by* Peter Morwyng of Magdalen College in Oxford (London, 1558), sigs. π2ʳ, π5ᵛ -π6ʳ. A revised edition, also prepared by Morwyng, appeared in 1561 and was subsequently reprinted in 1567, 1575, 1579, 1593, 1596 and 1615. Morwyng's translation was superseded by James Howell's polemical new version that opposed the readmission of the Jews into England, *The Wonderful, and most deplorable History of the Latter Times of the Jews, and of the City of Hierusalem. Beginning where the Holy Scriptures do end. Written first in Hebrew, and now made more Methodical, and corrected of sundry Errors* (London, 1653).

19. *A Sermon Preached at Paules Crosse on Barthelmew day, being the 24. of August. 1578* (London, 1578), 16, 19.

20. (London, 1584), sig. B5ᵛ. Cf. "The translator vnto the Reader," inserted

into *The Thirde Booke of the Ecclesiasticall Historye of Evsebivs*, in *The Auncient Ecclesiasticall histories of the First Six Hvndred Yeares after Christ, written in the Greeke tongue by three learned Historiographers, Eusebius, Socrates, and Euagrius*, trans. Meredith Hanmer, Maister of Arte and student in diuinitie (London, 1577), 42–44. Hanmer's note was intended as a mini-sermon: "I thinke it not amisse (gentle Reader) to note here vnto thee the infinite number of Iewes which perished, from the beginning of the warres, between the Romaynes, and the Iewes . . . to the ende we may beholde eyther the long suffering, and goodnes of God, for the amendement of our liues, by repentance, which winked so long at the wickednesse of these Iewes, to prouoke vs: or els the ire, wrathe, and heauy hand of God, ouer impenitent persons, to terrifie vs to feare his name, and tremble at his plagues" (42).

21. Op. cit., II: 34.

22. *The Stratagems of Ierusalem. With the martiall lawes and militarie discipline, as well of the Iewes as of the Gentiles. By Lodowick Lloyd Esquier, one of her Maiesties Serieants at Armes* (London, 1602), 229.

23. *A Sermon Preached at Paules Crosse* (1578), op. cit., 20–21.

24. *Christs Teares*, op. cit., II: 80, 174.

25. (London, [c. 1640]). "The mighty Emperour of Rome" comes with the intention of punishing the Jews for "dispatch[ing] / the liuing Lord of life."

26. On University drama, see Frederick S. Boas, *University Drama in the Tudor Age* (Oxford: Clarendon Press, 1914, repr. New York: Benjamin Blom, 1966); G. C. Moore Smith, *College Plays Performed in the University of Cambridge* (Cambridge: Cambridge University Press, 1923); Alan H. Nelson, *Early Cambridge Theatres: College, University, and Town Stages, 1464–1720* (Cambridge: Cambridge University, 1994); and idem, "Contexts for Early English Drama: The Universities," in *Contexts for Early English Drama*, ed. Marianne G. Briscoe and John C. Coldewey (Bloomington and Indianapolis: Indiana University Press, 1989), 137–49. On neo-Latin literature of the English Renaissance, see James Wallace Binns, *Intellectual Culture in Elizabethan and Jacobean England: The Latin Writings of the Age* (Leeds: Francis Cairns, 1990).

27. *A Very Fruitfull and Necessarye Sermon*, op. cit., sig. B8[r].

28. *The Famous and Memorable Workes of Josephus, A Man of Much Honour and Learning among the Jewes. Faithfully translated out of the Latin, and French, by Tho. Lodge Doctor in Physicke* (London, 1602).

29. Mark H. Curtis, *Oxford and Cambridge in Transition, 1558–1642: An Essay on Changing Relations between the English Universities and English Society* (Oxford: Clarendon Press, 1959); Hugh Kearney, *Scholars and Gentlemen: University and Society in Pre-Industrial Britain, 1500–1700* (Ithaca: Cornell University Press, 1970). On classics in university curriculum and early modern culture more generally, see *The History of the University of Oxford*, gen. ed. T. H. Aston, vol. III: *The Collegiate University*, ed. James McConica and vol. IV: *Seventeenth-Century Oxford*, ed. Nicholas Tyacke (Oxford: Clarendon Press, 1986 and 1997 respectively); J. H. M. Salmon, "Seneca and Tacitus in Jacobean England," in *The Mental World of the Jacobean Court*, ed. Linda Levy Peck (Cambridge: Cambridge University Press, 1991), 169–88; and David Womersley, "Sir Henry Savile's Translation of Tacitus and the Political Interpretation of Elizabethan Texts," *Review of English Studies*, 42 (1991), 313–42.

30. For an overview of partisan uses of Josephus, see Eva Matthews Sanford, "Propaganda and Censorship in the Transmission of Josephus," *Transactions and Proceedings of the American Philological Association*, 66 (1935), 127–45. On the

topicality of Josephus in sixteenth-century France, see Pauline M. Smith, "The Reception and Influence of Josephus's *Jewish War* in the Late French Renaissance with Special Reference to the *Satyre Mepippée*," *Renaissance Studies*, 13 (1999), 173–91. On the Israelite and Batavian paradigms of Dutch nationhood based, respectively, on scripture and on Tacitus, Pliny, and Strabo, see Simon Schama, *The Embarrassment of Riches: An Interpretation of Dutch Culture in the Golden Age* (London: Collins, 1987), esp. 44–125; on the implications of the Hebrew self-image for Dutch political thought, see Lea Campos Boralevi, "Classical Foundational Myths of European Republicanism: The Jewish Commonwealth," in *Republicanism: A Shared European Heritage*, vol. I: *Republicanism and Constitutionalism in Early Modern Europe*, ed. Martin van Gelderen and Quentin Skinner (Cambridge: Cambridge University Press, 2002), 247–61; the republican account of the Hebrew state by the professor of politics at Leiden, Petrus Cunaeus, *De republica Hebræorum libri III* (Lugduni Batavorum: Apud Ludovicum Elzevirium, 1617) was translated into English by Clement Barksdale as *Of the Commonwealth of the Hebrews* (London: T. W. for William Lee, 1653). On Dutch republicanism, see Martin van Gelderen, *The Political Thought of the Dutch Revolt, 1555–1590* (Cambridge: Cambridge University Press, 1992); and, idem, (ed. and trans.), *The Dutch Revolt* (Cambridge: Cambridge University Press, 1993). For a discussion of topical appropriation of Jewish history in the Iberian Peninsula, see David Hook, "The Legend of the Flavian Destruction of Jerusalem in Late Fifteenth-Century Spain and Portugal," *Bulletin of Hispanic Studies*, LXV (1988), 113–28.

31. Dana F. Sutton, "Justus Lipsius to Thomas Legge, January 1, 1585," *Humanistica Lovaniensia*, 40 (1991), 275–81.

32. H. C. Porter, *Reformation and Reaction in Tudor Cambridge* (Cambridge: Cambridge University Press, 1958), Part II: "The Puritans and Authority;" Collinson, "Andrew Perne and his Times;" James Bass Mullinger, *The University of Cambridge from the Royal Injunctions of 1535 to the Accession of Charles I* (Cambridge: Cambridge University Press, 1884); and the documents reproduced in *Cambridge University Transactions During the Puritan Controversies of the 16th and 17th Centuries*, ed. James Heywood and Thomas Wright, 2 vols (London: Henry G. Bohn, 1854).

33. In a letter to Burghley dated 14 December 1572, Vice-Chancellor Thomas Byng reported on the search of Dr. Caius's lodgings which turned up "muche popishe trumpery." See *Cambridge University Transactions*, op. cit., I: 123–25, at 125. For the accusations against Legge, the depositions of witnesses, and the protest of the master and president, see ibid, 314–41; and cf. Brooke, *History*, op. cit., 91–92.

34. In contrast to parts two and three, which are too long and repetitive to warrant stage presentation, the First Action is fully revised and stageable. One reason why Legge did not complete the task may have been the growing demands of his legal career that called for frequent absences from the college: he joined Doctors' Commons in 1590 and shortly thereafter became a Master in Chancery and a Cambridge JP. See Brooke, *History*, op. cit., 85–86.

35. Op. cit., II: 16.

36. On the so-called *Testamentum Flavianum*, a forged passage about Jesus interpolated into the Latin version of Josephus, see Feldman, *Josephus*, op. cit., pp. 680–703; Zvi Baras, "*The Testimonium Flavianum* and the Martyrdom of James," in Feldman and Hata (eds.), *Josephus, Judaism, and Christianity*, op. cit., 338–48.

37. "pudet, ah pudet / fixisse stipitis tonantis filium / ficto necis crimine, pater quem postea / sedes ad aethereas trahebat cum agmine / pulchro atque parte sui locabat dextera, solium ut sibi commune gnatus ouccupet" ["I am ashamed, yes I am ashamed to have crucified the son of the Thunderer on a falsified capital charge. Afterwards His Father lifted Him up to a heavenly seat among the beautiful company of angels and seated Him on His right hand, so that His son might share His throne" (the Third Action, IV.i.4234–39). This outburst seems incongruous in the context in which it appears.

38. See Abraham Wasserstein's Introduction to his edition of *Flavius Josephus: Selections from His Works* (New York: Viking Press, 1974).

39. *Compendious*, op. cit., sig. π6^r.

40. *A Very Fruitfull and Necessarye Sermon*, op. cit., sig. B4^v.

41. *Christs Teares*, op. cit., II: 60, 79. And further: "Onely the ambitious shaking of the yoke of the Romains was the bane of *Ierusalem*" (87).

42. Stephanus Junius Brutus, the Celt, *Vindiciae, Contra Tyrannos: or, concerning the legitimate power of a prince over the people, and of the people over a prince*, ed. and trans. George Garnett (Cambridge: Cambridge University Press, 1994), 46–50, at p. 48.

43. *Stratagems*, op. cit., 226.

44. For a character of Florus, see Josephus's *The Jewish War*, in *Josephus*, with an English translation by H. St. J. Thackeray, Loeb Classical Library, 8 vols (London: William Heinemann, 1926), II: 277–79 et passim.

45. Another example is the opening stage direction of II.iv: "*The soldiers carry over the stage Jewes tyed in ropes to their deathes*" (p. 44).

46. *Jewish War*, op. cit., II: 325–29.

47. Eleazar is an ambivalent figure: initially his impassioned call for defence of Jewish liberty appears impressive, but his refusal of gentile sacrifices and his violence against his own people alienate our sympathies. Conversely, an account of his steadfastness in the face of defeat in the final part of the trilogy momentarily revives our respect for him: alone of the three factious commanders, Eleazer dies a dignified death, committing suicide rather than groveling before the Romans and becoming a captive to be exhibited during the triumph.

48. In Josephus, his motives are less self-serving: "Agrippa was indignant at their narrative, but diplomatically turned his resentment upon the Jews whom at heart he pitied, wishing to humiliate their pride and, by appearing to disbelieve that they had been at all ill treated, to divert them from revenge" (*Jewish War*, op. cit., II: 336–42).

49. Sutton calls this scene a fabrication; but, as with his depiction of Nero's embassy, Legge draws on the *Yosippon* except that he attributes to Anani the warlike message that in the original comes from "bothe priestes, chief men, rulers, and all the noble men of *Iudea* with the reaste of the people." See Morwyng's *Compendious . . . History*, op. cit., Fol. xcvi^r.

50. Cf. Lloyd, *Stratagems*, op. cit., on Roman discipline: "Of the martiall lawes and military discipline of the Gentiles:" "The Romanes were somewhat more seuere against disobedient souldiers, especially against seditious & fugitive souldiers, and against them that forsooke theyr standart, and turned their backes to the enemies, and from the camp to flee to the enemie, these amongst the Romanes were punished with death" (p. 79).

51. Titus has already produced a gruesome spectacle of pretended Jewish refugees who have been mutilated on his orders: "*Let him shew foure with the right hand cut of*" (p. 422). Cf. *Jewish War*, op. cit., V. 446–53.

52. Sutton misses the point when he says, in a note on lines 9059 ff. of Eleazer's speech, that Legge "concocts an interesting mixture of Jewish soul-lore and Stoic views about the advantages of suicide" (p. 603).

53. In John Fletcher's *Bonduca*, the suicide of the eponymous British queen and her two daughters similarly elicits a mixed reaction from the Roman invaders. See *Bonduca* (Oxford: Malone Society Reprints, 1951), IV.iv.

54. "belli ducem quem elegeret anxius diu / Nero fuit, at mox Flavio acquiescit in / Vespasiano. prospere hic Britaniam / armis domuit et frigido quae subiacent / arcto, iugum illis victor imposuit suum" ["For a long time Nero fretted about what general to choose, but soon he settled on Vespasian the Flavian. This man had successfully reduced Britain by arms and the lands which lie under her cold sky, and as victor had imposed his yoke on her inhabitants"] (the Second Action, II.i.2621–25). In the First Action, Agrippa lists Britain among the various nations subdued by the Romans: "ignota prius his victa cessit Albion / divesque Gallus, Bosphoranus bellicus / et Graecus ingenio sagaci fascibus" ["Britain, previously unknown, has yielded to their fasces, as has the wealthy Gaul, the warlike inhabitant of the Bosphorus, and the ingenious Greek" (III.iii.1120–22). On Vespasian's and Titus's service in Britain, see William Camden, *Britain, or, a Chorographicall Description of the most flourishing Kingdomes, England, Scotland, and Ireland... Written first in Latine by W. Camden ... translated newly into English by Philemon Holland ... Finally revised, amended, and enlarged with sundry additions* (London, 1610), 42.

55. Ibid., 46.

56. *The Origins of Empire: British Overseas Enterprise to the Close of the Seventeenth Century*, ed. Nicholas Canny, vol. I of *The Oxford History of the British Empire* (Oxford: Oxford University Press, 1998); David Armitage, *The Ideological Origins of the British Empire* (Cambridge: Cambridge University Press, 2000).

57. Thus Camden: "This yoke of the Romanes although it were grevous, yet comfortable it proved and a saving health unto them: for that healthsome light of Iesus Christ shone withal upon the Britans, whereof more hereafter, and the rightnesse of that most glorious Empire, chased away all savage barbarisme from the Britans minds, like as from other nations whom it had subdued" (*Britain*, op. cit., 63–64). See Graham Parry, "Ancient Britons and Early Stuarts," in *Neo-Historicism: Studies in Renaissance Literature, History and Politics*, ed. Robin Headlam Wells, Glenn Burgess, and Rowland Wymer (Cambridge: D. S. Brewer, 2000), 153–78; Tristan Marshall, *Theatre and Empire: Great Britain on the London Stages under James VI and I* (Manchester: Manchester University Press, 2000); Jodi Mikalachki, *The Legacy of Boadicea: Gender and Nation in Early Modern England* (London: Routledge, 1998).

58. Protestant England's (later Britain's) imperial designs were framed in opposition to Spain's Catholic empire, and called for subjection of the Catholic Irish and conversion of New World natives to the correct brand of Christianity.

59. *Holinshed's Chronicles of England, Scotland, and Ireland*, 6 vols. (London, 1807), I: 494. No less apposite is Holinshed's "A catalog of causes or greeuances inciting the Britaines to rebell against the Romans, wherein is shewed what iniuries they susteined" (I: 495ff). Cf. Camden, *Britain*, op. cit.: "With these and such inducements, inciting and quickning one another, they take armes under the conduct of *Boadicia a Ladie of the roiall bloud* (for in matter of government in chiefe the Britans make no distinction of sex) *having stirred up the Trinobanes to Rebellion*" (op. cit., 50).

60. Op. cit., II: 82, 114.

61. *Holinshed's Chronicles*, op. cit., II: 140. Cf. Camden, *Britannia*: "the inland parts of Britaine, wasted rather with *Civil* wars and factions, than by the force of the Romans, after sundrie overthrows and slaughters of both sides, came at the length by little and little under the subjection of the Romans" (op. cit., 40).

62. Richard Beacon, *Solon his Follie, or A Politique discourse, Touching the Reformation of common-weales conquered, declined or corrupted* (Oxford, 1594).

63. *Classical Humanism and Republicanism in English Political Thought, 1570–1640* (Cambridge: Cambridge University Press, 1995), 74ff.

64. *Solon*, op. cit., p. 77.

65. Charles Wilson, *Queen Elizabeth and the Revolt of the Netherlands* (London: Macmillan, 1970).

66. By the early seventeenth century, the duty of Englishmen as God's chosen people to seek the conversion of Irishmen, Indians, Moors, and Jews, whether by means of trade or colonial expansion, had been firmly established. See, for example, Thomas Middleton's Lord Mayor's Show for 1613, *The Triumphs of Truth*; and Thomas Cooper's sermon, *The Blessing of Japheth, Proving the Gathering in of the Gentiles and Finall Conversion of the Jewes* (1615), preached before the Lord Mayor, Aldermen, and Sheriffs of the City of London, and the Commissioners for Plantations in Ireland and Virginia. For the Irish dimension of native history plays, see Christopher Highley, *Shakespeare, Spenser, and the Crisis in Ireland* (Cambridge: Cambridge University Press, 1997).

67. Cf. Nero's message in Morwyng's translation: "I assure unto you a faithful league, by the consent and counsel of the *Senate* of Rome, that hereafter there shall never Romaine captaine stirre hand nor fote against you, but rather your heades, rulers, & iudges, shal be al Jewes and of Jerusalem" (*Compendious . . . History*, op. cit., Fol. lxxxiii^r).

68. Op. cit., 505–506.

69. The Second Action, III.ii.3369–76; 3384–86; cf. Sutton's note on p. 577.

70. Legge's chief source here is Carlo Sigonio's *De Republica Hebræorum Libri VII, Ad Gregorium XIII Pontificem Maximum* (Frankfurt, 1583). William McCuaig's *Carlo Sigonio: The Changing World of the Late Renaissance* (Princeton: Princeton University Press, 1989) provides a useful overview of Sigonio's treatment of history but does not discuss the tract on the Hebrew Commonwealth. The Sanhedrin was abolished in the aftermath of the Jewish war.

71. In the 1650s, Cromwell and others considered a plan for a national assembly modelled on the Jewish Sanhedrin. See David S. Katz, *Sabbath and Sectarianism in Seventeenth-Century England* (Leiden: Brill, 1988), 2.

72. Cf. the many derogatory references to "zeal" in Richard Hooker's *Of the Laws of Ecclesiasticall Politie. Eyght Bookes* (London, n.d.). In the epistle addressed "To them that seeke (as they tearme it) the reformation of Lawes, and orders Ecclesiasticall, in the Church of ENGLAND," Hooker is sarcastic about "[t]he wonderful zeale and fervour wherewith ye haue withstood the receiued orders of this Church" (3); *The fift Booke* (1597) condemns "head-strong and inconsiderate zeale" (sig. A4^r) and traces superstition to "either misguided zeale or ignorant feare of diuine glorie." "Zeale," Hooker argues, "vnlese it be rightly guided, when it endeuoureth most busily to please God, forceth vpon him those vnseasonable offices which please him not" (7).

73. Cf. Hooker: "we shold be slow and vnwilling to change without very vrgent necessitie the aunciente ordinances, rites, and long approued customes of our venerable predecessors" (*Of the Laws*, Book V, op. cit., 12); and Nashe's tirade against

fruitless squabbles about forms of worship, against Puritans as a species of atheist, and against Englishmen's hankering after innovation in religion (Nashe's *Christ's Teares*, op. cit., II 133, 118, 134. For recent accounts of the English Reformation, see Patrick Collinson, *The Birthpangs of Protestant England: Religious and Cultural Change in the Sixteenth and Seventeenth Centuries* (Basingstoke: Macmillan, 1988); Eamon Duffy, *The Stripping of the Altars: Traditional Religion in England c. 1400–c. 1580* (New Haven: Yale University Press, 1992); Christopher Haigh, *English Reformations: Religion, Politics, and Society Under the Tudors* (Oxford: Clarendon Press, 1993); *England's Long Reformation, 1500:1800*, ed. Nicholas Tyacke (London: UCL Press, 1998); on Puritanism, see Christopher Hill, *Society and Puritanism in Pre-Revolutionary England* (London: Secker & Warburg, 1964); on religious controversy in Renaissance Cambridge, see *Cambridge University Transactions During the Puritan Controversies*, ed. Heywood and Wright; James Bass Mullinger, *The University of Cambridge from the Royal Injunctions of 1535 to the Accession of Charles I* (Cambridge: Cambridge University Press, 1884); H. C. Porter, *Reformation and Reaction in Tudor Cambridge* (Cambridge: Cambridge University Press, 1958); John Morgan, *Godly Learning: Puritan Attitudes towards Reason, Learning, and Education, 1560–1640* (Cambridge: Cambridge University Press, 1986); and *Andrew Perne: Quatercentenary Studies*, ed. McKitterick, op. cit.

74. "Of the Authority of the Church in things indifferent," in *The Works of John Whitgift*, ed. J. Ayre, 3 vols (Cambridge: Cambridge University Press for The Parker Society, 1851–53), I: 271. The corresponding marginal note reads: "The assertion of T. C. tendeth to Judaism." In the early sixteenth century Catholics accused Protestants of judaising; Luther, Melanchton, and Calvin leveled the charge at Protestant Hebraists. Jerome Friedman notes that, "[b]y the late 1530s . . . the term 'judaizer' came to have the same meaning among Protestants and Catholics ascribed to the term Jew when referring to Protestants" ("Sixteenth-Century Christian Hebraica," op. cit., 145).

75. *REED: Cambridge*, II: 1151–53; the original Latin text is reproduced in I: 315–16. For discussion, see David S. Katz, *Sabbath and Sectarianism* and idem, "Jewish Sabbath and Christian Sunday in Early Modern England," in *Jewish Christians and Christian Jews*, op. cit., 119–30.

76. In his introduction to *Solymitana Clades*, Sutton argues that the audience might well have associated sectarian passion depicted by Legge with Marian persecutions. This is unlikely. The only religious grouping that could be potentially identified with the Catholics would be the priests of the Temple and they are the persecuted, not the persecutors.

77. Cf. Hooker's *Of the Laws*: ". . . the plot of Discipline did not only bend it selfe to reforme ceremonies, but seeke farther to erect a popular authoritie of Elders, and to take away Episcopal iurisdiction together with all other ornaments and meanes wherby any difference or inequalitie is vpheld in the Ecclesiasticall order," op. cit., sig. A5r.

78. *Holinshed's Chronicles*, op. cit., IV: 379.

79. *The Life and Works of George Peele*, ed. Charles Tyler Prouty et al, 3 vols (New Haven: Yale University Press, 1952–1970), I: ll. 27, 34–36.

80. In a sermon of 1583, having stressed that the overthrow of Jerusalem was largely caused by internal divisions, and having reviewed other examples of bloody internecine strife, Bishop Jewel exclaimed: "But what needeth us to go to Hierusalem or to Turkey for examples? This kingdom of ours . . . could never yet be conquered by any enemy, but only at such time as the people were at variance

within themselves," *Certain Sermons*, in *The Works of John Jewel*, ed. John Ayre, 4 vols (Cambridge: Cambridge University Press for the Parker Society, 1845–50), II: 1028; cf. Bishop Sandys, *A Sermon Preached before the Queen*, in *The Sermons of Edwin Sandys*, ed. John Ayre (Cambridge: Cambridge University Press for The Parker Society, 1841), 92–111 at p. 101.

81. For an overview of theatrical representations of the fall of Jerusalem in medieval and Renaissance drama, see Stephen K. Wright, *The Vengeance of Our Lord: Medieval Dramatizations of the Destruction of Jerusalem* (Toronto: Pontifical Institute of Mediaeval Studies, 1989). Although his book appeared sixteen years after the discovery of *Solymitana Clades*, Wright is under the impression that the play is not extant and merely speculates on its contents.

82. *Records of Early English Drama: Coventry*, ed. R. W. Ingram (Toronto: University of Toronto Press, 1981), xix, 303–9, 332, 590; idem, "Fifteen Seventy-nine and the Decline of Civic Religious Drama in Coventry," in *The Elizabethan Theatre VIII: Papers given at the Eighth International Conference on Elizabethan Theatre held at the University of Walterloo, Ontario in July 1979*, ed. G. R. Hibbard (Port Credit: P. D. Meany, 1982), 114–28; Stephen K. Wright, "'The Historie of King Edward the Fourth': A Chronicle Play on the Coventry Pageant Wagons," *Medieval and Renaissance Drama in England*, 3 (1986), 69–82; and, more generally, Benjamin Griffin, "The Breaking of the Giants: Historical Drama in Coventry and London," *ELR* 5 (1999), 3–21.

83. Critics generally suppose that this was a play about the destruction of Jerusalem; there is, however, another possibility. Given that Vespasian and Titus had served in Britain, and that it was widely believed that Titus had saved his father's life during the British campaign, it is not inconceivable that the Strange's Men's script dealt with Roman-British rather than Roman-Jewish conflict.

84. E.g. by Ingram in *REED: Coventry*, op. cit., 587. The plagiarism story was first recorded in the posthumous entry on Legge, dated July 1607, in *The Annals of Gonville and Caius College by John Caius*, ed. John Venn (Cambridge: Cambridge Antiquarian Society, 1904), 214; and it was retailed by Thomas Fuller in *A History of the Worthies of England* (London, 1662), 276.

85. On Renaissance stage Jews, see Jacob Lopes Cardozo, *The Contemporary Jew in the Elizabethan Drama* (Amsterdam: H. J. Paris, 1925); James Shapiro, *Shakespeare and the Jews* (New York: Columbia University Press, 1996); David S. Katz, *The Jews in the History of England, 1485–1850* (Oxford: Clarendon Press, 1994), 103–5; Edgar Rosenberg, "The Jew in Western Drama," *Bulletin of the New York Public Library*, 72 (1968), 442–91. In the early seventeenth century, plays about Jewish history such as Elizabeth Carey's *Tragedy of Mariam* and William Heminges's *Jews' Tragedy* (the latter, like Legge's, focusing on the fall of Jerusalem) offered a secular and political rather than exclusively religious-ideological perspective on the Jews. There were also motions and drolls, which itinerant showmen exhibited throughout the country, that took the destruction of Jerusalem as their theme. Among the 'Spectacula Oxonij hoc anno" that Thomas Crosfield recorded on 15 July 1634, we find: "Hierusalem in it's glory, destruction—The Story devided into 5 or 6 parts, invented by Mr Gosling, sometimes scholler to Mr Camden, Enginer" [(*The Diary of Thomas Crosfield*, ed. Frederick S. Boas (London: Royal Society of Literature, 1935)], 71).

86. *A Sermon*, op. cit., 18.

87. "All the popish gentlemen in this country send their sons to him. He setteth sundry of them over to one Swale, also of the same house, by whom the youth of this country is corrupted" (cited in Venn, *Caius College*, op. cit., 78); *A Sermon Preached at Paul's Cross*, in *Sermons*, op. cit., 349.

88. *A Very Fruitful*, op. cit., sig. B8ʳ; *Christs Teares*, op. cit., 49. "[T]hey dydde as greatlye abhorre and deteste the name of a Heathen, as wee doe nowe the name of a Jewe or Turke, or shoulde doe the name of a Papiste": thus Stockwood in 1578 (op. cit., 13).

89. Cf. Nashe, *Christs Teares*, op. cit., I: 48 and Stockwood, *A Very Fruitful and Necessary Sermon*, op. cit., on the discontinuance of Jewish ceremonies.

90. These are reproduced by Sutton at pp. 605–6 and 607–8 respectively.

91. P. 607. (Cf. Nashe, *Christs Teares*, op. cit., II: 110, on the Pharisees' vainglory and hypocrisy of which the phylacteries are a sign.) This is followed by a note about the attire of priests and levites, based on Josephus's *Jewish Antiquities*, that directs the reader to a visual source: "this attire is pictured out in the king of Spaines great bible" (p. 608).

92. David S. Katz, *Philo-Semitism and the Readmission of the Jews to England, 1603–1655* (Oxford: Clarendon Press, 1982). On the Scottish perspective, see Arthur H. Williamson, "British Israel and Roman Britain: The Jewish and Scottish Models of Polity from George Buchanan to Samuel Rutherford," in *Jewish Christians and Christian Jews*, op. cit., 97–117; and idem, "The Jewish Dimension of the Scottish Apocalypse: Climate, Covenant and World Renewal," in *Menasseh Ben Israel and His World*, ed. Yosef Kaplan, Henry Méchoulan, and Richard H. Popkin (Leiden: E. J. Brill, 1989), 7–30.

93. Hooker responds to such charges in a passage accompanied by the following marginal gloss: "The forme of our Liturgie too neere the Papists, too farre different from that of other reformed Churches as they pretend" (*Of the Laws*, Book V, op. cit., 58). Throughout Book V, Hooker cites specific Jewish rites as legitimate forms of worship for those people at that time; but he insists that they have been superseded by new observances instituted by Christ and, in respect of what Whitgift called "things indifferent," by the Church. Although there is continuity, for instance regarding sanctity of churches, preaching, etc., the two dispensations are worlds apart. Thus to argue, as did some Puritan Judaizers, that Old Jewish Law is binding on contemporary Christians is misguided.

94. The work on this essay was made possible by the generosity of several institutions: the Folger Shakespeare Library where I held the Hanson Lee Dulin Senior Fellowship for 1999–2000; the University of Wales Aberystwyth which awarded me a grant from the College Research Fund in 2001; the Leverhulme Trust which awarded me a one-year Research Fellowship in 2002; and the Huntington Library, California, where I was the Mellon Foundation Fellow in the summer of 2003. For liberal help of various sorts I wish to thank Professors Christopher Brooke, Lawrence Greene, Robert D. Hume, David S. Katz, Bernard Wasserstein, David Wasserstein, Arthur H. Williamson, and Blair Worden. I am also grateful to the editors of this volume, Eric Buckley and Allen Michie, for their patience, kindness, and useful suggestions.

The Prince's Choice
Terence Hawkes

ONCE UPON A TIME THERE WERE THREE PARADOXES.

ROYAL HIGHNESS

We can begin with the paradox inherent in the political structure of the society called Great Britain. By and large, the British think of themselves as citizens of a democratic state. There is even an unexamined conviction that the British are the only begetters of modern democracy and that from thence springs the moral right—and duty—to enlighten and instruct other countries as to the virtues and necessities of this system of government.

But of course Britain is not, in any straightforward sense, a democracy, and its political system retains features that would have no place, for example, in the constitutions of France, Germany, Italy or the United States. In fact, the chief distinguishing characteristic of the British state continues to be its commitment to a monarchical system and the principle of a *de jure* right to govern on the basis of inheritance by blood, which that system sustains and justifies. Of the three main instruments of government in the British Isles: (the Crown, the House of Lords, and the House of Commons), two operate, wholly or in part, on the basis of blood inheritance. Admittedly, the House of Lords is currently, at the beginning of the second millenium, in the initial throes of reform. Yet even this late in the day, although hereditary peers have now lost their automatic right to membership, a number of them still sit there on the basis of having been chosen by their fellow peers. Eventually, if the present government has its way, selection rather than election will be the governing principle by which the House of Lords will be constituted. Only one institution, the House of Commons, is an assembly whose entire membership is elected on the principle of a single vote for each adult citizen. Even that arrangement can scarcely claim to be of long standing. It has only been fully operational since 1948.[1]

It is worth confronting the paradoxical nature of this situation, not for any immediate political reason (most of the British people bear the present system no ill will and have no pressing desire to live in the sort of democratic society they happily urge on others), but because of the light it sheds on a publication called *The Prince's Choice*, and the purchase this affords on the issue of the uses to which Shakespeare may nowadays be put.

Royal Family

The Prince's Choice offers a selection of passages, scenes, and speeches from Shakespeare's plays and sonnets, assembled by the present Prince of Wales. These are gathered under various headings, such as "Extraordinary People and Exceptional Language," "All Sorts and Conditions of Men," "Humour," "The Darker Side," and so on. Jacques' "All the world's a stage" supplies a Prologue, and Prospero's "Our Revels now are ended" an Epilogue. The selections are also available in the form of sound recordings, performed on cassette and compact disc, by "an outstanding cast" including "HRH" himself.

The domestic, social, and political context in which the book appeared (in November, 1995) is well-known and conveniently focuses attention on the second paradox; one whose complexity is most aptly summed up in the peculiarities of the phrase "Royal Family." Prince Charles is of course a central member of this institution. Although very little republican sentiment exists in Britain, the political situation of the present "Royal Family" has gradually become—though never precarious—slightly shaky. There are various reasons for this, some arising from the pressures of economic developments that led some years ago, for instance, to demands that the Queen's finances should attract at least a token degree of income tax. But most prominent in terms of the general public's perception has been the evident susceptibility of the Royal Family to the stresses and strains of what might be termed "ordinary" family life. These have generated predictably sad results. Over the years, the marriage of the Queen's sister has collapsed, as have those of three of her own children. Most notorious of all, the marriage of the heir to the throne, Prince Charles, ended in divorce, and the subsequent tragic death of his wife Princess Diana provoked a sympathetic surge of public emotion, some of it directed against the monarchy.

Whilst the marital rifts at stake are no more alarming or surprising than they would be in any contemporary family, the immoderate responses they produce amongst British subjects point to the heart of the incongruity in question. In order to sustain the fiction that a monarchy dependent on blood inheritance can have an acceptable role within a democracy, members of the royal household have chosen in recent decades, at least in their public life, to lay claim to dimensions of "ordinariness" unknown to previous incumbents. Obviously enough, the more those particular and ordinary "family" pressures are encouraged to reveal and to exert themselves, the less available the universalizing principle of a "royal" uniqueness, inherited by blood, becomes. And yet the grounding postulate of royalty requires the maintenance of precisely that distinction.

After all, the monarch's claim to be a monarch depends upon and embodies the *absence* of ordinariness. The notion of a "Royal Family" whose commitments are those of "ordinary" family life thus clearly involves a major contradiction, one which virtually turns the phrase itself into an oxymoron. Nobody can be both a member of a particular "family" subscribing to the duties and restrictions of wedlock (i.e., ordinary) and also an inhabitant of a larger "royal" dimension with quite different duties and restrictions (i.e., extraordinary).

Charles himself has spoken of the tensions that persistently dogged his marriage. Its semi-scandals, involving the commitment of the couple to other, nonroyal partners, became common knowledge. Running through all of this has been a disquieting sense that its results may finally bring about the end of the monarchy. So, although Charles is universally regarded as the person most likely to succeed to the British throne, important questions have been raised as to whether or not he ever will. Shortly after the publication of *The Prince's Choice*, the Prince's other choice, his wife, openly accused the Palace of stifling her "personal" development, freely doubted whether Charles would make an effective monarch, and proceeded to lay claim to racy, if ill-defined, titles such as "Queen of Hearts." Rarely have the changes on the "ordinary" and the "extraordinary" been so challengingly rung. When, at Diana's death, the Prime Minister informally bestowed on her the sobriquet "The People's Princess," his opportunistic yoking together of the two poles seemed entirely apt.

United Kingdom

The third paradox lurks at the heart of Charles's inherited title. As King, his realm would be the area known as the "United Kingdom of Great Britain and Northern Ireland." Within that sphere, Charles is currently Prince of Wales. This is a title that, since Edward I's conquest of Wales, Kings of England have regularly bestowed on their eldest sons. However, the claim to be a true "Prince of Wales" has also in the past been made by native-born Welshmen as part of a revolutionary rejection of English domination. The most famous example of this is the case of Owain Glyn Dwr who, anglicized as "Owen Glendower" in Shakespeare's second tetralogy of history plays, leads his Welsh rebels against Henry IV, making common cause with Hotspur, Northumberland and Mortimer in the process.

In the twentieth century, Princes of Wales have been no strangers to controversy. Charles's immediate predecessor went on to become King Edward VIII, but quickly renounced the crown because of an unsuitable relationship with an American woman. In the same month in which *The Prince's Choice* appeared, apparently convincing evidence came to light suggesting that during the 1930s Edward had become involved in dubious negotiations with Adolf Hitler with a view to his own restoration to the monarchy should Nazi Germany win the war. He is said to have advised the Führer that aerial bombardment of the British was likely to prove persuasive in this regard—a belief, to be fair, that was also widespread amongst senior British politicians, especially those who opposed Churchill.[2]

Sad to say, Charles seems to have inherited a similar, albeit less murderous, tendency toward contention. In a sense it has been inescapable. Leaving aside his domestic problems, there can be no doubt that his title links him in any case with one of the areas of the British Isles where the writ of "Englishness" does not, these days, comfortably run. The spirit of Owain Glyn Dwr haunts him as much as it did King Henry IV and Prince Hal. If we remember that the term "Britain" also includes areas of notable disaffection such as Scotland and, inevitably, Northern Ireland, then the contradictions inherent in the phrase "United Kingdom" might seem to match, in irony if nothing else, those already noted in "Royal Family." A similar clash between the claims of universal principle and the nuts and bolts of their particular application threatens to make oxymorons of both.[3]

The King of Shakespeare's Land

Prince Charles would certainly not be the first member of a British royal household to turn to Shakespeare at moments of evident discord. British Kings and Queens from Elizabeth I on have frequently bestowed upon the Bard their grateful patronage at the same time as they have tended to support the institution of the theater. Why not? Monarchy has, after all, a certain investment in display, ceremony, and the spectacular. It also remains the case that the one successful revolution mounted against monarchic rule in Britain notoriously moved, as part of its project, to close down the theatres. The restoration of the monarchy in 1660, that act of "collective, willed oblivion" marked, as Gary Taylor has pointed out, the restoration of Shakespeare's fortunes both in terms of text and of performance.[4]

However, the question of personal motivation is not at issue here. Charles's interest in Shakespeare may well simply reflect a deep-seated aesthetic response to the plays, and a corresponding educational commitment. It is not in any case a recent phenomenon. The Prince has served for some time as President of the Royal Shakespeare Company at Stratford and, more than a decade ago, founded the Prince of Wales Summer School which takes place annually in the town.

This is to say no more than that he clearly sees the Bard representative of what is best about Britain, and an emblem of what Britain has to offer the rest of the world. On a number of occasions he has recommended the plays as the basis for a command of the English language, that linchpin of national cohesion, confirmed by the Home Secretary in December 2001 after a summer of riots in northern cities, as a central means of easing racial tension in Britain. In 1991, delivering the annual Shakespeare Birthday Lecture in Stratford itself, and speaking from the stage of the Swan Theatre, Charles mounted an outspoken attack on the nation's educational standards and the growing neglect of what he termed "the cultural heritage of our country." "It is almost incredible," he lamented, "that in Shakespeare's land one child in seven leaves primary school functionally illiterate." He went on to denounce English literature syllabi which "prescribe no Shakespeare at all," and to complain that "Thousands of intelligent children leaving school at sixteen have never seen a play of Shakespeare on film or on the stage, and have never been asked to read a single word of any one of his plays."

But however personal and deeply felt such sentiments may be, they can hardly be drained of the political impulse that also properly resides within a person destined to become head of the British state. After all, such an evacuation would strike at the very nature of the monarchy itself. Like it or not, a Prince literally *embodies* a politics when his inheritance comes by blood and birth. The concepts of an overriding "private" life, or "private" opinions, cannot be genuinely appropriate to such an institution, and to lay claim to them is to undermine it. As King Richard II and King Lear discover, royalty cannot be renounced, even temporarily: An ex-king raises the issue of kingship as much as, maybe more than, a sitting tenant.[5]

No Holds Bard

To his credit, Charles seems clearly aware of the complexities of this situation. His short Introduction to *The Prince's Choice* pointedly expresses admiration for the Bard's ability, evident in Henry V's speech "Upon the King . . ." (IV. i. 218–72) to penetrate "into the mind of someone born into this kind of position."[6] In fact, Shakespeare's capacity for such penetration becomes a central theme of the essay, despite the charmingly self-deflating admission that the youthful and "largely unmoved" prince initially failed to perceive it, and that he at first "failed to realise just what fun Shakespeare could be."

Unsurprisingly, the fun has a serious side. The Prince's favorite play "happens to be" *Henry V*. Spellbound by Kenneth Branagh's Stratford performance, he has (with matching heroism) seen the actor's film of the play "at least three times."[7] What moves him most is the King's "humanity" and Shakespeare's ability to capture the "loneliness of high office," something that extends throughout modern society, afflicting "all those who shoulder great burdens, run industries or schools—or perhaps nurse invalid relatives."[8] A recent rereading of *Julius Caesar* made him appreciate "for the first time the fascination of that complex character Brutus, the reluctant revolutionary; the excitement and rhetoric of Antony's great speeches, and the extraordinary timelessness of Shakespeare's presentation and analysis of riot, revolution, intrigue and internecine strife which is at the heart of the play."[9] In this context, the Bard swiftly acquires all the qualities traditionally characteristic of national "genius."[10] He has an "all-encompassing view of mankind," his understanding of all ranges and types of human being in his plays is such that "All human life really is there" together with an "extraordinary range and subtlety of characterisation."[11] In addition, his "understanding of domestic life" is vast. No aspect of the minds of "soldiers and politicians, of the fundamental relationships between men and women" can escape him. The characters he draws are so universal, so "timeless," that "we find them alive and around us today, every day of our lives."[12] Indeed, so capacious is the Bard's understanding of humanity that it "remains eternally relevant," enabling his plays to "communicate wisdom through the evocation and study of human emotion, thought and behaviour."[13]

There is no need to continue. This is familiar territory, firmly staked out by ironclad and unalterable presuppositions. They can be readily summarized:

1. That Shakespeare is an all-wise, all-knowing genius, possessed of astounding capacities of insight into the human psyche.
2. That his plays present portrait galleries of individual human figures, exemplifying characteristic faults or virtues, which the Bard's insight permits him to probe and exhibit.
3. That his work is "timeless," universally valid, and speaks to human beings across the ages, as clearly now, had we the wit to see it, as it did then.
4. That to encounter his plays is thus finally to come across ourselves, to encounter a trenchant and accurate diagnosis of our failings and possibilities and, by implication, to develop the capacity to engage at last with the contours of our own nature. In the portentous words of Harold Bloom (to choose only the most recent voice in a chorus that extends back to Coleridge), the true "use" of Shakespeare (along with other great writers) is "to augment one's own growing inner self," a process that will bring "the proper use of one's own solitude, that solitude whose final form is one's confrontation with one's own mortality."[14]

These claims, it could be argued, rest on the following, perhaps even more dubious, and certainly deeply occluded principles:
(a) That human nature is permanent, one, and indivisible, regardless of place, race, creed and culture. In the end, under the skin, we are all the same and it is to this sameness that Shakespeare speaks.
(b) That neither the passage of time nor the exigencies of place, culture, or economics, make any difference to this. Indeed, construed aright, and analyzed with sufficient ingenuity, ap-

plication, vigor and flexibility, Shakespeare's plays are able to address all people at all times, and everywhere.

(c) That to deny any of the above is to reveal serious deficiencies in one's humanity, such as characterize the ravings of the deranged, the perverse, the envious, and the politically and socially deviant.

But perhaps the true value of the Prince's remarks lies nonetheless in their exquisite crassness, its inadvertence artlessly hinting at maneuvres that other projects more deftly conceal. One example looms up in the observation that those of us who speak English enjoy the "enormous good fortune that the world's greatest playwright—perhaps the world's greatest poet—wrote in our language." This then fuels the proposal that, although Shakespeare's lofty concern is with the "essential truths about the meaning and significance of life," and although "his message . . . is a universal, timeless one," the Bard somehow and simultaneously also manages to remain British to the core: "Shakespeare's language is ours, his roots are ours, his culture is ours—brought up as he was in the gentle Warwickshire countryside," etc.[15]

Shakespeare, in short, is "not just our poet, but the world's."[16] The contradiction is glaring. If Shakespeare's language, roots and culture are "ours," how can they also immediately and at the same time be "the world's"—that is, unless the world is prepared to admit that it is, even just a little bit, "ours" too? That seems, to say the least, an unlikely development. Leaving aside the connection between Shakespeare and a kind of generalized, portable "Englishness," manufactured for the purposes of empire and exported by means of that empire's commitment to the academic subject called "English," the truth is that statements such as "Shakespeare's language is ours, his roots are ours, his culture is ours" have a slightly hollow ring in the context of present-day Northern Ireland, Scotland, or—with particular irony—Wales.[17] And in racially-troubled England itself, particularly in the inner-city classrooms of large industrial conurbations, words like "ours" used in connection with notions of "language," "roots" and "culture" can—or should—no longer trip, unsifted, off the tongue.

How, then, can this intensely local Bard speak—effortlessly and forever—for "the world" at large: for times, places, regions and ways of life of which he could know nothing and whose cultures remain, in many cases, older and more complex than his own? This paradox, whereby that which is particular and rooted turns out also to be universal and sublime is not, as we have seen, unfamiliar in modern Britain. It enjoys a special status here. It is, of course, central to the notion of monarchy.

Playing the Shakespeare Card

That Shakespeare should by now begin to exhibit a certain resemblance to the heir to the British throne is, given the circumstances, not surprising. That his plays should so neatly reflect Charles's own range of contradictions—timeless yet also timebound; like us, with our language, our roots, our culture on the one hand; emphatically unlike us because of an ineffable "royal" dimension on the other—might even seem predictable. A balding, diffident transcendency is broadly strewn across the British pantheon.

Nevertheless, the Shakespeare card has always been a tricky one to play. We can presume that the Prince is aware of, and perhaps wishes to resolve, the paradoxes inherent in his situation. Yet *The Prince's Choice* finally serves only to confirm and reinforce their existence. Charles's unavoidable connection with Wales offers a good example. Its function—in terms of a United Kingdom—should be a bridging, binding and unifying one. Yet it turns out to be more likely to disturb the very stability at which such a project aims. Since Owain Glyn Dwr's revolt, and his self-proclamation as the true "Prince of Wales," Wales has presented a permanent challenge to the notion that those parts of the world that won't own up to being English are really just kidding.

Indeed, Wales offers a quite different reading of the complex text called "Britain." A land obsessed by lineage and genealogy, blood descent and complex, carefully nurtured family relations, its serpentine kinship and political structures seem destined, if not designed, to undermine linear English certainties. The major British political upheaval of the fourteenth century had, after all, climaxed in Wales. In the summer of 1399, the shattering deposition of Richard II, the ultimate *de jure* monarch of the old medieval order, removed the last king of Britain who ruled by undisputed hereditary right. Beyond Offa's Dyke, an English Prince of Wales can almost expect to find his title disputed by an *unheimlich* claimant. In *The Second Part of Henry IV*, a successor to the English crown, Bolingbroke, has to face the threat of a rival located in Wales: Mortimer, who has gone native.

Most seriously, the language the English speak and which makes the world over in their particular image, finds itself challenged in

Wales by an alarmingly different tongue: one that not only claims currency on the same small island, but also offers quite a different account of its history and structure. In this connection, the Welsh have of course long had their own tradition of Bards. Yet the English perception of that outlandish horde speaks tellingly of its irredeemable exclusion from civilization as we know it. The very word "Welsh" derives from the Old English *wælisc*, meaning, dismissively, "foreign." An "English" Prince of Wales cannot therefore help but be a virtual contradiction in terms. Talk of "we," "us," "our language," and "our poet," rooted "in the gentle Warwickshire countryside," turns Shakespeare's Prince of Wales into an actual one. At best, it becomes a kind of whistling in the dark.

Shakespeare's carefully constructed version of an English past in both of the tetralogies shares with Glyn Dwr's revolutionary project a large commitment to art's central role in the manufacture of history. But, as part of the same process, his plays also frequently deny the easy certainties expected from them. The scene in *Henry IV*, in which Falstaff and Hal put on the little drama whereby each alternately takes on the roles of the Prince of Wales and the King, seems at first blush to underwrite Hal's burgeoning authority (2.4.371 ff.). But it also manages in the process to undermine it by generating no less than three Princes of Wales on the stage at the same time: Hal himself; Hal 'as' Hal; and Falstaff as Hal. *The Prince's Choice* not only makes this scene one of its main selections (in the section "Public Life and Leadership"), it also includes it in the recorded version with, inevitably, Prince Charles electing to take on the role of Prince Hal himself. The result, equally inevitably, is that the Welsh multiplier goes into overdrive and the scene becomes worryingly cluttered, as no less than four Princes of Wales (Charles, Charles as Hal, Hal as "Hal," Falstaff as "Hal") play out the scene. Worse, there remains, as we know, a revolutionary fifth figure, claiming to be the "true" Prince of Wales, Owain Glyn Dwr, waiting in the wings for the scene which immediately follows (3.1).

In short, despite the best efforts of *The Prince's Choice*, the Principality's multifariousness directly subverts the reassuring single vision of English certainties. It reinforces the contradictions that undermine the concept of a "United Kingdom" and that of a "Royal Family" which rules over it. Charles may claim that Shakespeare's art, like that of other great artists, "provides us with access to some of the essential truths about the meaning and significance of life."[18] But has the meaning and significance of *five* Princes of Wales eluded him? One thing is sure, the use of the Bard cannot resolve such paradoxes. The plays after all deal in them. Like all art, they play the Welsh game in which nothing is simple or single or availably grounded in one coherent "truth." The happy result, as *The Prince's Choice* inevitably reveals, is that, in Shakespeare's land, nothing can be appropriated without the possibility of fearful, proliferating, undermining consequences. And this means that no one there—Princes least of all—can expect to live happily ever after.

Notes

1. The argument that the House of Commons is the only arm of government that "really counts" fails to allow that the delaying tactics open to the other two can, when time presses, prove capable of directly influencing legislative programs by necessitating the withdrawal of proposed measures. Not infrequently, it transpires that time is unavailable for their re-presentation. It's also worth reflecting that, at the State opening of parliament, the monarch prefaces each item of the forthcoming legislative program with the formula "My government will . . ." The notion that the monarch is completely without power is one of the central delusions of the British. Each Bill requires the "Royal Assent" in order to become law. It's also worth pondering why, if such instruments of government have no power, proposals for their removal always meet with such a strong chorus of objection.

2. See Anthony Cave Brown, *"C": The Secret Life of Sir Stewart Manzies* (New York and London: Macmillan, 1987), 680.

3. The post-1999 development of "devolution," and the establishment of parliaments or assemblies in Scotland and Wales matching that in Northern Ireland, have gone some way toward easing tensions, but have also inevitably generated anomalies of their own. At present, for instance, there is no English parliament.

4. See Gary Taylor, *Reinventing Shakespeare* (London: The Hogarth Press, 1990), 10–51.

5. The argument of E. H. Kantorowicz [*The King's Two Bodies: a Study in Medieval Political Theology* (Princeton: Princeton University Press, 1957)] concerning notions of the King's simultaneous existence on more than one level does not, in my view, affect this case.

6. Charles, Prince of Wales, *The Prince's Choice: a Personal Selection from Shakespeare with an Introduction by HRH the Prince of Wales* (London: Hodder and Stoughton, 1995), 2–3.

7. Ibid., 2.
8. Ibid., 2–3.
9. Ibid., 1.
10. Ibid., 3.
11. Ibid.
12. Ibid., 1, 3.
13. Ibid., 3, 4.
14. Harold Bloom, *The Western Canon* (New York and London: Harcourt Brace, 1994), 30 ff. See my Introduction to *Alternative Shakespeares 2* (New York and London: Routledge, 1996), 9–10, where these issues are discussed in similar terms and at greater length.

15. Charles, *The Prince's Choice*, 5.
16. Ibid.
17. See Chris Baldick, *The Social Mission of English Criticism 1848–1932* (Oxford: Clarendon Press, 1983), 70–73.
18. Charles, *The Prince's Choice*, 4.

Contributors

MARTINE WATSON BROWNLEY is Goodrich C. White Professor of English and Winship Distinguished Research Professor at Emory University, where she is also Director of the Center for Humanistic Inquiry. She has published on Clarendon and Gibbon, and her most recent book is *Deferrals of Domain: Contemporary Women Novelists and the State* (2000).

JOHN CAREY is Emeritus Merton Professor of English Literature at Oxford University. His books include studies of Donne, Milton, Dickens, and Thackeray, also *The Intellectuals and the Masses* (1992) and *Pure Pleasure* (2001).

MAURICE CHARNEY is Distinguished Professor of English at Rutgers University. He has been President of the Shakespeare Association of America and the Academy of Literary Studies. He also received the Medal of the City of Tours in France. Some publications are *Shakespeare on Love and Lust* (2000) and *All of Shakespeare* (1993), *Style in Hamlet* (1969), *Shakespeare's Roman Plays: the Function of Imagery in the Drama* (1961), and *Comedy High and Low: an Introduction to the Experience of Comedy* (1978). He also published a critical book on Joe Orton (1984) and a study of *Titus Andronicus* (1990).

MANUEL J. GÓMEZ-LARA is a Senior Lecturer of the Department of English and American Literature at Seville University. His publications include *The Ways of the Word: an Advanced Course on Reading and the Analysis of Literary Texts* (1994), *Stylistica: I Semana de Estudios Estilísticos* (1987), and several books and essays on Baroque public ceremonies and medieval, Renaissance and Restoration English Drama. He has co-edited Shadwell's *The Virtuoso* (1997) and *Epsom Wells* (2000), as well as J. Arrowsmith's *The Reformation* (2003). At the moment he is engaged in "The Restoration Comedy Project," a collaborative work aimed at compiling a full catalogue of comedies written between 1660 and 1700, and editing neglected plays from the period.

TERENCE HAWKES is an Emeritus Professor of English at Cardiff University. He is the author of a number of books on Shakespeare, including *That Shakespeherian Rag* (1986), *Meaning by Shakespeare* (1992) and *Shakespeare in the Present* (2002). He is also General Editor of the Accents on Shakespeare series published by Routledge.

PAULINA KEWES is a Fellow and Tutor of Jesus College, Oxford. Her publications include *Authorship and Appropriation: Writing for the Stage in England, 1660–1710* (1998) and essays on Shakespeare, Dryden, and the drama of the Renaissance, Restoration and eighteenth-century drama. She has edited a volume of essays on *Plagiarism in Early Modern England* (2003), and she is now completing a book on the staging of history in Elizabethan and Stuart drama and civic pageantry.

ARTHUR F. KINNEY is Thomas W. Copeland Professor of Literary History and the Director of the Massachusetts Center for Renaissance Studies at the University of Massachusetts, Amherst. Among his many books are *Humanist Poetics: Thought, Rhetoric, and Fiction in Sixteenth-Century England* (1986), *Continental Humanist Poetics: Studies in Erasmus, Castiglione, Marguerite de Navarre, Rabelais, and Cervantes* (1989), *John Skelton, Priest as Poet: Seasons of Discovery* (1987), *"Lies Like Truth": Shakespeare, Macbeth, and the Cultural Moment* (2001), and *Shakespeare by Stages: an Historical Introduction* (2003). He has also edited primary documents as well as the *Cambridge Companion to English Literature 1500–1600* and the *Blackwell Companion to Renaissance Drama*.

RICHARD LEVIN is Professor Emeritus of English at the State University of New York at Stony Brook. He is the author of *The Multiple Plot in English Renaissance Drama* (1971) and *New Readings vs. Old Plays: Recent Trends in the Reinterpretation of English Renaissance Drama* (1979), and he has just published a collection of his recent essays titled *Looking for an Argument: Critical Encounters with the New Approaches to the Criticism of Shakespeare and His Contemporaries* (Fairleigh Dickinson University Press, 2003).

ROBERT MARKLEY is Professor of English at the University of Illinois and Editor of *The Eighteenth Century: Theory and Interpretation*. His books include *Two-Edg'd Weapons: Style and Ideology in the Comedies of Etherege, Wycherley, and Congrove* (1988), *Fallen Languages: Crises of Representation in Newtonian England, 1660–*

1740 (1993), and *Virtual Reality and Its Discontents* (1996). His study of European-Asian relations from 1500 to 1800 is forthcoming.

ALLEN MICHIE is an Assistant Professor of English at Iowa State University. He is the author of *Richardson and Fielding: the Dynamics of a Critical Rivalry* (Bucknell University Press, 1999), as well as studies of Bunyan, Locke, and Sarah Fielding.

MICHAEL NEILL is Professor of English at the University of Auckland, New Zealand. His publications include *Issues of Death* (1997), *Putting History to the Question* (2000), and essays on Renaissance and Restoration drama, as well as Postcolonial and Irish Literature. He has edited *Anthony and Cleopatra* for the Oxford Shakespeare, and he is currently completing *Othello* for the same series.

DAVID NORBROOK is Merton Professor of English Literature at the University of Oxford. In addition to books and articles on Renaissance poetry and politics, he has published occasional poems in *Oxford Poetry, Oxford Magazine,* and elsewhere.

LINDA WOODBRIDGE is Distinguished Professor of English at Pennsylvania State University. Her books include *Women and the English Renaissance: Literature and the Nature of Womankind, 1540–1620* (1984); *Shakespeare: A Selective Bibliography of Modern Criticism* (1988); *True Rites and Maimed Rites: Ritual and Anti-Ritual in Shakespeare and His Age of Shakespeare* (co-editor, 1992); *The Scythe of Saturn: Shakespeare and Magical Thinking* (1994); *Vagrancy, Homelessness, and English Renaissance Literature* (2001). She is the former President of the Shakespeare Association of America and a former member of the editorial board of Papers of the Modern Languages Association.

BIBLIOGRAPHY

Ames, Richard. *Islington-Wells, or, The threepenny-academy, a poem.* London, 1691.

Anderson, Judith H. *Biographical Truth: The Representation of Historical Persons in Tudor-Stuart Writing.* New Haven: Yale University Press, 1984.

Aquinas, St. Thomas. *Summa Contra Gentile sof Saint Thomas Aquinas, Literally Translated by the English Dominican Fathers from the Latest Leonine Edition.* London: Burns, Oates and Washbourne, 1929.

Aristotle. *Poetics.* Trans. Ingram Bywater. In *The Basic Works of Aristotle*, edited by Richard McKeon, 1453–87. New York: Random House, 1941.

Aston, Margaret. *The King's Bedpost: Reformation and Iconography in a Tudor Group Portrait.* Cambridge: Cambridge University Press, 1994.

Baker, Thomas. *Tunbridge-Walks: or The Yeoman of Kent.* London, 1703.

Barnard, John, ed. *The Man of Mode.* London: Ernest Benn, 1979.

Billson, Marcus. "The Memoir: New Perspectives on a Forgotten Genre." *Genre* 10 (1977): 259–82.

Birdsall, Virginia Ogden. *Wild Civility: the English Comic Spirit on the Restoration Stage.* Bloomington: Indiana University Press, 1970.

Bloom, Harold. *Shakespeare: The Invention of the Human.* New York: Riverhead, 1998.

———. *The Western Canon.* New York and London: Harcourt Brace, 1994.

Blunden, Edmund. *On the Poems of Henry Vaughan; Characters and Imitations, with His Principal Latin Poems Carefully Translated into English Verse.* London: R. Cobden-Sanderson, 1927.

Bond, Donald F., ed. *The Tatler.* Oxford: Clarendon Press, 1987.

Bosch, Peter. *Agreement and Anaphora: A Study of the Role of Pronouns in Syntax and Discourse.* London: Academic Press, 1983.

Brathwait, Richard. *A Survey of History: Or, a Nursery for Gentry.* London, 1638.

Briggs, John and F. David Peat. *Turbulent Mirror: An Illustrated Guide to Chaos Theory and the Science of Wholeness.* New York: Harper & Row, 1989.

Brome, James. *Travels over England, Scotland and Wales.* London, 1700.

Brooke, Christopher. "Thomas Legge and the Elizabethan College." In *A History of Gonville and Caius College.* Woodbridge: Boydell, 1985. Reprinted with addenda 1996: 79–93.

Brown, Laura. *English Dramatic Form, 1660–1760: An Essay in Generic History.* New Haven: Yale University Press, 1981.

Burnet, Gilbert. "The Preface." *Memoires of the Lives and Actions of James and William Dukes of Hamilton and Castlehearld, &c.* London, 1677.

Byfield, T. *A Short and Plain Account of the Late-Found Balsamich Wells at Hoxdon*. London, 1687.

Canfield, J. Douglas. *Nicholas Rowe and Christian Tragedy*. Gainesville: University Press of Florida, 1977.

———. "Shadwell at the Crossroads of Power: Spa as Microcosm in Epsom-Wells." *Restoration* 20 (1996): 135–48.

———. *Tricksters and Estates: On the Ideology of Restoration Comedy*. Lexington: University Press of Kentucky, 1997.

Carey, John. "Introduction." In *John Donne: The Major Works*, xix–xxxii. Oxford: Oxford University Press, 1990.

———. *John Donne: Life, Mind and Art*. New York: Oxford University Press, 1981.

Castiglione, Baldassare. *The Book of the Courtier*. Trans. Sir Thomas Hoby. London: Dent, 1928.

Charles, Prince of Wales. *The Prince's Choice: a Personal Selection from Shakespeare with an Introduction by HRH the Prince of Wales*. London: Hodder and Stoughton, 1995.

Cibber, Colley. *An Apology for the Life of Colley Cibber*. Ed. B. R. S. Fone. Ann Arbor: University of Michigan Press, 1968.

Clodd, Edward. *Magic in Names and in Other Things*. London: Chapman and Hall, 1920.

Coffin, Charles Monroe. *John Donne and the New Philosophy*. Morningside Heights, N.Y.: Columbia University Press, 1937.

Congreve, William. *The Complete Plays of William Congreve*. Ed. Herbert Davis. Chicago: University of Chicago Press, 1967.

———. *The Way of the World*. In *The Comedies of William Congreve*, edited by Eric S. Rump. Harmondsworth: Penguin, 1985.

Cooper, Anthony Ashley, Earl of Shaftesbury. *Characteristics of Men, Manners, Opinions, Times* [1711]. Ed. John M. Robertson. Indianapolis: Bobbs-Merrill, 1964.

Corman, Brian. *Genre and Generic Change in English Comedy, 1660–1710*. Toronto: University of Toronto Press, 1993.

Covino, William A. *Magic, Rhetoric, and Literacy: An Eccentric History of the Composing Imagination*. Albany: State University of New York Press, 1994.

Crawford, Patricia. *Denzil Holles, 1598–1680: A Study of his Political Career*. London: Royal Historical Society, 1979.

Cunaeus, Petrus. *De republica Hebræorum libri III*. Lugduni Batavorum: Apud Ludovicum Elzevirium, 1617.

———. *Of the Common-wealth of the Hebrews*. Trans. Clement Barksdale. London: T. W. for William Lee, 1653.

Curtis, Mark H. *Oxford and Cambridge in Transition, 1558–1642: An Essay on Changing Relations between the English Universities and English Society*. Oxford: Clarendon Press, 1959.

Davies, Stevie. *Henry Vaughan*. Bridgend, Mid Glamorgan, Wales: Seren, 1995.

Defoe, Daniel. *A Tour through the Whole Island of Great Britain*. Ed. Pat Rogers. Harmondsworth: Penguin, 1971.

De Grazia, Margreta. "Hamlet's Thoughts and Antics." *Early Modern Culture* 1.1 (2001).

Desmet, Christy. *Reading Shakespeare's Characters: Rhetoric, Ethics, and Identity*. Amherst: University of Massachusetts Press, 1992.

Donne, John. *Devotions Upon Emergent Occasions*. Ed. Anthony Raspa. Montreal and London: McGill-Queen's University Press, 1975.

———. *The Divine Poems*. 2d ed. Ed. Helen Gardner. Oxford: Clarendon Press, 1978.

———. *The Elegies and the Songs and Sonnets*. Ed. Helen Gardner. Oxford: Clarendon Press, 1965.

———. *The Epithalamions, Anniversaries and Epicedes*. Ed. W. Milgate. Oxford: Clarendon Press, 1978.

———. *The Major Works*. Ed. John Carey. Oxford: Oxford University Press, 1990.

———. *The Satires, Epigrams and Verse Letters*. Ed. W. Milgate. Oxford: Clarendon Press, 1967.

———. "Selected Prose." In *Selected Prose*. Ed. Helen Gardner, Evelyn Simpson, and Timothy Healy. Oxford: Clarendon Press, 1967.

———. *The Sermons of John Donne*. Ed. Evelyn M. Simpson and George R. Potter. Berkeley and Los Angeles: University of California Press, 1953.

Donoghue, Denis. "Doing Things with Words: Criticism and the Attack on the Subject." *Times Literary Supplement* 4763 (15 July 1994).

Dryden, John. "An Essay of Dramatic Poesy," in *English Critical Essays: Sixteenth, Seventeenth,and Eighteenth Centuries*. Ed. Edmund D. Jones. London: Oxford University Press, 1947.

———. *John Dryden*. Ed. Keith Walker and Frank Kermode. Oxford: Oxford University Press, 1987.

D'Urfey, Thomas. *The Bath, or The Western Lass*. London, 1701.

Dyche, Thomas. *A New General English Dictionary*. 1735.

Eliot, T.S. *The Complete Poems and Plays 1909–1950*. San Diego: Harcourt Brace Jovanovich, 1950.

An Exclamation From Tunbridge And Epsom Against The Newfound Wells At Islington. London, 1684.

Fish, Stanley. "Consequences." In *Against Theory: Literary Studies and the New Pragmatism*, edited by W. J. T. Mitchell, 106–131. Chicago: University of Chicago Press, 1985.

———. *Self-Consuming Artifacts: The Experience of Seventeenth-Century Literature*. Berkeley and Los Angeles: University of California Press, 1972.

———. *Surprised by Sin: The Reader in* Paradise Lost. Baltimore: Johns Hopkins University Press, 1967.

Flos Ingenii vel Evacuatio Discriptionis. Being an Exact Description of Epsam, and Epsam Wells. London, 1674.

Fowler, Alistair. *Kinds of Literature: An Introduction to the Theory of Genres and Modes*. Cambridge: Harvard University Press, 1982.

Foxe, John. *Two Latin Comedies by John Foxe the Martyrologist: Titus et Gesippus and Christus Triumphans*. Ed. and trans. John Hazel Smith. Ithaca and London: Cornell University Press, 1973.

Fuller, Thomas. *The History of the Worthies of England*. London, 1662.

Gill, Pat. *Interpreting Ladies: Women, Wit, and Morality in the Restoration Comedy of Manners*. Athens: University of Georgia Press, 1994.

Gorion, Joseph Ben. *A Compendious and most marveilous History of the latter tymes of the Jewes commune weale, beginnynge where the Bible or Scriptures leave, and continuing to the utter subversion and laste destruction of that countrey and people: Written in Hebrew by* Ioseph Ben Gorion, *a noble man of the same countrey, who sawe the most thinges him selfe, and was auctour and doer of a great part of the same. Translated into Englishe by Peter Morwyng of Magdalen College in Oxford, London, 1558*. London: 1558.

———. *The Wonderful, and most deplorable History of the Latter Times of the Jews, and of the City of Hierusalem. Beginning where the Holy Scriptures do end. Written first in Hebrew, and now made more Methodical, and corrected of sundry Errors*. Trans. James Howell. London, 1653.

——— *The Wonderful and Most Deplorable History of the Later Times of the Jews: With the Destruction of Jerusalem*. London, 1678.

Grove, Allen W. "Sexual Chaos: The Gothic 'Formula' and the Politics of Complexity." In *Disrupted Patterns: On Chaos and Order in the Enlightenment*, edited by Theodore E. D. Brown and John A. McCarthy, 107–18. Amsterdam and Atlanta: Rodopi, 2000.

Guibbory, Achsah. "John Donne." In *The Cambridge Companion to English Poetry: Donne to Marvell*. Ed. Thomas N. Corns, 123–47. Cambridge: Cambridge University Press, 1993.

Guidott, Thomas. *A True and Exact Account of Sadlers Well: or The New Mineral-WatersLately Found out at Islington*. London, 1684.

Hanmer, Meredith, trans. *The Auncient Ecclesiasticall Histories of the First Six Hundred Yeares After Christ Wrytten in the Greeke Tongue by Three Learned Historiographers, Eusebius, Socrates, and Evagrius*. London, 1577.

Harvey, Gideon. *A Discourse of the Plague . . . With several waies for purifying the air in houses, streets, &c*. London, 1665.

Hawke, Kathleen, comp. *Cornish Sayings, Superstitions, and Remedies*. Penzance: Headland, 1973.

Hawkins, Harriett. *Classics and Trash: Traditions and Taboos in High Literature and Popular Modern Genres*. Toronto: University of Toronto Press, 1990.

———. *The Devil's Party: Critical Counter-Interpretations of Shakespearian Drama*. Oxford: Clarendon Press, 1985.

———. "The 'Example Theory' and the Providentialist Approach to Restoration Drama: Some Questions of Validity and Applicability." *The Eighteenth Century: Theory and Interpretation* 24, no. 2 (1983): 103–14.

———. *Likenesses of Truth in Elizabethan and Restoration Drama*. Oxford: Clarendon Press, 1972.

———. *Measure for Measure*: A Critical Introduction. Brighton: Harvester, 1987.

———. " 'Players and Scorecards': Some Principles of Exposition in English Drama." In *From Renaissance to Restoration: Metamorphoses of the Drama*, edited by Robert Markley and Laurie Fincke, 16–32. Cleveland: Bellflower Press, 1984.

———. *Poetic Freedom and Poetic Truth: Chaucer, Shakespeare, Marlowe, Milton*. Oxford: Clarendon Press, 1976.

———. *Strange Attractors: Literature, Culture, and Chaos Theory*. New York: Prentice-Hall, 1995.

Hellegers, Diseree. *Handmaid to Divinity: Natural Philosophy, Poetry, and Gen-*

der in Seventeenth-Century England. Norman: University of Oklahoma Press, 2000.

Herbert, Sir Thomas. *Memoirs of the Two Last Years of the Reign of King Charles I.* London, 1813.

Heywood, James and Thomas Wright, eds. *Cambridge University Transactions During the Puritan Controversies of the 16th and 17th Centuries.* 2 vols. London: Henry G. Bohn, 1854.

Holland, Norman. *The First Modern Comedies: The Significance of Etherege, Wycherley, and Congreve.* Cambridge: Harvard University Press, 1959.

Holland, Peter. *The Ornament of Action: Text and Performance in Restoration Comedy.* Cambridge: Cambridge University Press, 1979.

Holles, Denzil. *Memoirs of Denzil Lord Holles.* 1699. Cambridge: Cambridge University Press, 1979.

Hughes, Derek. *English Drama 1660–1700.* Oxford: Clarendon Press, 1996.

Hughes, John. Preface to *A Complete History of England.* 2d ed. London, 1719.

Hume, Robert. *The Rakish Stage: Studies in English Drama, 1660–1800.* Carbondale: Southern Illinois University Press, 1983.

Hunter, Heidi. *Colonial Women: Race and Culture in Stuart Drama.* New York: Oxford University Press, 2001.

James I. *Daemonologie.* 1597. Reprint, New York: Barnes and Noble, 1966.

Jones, T. Gwynne. *Welsh Folklore and Folk-Custom.* Woodbridge, Suffolk: D. S. Brewer, 1930.

Josephus. *The Famous and Memorable Workes of Josephus, A Man of Much Honour and Learning among the Jewes. Faitfully translated out of the Latin, and French, by Tho. Lodge Doctor in Physicke.* London, 1602.

———. *Flavius Josephus: Selections from His Works.* Ed. Abraham Wasserstein. New York: Viking Press, 1974.

———. *History of the Jewish War.* Basle, 1544.

———. *Jewish Antiquities.* Basle, 1544.

———. *Josephus.* Trans. H. St. J. Thackeray. Loeb Classical Library. 8 vols. London: William Heinemann, 1926.

Kearney, Hugh. *Scholars and Gentlemen: University and Society in Pre-Industrial Britain, 1500–1700.* Ithaca: Cornell University Press, 1970.

Keats, John. *Poetical Works.* Ed. H. W. Garrod. 2d ed. Oxford: Clarendon Press, 1958.

Keenan, Elinor. "Norm-makers, Norm-breakers: Uses of Speech by Men and Women in a Malagasy Community." In *Explorations in the Ethnography of Speaking,* ed. Richard Bauman and Joel Sherzer, 125–43. Cambridge: Cambridge University Press, 1974.

Lamentatio Civitatis or, Londons Complaint Against her Children in the Countrey. London, 1665.

Larson, Deborah Aldrich. *John Donne and Twentieth-Century Criticism.* Rutherford, N.J.: Fairleigh Dickinson, 1989.

Legge, Thomas. *Destruction of Jerusalem.* Cambridge University Library Add. 7958.

———. *Richardus Tertius.* Ed. Robert J. Lordi. In *Renaissance Latin Drama in*

England, ed. Marvin Spevack, J. W. Binns, Hans-Jürgen Weckermann. Second Series: 8. Hildesheim: Georg Olms Verlag, 1989.

———. *Solymitana Clades*. Ed. Robert J. Lordi and Robert Ketterer. In *Renaissance Latin Drama in England*, ed. Marvin Spevack, J. W. Binns, Hans-Jürgen Weckermann. Second Series: 8. Hildesheim: Georg Olms Verlag, 1989.

———. *Thomas Legge: The Complete Plays*. Ed. Dana F. Sutton. 2 vols. New York: Peter Lang, 1993.

Leigh, William. *Queene Elizabeth, Paraleld in her princely virtues, with David, Iosua and Hezekia*. London, 1612.

Lennard, Reginald. *Englishmen at Rest and Play: Some Phases of English Leisure (1558–1714)*. Oxford: Clarendon Press, 1931.

Lloyd, Lodowick. *The Stratagems of Ierusalem. With the martiall lawes and militarie discipline, as well of the Iewes as of the Gentiles. By Lodowick Lloyd Esquier, one of her Maiesties Serieants at Armes*. London, 1602.

Lodge, Thomas. *An Alarum against Usurer*. London, 1584.

Mackaile, Matthew. *Moffet-Well: Or, A Topographical-Spagyricall description of the Mineral Wells, at Moffet in Annandale of Scotland*. Edinburgh, 1664.

MacKerness, E. D. "'Christ's Teares' and the Literature of Warning." *English Studies* 33 (1952): 251–54.

Macky, John. *A Journey through England in Familiar Letters from a Gentleman Here to his Friend Abroad*. London, 1732.

Madan, Pat. *A Philosophical and Medicinal Essay of the Waters of Tunbridge*. London, 1687.

Major, John Campbell. *The Role of Personal Memoirs in English Biography and Novel*. Philadelphia: University of Pennsylvania Press, 1935.

Manley, Lawrence. "From Matron to Monster: Tudor-Stuart London and the Languages of UrbanDescription." In *The Historical Renaissance: New Essays on Tudor and Stuart Literature and Culture*, edited by Heather Dubron and Richard Strier, 347–74. Chicago: University of Chicago Press, 1988.

Markley, Robert. *Two-Edg'd Weapons: Style and Ideology in the Comedies of Etherege, Wycherley, and Congreve*. Oxford: Clarendon Press, 1988.

Martin, L. C. "Henry Vaughan and Hermes Trismegistus." *Review of English Studies* 18 (1942): 301–7.

McCartney, Eugene S. "Praise and Dispraise in Folklore." *Papers of the Michigan Academy of Science, Arts, and Letters* 28 (1942): 567–93.

McKeon, Michael. "Marxist Criticism and 'Marriage a la Mode'." *The Eighteenth Century: Theory and Interpretation* 24 (1983): 141–62.

Medawar, Peter. *The Art of the Soluble*. London: Methuen, 1967.

Meres, Francis. *Palladis Tamia*. London, 1598.

Milton, John. "Areopagitica." In *Complete Poems and Major Prose*, edited by Merritt Y. Hughes, 716–749. New York: Odyssey Press, 1957.

———. "A Mask (Comus)." In *Complete Poems and Major Prose*, edited by Merritt Y. Hughes, 86–114. New York: Odyssey Press, 1957.

Morris, Christopher, ed. *The Journeys of Celia Fiennes*. London: The Cresset Press, 1949.

Morton, Thomas. *Salomon, or a Treatise Declaring the State of the Kingdom of Israel*. London, 1596.

Nashe, Thomas, *Christs Teares over Jerusalem* (1593). In *The Works of Thomas Nashe*, edited by R. B. McKerrow and Rev. F. P. Wilson, vol. 2. 5 vols. London, 1904. Reprint, Oxford: Basil Blackwell, 1958.

———. *The Works of Thomas Nashe*. Ed. R. B. McKerrow, rev. F. P. Wilson. 5 vols. London, 1904. Reprint, Oxford: Basil Blackwell, 1958.

Neill, Michael. "Heroic Heads and Humble Tails: Sex, Politics, and the Restoration Comic Rake." *The Eighteenth Century: Theory and Interpretation* 24 (1983): 115–39.

Nelson. Alan H., ed. *Records of Early English Drama: Cambridge*. 2 vols. Toronto: University of Toronto Press, 1989.

Opie, Iona and Peter. *The Lore and Language of Schoolchildren*. Oxford: Clarendon, 1961.

Osborne, B. and C. Weaver. *Aquae Britaniae: Rediscovering Seventeenth-Century Springs and Spas in the Footsteps of Celia Fiennes*. Malvern: Aldine Press, 1996.

Ó Súilleabháin, Seán. *Irish Folk Custom and Belief*. Dublin: Cultural Relations Committee, n.d.

Paracelcus. *The Hermetic and Alchemical Writings of Aureolus Philippus Thoephrastus Bombast of Hohenheim, Called Paracelsus the Great*. Ed. A. E. Waite. 2 vols. London: James Elliott, 1894.

Paster, Gail Kern. *The Body Embarrassed: Drama and the Disciplines of Shame in Early Modern England*. Ithaca: Cornell University Press, 1993.

Peltonen, Markku. *Classical Humanism and Republicanism in English Political Thought, 1570–1640*. Cambridge: Cambridge University Press, 1995.

Pepys, Samuel. *Diary, 1660–69*. Eds. R. Latham and W. Matthews. London: Bell, 1970–1983.

Perkinson, Richard H. "Topographical Comedy in the Seventeenth Century." *English Literary History* 3 (1936): 270–90.

Peter, John. *A Treatise of Lewisham (But Vulgarly called Dulwich) Wells In Kent . . . with Directions for the Use of them*. London, 1681.

Pipkin, John S. "Space and the Social Order in Pepy's Diary." *Urban Geography* 11 (1990): 153–75.

A Poem on the New Wells at Islington. London, 1684.

Poor-Robin. *News from Epsom: Or, The Revengeful Lady . . . A Novell . . . In imitation of Monsieur Scarron*. N.p., 1679.

Porter, Enid. *The Folklore of East Anglia*. London: Batsford, 1974.

Porter, H. C. *Reformation and Reaction in Tudor Cambridge*. Cambridge: Cambridge University Press, 1958.

Prat, E. *A Short Treatise of Metal and Mineral Waters, wherein is described their bad as well as good qualities, with the dangers of Peoples too frequent and unadvisedly Drinking them. Mirabilis in Aquis Dominus*. London, 1684.

Rawlins, Thomas. *Tunbridge-Wells, or, A Days Courtship*. London, 1678.

Rochester, John Wilmot, Earl of. "Tunbridge Wells." In *Complete Poems*, edited by David M. Vieth. New Haven: Yale University Press, 1968.

Rowzee, Lodwick. *The Queenes Welles. That is, A Treatise of the nature and vertues of Tunbridge Water*. London, 1632.

Sack, Robert David. *Human Territoriality: Its Theory and History*. Cambridge: Cambridge University Press, 1986.

———. *Homo Geographicus: A Framework for Action, Awareness, and Moral Concern*. Baltimoreand London: The Johns Hopkins University Press, 1997.

Schellinks, William. *The Journal of William Schellinks: Travels in England 1661–1663*. Ed. M. Exwood and H. L. Lehman. London: Royal Historical Society, 1993.

Shadwell, Thomas. *Epsom Wells*. Ed. Juan A. Prieto-Pablos, Mara Jos Mora, Manuel J. Gomez-Lara, and Rafael Portillo. Sevilla: Secretariado de Publicaciones de la Universidad de Sevilla, 2000.

Shakespeare, William. *The Complete Works of Shakespeare*. Ed. David Bevington. 4th ed. New York: HarperCollins, 1992.

———. *The Riverside Shakespeare*. Ed. G. Blakemore Evans and others. 2d ed. Boston: Houghton Mifflin, 1997.

Sherwood, Terry G. *Fulfilling the Circle: A Study of John Donne's Thought*. Toronto: University of Toronto Press, 1984.

Siebers, Tobin. *The Mask of Medusa*. Berkeley: University of California Press, 1983.

Sigonio, Carlo. *De Republica Hebræorum Libri VII, Ad Gregorium XIII Pontificem Maximum*. Frankfurt, 1583.

Smith, Nigel, ed. *A Collection of Ranter Writings from the Seventeenth Century*. London: Junction Books, 1983.

Spenser, Edmund. *The Faerie Queene*. Ed. P. C. Bayley. London: Oxford University Press, 1965.

Stockwood, John. *A Sermon Preached at Paules Crosse on Barthelmew day, being the 24. of August. 1578*. London, 1578.

———. *A Very Fruitful and Necessary Sermon of the most Lamentable Destruction of Jersualem*. London, 1584.

Stoppard, Tom. *Arcadia*. London: Faber & Faber, 1993.

Sutton, Dana Ferron. "Justus Lipsius to Thomas Legge, January 1, 1585." *Humanistica Lovaniensia* 40 (1991): 275–81.

Sympson, W. *The History of Scarbrough-Spaw*. London, 1679.

Taylor, Gary. *Reinventing Shakespeare*. London: The Hogarth Press, 1990.

Thompson, James. "Dryden's *Conquest of Granada* and the Dutch Wars." *The Eighteenth Century: Theory and Interpretation* 31 (1990): 211–26.

———. "Histories of Restoration Drama." *The Eighteenth Century: Theory and Interpretation* 24 (1983): 163–72.

———. *Language in Wycherley's Plays: Seventeenth-Century Language Theory and Drama*. Tuscaloosa: University of Alabama Press, 1984.

———. *Models of Value: Eighteenth-Century Political Economy and the Novel*. Durham: Duke University Press, 1996.

Thompson, Stith. *Motif-Index of Folk-Literature*. Rev. ed. Bloomington: Indiana University Press, 1955–1958.

Toland, John. *A Voyce from the Watch Tower; Part Five: 1660–1662*. Camden 4th ser., 21. London: Royal Historical Society, 1978.

Traversi, Derek. *An Approach to Shakespeare*. New York: Doubleday, 1969.

———. *Shakespeare: The Last Phase*. Stanford: Stanford University Press, 1965.

———. *Shakespeare: From* Richard II *to* Henry V. Stanford: Stanford University Press, 1957.

———. *Shakespeare: The Roman Plays*. Stanford: Stanford University Press, 1963.

Tumbleson, Raymond D. *Catholicism in the English Protestant Imagination: Nationalism, Religion, and Literature 1600–1745*. Cambridge: Cambridge University Press, 1998.

Underwood, Dale. *Etherege and the Seventeenth Century Comedy of Manners*. New Haven: Yale University Press, 1957.

Vaughan, Henry. *The Complete Poems*. Ed. Alan Rudrum. London: Penguin, 1977.

———. *The Works of Henry Vaughan*. Ed. L. C. Martin. 2d ed. Oxford: Oxford University Press, 1957.

Vaughan, Thomas. *The Works of Thomas Vaughan: Eugenius Philalethes, Edited, Annotated and Introduced by A. E. Waite*. London: Theosophical Publishing House, 1919. Venner, Thomas. *The Baths of Bathe*. London, 1628.

Waldrop, M. Mitchell. *Complexity: The Emerging Science at the Edge of Order and Chaos*. London: Penguin, 1992.

Walpole, Horace. *A Catalogue of the Royal and Noble Authors of England*. Edinburgh, 1796.

Ward, Edward. *A Walk to Islington: with a Description of New Tunbridge-Wells and Sadler's Music-House*. London, 1699.

———. *A Step to the Bath*. London, 1700.

Warwick, Sir Philip. *Memoirs of the Reign of King Charles the First*. Edinburgh: Ballantyne, 1813.

Weber, Harold. *The Restoration Rake-Hero: Transformations in Sexual Understanding in Seventeenth-Century England*. Madison: University of Wisconsin Press, 1986.

Wellwood, James. "To the Reader." In *Memoirs of the Most Material Transactions in England*. London, 1700.

White, Paul Whitfield. *Theatre and Reformation: Protestantism, Patronage, and Playing in Tudor England*. Cambridge: Cambridge University Press, 1993.

———, ed. *Reformation Biblical Drama in England: The Life and Repentaunce of Mary Magdalene & The History of Iacob and Esau (An Old-spelling Critical Edition)*. New York and London: Garland, 1992.

Williams, Aubrey. *An Approach to Congreve*. New Haven: Yale University Press, 1979.

Wilmont, John. *The Poems of John Wilmot, Earl of Rochester*. Ed. Keith Walker. Oxford: Shakespeare Head Press/Basil Blackwell, 1984.

Wilson, Charles. *Queen Elizabeth and the Revolt of the Netherlands*. London: Macmillan, 1970.

Woodbridge, Linda. *The Scythe of Saturn: Shakespeare and Magical Thinking*. Champaign: University of Illinois Press, 1994.

Index

Adler, Max K., 96 n. 6
aesthetics, 13, 15, 17
affectation, 182, 193, 194–95, 198–99
Agrippa, Henry Cornelius, 241
Agrippa, King, 229, 236, 241
Althusser, Louis, 48
Anani, 241, 250
Anderson, Judith H., 145
Anglo-Saxon, 97 n. 7
anthropology, 202
Aquinas, Thomas, 75
Archilochus, 40
art and nature, 15, 59, 108, 181–84, 188–89, 194
artifice, 15, 56, 181–82, 187–93, 195, 197–98
Aston, Margaret, 230
Athens, 246
Augenbraum, Harold, 111 n. 1

Bacon, Francis, 50
Bacon, Sir Nicholas, 230
Bamborough, John, 18
Barker, Francis, 134 n. 26
Bartholomew Fair, 211
Bath, 206, 208, 209, 211, 225 n. 56
Bauthumley, Jacob, 76
Beacon, Richard, 246
Behn, Aphra, 45, 147
Bennett, Josephine Waters, 32
Billson, Marcus, 137
Blake, William, 65
Blasphemy Act, 76
Bloom, Harold, 128, 133 n. 23, 273
Blunden, Edmund, 69, 82
Bohr, Neils, 33
Brathwait, Richard, 137, 141
Brecht, Bertolt, 39, 48
British Academy, 16
Brontë, Emily, 11
Brook, Peter, 116, 132 n. 8

Brooke, Christopher, 235
Brown, Laura, 48, 53 n. 21
Browning, Robert, 94
Buckley, Eric, 17
Burnet, Gilbert, 136, 141, 148 n. 17
Burton, Robert, 224 nn. 36, 50
Byfield, T., 207
Byrd, William, 228

Cad Goddea, 90
Caesar, Julius, 141–42, 200 n. 28, 243, 246–47; *Commentaries*, 141
caesura, 100
Caius, John, 228, 235
Calvin, John, 264 n. 74
Camden, William, 137, 243, 262 n. 57; *Britannia*, 243
Canfield, Douglas, 48, 204
canonization, 13
Carey, Elizabeth, 265 n. 85
Carey, John, 174 n. 1
Cartwright, Thomas, 235, 251
Caruthersville, MO, 16, 17
Cassius, Dio, 100, 234
Castiglione, Baldassare, 181, 184, 186, 192, 194–95; *The Courtier*, 184, 188
Catholicism, 159, 234, 247, 257 n. 12, 262 n. 58, 264 n. 74
Cavell, Stanley, 214
Cestius, 236–38, 241
chaos theory, 14, 18, 34, 39, 42, 44, 49–50, 52, 151, 157–58, 160–61, 164, 166, 168, 170, 173
Charles, Prince of Wales, 15, 268, 271, 276; *The Prince's Choice*, 15, 267–77
Charles I, 10, 136, 182
Charles II, 10, 182
Chaucer, Geoffrey, 44, 51, 143
Chekhov, Anton, 30, 38
Christopher Hill, 19, 47
Church of England, 230, 252, 255

291

Ciaconnius, Petrus, 234
Cibber, Colley, 145
Claudius, 114–15, 118, 120, 122–26, 128–31, 243
Clodd, Edward, 90
Collier, Jeremy, 47
Collinson, Patrick, 230
colonialism, 15
Congreve, William, 45–47, 49–51, 189, 200n. 29
Cooper, Anthony Ashley, Earl of Shaftesbury, 147n. 5, 148n. 8
Corman, Brian, 48, 54n. 21
Crawshay, Rose Mary, 16
Crichton, Michael, 18
Cromwell, Oliver, 10, 139, 142, 146, 263n. 71
Crosfield, Thomas, 265n. 85
Crowl, Samuel, 132n. 8
Curll, Edmund, 136, 148

Daud, Abraham Ibn, 231
Davies, Stevie, 69
deconstruction, 51, 140
Defoe, Daniel, 136, 147, 203, 209–10, 212, 218, 222n. 8
De Man, Paul, 86
Dennis, John, 189
Dial, The, 69
Diana, Princess of Wales, 268
Dodd, William, 133n. 24
Donne, John, 14, 150–74
Donoghue, Denis, 86
Drake, Sir Francis, 252
Dryden, John, 9–10, 12, 15, 39, 141, 148, 182–85, 187–88, 191–92, 194, 197–98, 200nn. 2, 13, 201nn. 38 and 40; *All for Love*, 39, 184; *Aureng-Zebe*, 184; *Essay of Dramatic Poesy*, 15, 182, 188, 198
Dyche, Thomas, 136

Earl of Tyrone, 247
East Anglia, 230
Edward VIII, 270
Egypt, 17, 55, 97n. 13
Eleazer, 236, 239–40, 242, 249, 252
Eliot, T.S., 13, 35, 69, 70–71, 82
Elizabeth I, 136, 229–231, 246, 252, 256n. 4, 258n. 13, 271
eloquence, 13–14, 99–110

Emory University, 17
English Review, The, 12, 17, 19, 55, 60
entropy, 50
enueg, 132n. 6
epithets, 13, 87–88, 91, 122, 124, 128
Epsom, England, 202–4, 208–14, 217–19, 221, 226, 227n. 100
Etherege, George, 15, 42–43, 45–46, 50–51, 182, 188–89, 191–92, 194, 197–98, 200n. 24; *Man of Mode*, 15, 42, 49, 182, 188, 190, 193, 198
Eucherius, 81
euphemism, 13, 87, 90, 92, 97n. 6
Evelyn, Mary, 224n. 39
evil-eye belief, 84–86, 91, 93
Exclusion Crisis, 147n. 5
Ezechias, 230–31

Farquhar, George, 45
fashion, 9–11, 15, 52, 184, 190–91, 205, 210, 212
feminism, 17, 44
Fielding, Henry, 48
Fiennes, Celia, 203, 224n. 51
Fletcher, John, 192, 243, 262n. 53
Florus, Cestius, 236–41, 249
Flos Ingenii vel Evacuatio Discriptionis. Being an Exact Description of Epsam, and Epsam Wells, 214
Fogle, Richard, 16
folklore, 95, 97n. 12, 98n. 19
Fowler, Alistair, 145
fractals, 14, 52, 150, 152–58, 160–62, 164–69, 171–72
Frayn, Michael, 33
Frazer, Sir James, 98n. 19
Freud, Sigmund, 95; Freudianism, 37, 133n. 21, 226n. 81

Galba, Servius Sulpicius, 244
Gardner, Dame Helen, 18
Garner, Ross, 83n. 1
geography, 15, 202
George I, 222n. 8
Gertrude, 114–15, 122, 131
Ghost, 37, 113–16, 118–19, 122, 125–26, 128
Gifford, George, 251
Gill, Pat, 48, 54n. 21, 226n. 82
Glyn Dwr, Owain, 270, 275–76

grammar, 13, 36, 84, 86–87, 92, 94–95, 234
Granville-Barker, Harley, 133 n. 19
Greene, Robert, 238, 254
Guggenheim Fellowship, 16
Gurgunt, 252

Hanmer, Meredith, 259 n. 20
Harington, Sir John, 226 n. 75
Hawkins, Harriett, 9, 11–12, 14, 16–18, 19, 30–52, 150–52, 154, 157, 159, 161, 163, 190; *Classics and Trash*, 17, 33, 39; *The Devil's Party*, 9, 17, 33, 36–40; *Measure for Measure*, 17; *Poetic Freedom*, 16, 30, 34, 42, 43–44; *Strange Attractors*, 14, 17, 44, 150, 156
Heisenberg, Werner, 33–34
Hellegers, Desiree, 49
Heminges, William, 265 n. 85
Henry VII, 229, 252
Henry VIII, 252
Herbert, George, 69–70, 72, 80–82, 136
Herbert, Sir Thomas, 69–70, 72, 80–82, 136
Hermeticism, 69, 74, 97 n. 12
Heywood, Eliza, 36
Hezekiah, 230–231
Hirsh, James, 132 n. 5, 133 n. 24
Hitler, Adolf, 161, 270. *See* Nazi Party
Hobbes, Thomas, 38
Holinshed, Raphael, 245–46, 248, 250; *Chronicle*, 245, 248
Holland, 185, 190, 234, 247, 260 n. 30
Holland, Norman, 45
Holland, Peter, 48, 53 n. 21
Holles, Denzil, 14, 135–47
Holmes, Elizabeth, 83 n. 1
Hooker, Richard, 255, 264 n. 77, 266 n. 93
Hopkins, Gerard Manley, 72
House of Commons, 140, 143, 146, 267, 277 n. 1
House of Lords, 143, 267
Howard, Leon, 134 n. 25
Hoxdon, England, 207–9
Hughes, Derek, 48, 54 n. 21
Hughes, John, 141
Huguenots, 239
Hume, Robert, 48, 53 n. 21

Hunter, Joseph, 133 n. 19
Huntington Library, 16

imagery, 12–14, 109, 121, 142, 150, 152, 163–65, 169
India, 84, 87
interiority, 127–28, 131
internal action, 119–21, 123
Ireland, 15, 90, 97 n. 12, 140, 243, 246–49, 262 n. 58, 263 n. 66, 270, 274
Islington, 230, 236, 239, 251, 258
Israel, 208–9, 212, 258 n. 13, 14

Jack Straw's Rebellion, 250
James I, 33, 96 n. 1, 136, 209
James VI, 243
James, Duke of York, 147 n. 5
Jechochanan, 249, 252
Jerusalem, 15, 228–34, 236–38, 241–44, 246, 248, 253–54, 256
Jesus, 74–75, 79, 87, 156, 165–68, 230–32, 237–38, 254, 260 n. 36, 266 n. 93
Jewel, Bishop John, 264 n. 80
Jewish rebellion, 233–34, 239, 245, 253, 256
Jewish-Roman conflict, 253
Jones, Gwynne T., 19
Jonson, Ben, 42, 183–85, 234; *The Silent Woman*, 183, 185
Josephus, Flavius, 230–31, 233–35, 237–41, 243–44, 247–50, 252, 259 n. 30, 260 n. 30, 260 n. 36, 266 n. 91; *The Jewish War*, 238, 241
Judaism, 15, 75, 229–42, 244–45, 247–49, 251, 253–55, 263, 265–66

Keats, John, 40, 55–56, 72
Ken, Thomas, 223 nn. 24 and 29
Kermode, Frank, 131 n. 3

Latin, 101, 114, 116, 129–31, 259 n. 26
Laud, Archbishop William, 69
Legge, Thomas, 15, 228–56, 257 n. 12, 260 n. 34, 262 n. 52, 84; *Richardus Tertius*, 228–29, 235; *Solymitana Clades*, 228–56
Lennard, Reginald, 203
Levin, Richard, 14, 44

294 INDEX

Levisham, 209
Lewis, Matthew, 11
Linacre College, Oxford, 16–18, 45
Lipsius, Justus, 234
Llyod, Lodowick, 232, 239
Lodge, David, 45
Lodge, Thomas, 233, 238
London, 10, 16, 97 n. 13, 143, 146, 185, 198, 202–3, 208–12, 217, 228, 230–33, 236, 238, 253
Lucan, 228
Ludlow, Edmund, 60, 135
Luther, Martin, 264 n. 74
Lyly, John, 36

Machiavelli, Nicolo, 31, 246
Maclean, Norman, 133 n. 22
Madan, Pat, 207, 227 n. 92
Maher, Mary Z., 132 n. 8
Malagasy, 91
Manley, Lawrence, 72, 210
Marlowe, Christopher, 11, 51, 87, 94, 154, 230, 254; *Dr. Faustus*, 87, 94
Martin, L.C., 69–71, 73, 77–78
Marx, Karl, 33, 48
Marxism, 37
Maseres, Francis, 139, 148 n. 15
Massachusetts Center for Renaissance Studies, 18
McKeon, Michael, 48
Medawar, Sir Peter, 51
Melanchton, Philipp, 264 n. 74
Melville, Herman, 11
memoirs, 14, 135–47
Memphis, TN, 16
Meres, Francis, 228; *Palladis Tamia*, 228
Middleton, Thomas, 43, 130
Miller, J. Hillis, 86
Milton, John, 12, 44, 47–48, 51, 55–56, 60–65, 143, 145, 157, 183, 201 n. 37; *Areopagitica*, 65; *Comus*, 56, 60–65; *Paradise Lost*, 18, 44, 56, 60, 158, 161
mimesis, 108
mind maps, 222 n. 9
Miner, Earl, 201 n. 36
Montaigne, Michel de, 201 n. 36
Morgann, Marurice, 39
Moron, A.L., 47

Morwyng, Peter, 231–33, 238
Mowat, Barbara A., 134 n. 26

Nashe, Thomas, 228, 232–33, 236–37, 239, 246, 254
National Endowment for the Humanities, 16
Nazi Party, 97 n. 7, 270. *See* Hitler, Adolf
Neill, Michael, 15, 48
Nero, 236–37, 243, 247–48, 250
New Historicism, 32, 44
New World, 243, 247
nicknames, 91–92
Norris, Sir John, 252
nouns, 13, 86–90, 92–93, 95
Novak, Maximillian E., 147 n. 7

Oates, Titus, 147 n. 5
Ophelia, 37, 116, 118, 129
Origen, 70
Osborne, Bruce, 136, 203
Otho, Marcus Salvius, 244
Otway, Thomas, 45
Ovid, 190, 200 n. 30
Oxford English Dictionary, 99, 107, 110, 136
Oxford University, 12, 16–19, 43, 45, 99, 107, 110, 253
Oxford University Press, 16–17, 19, 43

pamphlets, 15, 135, 205, 214, 230–33, 236, 246, 254
Paracelsus, 75
paralinguistics, 106
Paster, Gail Kern, 213–14
Peacham, Henry, 225 n. 52
Peele, George, 228, 252
Peltonen, Markku, 246
Pepys, Samuel, 203, 217, 226 n. 71, 227 n. 100
peripeteias, 103
Perkinson, Richard H., 204
Perne, Andrew, 251
Peter, John, 207, 211
Philip II, 231, 247
Pile, Steve, 222 n. 9
Pipkin, John S., 221
Plato, 38, 59
plots, 15, 60, 101, 114, 116–17, 123,

126, 128–29, 131, 189, 197, 203–4, 241
Polonius, 114, 116, 118, 129
Poor Law of 1572, 206
"Poor-Robin," 219
Popish Plot, 147n. 5
Popper, Karl, 33, 38
popular culture, 16–17, 42, 150
Post, Jonathan F.S., 83n. 1
prepositions, 71–73, 95
Project on the Rhetoric of Inquiry, 174n. 1
pronouns, 13, 86–95
prosopopeia, 86
Protestant Reformation, 205, 230, 238, 246, 252, 255, 264n. 74
Puritans, 15, 76, 229–30, 235, 251–53, 255, 264n. 73, 266n. 93
Pushkin, Alexander, 30

Radcliffe, Ann, 11
Rawlins, Thomas, 209, 225n. 64
relativism, 50
Restoration, 9–13, 15–17, 19, 42–49, 52, 181–82, 188, 192, 202–3, 220–21
rhetoric, 10, 13, 43–44, 105, 137–40, 142, 145–47, 172, 234, 272
rhyme, 183–84, 186–87, 189, 192
Richardson, Samuel, 48
Roach, Joseph R., 201n. 44
Rochester, John Wilmot, Earl of, 181–82, 188–89, 195, 199, 218, 226n. 82
Romans, 15, 55, 75, 85, 99–100, 102, 143, 229–30, 232, 234, 236–49, 252–53, 255, 261n. 41, 262n. 59, 265n. 83
Rowling, William, 43
Rowzee, Lodwick, 206–7, 211–13, 216, 224n. 49
Rudrum, Alan, 69
Rumpelstiltskin, 90–91

Sack, David, 204–5
Sandys, Bishop Edwin, 254
Sanhedrin, 249–50
Schellink, William, 203, 213, 217
Schimeon, 249, 252
Scotland, 84–85, 90–91, 142, 144, 146, 205, 243, 270, 274, 277n. 3
Scouten, A.H., 44, 51, 53n. 5
Sedley, Sir Charles, 200n. 24, 221

Shadwell, Thomas, 189, 202–4, 222n. 8; *Epsom Wells*, 202–4, 208, 210, 213, 219, 221
Shakespeare Survey, 17
Shakespeare, William, 12–18, 30–31, 33–40, 42, 44–45, 49, 51, 56, 84, 86–87, 92–95, 99–100, 102–4, 106–19, 125, 127, 130, 133n. 19, 183–84, 192, 228, 230, 243, 250, 254, 266, 268, 270–77; *Antony and Cleopatra*, 55–56, 95, 103–4, 110, 161; *Hamlet*, 14, 37–39, 99–103, 106, 113–31, 132nn. 4, 6, and 7, 133nn. 12–13, 15–20, and 22, 134n. 26; *Henry IV, Part One*, 104–5, 253, 270, 275–76; *Henry V*, 13, 69, 229, 252–53, 272; *Henry VI, Part 2*, 250; *Julius Caesar*, 49, 92–95, 99–100, 103–4, 246, 272; *King Lear*, 38, 101, 106–7, 109, 132n. 6, 133n. 22, 272; *Macbeth*, 33, 84–94, 96n. 7, 97n. 9, 106; *Measure for Measure*, 17, 30–32, 34–36, 106; *The Merchant of Venice*, 96n. 1, 230; *The Merry Wives of Windsor*, 96n. 1; *A Midsummer Night's Dream*, 111; *Much Ado about Nothing*, 106; *Othello*, 96n. 3, 97. n. 12, 98n. 19, 106–7, 133n. 22; *The Rape of Lucrece*, 84–85, 93–94; *Romeo and Juliet*, 30, 37, 49, 132n. 11; *The Tempest*, 94, 189; *Troilus and Cressida*, 106
Siebers, Tobin, 84
Sigonio, Carlo, 234
Smith, John, 172, 253
Smyth, John, 251
soliloquies, 14, 89–90, 92, 93, 105, 113–31, 239, 258
Solzhenitsyn, Alexander, 43
Spain, 188, 234, 247, 249, 262n. 58
spas, 15, 202–6, 208–10, 212–18, 220, 221
Speech Act Theory, 86
Spenser, Edmund, 12, 56, 58, 59
Stalin, Joseph, 43
St. John, Oliver, 142, 228
Stockwood, John, 232–33, 237–38, 254
Stoicism, 262n. 52
Straus, Ralph, 148
stylistics, 10
Suetonius, 234

suicide, 104, 110, 115–16, 120, 130, 238, 242
superstition, 13, 84, 90–91
Sutton, Dana, 229–30, 241, 247, 261 n. 49, 262 n. 52, 264 n. 76, 266 n. 90
Swarthmore College, 16
Swift, Jonathan, 226 n. 82
synonyms, 13, 87
syntax, 69, 71–73, 76–77, 95, 99, 119, 122–25, 127, 160

Tacitus, Cornelius, 143, 234
Thompson, James, 48, 90–91, 142
Thompson, Stith, 90–91
Thurber, James, 51
Titus, 130, 147, 242–43, 245, 253, 255, 261 n. 51, 54, 262 n. 54, 265 n. 83
Toland, John, 135, 142, 146, 203, 224 n. 51
Tolstoy, Leo, 30
Tourneur, Cyril, 43
Traversi, Derek, 49
Tulane University, 16
Tumbleson, Raymond, 49
Tunbridge, England, 206–9, 211–12, 217–19, 227 n. 92, 232

Udall, Nicholas, 231
Underwood, Dale, 45

Vanbrugh, John, 45
Vassar College, 16–17, 42–43, 45, 49
Vaughan, Henry, 13, 69–82

Venner, Thomas, 211, 223 n. 33
verbs, 13, 71–73, 82, 86–89, 92–93, 95, 143, 146, 160
Verdi, Giusippe, 39
Vespasian, Titus Flavius, 243, 245, 253, 258 n. 15, 265 n. 83
Vindiciae, contra Tyrannos, 239, 245
Vitellius, Aulus, 244
Voadicia, 245

Wales, 80, 90–91, 270, 274–77, 277 n. 3
Walker, Anthony, 223 n. 25
Waller, Edmund, 188–90
Walpole, Horace, 139, 148 n. 10
Ward, Edward, 212
Warwick, Sir Philip, 136
Washington University, 16
Weaver, Cora, 203
Weber, Harold, 48, 54 n. 21
Webster, John, 43
West, Mae, 104
Whitgift, John, 234–35, 251
wildness, 192–95, 197, 199
Williams, Aubrey, 46–49
Wilson, John Dover, 133 n. 19
Worden, Blair, 147 n. 3
Wycherley, William, 45–46

Yosippon, 231, 233, 247

Zealots, 229–30, 236, 240, 248, 251–52
Zitner, S.P., 134 n. 26